General Sir James Scarlett

General Sir James Yorke Scarlett (1799–1871) by Edmund Havell, 1868.

General Sir James Scarlett

The Life and Letters of the Commander of the Heavy Brigade at Balaklava

Martin Sheppard

Pen & Sword
MILITARY

First published in Great Britain in 2022 by
Pen & Sword Military
An imprint of
Pen & Sword Books Ltd
Yorkshire – Philadelphia

ISBN 978 1 39908 998 2

A CIP catalogue record for this book is
available from the British Library.

Typeset by Mac Style
Printed and bound in the UK by CPI Group (UK) Ltd,
Croydon, CR0 4YY.

Pen & Sword Books Limited incorporates the imprints of Atlas,
Archaeology, Aviation, Discovery, Family History, Fiction, History,
Maritime, Military, Military Classics, Politics, Select, Transport,
True Crime, Air World, Frontline Publishing, Leo Cooper, Remember
When, Seaforth Publishing, The Praetorian Press, Wharncliffe
Local History, Wharncliffe Transport, Wharncliffe True Crime
and White Owl.

For a complete list of Pen & Sword titles please contact

PEN & SWORD BOOKS LIMITED
47 Church Street, Barnsley, South Yorkshire, S70 2AS, England
E-mail: enquiries@pen-and-sword.co.uk
Website: www.pen-and-sword.co.uk

Or

PEN AND SWORD BOOKS
1950 Lawrence Rd, Havertown, PA 19083, USA
E-mail: Uspen-and-sword@casematepublishers.com
Website: www.penandswordbooks.com

Contents

Illustrations

Text Illustrations

Illustration Acknowledgements

The author and publisher are grateful to the following for permission to reproduce illustrations: the Defence Academy of the United Kingdom, 30; Guildford Borough Council's Heritage Service, p. 39; the Royal Dragoons, 34, 37 and 38; the Royal Dragoon Guards Museum, York, 22, 35, 36; Roger Scarlett-Smith, 28; Towneley Hall, Burnley, p. ii and plates 20, 23, 38. The William Simpson watercolours of the Crimea are available on Wiki Commons and the Roger Fenton photographs of the Crimea on the Library of Congress website. Both are in the public domain. All other illustrations are from images or photographs in the author's possession. I am grateful to Samuel Bates, Charles Mackain-Bremner, Mary Ann Combes, Sarah Fairhurst, Jack French, Aneta Imrie, Roger Scarlett-Smith, Aline Staes and Mike Townend for their help with the illustrations.

People and Places

Abinger, Lord, *see* James Scarlett; Robert Scarlett; William Scarlett

Abinger Hall, Abinger, Surrey, country house belonging to Scarlett family

Bank Hall, Burnley, house belonging to James Yorke Scarlett

Beatson, William, colonel, aide de camp to James Yorke Scarlett

Burton, *see* Hallyburton Campbell

Cally, *see* Caroline Orde

Cambridge, George, Duke of (1819–1904), army officer, later Commander in Chief, British Army

Campbell:

    Cecilia (Cecie) (1835–1927), third daughter of John and Mary Campbell

    Dudley (1833–1900), youngest son of John and Mary Campbell

    Hallyburton (Hally, Burton) (1829–1918), second son of John and Mary Campbell

    John, Sir John Campbell, first Lord Campbell (1779–1861); husband of Mary Scarlett, Lady Stratheden; father of Cecilia, Dudley, Edina, Frederick, Hallyburton, Louisa and Mary Campbell

    Louisa (Louy, Lou) (1823–1916), eldest daughter of John and Mary Campbell; married William Spranger White in 1850

    Mary, Lady Stratheden (1796–1860), elder daughter of James, first Lord Abinger; sister of James Yorke Scarlett; wife of John Campbell; mother of Cecilia, Dudley, Edina, Frederick, Hallyburton, Louisa and Mary Campbell

    Mary (Molly, Poll, Polly) (1827–1916), second daughter of John and Mary Campbell

Cardigan, James Brudenell, seventh Earl of Cardigan (1797–1868), commander of the Light Brigade

Cattell, Dr William, surgeon, 5th Dragoon Guards

Cliviger, near Burnley; *see* Ormerod Hall; Holme Chapel

Conolly, James, brigade major, Heavy Brigade

Currey, Louise, Lady Currey, sister of James Yorke Scarlett, wife of Sir Edmund Currey

Charlotte, Aunt, *see* Charlotte Scarlett

Stratheden House, Knightsbridge, London house belonging to Campbell
   family
Thursby, Eleanor, née Hargreaves, sister of Charlotte Scarlett
Thursby, John, nephew of Charlotte Scarlett, aide de camp to James Yorke
   Scarlett
Thursby, William, husband of Eleanor Thursby, née Hargreaves
Torlundie or Torlundy, house near Fort William, later Inverlochy Castle
Towneley, John, of Towneley Park, principal landowner in Burnley
Uncle Campbell, *see* John, Lord Campbell
Uncle Jim, *see* James Yorke Scarlett
Varna, town on the west coast of the Black Sea
West, Georgina, Henry, Jane and Richard, friends of Frances Scarlett
Willy, *see* William Scarlett
Yorke, John, colonel, 1st Dragoons

To Louise Berridge

Vestigia Nulla Retrorsum

It was a mighty affair and, considering the difficulties under which the Heavy Brigade laboured, and the disparity of numbers, a feat of arms which, if it ever had its equal, was certainly never surpassed in the annals of cavalry warfare, and the importance of which in its results can never be known.

Lord George Paget on the Charge of the Heavy Brigade

Introduction

At dawn on 25 October 1854 a force of over 20,000 Russians attacked the British supply lines in the Crimea, taking their enemies unprepared. Three hours later, at about 9 o'clock, Brigadier General James Yorke Scarlett was leading four regiments of the Heavy Brigade towards the port of Balaklava, the defence of which was vital to the British campaign. Suddenly, his aide de camp, Alexander Elliot, pointed out a large body of Russian cavalry coming into view on the hill above them.

Scarlett at once put himself ahead of the three hundred men nearest to him. After dressing them to the right, and followed by Elliot, and by his trumpeter and orderly, he charged uphill at the Russians, being the first into their ranks. In Scarlett's own words:

> I ordered the advance. The ground was bad, uphill and some of the picket ropes of the Light Brigade camp interfered, but we got into a trot and gallop and went right at them before they had time to deploy, which they were in the act of doing. They did not advance to meet us but stood still and we were soon hand to hand and deep into them in regular mill.[1]

The men of the Scots Greys and Inniskillings were quickly supported by the other regiments of the Heavy Brigade, the 4th and 5th Dragoon Guards and the Royals, charging in from different angles.

The Russians, who outnumbered the seven hundred men of the Heavy Brigade by at least three to one, failed to make use of their overwhelming advantages of numbers, position and surprise. They halted and seemed uncertain what to do. This handed Scarlett the initiative. After less than ten minutes of hand-to-hand fighting, the Russians retreated. Their attempts to reform were thwarted by accurate fire from a battery of Royal Horse Artillery. Astonishingly, both Scarlett and Elliot survived the charge, although the former received five wounds and the latter fourteen.

Poorly commanded, the Russian cavalry showed itself unable to react flexibly to an unexpected challenge on the battlefield. Its ranks were so tightly packed as to inhibit an effective response to the British charge. The horses of the Russians were smaller than those of the British and their swords were remarkably blunt, which accounts for the low number of fatalities they inflicted. In contrast, Scarlett showed decisive leadership at a critical moment and inspired his men by his personal example. The men of his brigade responded with professionalism and belief in themselves, reflecting high morale. Scarlett's brigade, however, won the encounter by itself, without the help of the Light Brigade. Commanded by the Earl of Cardigan, the Light Brigade was nearby but failed to support the Heavies. Cardigan afterwards claimed, contradicting the commander of the cavalry division, the Earl of Lucan, that he had been ordered only to defend the position that he and the Light Brigade were in.

This remarkable encounter was by no means the end of General Scarlett's day. Two hours later, Scarlett and the Heavy Brigade were lined up behind the Light Brigade to follow them down the Valley of Death. As instructed by the Commander in Chief Lord Raglan's fatal order to Lucan, the whole cavalry division was ordered to attack, not just the Light Brigade. Scarlett himself was already advancing ahead of his brigade, and under heavy fire, when Lucan ordered the Heavy Brigade to halt, to the surprise of its own commander.

Lucan had not hesitated, on receiving Raglan's order, in sending his hated brother-in-law, the Earl of Cardigan, and the Light Brigade to charge the Russian battery at the end of the valley through crossfire from both sides. Now, at the very last minute before the Heavy Brigade was committed to following in the Light Brigade's wake, Lucan had second thoughts. He excused himself from any responsibility, saying to Lord William Paulet, the assistant adjutant general, who was with him, 'They have sacrificed the Light Brigade. They shall not have the Heavy, if I can help it.'[2] In stopping Scarlett and the Heavy Brigade coming to the support of the Light Brigade, Lucan reversed what had had happened two hours earlier, when the Light Brigade had failed to come to the support of the Heavy Brigade.

Paradoxically, if the Heavy Brigade had followed the Light Brigade down the valley, this might have led to victory. The Light Brigade had achieved its objective, knocking out the Russian battery they had attacked, and a number of its men had ridden well beyond the battery. While the first line of the Light Brigade had indeed suffered severe losses, the second and third lines had lost many fewer men and horses. At the time the Heavy Brigade were about to charge, the Russian battery of the Fedoukine Heights, on the western side of the valley, was put out of action by the French cavalry. The Heavy Brigade would therefore have arrived beyond the destroyed central battery relatively unscathed. The men of the Light Brigade were expecting the support of the Heavy Brigade and only Lucan stopped them from having it.

Meanwhile the Russian cavalry behind the central battery were in disarray. They had been astonished by the Light Brigade's attack. Even the small number of men of the Light Brigade behind the guns had induced them to panic. The arrival of a second British brigade, in good order and at almost full strength, would have turned Russian disorder into a rout. Fleeing towards the Traktir Bridge, at the end of the valley, many Russians would have been killed. This would have made the charge of the British cavalry division a triumphant success. The victorious British would then, when returning up the valley, have been able to carry away the guns they had charged as trophies.

Balaklava, however, will be remembered for the Charge of the Light Brigade, the ultimate example of glorious and heroic failure. Victory would have been far less memorable.

Although by 1850 Britain was the leading industrial power in the world, with a global empire, Britons liked to think of themselves as plucky amateurs, up against the odds, showing a casual disregard of danger that almost amounted to foolhardiness. They put their success down to character and resolve, virtues they thought were seldom displayed by other nations in Europe, let alone outside it. This belief gave them a comforting awareness of their own worth and a confidence that Britons came from a superior stock. This sense of superiority was shared by their soldiers and sailors, ensuring high morale in battle and gratification to those reading about their exploits at home.[3] A British soldier, in this view, would rather die than face dishonour and was more than willing to shed his blood as a sacrifice for his country. As Thomas Babington Macaulay had written in *Horatius*, reflecting the Victorians' self-identification with the Romans:

> How can a man die better
> Than facing fearful odds
> For the ashes of his fathers
> And the temples of his gods?[4]

Where the British suffered a reverse, unless greatly outnumbered, this was never due to the superior calibre of their opponents but only to their own blunders or to appalling bad luck. In this spirit, Tennyson's 'The Charge of the Light Brigade', written six weeks after Balaklava, epitomised a national consensus.

Even if the joint charge of the British cavalry division had led to an unlikely victory, it would not have had much effect on the overall outcome of the war. What, however, has not previously been noted is the strategic importance of the Charge of the Heavy Brigade. Had Scarlett been defeated earlier in the day, the road to Balaklava would have lain open to a Russian attack by infantry and artillery, as well as cavalry. If Russia had then captured Balaklava and gained control of the British supply line, the British would have had to abandon the siege of Sebastopol and would have suffered a humiliating defeat at the hands of the Russians.

The concentrated attention on the Charge of the Light Brigade at Balaklava has led to a false perspective on the battle. In this, the Charge of the Heavy Brigade is usually mentioned as no more than a prelude to the main event. There has been little focus on the cavalry division as a whole in the battle, despite Raglan's orders being issued to all of the division, not just part of it. This has led to the importance of the Charge of the Heavy Brigade being ignored and the part played by the Heavy Brigade in the Charge of the Light Brigade being underestimated.

The Heavy Brigade is indissolubly linked with the name of its commander, James Yorke Scarlett, yet little has been written about him. While nearly all histories of the Crimean War, from Kinglake on, mention the Charge of the Heavy Brigade, and give Scarlett credit both for bravery and for professionalism, they naturally concentrate on his ten minutes of glory at Balaklava rather than the rest of his life. He occupies centre stage for a few pages, usually with a stock description as a stoutish, bewhiskered, ruddy-faced, short-sighted, fifty-five-year-old officer who had never previously been engaged in battle. Despite his contemporary fame, no biography of James Yorke Scarlett has ever been written. Fascination with military blunders, and the public appetite for heroic failure, has led to an overwhelming concentration on the Charge of the Light Brigade, and on the characters of Cardigan and Lucan, at the expense of Scarlett and the Heavy Brigade.

Scarlett's low profile is reflected in the 1968 Tony Richardson film, *The Charge of Light Brigade*, from which the Charge of the Heavy Brigade itself and the Heavy Brigade's part in the Charge of the Light Brigade are both omitted. To add insult to injury, Scarlett, knighted incorrectly before the Crimean War, is given a non-speaking part as 'Sir John Scarlett'.[5] In at least appearing in the film, Scarlett did better than in the Michael Curtiz 1936 film of *The Charge of the Light Brigade*, starring Errol Flynn as Major Geoffrey Vickers, in which there was no place for him. More even-handedly, Raglan, Lucan, Cardigan and Nolan are also omitted. In the charge scene, filmed in Mexico, where the laws on the treatment of animals were lax, the death of twenty-five horses, out of one hundred and twenty-five brought down by tripwires, caused Flynn, an accomplished horseman, and Curtiz to come to blows.

Who, then, was General Scarlett? The basic details of his life and career are not hard to find. General Sir James Yorke Scarlett (1799–1871) was the second son of James Scarlett, a hugely successful barrister and significant politician, who became the first Lord Abinger in 1835. Born in London and educated at Eton and Trinity College, Cambridge, James Yorke Scarlett was Tory MP for Guildford from 1837–41, near his family's country house, Abinger Hall, just outside Dorking. In 1835 he had married a wealthy heiress, Charlotte Hargreaves, whose family owned the most valuable mines in Burnley in Lancashire. Sadly, the marriage was childless. Scarlett's home from then on, despite long absences away on duty, was at Bank Hall in Burnley.

A reluctant politician, Scarlett was a dedicated professional soldier who made the 5th Dragoon Guards, which he commanded for fourteen years, an outstanding regiment in both morale and efficiency. A wealthy man, he undoubtedly spent heavily if unostentatiously upon it, although no record exists of this. What is certain is that he made himself outstandingly popular with the men he commanded. In bidding his regiment farewell, when he relinquished his formal ties with it on his promotion, he wrote:

> Though this promotion is most flattering to the major general as a reward for his services performed in the field, he cannot see the connection which has so long existed between him and the regiment he has had the honour and pleasure to command dissolved without feelings of pain and regret. It has during his command been the pride and delight of his life to have received from every general officer who has inspected the 5th Dragoon Guards their full approbation of the regiment, and to have been able to place on their records the special approbation of the greatest soldier of the day, the late Duke of Wellington.[6]

The Charge of the Heavy Brigade made James Yorke Scarlett a household name in Victorian Britain. He received congratulations from the Queen and from Parliament. He was promoted to major general and knighted. In Burnley, his visit in May 1855 was marked by the presentation of a sword and a banquet in his honour. He returned to command the cavalry division in the Crimea, rebuilding it to more than its original strength, but had no further opportunity to lead it in battle against the Russians. After the war, he had a distinguished career, holding some of the most senior army appointments and retiring as commandant of Aldershot in 1869. On his death in 1871, the funeral route in Burnley was lined by 60,000 people.

There is not, however, enough material available to write a full biography of General Scarlett, as for many years of his life little information has survived. He did not keep a diary and wrote neither an autobiography nor an account of his time in the Crimea. There is, however, more material than has usually been supposed. Childless as he was, the General was a member of a close-knit family. He was always on excellent terms with his father and mother. He had two brothers and two sisters, all of whom had children. Before, during and after the Crimean War, he corresponded with many of them. While most of these letters have disappeared, a substantial number of previously unpublished letters survive. These make up the heart of this book.

The letters tell us a great deal about the General's character. They testify to his professionalism and high standards, and to the interest he took in his men. They combine the personal and professional, with details of his experiences before, during and after the Crimea. They give his views on the progress of the war and on its likely outcome. They display an unfailing interest in the people and places around him, combined with a sense of humour. Of the letters from the time of the Crimean War, one is of especial interest. In a previously unpublished letter to Colonel James Chatterton, the one-time commander of the 4th Dragoon Guards, and written six weeks after Balaklava, Scarlett describes his experiences on 25 October at length.[7]

The portrait which emerges of the General, from his letters and from many other sources, is a remarkably consistent one. Not only was James Yorke Scarlett a brave and highly competent soldier, he was liked and admired by everyone who came in touch with him. This ranged from Queen Victoria herself, who referred to him as 'a most amiable sensible man, and an excellent officer',[8] to the officers and men of his regiment and brigade, and to his family. When the men of the 5th Dragoon Guards, arriving at Constantinople in the *Himalaya*, saw him approaching in a small boat, their reaction was immediate. 'As soon as he was seen, the men cried out, "The General", and in a moment those on board seemed to come from all parts of the ship, crowding round the gangway, cheering, clapping their hands and acting in a very boisterous and somewhat unusual manner – more like a lot of schoolboys than soldiers.'[9] As George Ryan wrote about him in 1855, 'The private character of General Scarlett is so well known in the greater part of the United Kingdom that to dwell upon it would be superfluous – we can only repeat the opinion of his friends: "He has no enemies except the Russians".'[10]

One of the revelations in the General's letters from the Crimea is his constant concern for his wife Charlotte, who clearly suffered from major attacks of depression. He was torn between his responsibilities as the commander of the Heavy Brigade, and then of the cavalry division in the Crimea, and his conviction that only he would be able to comfort his wife in her affliction. It was because of her that he returned to England for two months in the spring of 1855. His niece, Frances Scarlett, wrote about the wish of Lord Hardinge, the Commander in Chief of the British Army, to send the General back to the Crimea:

it would place Uncle Jim in a very hard position. He is not a man to be moved by worldly honour, and he will consign himself to oblivion if he thinks he sees that that is his duty. He may be moved by the cry 'the country needs you', but he is too modest about himself to think he is absolutely necessary.[11]

He returned reluctantly, greatly worried about Charlotte, to the Crimea in June 1855.

Besides the letters from General Scarlett himself, many other letters from members of his wider family survive, such as the one written by Frances Scarlett above. These often mention 'the Colonel', who later became 'the General'. For the Crimean War these letters provide a valuable source of information about the home front, including how news of the General's exploits was received by his own family.

His family indeed had a double interest in the Crimea in that the General's nephew, William Scarlett, later the third Lord Abinger, was an officer in the Scots Fusilier Guards. After being in the thick of the fighting at the battle of the Alma, a month before Balaklava, William Scarlett became one of his uncle's aides de camp, seeing him on a daily basis. His letters constitute a commentary on the history of the war, as William Scarlett was either near Varna or in the Crimea from June 1854 until the end of the war, other than for a short home leave in early 1856. His letters are clear, graphic and varied.[12] They also make multiple references to the General and indeed include a letter sent to the latter while the General was on leave in England in 1855.

In addition to these letters, Frances Scarlett, the General's niece who was William's younger sister, kept a lively and detailed diary between 1842 and 1854. Close both to her brother and her uncle, the diary describes the departure of William Scarlett with the Scots Fusilier Guards from Portsmouth and later that of the James Yorke Scarlett (still formally a colonel) from Marseilles, after a joint trip across France by the General, his brother and sister-in-law, and his niece. When he sailed east on board the *Oronte*, 'We watched till the high ground hid her from our sight and we could no longer see the Colonel at the stern standing waving his handkerchief.'[13]

This book is the story of a remarkable man as much as an account of a highly successful military career. It does not attempt to assess James Yorke Scarlett's term as Adjutant General between 1860 and 1865, partly because of the impossibility of consulting the sources for this phase of his career at the National Archives during the pandemic. The book indeed reflects the sources from which it has been written, above all James Yorke Scarlett's own letters and letters from other members of his family. These have survived since his death in 1871 in a private archive, owned by a succession of family members over the years. In this archive, which contains over a thousand

xxii   General Sir James Scarlett

nineteenth-century letters, as well as photograph albums and many other items, the General's letters form no more than a small part.[14]

One of the main recipients of the General's letters was his sister-in-law, Sarah Scarlett, Lady Abinger, who assembled the collection initially. As her son, William Scarlett, wrote to his father, Lord Abinger, from the Crimea in June 1855:

> Will you please give this letter to Mother, and all my letters, to keep, as I wish to look at them when I get home. A journal is too much trouble to keep; and Mother is very methodical with her papers.[15]

On the death of Sarah, Lady Abinger, in 1878 the archive passed to her daughter Frances Smith, née Scarlett, who lived at Brampton Ash in Northamptonshire, where her husband was rector for fifty-nine years, and then at South Bank, her house in Hereford after her husband's death in 1903. Frances Scarlett, who was on affectionate terms with her uncle, had herself been the recipient of many of the General's letters. As well as writing her diary, Frances kept up a surviving correspondence with her first cousin and best friend, Mary Campbell (another of the General's nieces), which runs to over two hundred letters and 125,000 words. In later life, she wrote a detailed account of the Scarlett family and the other families connected to it.[16]

The archive was inherited on his mother's death in 1920 by Frances' eldest son, Harold Yorke Lidderdale Smith, and subsequently, on Harold's death in 1939, by his eldest daughter, Hester Smith.[17] Hester Smith, who spent much of her life as a missionary teacher in southern India but kept a house in London, lived in her final years with two of her first cousins, both granddaughters of Frances Smith. She and her cousin Cilla Douglas-Jones, who lived at Glyndyfrdwy near Llangollen in north Wales, spent many happy hours reading parts of the archive. They even produced a small photocopied and illustrated book, entitled *Fanny Scarlett*, which has a short chapter on the General. This included several of his letters, taken from copies made by their grandmother during the First World War.[18]

Following the death of Cilla Douglas-Jones, Hester Smith moved to Bath to live with Cilla's youngest sister, Audrey Sheppard. She brought the archive with her and Audrey inherited it on Hester's death in 1986. Audrey clearly spent a great deal of time in her final years reading the letters. After her death at the age of ninety-eight in 2013, nearly all of them were found sorted into groups, tied together with ribbon and labelled by her in pencil. The letters were inherited by Audrey's three children, my brother Peter, my sister Sarah and myself.[19]

As someone with a long-term interest in history, and as the author of several history books, I have very much enjoyed working on the archive. I soon identified a number of the General's letters and subsequently found other letters from the General and about him both in the archive and elsewhere. Having transcribed these letters, I annotated them, identifying the people, places and events to which they referred. In transcribing them, I have followed the originals as closely as possible but have modernised the punctuation where this has made the sense clearer. As well as reading books about the history of the Crimean War, I became a member of the leading society for those interested in the war, the Crimean War Research Society. After joining the society, I wrote to Louise Berridge, the editor of its quarterly journal, the *War Correspondent*, telling her about General Scarlett's letters.

Louise responded immediately and asked me to write a series of articles about General Scarlett for the *War Correspondent*. During the preparation of these articles, which made me focus closely on the General's life and career, and on the Charge of the Heavy Brigade itself, Louise was unfailingly encouraging and helpful. Our correspondence on the Crimea, the General and many other matters was highly enjoyable. Louise helped me think about how to turn the General's letters into a book. This book is dedicated to her.

Many other people have also helped and encouraged me. As well as to my brother and sister, I am grateful to my cousins Jamie Abinger and Roger Scarlett-Smith for allowing me to reproduce letters from the General in their possession. Jamie was most hospitable to me on a visit to Frahan, in Belgium, where he himself has a sizeable archive of items reflecting Scarlett family history. Roger has allowed me to copy all the family letters in his possession and to reproduce an original water colour of the General's hut in the Crimea. Sarah Scarlett and I spent a fruitful day together exploring the archive of the Scots Greys in Edinburgh Castle. Together with Chris, Georgie and Rob Matthew, Peter Sheppard and I visited Burnley together, seeing the site of Bank Hall, Towneley Hall and the General's grave at Cliviger. Mary Ann Combes and I together visited the Surrey History Centre in search of references to the General. We also recently visited Guildford Museum, where we were shown the election posters for the 1837 and 1841 Guildford elections by Sarah Fairhurst.

In October 2019, on a visit to British Columbia, I enjoyed the hospitality of Mary Berg, David and Gwen Gaddes, and Sandy Wilson, the Canadian descendants of William Scarlett, all of whom own significant archives of material to do with family history. I am sorry never to have met Boyce Gaddes, the father of David and Mary, who worked extensively on Scarlett family history and who would have enjoyed this book. From Melbourne, another cousin, Ann Constable, has commented incisively on my work on family history. She also sent me the original of a letter from the General I had not previously seen. Irene Moore of Pen & Sword edited the text ably and sympathetically, indulging my liking for making changes on paper rather than on screen. I also wish to thank Matt Jones of Pen & Sword for overseeing the production of this book.

This book has already led me on to other projects. I discovered that the General had written to William Duckworth, the father of an officer in the 5th Dragoon Guards, to tell him that that his son George had died of cholera at Varna in August 1854. As I thought it unlikely that such a letter would have been thrown away lightly, I looked for and found it in the Duckworth family collection in the Somerset Archives. This archive proved itself to contain not just one but two letters from the General (Letters 14 and 27 below). It also contained a series of letters from and to George Duckworth and the diary he kept for the last three months of his life. I have now published an edition of these letters and the diary as *Crimean Tragedy: George Duckworth, 1826–1854*. For their help on both books I wish to thank Katy Horton-Fawkes, Henri Le Boëdec, Alastair Macleay and Michael McGarvie.

In Burnley, the General's adopted home, Ramon Collinge took me around a variety of sights to do with the Scarletts, and introduced me to three other historians of Burnley, Roger Frost, Mollie Haines and Ken Spencer. Ken arranged for Burnley Library to produce a number of relevant documents during my visit. At Towneley Hall, Mike Townend showed me the extensive collection of items to do with the General held there.

In York, at the Royal Dragoon Guards Museum, Graeme Green got out the General's Balaklava helmet from the display, so that I could inspect its dents. He, Aline Staes and Charlotte Hughes made my visits to the archive there in June 2019 and July 2021 productive and enjoyable. Tim Wright, and the other officers of the Royal Dragoons, the successor regiment to the 5th Dragoon Guards, were most hospitable on a visit to Catterick in November 2019, showing me the portrait of General Scarlett by Sir Francis Grant which presides over their mess and the magnificent silver centrepiece the General presented to the regiment. Charles Mackain-Bremner and Samuel Bates subsequently sent me photographs of both. I would also like to thank Edwin Rutherford of the Royal Scots Dragoon Guards Museum in Edinburgh and Peter Storer of the Household Cavalry Museum Archive in Windsor.

Anyone writing about the Crimean War is in debt to the members of the Crimean War Research Society. Its quarterly periodical, the *War Correspondent*, is a cornucopia of information about all aspects of the war.

Tony Margrave's invaluable list of *British Officers in the East, 1854, 1855, 1856*, published by the society, is supplemented every month by the detailed sources Tony circulates to those actively involved in research on the war. Amongst other members of the society, I wish to thank Douglas Austin, Glenn Fisher, Mike Hinton, David Jones, Colin Robins, Ken Tough and Lee Tough.

Astonishingly, there are two biographical dictionaries of the men who took part in the Charge of the Heavy Brigade: Roy Dutton, *Forgotten Heroes: The Charge of the Heavy Brigade* (2008), and Lawrence W. Crider, *In Search of the Heavy Brigade* (2012), both of which have been invaluable.

Brian Earl, Farquhar McKay and Tony Morris have proved themselves outstanding sounding-boards for my ideas about the Charge of the Heavy Brigade. Alison Kemp and Eva Osborne have followed the progress of this book sympathetically during its gestation, as have my daughters, Catherine, Eleanor and Matilda. My eldest grandson, Sandy Morrison, has shown a persistent and gratifying interest in the Crimean War. My wife, Lucy, has made the whole project possible. Finally, Phil Sidnell of Pen & Sword and I have a shared interest in warhorses going back over fifteen years. I am glad to have been able to reaffirm this interest by this book.

Chapter 1

Early Life

James Yorke Scarlett was born in London on 1 February 1799. He was christened at St Marylebone parish church three months later, on 2 May. Named James after his father, he was called Yorke after his great aunt.[1] He was the fourth out of three boys and three girls.[2] When he was born his parents were living at 74 Guildford Street in London, just north of the Inns of Court, convenient for his father's work as a barrister. While little or nothing else is known about the first ten years of his life, he was born into a talented, wealthy and loving family.

His father, James Scarlett (1769–1844), had not been born in England but at Duckett's Spring in Jamaica, a sugar plantation near Montego Bay. The Scarletts, originally from Sussex, had been in Jamaica since its conquest by a Commonwealth fleet under Penn and Venables in 1655. James's youngest brother, Sir William Anglin Scarlett, stayed in Jamaica and became chief justice of the island. Another brother, Dr Robert Scarlett, studied medicine in Edinburgh. According to James Scarlett himself, 'he had never known any cleverer man than his own brother Robert, and when he said this, he had seen all the men of his time'.[3]

James Scarlett himself came to England in 1785 to enrol in the Inns of Court and to complete his education at Trinity College, Cambridge. After doing well at Trinity, he enjoyed a rapid and remarkable success at the Bar, becoming the highest earning barrister of the day. He was described as

> an amiable, popular man, of respectable character and genial disposition. His voice was low and mellifluous, his manner persuasive and easy, his face was round, jolly, rubicund and intelligent in expression. In later life he became very portly. Cautious, wary, astute, clear in his discernment, almost infallible in his judgement, he was an unrivalled *nisi prius* counsel, and his success with juries was almost miraculous, though not given to oratorical or any other form of display.[4]

James Scarlett made many friends while at Trinity, one of whom, Peter Campbell of Kilmory, introduced him in 1785 to his sister, Louise Henrietta Campbell (1772–1829): 'At Christmas I had engaged myself to visit a family at Tittenhanger Park, near St Alban's, the property of the Earl of Hardwicke. There I first met the lady to whom, after an attachment of nearly seven years, I was married.'[5]

He had proposed to her at Richmond, Yorkshire, on the banks of the River Swale, where she was staying with her cousins, the Yorkes. The couple were married in St Marylebone church on 22 August 1792. While the father of Peter and Louise Campbell owned Kilmory Castle in Argyll, they had also both been born in Jamaica, at Paradise Estate, near Montego Bay. It was a happy marriage. As James Scarlett recalled in his memoirs, Louise

> had been the object of my early and constant attachment, and had from my first acquaintance with her exercised a strong influence over my conduct.
>
> Her children, for whom these memories are intended, lived to witness her sweet disposition, her divine temper, and consummate discretion. I lived with her in uninterrupted comfort and happiness from the time of our marriage to the month of March 1829 and have lived ever since to lament her loss.[6]

In their links with slavery, the Scarletts and Campbells were by no means unusual. Many propertied families in Britain had at least some connection with the plantations in the West Indies. Nor, to many people, was slavery seen as unacceptable before the success of a long-term Evangelical campaign resulted in the Abolition of the Slave Trade in 1807 and the Abolition of Slavery itself in 1833. James Scarlett's fortune was made in the law, rather than from inherited Jamaican wealth, but Louise Campbell inherited £5000 and may have brought more as a dowry.[7] Although there is no easy equivalence, Jamaican wealth and talent contributed in many ways to the life of nineteenth-century Britain. The careers of the first Lord Abinger and of his sons, James Yorke Scarlett and Peter Campbell Scarlett, are cases in point.

As James Scarlett's success grew, the family moved to a house in Westminster, No. 4 Spring Gardens, New Street.[8] He also bought a country house at Abinger, near Dorking, in 1810. Besides his career as a barrister, James Scarlett was an active politician. MP for Peterborough from 1819 to 1830, then for Cockermouth and Norwich, he was Attorney General under Canning and Wellington. He was particularly close to George Canning, Prime Minister for 119 days, whose early death in 1828 checked Scarlett's political career. He was, however, never as successful a speaker in Parliament as he had been an advocate in the courts. Initially a Whig, his opposition to the Reform Bill led to his becoming a Tory. He became Chief Baron of the Exchequer under Peel in 1834 and was ennobled as Lord Abinger in 1835.

Although there are no records of his relationship with his own sons and daughters when they were young, James Scarlett seems always to have been at ease with children, as the memoirs of his granddaughter, Frances Scarlett, who lived with her parents and grandfather in London, testify:

> Very early in my life, when I was perhaps twelve, I was established as reader to Grandpapa. Every morning when he was at breakfast, a very simple meal consisting of toast and an egg, or a small piece of bacon, previous to his going to the court, I read the leading articles in the *Times* to him. They lasted generally until he had finished, and then kissing and thanking me he hurried off. I always look back on this morning reading as the best part of my education. I acquired an interest in the outside world not generally awakened in little girls, and a fair knowledge of subjects which would have been on ordinary lines supposed to be out of the reach of my comprehension. Sometimes, not often, I was a little late and then the family butler, Davis, who was really the most benevolent of men, would regard me rather sternly: 'This won't do at all, Miss Fanny', he would say. I was much more afraid of him than of Grandpapa.
>
> At Abinger there was more leisure and Grandpapa breakfasted with the family at 10 o'clock. I read to him before breakfast. On some especially fine mornings he would propose that we should walk on the terrace, or in the garden, instead of reading. These walks were delightful to me. He would tell me the tales of Shakespeare's plays, or the incidents of *Paradise Lost*. I remember he told me the story of *Cymbeline* on a lovely September morning, when the spiders' webs were floating in the air and the dew shone upon the ground. Ever since floating webs and sparkling dew have called up *Cymbeline* to my mind.[9]

James Yorke Scarlett, his elder brother Robert and his younger brother Peter were sent to school at Temple Grove School in East Sheen. All three then went to Eton, before going on to Trinity College, Cambridge. Their father took a close interest in their studies. A surviving notebook kept by Peter Scarlett at his father's behest gives a blow-by-blow account of his scholarly progress. On his first day at Eton, Peter wrote:

> My dear Father, This is the first day of my arrival at Eton and, to let you see I have not forgot your injunctions, I have set myself down to write you a few lines before I go to bed. My tutor, after I had accomplished some verses and a theme, examined me in Greek. The questions he put to me were not difficult and I answered most of them

without hesitation. I first construed him some Herodotus, after which I said some rules in the Greek grammar. Having shown up my verses to Keate,* I was entered into the upper remove of Eton.[10]

No such notebook by either of Peter's elder brothers, Robert and James, survives, but it is clear that their father took an exceptionally close interest in his children's lives and studies. Testimony that it was a positive relationship is provided by James Yorke Scarlett's reaction after the success of the Charge of the Heavy Brigade, writing to his sister-in-law:

I am overpaid by the praises I have received for the acts performed; but, as one works a long time in the dark and obscurity without notice, perhaps one should consider the payment for the present as partly for the past – the feeling I have strongly implanted in my mind, which is the satisfaction which any distinction I may gain would have given to my dear father, who set a high value on reputation and distinction.[11]

At Eton, where he was for six years, James Yorke Scarlett was in the same class as an almost exact contemporary, Edward Smith-Stanley (1799–1869), later fourteenth Earl of Derby and three times Prime Minister in 1852, 1858–59 and 1866–68. They were friends throughout their lives. Only illness prevented Lord Derby, two months before his own death, from attending a presentation by the Conservative Working Men of Burnley to the General in August 1869:

if I could have been tempted on any occasion to break through my rule, it would have been for the purpose of joining in a mark of esteem for Sir James Yorke Scarlett, who fifty-five years ago was my most intimate friend at Eton, and for whom, during that long period, I have entertained an increasing regard.[12]

Another friend made by James Yorke Scarlett was Walter Scott, the son of Sir Walter Scott and a fellow officer in the 18th Hussars. Sir Walter recorded in his diary on 19 December 1825, 'Dined at Lord Chief Baron's –

---

* John Keate, headmaster of Eton, 1809–34. According to Alexander Kinglake, the historian of the Crimean War: 'He was little more (if more at all) than five feet in height, and was not very great in girth, but within this space was concentrated the pluck of ten battalions. You could not put him out of humour, that is out of the ill-humour which he thought to be fitting for a Head Master. His red, shaggy eyebrows were so prominent that he habitually used them as arms and hands for the purpose of pointing out any object towards which he wished to direct attention. He wore a fancy dress, partly resembling the costume of Napoleon, partly that of a widow woman.' Alexander Kinglake, *Eothen* (Oxford, 1982), p. 203.

Lord Justice Clerk, Lord President, Captain Scarlett, a gentlemanlike young man, the son of the great counsel and a friend of my son Walter.'[13]

James Yorke Scarlett's common sense and pleasure in his family are evident in two letters he wrote to his mother from Eton. These also display his ability to write a good letter from an early age. The first explains that he had been unable to see the Tsar and the King of Prussia in Windsor because of having no suitable coat. The second states categorically his confidence in the love and support given to him by his parents.[14] From Trinity College, Cambridge, where he was from 1816–18, he wrote a letter to his brother Robert which displays a remarkable maturity.[15] It shows a conciliatory approach, and a willingness to settle differences amicably, which served him well in later life.[16]

When choosing a career, James Yorke Scarlett rejected two obvious choices. Unlike both his brothers, he did not become a barrister.[17] He also did not go into the church. There was no family living available and no tradition of ordination in the family. He was also brought up before the broad church of the eighteenth century had been both revived and divided by high-church ritual and low-church enthusiasm. His early attitude to religion is expressed in one of his letters from Eton:

> The bell is ringing for church. I shall not send this till after one. Then, perhaps, I shall have somewhat more to say. I am just come from the tiresome ceremony of kneeling down, getting up again, and performing many of the evolutions which have been performed in the same manner, with as little meaning, for this last six years.[18]

While this was a Regency rather than a Victorian attitude to Anglican devotion, in later life James Yorke Scarlett became a staunch supporter of the Church of England and a vigorous opponent of the disestablishment of the Church of Ireland.

Instead, he determined to make a career in the army. The first mention of this aim is in his letter to his brother Robert from Trinity. 'With respect to Malorti, he is Master of Fortification at Woolwich and also takes private pupils who have nothing to do with the college.'[19] He also did not wish to stay in Cambridge. 'I have no chance of being high enough at examination to make it worthwhile staying here. I certainly shall not acquire much fresh knowledge on the subjects, and I may acquire a great deal of fortification, or to a great extent, in the same time.'[20] While there was no recent tradition of soldiering in his family, other than that of commanding militia regiments in Jamaica, nearly all of James Yorke Scarlett's life had been spent at a time when Britain was at war with France. Britain's long struggle at sea and in the Spanish peninsula had helped bring about the defeat and abdication of Napoleon in 1814. Victory at Waterloo in 1815, following Napoleon's escape from Elba, made the Duke of Wellington a national hero and gave the army a prestige which it has seldom had before or since.

One factor in his decision to make his career in the army may well have been that James Yorke Scarlett was an outstanding horseman:

> From his boyhood he evinced a passion for horsemanship, and when but a youth his judgment as to the 'points' of the noble animal he was one day to bestride so well was considered not only excellent but up to that of the 'Corner' veterans. One of the best riders in his regiment, and delighting in the chase, his own stud was always conspicuous for their performances in the field.[21]

Becoming an officer in the British Army was not a cheap option. Commissions had to be bought and were important property rights. This system was defended, particularly in the years after the French Revolution, by the argument that giving army officers a stake in the existing system was a bastion against revolution. Becoming an officer in a fashionable regiment cost more than in a provincial one. The Guards and the cavalry were the most prestigious of all. Fortunately for James Yorke Scarlett, his father was in a good position to provide him with an entry into the army and to support his progress when there.

1

James Yorke Scarlett to Louise Scarlett
Eton, 10 June 1814

Friday evening, Eton College, Bucks, 10 June 1814

My dearest Mother, I suppose you know that we have got all the Emperors and Kings here at Windsor, and you cannot imagine how gay the good people are in the blessed town.[22] The Queen has got all the boys leave to walk in Frogmore Gardens tonight, that they may have a view of these great personages who are to be there.[23] You will wonder why I am not there then, as you know I have as much curiosity as other folks. To tell you the truth, at this present time I am dressed out very gay, only the taylor has sent down to say he cannot possibly get my coat done tonight. What can I do? I cannot appear in my Montem coat, which is the only one I have got; at least, as my old one is out of the question, as we are to appear in full dress.[24] Why, the only thing I can do is to stay at home; and, while others are walking and showing off their fine cloths, to write to you; and then tomorrow I shall be as happy as the rest of them. It is no use to bewail this dire mishap; for, as the proverb says, 'What can't be cured must be endured.'

I have not heard from you lately. Pray write soon. What are your plans for the summer? Shall you be in town during my holydays? I hope not. I envy Master Peter a little his coming home so soon.[25] It does not want above ten days to his vacation. I have to look forward to seven long dull weeks. I see from my aunt's letter to Robert that she intends going to Tunbridge soon.[26] I cannot tell her exactly the day her son will be at home, but I think it will be about the twenty-sixth or thirtieth of July.

The maid has just opened my door and is staring with astonishment to see me writing a letter here, instead of being out at the gardens, and declares it is a great shame of the taylor to disappoint. The Ascot Races are this week, so that there is another cause of gaiety: every ten minutes we see carriages and horses coming through here on their way. Everybody seems to be so pleased about something or other, I can't tell what, but this I know: that these fine doings, at least fine to those that like them, have completely turned me out of my course; and I know not when I shall get back to it again.

It is just striking eight o'clock; at nine they must all come down, and I suppose I shall be overwhelmed with different accounts, but I have made up my mind to believe only those who tell me there was nothing worth seeing there. A rumour has been spread about here that, on the day Peace is proclaimed at Windsor, we shall have a day to ourselves without any absence or church.[27] Now of this I do not believe a word; but, if it should be so, I should be very much inclined to get on the outside of an early coach and pay you a visit, and then return by the four o'clock stage, which stops at Slough. But I fear I am writing of things that will never happen; but if it should be [the case] it would make up for all the disappointments twenty [times]. [You say] Gardener is going to be married.[28] Pray, is it to Mrs Martha or someone else? I have not heard from Bob this time. I was in hopes I should see him here, but I suppose he is still at Cambridge, though I believe the term is ended. Little Bob is very well and is gone up with some of his friends.[29] He can shift for himself now as well as the best of them.

You must excuse this scrawl. For, besides the badness of my pen, it is so dark I can hardly see. The trees have grown so much as to render my room, before one of the lightest, very nearly the darkest. Give my love to Papa, sisters and Anglin, and believe me, dear Mother, your ever affectionate and dutiful son J.Y. Scarlett.[30]

Cover, Mrs J. Scarlett, No. 74 Upper Guildford Street, Queen Square, London. Postmark, 13 June 1814.

* * *

2

James Yorke Scarlett to Louise Scarlett
Eton, 29 June 1814

My dearest Mother, It seems to me a long time since I have had the pleasure of seeing your writing, but I can account for that, as you suppose that Robert and Peter have told me all the news of Guildford Street.[31] I was much pleased and not less astonished to behold them opening my door on Sunday morning, as Robert had mentioned next Saturday for their visit. I need not tell you how glad I was to see them both, but I fear they spent a very dull time of it, the weather proving most provokingly bad.

In little more than four weeks, I expect to be with you again. Election Monday will be on the twenty-ninth of next month.[32] I have some little hopes to see you here then. I both wish it and fear it. I shall most probably speak Greek, therefore you will not understand me, and I think I shall gain by that circumstance. It is my opinion that there will be no great display of eloquence, as we have but one good speaker in the sixth form at present.

From all I hear, it is quite an uncertainty where you are to pass the summer this year; but, wherever it may be, the place will be pleasant to me if you are all there. That alone is sufficient to make any spot delightful. I return many thanks to Loo for her last letter.[33] I have nothing to amuse her or I should have not been so long in her debt. As for her sister Molly, I know she is a very naughty, idle little girl, and I have not had a single line from her, but I do not love her a bit the less for not writing, if she does not forget to love me.[34]

My dame has been questioning me about leaving her house at Election. I have told her that I could not tell her with certainty, for my father had not decided, but that I supposed I should be able to tell her before the holydays. I have hopes that she will be more flourishing soon. Three new boys are coming directly. I should be glad to see her house full, for she means very well, though she has strange ideas of good manners and politeness.

I have sustained an heavier loss than Bob and have not been as fortunate in my searches.[35] I suppose you have heard how he lost the stone of his seal and how we found it again; but I am more unfortunate. The morning after he went, I missed my purse with two one pound notes in it. I remembered that it was in the pocket of the trousers I had pulled off the night before. I directly asked for the trowsers, which the maid had taken down into the laundry. They were to be found easy enough, but the purse not so easily.

The maid, the washerwoman, offered to be searched, to swear and all other things that could prove them innocent. I suspect the latter, but to no purpose, for I fear it is irrecoverably lost. My dame and myself have made all sorts of inquiries about it. In the mean time I have only a few shillings left. I should not ask you for more, but I owe £3 10s. for some things I have had here, and therefore I may as well write when I am in want. If you will send me £5, there will be £1 10s. to keep me in rolls and butter till Election. I fear you will think that I cost you more by a great deal than I am worth, and perhaps you will think quite [right].[36]

The bell is ringing for church. I shall not send this till after one. Then, perhaps, I shall have somewhat more to say. I am just come from the tiresome ceremony of kneeling down, getting up again, and performing many of the evolutions which have been performed in the same manner, with as little meaning, for this last six years.

I have been reading the *Diable* with my French master.[37] I begin to understand the language better, but find that I do not gain much from a master which may not be acquired alone just as well. I cannot finish my letter till I have mentioned one thing. Robert tells me that a letter of mine gave you some uneasiness. He says, from my expressions, I seem to think I am neglected by my friends at home. Now, whether this be the case or not, I must assure you that nothing was ever farther from my thoughts. I know very well that I have been treated not only with that kindness which a son generally receives from his parents, but with much more than most sons; and with much more, if what Bob says is true, than I have ever deserved. Therefore I must beg you to excuse anything I may have said; and, believe me, I shall always remain, dearest Mama, your ever dutiful and affectionate son, JYS.

Love to all.

Cover, Mrs Scarlett, No. 74 Upper Guildford Street, Russell Square, London. Postmark, 29 June 1816.

* * *

3

James Yorke Scarlett to Robert Scarlett
Trinity College, Cambridge, 19 April 1818

Trinity College, 19 April

My dear Robert, I am very much obliged to you for your letter and the information it contains. I am now much better acquainted with my own affairs than I was before.[38] With respect to Malorti, he is Master of Fortification at Woolwich and also takes private pupils who have nothing to do with the college.[39] My information is derived from J. Bigge, from whom I had a letter on the subject.[40]

I cannot help feeling hurt at the first few lines of your letter. There seems to be some cloud between you and me which prevents us from seeing each other in a proper light. We shall no doubt, in our progress thro' life, have enough to contend with without increasing our ills by domestic quarrels. I am anxious therefore to take this opportunity to remove, as much as I am able, all causes of dispute between us.

You seem to think I have no confidence or faith in you, which is quite a mistaken notion. The only thing I take amiss is your coldness and reserve. If you wished to break off all intercourse between us, you could not have taken a more effectual method; for there is something in my temper which makes me fly the society of a person who appears to place any restraint upon himself which is wholly unnecessary. I suppose you have some reason for all you do. I therefore conclude I have done something to offend. Tell me what it is and it shall not be my fault if things are not put at rights again. I never in my life could live with a person upon half and half terms, if you can understand what I mean. It is like my dame's meat used to be: *hotty-cold*, which, you no doubt must remember, was by no means nice.[41]

I have no doubt but that all this arises from my want of reflection and temper, and therefore I am the first to propose that for the future we should on both sides leave off looking so very reserved at each other, lest what I believe is now only assumed should grow habitual.

I had yesterday written a much graver and longer letter, but I really was ashamed of the subject and burnt it. Write to me soon and do not let me begin my career with such a drawback. I myself think that, indeed I know that, I have no chance of being high enough at examination to make it worthwhile staying here. I certainly shall not acquire much fresh knowledge on the subjects, and I may acquire a great deal of fortification, or to a great extent, in the same time. The only chance I have of getting before other men is by having a better knowledge of my profession.[42]

With love to all the party, I am, dear Robert, your ever affectionate brother, J.Y. Scarlett.

Written on inside of the cover:

> The age was hard and men were rude
> Their cruel hands oft stained with blood.
> When [crossed out words] comfort and delight
> No stronger tie than brotherhood.[43]

Cover, R.C. Scarlett Esq., No. 2 King's Bench Walk, Temple.[44] Postmark, 20 April 1818.

* * *

Chapter 2

Cavalry Officer

In the nineteenth century, in a society where the horse was still ubiquitous, the cavalry remained what it had always been: with the Guards, the most prestigious part of the army. Cavalry regiments had played a distinguished part in the Napoleonic Wars, with the charges of the Dragoons at Salamanca and the Scots Greys at Waterloo part of military and Romantic legend.[1] Although increasingly vulnerable to guns, cavalry was considered vital on campaign for the gathering of intelligence and, when the moment was right, for delivering a devastating charge and then turning the beaten enemy's retreat into a rout.

In the eighteenth century the cavalry had become divided into two: light cavalry or hussars for scouting and heavy cavalry or dragoons for charging.[2] During the Napoleonic Wars and afterwards these gradually lost their separate identities. Both branches were ready to fulfil either function.

James Yorke Scarlett gained his commission at a time when all the branches of the army establishment were being reduced, although the cavalry was not reduced as much as the infantry.[3] On leaving Cambridge, he joined the 18th Hussars at Maidstone as a cornet, after the regiment returned from France in 1818. He must have made a good impression as 'shortly after joining, though junior cornet, he commanded the corps, then a thousand strong, on its march to Newcastle-on-Tyne.'[4] He served with the regiment for three years, including in Ireland, before it was disbanded. His uncertainty as to the course his future career is expressed in a letter of 1821 to his brother Robert.[5] While he clearly preferred to remain in England or Ireland, he also recognised the alternative: service in India.

After a short time on half-pay, he transferred to the 6th Dragoon Guards, known as the Carabiniers, in December 1822, with whom he served until June 1830.[6] His commitment to his profession was clearly demonstrated by his determination to improve his knowledge of warfare. According to a short biography printed in 1855:

> He at length obtained a half-pay majority and took advantage of the privilege of field officers to complete his military studies at Sandhurst, in mathematics and fortification. This was the act of a man who had

entered the service with an intention of being duly qualified to do it credit. His study was close, his progress rapid. Application had achieved for him its reward. But half the usual time considered necessary to the mastery of the solid science of war had expired when Scarlett was appointed to a full-pay majority in the 5th Dragoon Guards. The regiment being in Ireland (at that time in a disturbed state), the new major, anxious to join, offered himself for immediate examination at the end of his six months at Sandhurst. He went through the ordeal swimmingly. There had been no 'cramming': it was aptitude, he had buckled himself to the work, and it was done. On obtaining a certificate of proficiency, he was further honoured by a letter from the Horse Guards commending his zeal.[7]

As he knew from his time in Ireland with the 18th Hussars, home service in the cavalry in peacetime involved little scouting and no charging. As Elizabeth I's minister Lord Burleigh had presciently said in 1561, 'Soldiers in peace are like chimneys in summer'.[8] Between the end of the Napoleonic Wars in 1815 and the outbreak of the Crimean War in 1854, the principal role of the cavalry, except in India, was to support the civil authorities in keeping law and order. At a time of frequent political and industrial unrest, and before a regular police force took over handling all but the most serious incidents of riot, bodies of horsemen were remarkably successful in controlling and dispersing crowds. According to the Duke of Wellington:

> It is much more desirable to employ cavalry for the purposes of police than infantry; for this reason: cavalry inspires *more terror*. At the same time it *does much less mischief*. A body of twenty or thirty horse will disperse a mob with the utmost facility, whereas 400 or 500 infantry will not effect the object without the use of their firearms, and a great deal of mischief may be done.[9]

Over the twenty-four years of his service with, and in command of, the 5th Dragoon Guards, the regiment was nearly always spread out in detachments in either England or Ireland. It was in England from 1830 to 1841 and again from 1844–1850. It was in Ireland from 1841 to 1844 and from 1850 to 1854. The 5th Dragoon Guards' service record provides an outline of where the regiment was each year; and of particular incidents and events.[10] The regiment frequently changed its headquarters, from which individual troops were often at a distance and indeed split into detachments. In September and October 1830, the Dragoon Guards were deployed to help deal with the rural unrest near Oxford and the Swing Riots in the southern counties.

Four troops of the regiment were despatched to Oxford for the purpose of aiding the civil power, a riot having taken place at Otmoor in the vicinity of that city. Two of those troops returned to Windsor a few days afterwards, the others remained until later when they received a route to march the same day for Chatham in consequence of disturbances, caused by incendiaries in the counties of Kent, Surrey, Sussex, Hants etc. On 5 November the troops at Windsor marched for the same destination in aid of the civil power.

The troops were greatly harassed during this winter, in consequence of the opposition manifested by the lower orders to the payment of tithes; they assembled in great multitudes, setting on fire and causing great destruction to private property.

Amongst other places to which the regiment furnished detachments the following may be mentioned: Tunbridge, Seven Oaks, Rothersfield, East Grinstead, Battle, Hailsham, Cuckfield, Uckfield, Mayfield, Aylesford etc.[11]

In July 1837 they had to deal with an election riot in Birmingham: 'On the 25th and 26th a violent riot took place after the election for the borough of Birmingham and the aid of the regiment for its suppression was required by the magistrates … but by good conduct and the steadiness of that troop, the lieutenant colonel was able to suppress the riot without injury or bloodshed, and restore order for that night.'[12] In 1839, 'During the greatest part of this year, the North of England was kept in a very unsettled state, by the tumultuous proceedings of great bodies of men calling themselves Chartists. To suppress the riotous proceedings of these men, the regiment sent detachments to Derby, Loughborough, Arnold, Redhill, Mansfield, Bulwell, Stamford and other places in the more immediate neighbourhood of headquarters.'[13]

In Ireland, Scarlett and the 5th Dragoon Guards were fortunate not to face the rebel uprisings of the Napoleonic Wars or the later Fenian terror campaigns. They were also in England, not Ireland, during the terrible years of the potato famine of 1845–49. There were, nevertheless, frequent calls on their services, particularly at the time of elections. In 1841:

The regiment was called on to aid the civil power in preserving peace and enabling the electors to exercise unmolested their franchise. In performance of this difficult and delicate duty, rendered more than usually arduous from the excited state of public feeling and the violence of some parties in the state, the regiment was dispersed over a considerable tract of country in small detachments extending from

Wexford to Dingle, a distance of about two hundred miles and from Cork to Ennis, covering seven counties.

The reduced number of the British cavalry in Ireland rendered more than common exertions necessary and several detachments were forced to make marches of thirty and occasionally forty miles in the day to enable them to meet the demands made for their services.

To relate the causes or particularize the parties which rendered the elections in some places a scene of disgraceful riot and bloodshed does not come within the province of a military record; suffice it to say that under circumstances which imposed on the regiment the most disagreeable and harassing duties without the prospect of adding to its military renown, the temper and discipline displayed by the men, the zeal and discretion of the officers and general efficiency of the corps were fully acknowledged ...[14]

The regiment's actions were successful. There was no repetition of the disaster of August 1819, when the 15th Hussars, coming to the support of poorly disciplined Yeomanry, had killed eighteen men and women and injured large numbers while trying to disperse a large Radical meeting at St Peter's Field in Manchester, subsequently known as the Peterloo Massacre. Successful policing required considerable tact, not the panic which had induced the Manchester magistrates to send in the Hussars with sabres drawn. The 5th Dragoon Guards record contains the thanks of various civil authorities congratulating their officers and men on their conduct.

There were also regular reports of the high standards shown by the regiment at inspections. Praise for the regiment culminated in 1849:

On 7 August the regiment was inspected by Major General Brotherton CB, Inspector General of Cavalry, who was pleased to express his entire approbation of the appearance and discipline of the regiment in every respect. The regiment had a further gratification of receiving the approbation of His Grace the Duke of Wellington, Commander in Chief, conveyed to them by the Adjutant General, through the Inspector General, in the following words:

The efficient and perfect state of discipline of the 5th Dragoon Guards has appeared to the Commander in Chief as in the highest degree creditable to the Commanding Officer of this Corps, as well as to the admirable system established in it, and I am to request you will be pleased to communicate this expression of His Grace's satisfaction to Lieutenant Colonel the Honourable J. Yorke Scarlett.[15]

Henry Franks (1818–1909) enlisted in the 5th Dragoon Guards at Nottingham in 1839 and served in the regiment, including at Balaklava, until 1862, becoming a serjeant major. His memoirs, *Leaves from a Soldier's Note Book*, although not published until 1904, give a vivid account of life in the regiment and of James Yorke Scarlett as its commanding officer. Franks' independent witness from inside the regiment is doubly valuable in that it comes from a non-commissioned officer:

> We left Nottingham on 19 May 1840 and marched to Manchester – five days' march. Colonel Wallace now left the regiment and Major Scarlett became lieutenant colonel. There was a great rejoicing amongst the men, for the new colonel was very popular with all ranks. Although a strict disciplinarian, he was a thorough English gentleman and beloved by everyone.[16]

*   *   *

Colonel Scarlett began to introduce a number of reforms into the interior economy, and other matters in connection with the messing and cooking of the men's rations, which gave great satisfaction, were very beneficial and, being ably assisted by both adjutant and quartermaster. The colonel soon had the satisfaction of seeing a wonderful improvement. No doubt he was very much gratified by the results, and the men took every opportunity of shewing him that they greatly appreciated his kind efforts for their welfare. It was soon seen by the remarkable change that took place in the general conduct of the troops and, when the half-yearly inspection took place soon afterwards, General Wemyss complimented the regiment on the almost complete absence of crime; in fact it became patent to everyone that the colonel's efforts had been a success, and things were very pleasant all round. The 5th Dragoon Guards acquired a good name, soon became very popular in Manchester, and were respected generally by the inhabitants.[17]

The regiment was equally outstanding in Ireland:

> His Royal Highness the present Duke of Cambridge, then a young man of about thirty, was in command of the Dublin Garrison at that time. He was quartered in the Royal Barracks, where the 5th Dragoon Guards were also. I remember when he was inspecting another regiment, in making some comments upon its conduct, he remarked: 'I know a regiment that is now stationed in the Garrison, and the general conduct of that same corps has been so good for the last twelve months

they have not had a man tried by court martial. That regiment', he added, 'is the 5th Dragoon Guards.'[18]

In his many travels with his regiment, when posted in Burnley in Lancashire, James Yorke Scarlett had met his wife. Charlotte Anne Hargreaves was the younger daughter of Colonel John Hargreaves, a rank held in the local militia. Colonel Hargreaves had inherited a substantial mining interest in Burnley, as well as two large houses, Ormerod House, in Cliviger, just outside Burnley, and Bank Hall, near its centre. The beginning of the acquaintance between James Yorke Scarlett and Charlotte Hargreaves must have been well before their wedding, as clearly Scarlett knew his father-in-law, who died in 1834, well.

The couple were married in St Peter's church in Burnley on Saturday 19 December 1835, with the service performed by the bride's brother-in-law, William Thursby.[19] Having spent their honeymoon at Abinger Hall, the couple made their home at Bank Hall when not away with the regiment. The marriage made James Yorke Scarlett a very wealthy man. He and William Thursby, who lived with his wife Eleanor, Charlotte's elder sister, at Ormerod House, controlled the main mines in Burnley, employing over five hundred men.

Charlotte Scarlett remains a somewhat shadowy figure, though clearly very well respected in Burnley. A later tribute testified to the esteem with which Charlotte and her sister Eleanor were held in the town:

> Even in early youth the Misses Hargreaves were distinguished for their solicitude for the poor, and during the past two days many of the older inhabitants have been busy recalling incidents which bespeak the deep sympathy of these ladies with those in want and suffering. Their visits to the homes of those afflicted or in poverty, no less than their ready response to an appeal on behalf of any worthy object, endeared the young ladies from Bank Hall to the inhabitants at large.

The marriage was a love match, though sadly childless, other than for a stillborn daughter. A poignant newspaper notice in 1839 recorded: 'On the 15 Inst., at Birmingham, the Honorable Mrs Yorke Scarlett, of a daughter, still-born.'[20] The relationship between the couple was clearly a very close one, perhaps reinforced by the tragedy of the stillbirth and the absence of children. General Scarlett spoke about his wife at a presentation to her in 1869.

> General Scarlett, in the appropriate response made by him on behalf of his lady, said she disclaimed any merits such as Mrs Parker had

attributed to her.[21] Still, continued the gallant General, whilst she took no merit to herself, he knew that her heart overflowed with kindness, and he was quite certain that she deserved everything that could possibly be done for her, because a better daughter or a better wife never blessed the home of any man.

For thirty years they had lived together, and during that time he had never had a fault to find with her except on one occasion when her great affection overpowered her for a short time. At that time, grieved as she was, when she was asked whether she wished General Scarlett to remain at home or return to his duties in the Crimea, she gave no answer, nor could anyone persuade her at that moment to give an answer, but to him she afterwards said, 'How could I say I wished you to go out; or how could I wish you not to go out when it was your duty to go?' Knowing the effect which his having been there, and his going there again, had upon her, he thought the resolution which she showed on that occasion was worthy of her father, who was one of the most gallant men that ever existed.[22]

Charlotte Scarlett, however, suffered serious and prolonged bouts of depression. As her husband wrote, when expressing condolences on a family bereavement, 'Charlotte, who has suffered deeply and is too well acquainted with grief, feels I think as sensibly as I do how much you have to deplore and is as anxious to hear of you.'[23]

Two years after his marriage, James Yorke Scarlett became the Conservative MP for Guildford. He held the seat for four years but was defeated by the Liberal James Mangles in 1841. Although consistently voting with his party, which was in Opposition during these years, he spoke very rarely and took little active part in Parliamentary business. His longest speech, in April 1838, was on a family matter to do with Jamaica. He complained about the sudden emancipation of the apprentices upon the estate of his first cousin, Philip Anglin Scarlett.

Mr Scarlett had suffered in the rebellion of 1830, having fled before the insurgents for his life, with the loss of all his property. However, he had settled on another estate, where, by an accident of fire, he a second time lost his all and was utterly ruined. Nothing but his buoyancy of spirits enabled him to rise above these repeated calamities, and the present motion related to no fewer than 107 negroes, who he declared had been illegally and unduly declared free.[24]

An admirer of Sir Robert Peel, Scarlett was dismayed at the split in the Conservative Party caused by the Repeal of the Corn Laws.[25] As a supporter of his long-term friend, Lord Derby, he also almost became involved in another Parliamentary election in 1852, in the county seat of North Lancashire. For many years, the two-member constituency had been shared without a contest between the Whigs and Tories. This equilibrium was threatened when the Conservatives persuaded Scarlett to stand as a second Conservative candidate. The Liberals, however, responded by threatening to put up a second candidate of their own, Richard Fort. In the event, with uncertainty about the likely outcome, Scarlett and Fort both withdrew before nomination. At a series of meetings prior to this, Scarlett expressed his political views:

> Gentlemen, in politics I am a Conservative, because I love the institutions of Great Britain. Under these institutions we have attained to the position which we now occupy — the most extended empire in the world — powerful and respectable. If these institutions had been bad, we could not now have had extended empire, we could not have had that security for property and life, that freedom of action which is the boast of every Englishman, and, therefore, I highly value and reverence those institutions.
>
> At the same time, l am not one of those people who fancy that because a thing is good now, or is good tomorrow, that it will be good for all time. Times change, people alter, society advances, and occasional improvements and alterations are required. I am not so bigoted as not to see this, or to refuse to take into my consideration any of those necessary improvements or required alterations, at the same time adhering strictly to the main principles of the British Constitution.
>
> For the same reasons I may say I am a supporter of Lord Derby's government. The members of that government are men of high honour and principle, who have no other object in view but the good of their country. They are no mere adventurers – they are men of talent, educated men, whose sole object is to serve their country. I allude more particularly to the premier, who is a nobleman of high birth, of large property and of great ability. I would ask, what can he gain by undergoing all the toil and anxiety of office (and you can have very little idea how great that toil and anxiety is)? What can such a man as he gain, except the honour, the glory and credit of serving his country?[26]

James Yorke Scarlett's letters from this period of his life, addressed mostly to his brother and sister-in-law, are domestic rather than military. They reflect the social life of a cavalry officer in Ireland and England rather than his duties. Staying at the homes of the Irish aristocracy, and joining in the pleasures of hunting, fishing and racing, with balls and country house parties, was the soft side of the cavalry's important role in keeping law and order in Ireland and the seats of the Ascendancy safe. It clearly brought the Scarletts into contact with a variety of eccentrics, including the Marquess of Waterford, who had originated the term 'to paint the town red' by literally doing so in Melton Mowbray; and a parson who travelled with two nightingales and a spoonbill.[27]

The letters are also mainly from only a few years rather than spread over the whole period from 1818 to 1854. Country house parties are more in evidence than civil disturbances. There are, however, a number of items of military interest. The first letter from Scarlett's time in the army is a serious consideration about his prospects in it, while two later letters contain advice to his brother on how his nephew, William Scarlett, should apply for a commission in the 5th Dragoon Guards.[28] They also contain more mundane matters, including a drunken butler, as well as topics of family interest. His life-long interest in education is demonstrated by his attendance, recounted in a letter, at a prize-giving at a school for his soldiers' children.[29]

While there are a number of references to books in his letters, Scarlett also puts the case in one of his letters against reading in an age that was no longer one for action, and in which men and women got emotional satisfaction from books rather than real life:

The weather has become cold and chilly and it is very good fun to sit by the fire and read nonsense of any kind. I believe that reading is a very idle amusement and prevents people acting. Some people travel in books. Some are charitable in books. Some are good and some are bad in books. We weep and we laugh in books. We live in an unreal world of imagination. Our doings are all imaginary. We grow fat on the toils, travels, danger and thirst of a polar expedition. Our fighting propensities expend themselves on the history of the Duke's campaigns without danger to our precious limbs.[30] We satisfy our charity in devising a remedy against poverty and reading the arguments in the *Times*. Depend upon it a very reading age is not a very brilliant one for exploits of any sort or kind.[31]

He himself, after a long peacetime career in soldiering, was to show at Balaklava that the age of heroism was not dead.

4

James Yorke Scarlett to Robert Scarlett
Ireland, 1821

Many thanks, my dearest Robert, for your kind letter, which I have just received.[32] Probably, had I not thought you too much otherwise engaged, I should have written to you ere this. I think I understand what news you allude to – let what will happen, you have my most affectionate wishes for your happiness in public and private life.[33] With respect to my own fate, in which you take so kind an interest, I scarcely know what to think.

As long as my friends wish to keep me in this hemisphere, I can have no wish to be in another.[34] It is only when I think I am an unnecessary incumbrance that I feel any inclination to take so long a voyage. It does not appear to me certain at all that the 18th will go to India. Davy, who is a great rascal, would be glad to send us there, but there are several obstacles to our going.[35] In the first place, it is not our turn and the Horse Guards, according to all the information we obtain, are convinced that Sir David Ochterlony has acted most unjustly to the regiment.[36] Next, our appointment and uniform must be changed, which would be a considerable expence to government and the colonel of the regiment. Then there are several Light Dragoons in perfect trim for India. The report at present is very strong that the 3rd, Mackenzie's Regiment, go instead of us.[37] We have no *official* order for India, tho' I know that we were destined for that quarter at the Horse Guards.

Supposing we do go, we shall not get back before the early part of next year and we shall be in England in the autumn.[38] It is a great bore to begin at the bottom of the cornets after having been three years in the service. I am sure of a lieutenancy before we embark. The augmentations will take place a month or two previous to that event. Then will be the time to get an exchange. There may be some difficulty perhaps in getting leave to exchange when we are under orders, but they allowed several of the 11th, who went out on the return of the troops from France, to do so.

You may, if you can, contrive to find out what difference the cornets in the Life Guards expect to receive. The *only advantage* in being in the Life Guards is that they are always in London. On the whole I prefer the Light Cavalry service, and would prefer an exchange into any Hussar, Lancer or Light Dragoon corps.[39] I find the difference in price of a commission (a cornetcy) in the Life Guards and any other Dragoon regiment is £425.[40] Probably the gentleman might ask more for the exposure of his complexion and the chance of sea-sickness etc, etc.[41]

Exchange into some other corps probably might be had for less, but I do not wish to exchange as a cornet if I can avoid it. I would rather go on half pay as a lieutenant, to avoid going out, if I cannot then find an exchange on full pay. By going on half pay for the regulation difference after I got my lieutenancy in the 18th, I should have £450 in my pocket; and, by adding about £400 more, I should be sure of getting on full pay again as lieutenant in some other corps. Of course all the negotiations must be carried on under the rose. For, tho' there is now no such thing scarcely as getting commissions for the regulation, yet it is death without benefit of clergy (i.e. cashiering) to be known to have given or received more or less. A sub lieutenant in the Life Guards is but a cornet in the army and can only exchange with a cornet. The title of sub lieutenant is an empty name and an officer is not any higher in the army for holding it. The Guards (Foot Guards) have in the army the rank next above that they actually hold in their regiments: i.e. an ensign and lieutenant in the Guards can exchange with a lieutenant in any other corps.[42]

On the whole, it appears to me that we had better wait a little time before we commence any negotiations to see how matters stand. It is worthwhile, however, ascertaining, if you can:

1. What the officers in the Life Guards expect as a difference.
2. What chance of promotion there is in the corps at this moment.

The army is such a lottery that perhaps I might at the end of a year find myself as high by entering the Life Guards as junior cornet as I should by awaiting a lieutenancy in this regiment. Of course, I should get my lieutenancy in this regiment for nothing; but that advantage is to be balanced by the inability to sell any commission you do not purchase. So it comes pretty much to the same thing. On the whole, it is better to buy, if you have the money, a commission for the regulation than get it for nothing, because if you get it for the regulation, you have a good chance of getting much more for it when you want to sell out. If you get it for nothing, you must sell it for nothing. Ex nihilo nihil fit.[43]

I shall probably be in England sometime in August and September.[44] At least, at present I have a plan of meeting my father when he is on the Northern Circuit, towards the end of it, and getting franked up to London by means of a seat in his carriage, if it is not better occupied.[45] I can do this easily, as I can land at Liverpool, which is but a few hours travelling from Lancaster. I hope he will have no objection to my scheme. Its execution will of course depend upon circumstances and the good story I shall make out to persuade that old scoundrel Davy to give me leave.[46]

Machell, the officer whose folly has caused all our woes, you see has been replaced and reinstated in all his honours, which is a sign the Horse Guards do not view the case in the light Sir David represented it and which at first induced them to remove Machell from the service without even a hearing.[47] Hughes has acted with great spirit in attempting, as senior officer at our mess, to refute the charges of intemperance which the Scot brought against us.[48] He has sent in no less than two memorials, both of which Sir David returned and refused to forward to the Duke of York, because they were not sufficiently respectful to him (Davy); and, instead of excusing and palliating and throwing ourselves on his mercy, we boldly asserted our perfect innocence and denied that the excess of an individual of peculiar character was the anterior of our general habits.[49] I believe Hughes has …

Latter part of letter missing.

*   *   *

5

James Yorke Scarlett to Sarah Scarlett
Burnley, 25 September 1838

Burnley, 25 September 1838[50]
My dearest Sally, You have suffered a heavy blow and it is in vain to attempt a letter of condolence to you.[51] I would not prevent the flowing of one tear to the memory of those who loved you so well and to whom you were so truly attached. It must be some little consolation to you to remember that their kindness and affection (as I can bear witness) were never thrown away upon you; and, if your aunts sought every opportunity of showing their love for you, they never met with any but the most grateful return.

I had not the good fortune to be on terms of intimacy with them, but the evident love and attachment you on all occasions displayed towards them fully convinced me of their worth. We cannot restore them to you. All we can do is to assure you that you have still remaining relations whom your own merit has won over to you so thoroughly that we look upon you as if it was as natural and a feeling imbibed from the cradle.

Charlotte, who has suffered deeply and is too well acquainted with grief, feels I think as sensibly as I do how much you have to deplore and is as anxious to hear of you.[52] She is writing and will tell you what little there is to be told about ourselves. I shall therefore only add that, with the sincerest affection, I remain yours J. Yorke Scarlett.

Cover, The Hon. Mrs Scarlett, Abinger Hall, Dorking. Postmark, 27 September 1838.

*   *   *

6

James Yorke Scarlett to Sarah Scarlett
Mitchelstown Castle, County Cork, 3 July 1841

Mitchelstown Castle, 3 July

My dearest Sally, I do not know whether you are in my debt or I in yours, but I will be generous and pay beforehand for a letter from you, the more that I want to know something about the school Jimmy and Hally were at – Mr Joyce's I think it was.[53] Anything you will tell me I will make known to Lady Mountcashel, who is very desirous to send a young son to a quiet school for a year or two.[54]

I am now writing from Lord Kingston's, who is the most hospitable as well as the *oddest* of men. We are a military party almost, as there are here no less than four officers and three wives; one is coming here today. Lady Mountcashel, Lady Jane Moor, Mrs Cox and Massey Dawson, Mr and Mrs Matlock, and a few more I can't remember, are the party, which does not seem large in this immense house.[55] Lord Kingston so thoroughly puts at defiance all notions of *good* living that everybody has got reconciled to boiled mutton and turnip, ham and chickens, a sirloin of beef and greasy soup, served up on every and any kind of dish. Forks and spoons of any pattern or metal, no matter. Massey Dawson, your rector, has brought his cook here today and has ordered dinner, so that today we shall fare sumptuously. I daresay Charlotte will amuse you someday with many an anecdote, but in the meantime keep all this to yourself, for I should not like to repay the excessive kindness of Lord Kingston by spreading abroad any stories at his expense. We go to Cahir tomorrow.[56]

The breakfast went off admirably, in spite of the rain. Everybody came and the whole affair succeeded to our hearts' content and cost us less than a London dinner party, with much more amusement for the money. I am sorry to say that accounts from Lancashire are anything but agreeable. There is little or no trade. Vast Chartist meetings, though hitherto they depart quietly.[57] I fear such doctrines are being instilled which will produce ill fruit, if the change for the better does not take place before winter. I heard much in Henrietta's praise from Mrs Villiers Stuart, who came to our party and was, as usual, very lively and agreeable.[58] I can't imagine how the House of Commons have agreed to let Roebuck to establish the Star Chamber inquisition, but it will not expose the Tories so much as the Whigs.[59]

Are you going to Scotland?[60] With best love to all, will you believe me ever your very affectionate JYS.

Massey Dawson has brought in his phaeton two dogs, two Virginian nightingales and a spoonbill. Do you know anything of a Mr Joyce, rector of Dorking?[61] Lady Mountcashel has two sons for school, one of ten years and one of fifteen. Both require *quiet* schools, not being in strong health. If you know any other schools I will thank you for any information, terms, system, treatment; age of scholars and number etc.

No cover.

*   *   *

7

James Yorke Scarlett to Sarah Scarlett
Cahir, Tipperary, 19 September 1841

Cahir Barracks, 19 September 1841
My dearest Sally, I do not boast of being a good correspondent, but I am going to improve. Charlotte and I have been prevented going to Doonass by the expectation of Sir Edward Blakeney's promised visitation of the regiment, which keeps me in an uncertain state, for he may pop down any day and I should not like to be absent from my post when he comes.[62]

I have just heard from Captain Bolton that his elder brother is going to Abinger rectory on a visit to Dawson.[63] Should you see him with his reverence, be civil to him for the sake of my captain, who is a good fellow, and tell Dawson I feel exceedingly obliged to him for his invitation to us and was very sorry we were not able to accept it; and were also prevented meeting him at Lord Kingston's, as we were in the act of moving into our present abode that very day and I could not leave Charlotte to take possession by herself, in view of all the disagreeables, whilst I went to amuse myself with the good company at Mitchelstown.

We have had very uncertain weather here. Some bright warm gleams, much wind and rain, but mild withal. The barracks is exposed and when it is very quiet below we have a breeze here. I expect a visit from Felix tomorrow.[64] I wish he could have got what he wanted at the Castle, but the fact is that all great men have a great lot of relations to give away to.[65] I wish somebody would give me something, but I think that so unlikely that I have not made up my mind what to ask for. I do not think Charlotte would ask for a military appointment; for, though she faces inconveniences willingly, I think she would willingly be out of the way of them too. I think Peter should not ask for anything diplomatic but try to get some home office.[66]

I have heard nothing lately from Guildford and conclude they mean to put up with their beating, which is I suppose more palatable than paying for a petition.[67] What I shall have to pay I dread to think when I hear Horsham costs £1700 without a contest.[68] We had better trouble our heads no more about elections but draw a plan for a house at Inverlochy.[69]

Send me all the political, civil, military news you hear and more especially the news that her Royal Highness of Gloucester has got something for Currey and Louise.[70] I fear that there is a considerable sprinkling of Whigs in the new Lord Chamberlain's household. I think our people deserve to be kicked for showing the slightest fancy to the party who have reviled and abused and misused them. They do not conciliate the Whigs and the opportunity of obliging their friends is circumscribed by it. With best love to my Lord and all your party. Believe me ever, my dear lady, yours affectionately, JYS.

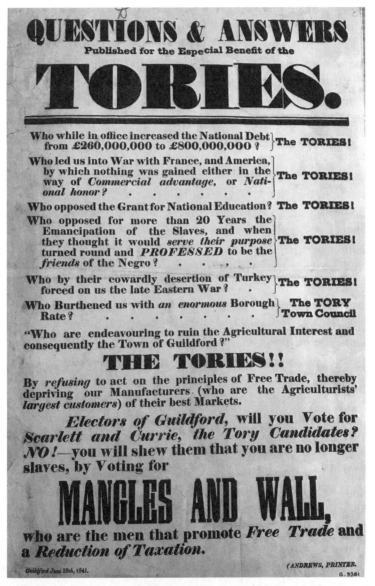

James Yorke Scarlett became Tory MP for Guildford in 1837, when the Conservatives lost the general election, but lost his seat in 1841, when a Tory government was returned under Sir Robert Peel.

8

James Yorke Scarlett to Sarah Scarlett
Cahir, Tipperary, 20 January 1842

My dearest Sally, Whether I owe you a letter or you are in my debt I don't know, but this I do know: it is a long time since I heard how the world went on *chez vous*. Some balls or rumours of balls, of bringings out or comings out, I have heard or read in a newspaper yclept *Surrey Standard* and should esteem it a favour if some intelligence of an official nature should reach the eyes and ears of us – sojourners in a foreign land; alien from England in blood and in religion.[71] How true a saying was that: how much commented on and with what very little effect and regard for truth palliated or denied. It was a true saying and will be proved more true if you don't contrive to clip O'Connell's wings before this time next year.[72] His worship the Lord Mayor is kicking up a riot you may depend, but what has that to do with Dorking balls and parties at Abinger?[73] And what can it matter to a lady recumbent on a fauteuil in London what storms are impending over the sweet city of Dublin and the Emerald Isle.

Are you asked to the christening or have you a hint to stay away?[74] Is Sir Robert Peel a favourite with Her Majesty or does she look askew at him as if he was soon to set her teeth on edge?[75] I want to know all this and a great deal more, which of course every lady who lives in London or near it knows, whilst to us everything comes across the water distorted by the sea fogs and we don't know whether to believe our eyes or trust our ears unless we get intelligence in a 'private letter'.

We have been going on very quietly. I don't know where our history was left off but we have been to Loughcoole (Lord Gort's); to Mitchelstown (Lord Kingston's); to Moor Park (Lord Mountcashel's); to Lismore (Mr Currey's); and to Dromana (Mr Villiers Stuart's).[76] All very pleasant visits of a day or two. We have dined with a Mr Perry and his pretty wife and are going tomorrow to dine at the Moors' near Clonmel, to go to the Clonmel ball of which they have made me a steward with others, the Marquis of Waterford among them.[77] I have had some hunting with the Marquis, who is quiet enough in the field, though an admirable rider; and as far as he has come under my ken a very good fellow and very good looking withal.* Poor Ingestre

---

* Henry de la Poer Beresford, third Marquess of Waterford (1811–1859), had in his youth a well-deserved reputation for rowdyism. He is said to have originated the phrase 'to paint

broke his leg and is now at Rockwell with Lady Sarah, but doing well and will I hope be able to get to town in time for the meeting of Parliament.[78] As he came here purposely to enjoy hunting, this broken leg is doubly annoying.

Today I have been very busy and somewhat bored by an examination of the soldiers' children in reading, writing and arithmetic, distributing prizes etc; but I am so far satisfied that I never saw a better conducted school or better taught scholars of their age at any other, gentle or simple. It really was a gratifying sight to see them well clothed, fed and taught; and drilled into something like good manners instead of running about ragged, lean and destitute as the children of the corresponding ranks in private life are frequently found. I got Charlotte, the parson's wife and daughter, and some other people, to make a party to be bored with me and it went off very well with a lunch at the end of it.

I believe we shall be in Dublin this spring and I think you had better make a tour into Ireland to see Wicklow and Killarney on your way to Inverlochy – Dublin and the 5th Regiment. Whether I will take a house there or not I have not quite made up my mind, for I am at present not in good humour with Mr Saunders, who has become so ill tempered with the other servants, and so much inclined to drink enough to make him irritable, that I see I shall have to part with him.[79] He will be a loss, as he is so very active when anything is to be done; but my confidence in his steadiness is gone.** If you should hear of a jewel of a butler who won't drink and will not mind moving

---

the town red'. After a heavy day's drinking at the Croxton Races, he and a number of fox-hunting friends arrived at Melton Mowbray early in the morning of 6 April 1837. When a tollhouse-keeper refused to open his gate for them before being paid, they used ladders, brushes and paint lying nearby to paint the keeper and a local constable red, as well as the door of the tollhouse, before moving on to paint other doors and inn signs in the town red. Although acquitted of riot, they were each fined £100 for common assault.

** James Yorke Scarlett's lenient treatment of offending servants is evident in a case in 1840. 'The severity of pecuniary penalties to the very poor, and the nullity of them to the rich, or to persons protected by the rich, has been the subject of frequent remarks in this journal. A fresh example point is now before us. The coachman of Colonel Scarlett was convicted of an assault on a police officer, and sentenced to a fine of £3 by Mr Burrell, the Queen Square magistrate.

Upon this the man's master, Colonel Scarlett, *interposed*, saying "The man is a very steady, careful man, and I shall pay the fine for him. Have you three pounds about you, Thomas?" Defendant: "Yes, Sir." Colonel Scarlett: "Then pay the fine, and I will settle with you and bye and bye." The magistrate's sentence on the offender was thus nullified by Colonel Scarlett, who, to make the exhibition richer, is the son of a judge! (Lord Abinger.) Had the offender been poor hackney coachman, he would probably have gone to gaol for a couple of months, in default of the penalty, or, if he could have mustered the sum, his family would have had to starve for a month from the loss of it.' *Taunton Courier and Western Advertiser*, 15 July 1840.

now and then, and is respectable in manner and look, pray let me know. The other servants have all behaved well and fit into our barrack quarter as well as in Dartmouth House.[80] I doubt whether they were so well put up before. Nor have we found the slightest inconvenience or interruption, but all barracks are not like these separate houses. Love to all from both of us, yours affectionately, JYS.

Cover, The Honorable Mrs Scarlett, 4 New Street, Spring Gardens, London (Abinger Hall, Dorking crossed out). Postmark, Cahir, 20 January 1842; Dorking 25 January 1842.

* * *

9

James Yorke Scarlett to Sarah Scarlett
Cahir, Tipperary, 14 April 1842

Cahir, 14 April 1842
My dearest Sally, The general impression that no news is good news, being confirmed by Robert's instruction that if 'I did not hear I was to consider my father improving', renders me more contented under the silence from New Street than I might otherwise be.[81] Still I cannot help being anxious to know how he is going on. One letter from Robert to tell me he was ill; one from you to say the complaint was subdued. I hope therefore to see his name as usual in the papers as 'on the bench', which will be much more congenial to his nature than being 'on the shelf'.

We have had some warm days but, as usual, only enough to make us more angry with the east wind which now dries up one's bones and skin. Give my love to Henrietta and congratulate her on what may be a happiness or not as she uses it – her introduction into the great world: great in quantity but little in quality, I think; all which cynicism arises from the wind NE.[82] Who is the youth that you appear to think has made an impression? Is it No. 10 or No. 9? We doubt but prefer that it should be No. 10. And she, I think, will like the airs from Devon better than the blasts from Scotia.[83] Do not be in a hurry, however, to draw conclusions. Many a fish nibbles at a beautiful fly on the surface and after all plunges down and swallows some put at the bottom that no one ever thought of.

I hear Felix is at Doonas and the farm there is I see advertised for immediate sale.[84] What a pity Charlotte (not my Charlotte) cannot prove herself of the male sex and keep that pretty place with a river that is not to be equalled for fish and beauty. What will Lady Massey do? Take a house at Cheltenham and have Felix and his family to live in it?

I read the debates with very little less disgust than I had to listen with. I can't say I like being taxed, because my nominal income is very much larger than my real income, but I suppose it cannot well be avoided and it is to be hoped won't last. I must be as stingy to everybody as my nature permits. I shall have many who will keep me in countenance in grinning and bearing it no doubt.

What is Peter about? Tell him that there is no White's Club here. Neither is there a Carlton or a St James's Street where the news and *on dits* grow, so I can send him no such flowers from hence.[85] But it may please him to know that I have sent twelve men to India to fight Ackbar Mahommed;[86] have bought thirty-two very fine three-year-old colts this summer; and that my men only get drunk when the whiskey overpowers them; and that I have hung up my hunting whip and greased the double bands and commenced for to drill. In return for which *news* I require him to write to me frequently and tell me all the things which are and are not true in and about London.

I have arrived at last nearly to my last home and chair in the United Services, having received intimation that I have found favour (which Lord Cardigan did not) and been elected a member.[87] It strikes me that the person who wrote me down in the book some eleven years since was Elphinstone, who I hope for his own comfort is no more, though I believe that he will (if alive) be able to prove that he disapproved of the conduct of the past government and never felt secure.[88]

Since writing the above, we have been out to ride and the east wind caused my dog to run under my horse's feet, whereby his toe was cut off. I have had to carry him home and doctor him. Luckily he was a little one and so was the toe. Best love to all in New Street. Write to say how my Lord is and believe me ever, my dearest Sally, yours affectionately, J. Yorke Scarlett.

Cover, The Honorable Mrs Scarlett, 4 New Street, Spring Gardens, London. Postmark, Cahir, 14 April 1842.

* * *

10

James Yorke Scarlett to Sarah Scarlett
Cahir, Tipperary, 30 July 1842

Cahir, 30 July
My dearest Sally, I am afraid your letter of this morning will not admit of any rational hope being indulged of poor Currey's recovery; and I anticipate the worst news in your next.[89] Poor fellow! So kind and cheerful and with so many good qualities. I cannot bear to think that all must be silenced in the grave, as I feel as if I have not half enough sympathised with his distresses and difficulties against which he struggled with courage, though I could frequently see that they affected him. I fear that he will not leave a very prosperous state of affairs and that poor dear Lou will have her grief added to by this circumstance. She fortunately is so dearly loved by all her own family – and I reckon you as thoroughly identified with us – that she will not want as much consolation as our affection can give; but it is a sad change to lose the *one* who occupied the chief place and whose affections were not given in the same degree to others.

Send me a line as soon as you can to say what takes place. I dare not hope. Charlotte has told you of our change of plans, or the change made for us by Sir Edward Blakeney.[90] I am writing from the sofa, lame from the inflammation of a corn extending up my leg; not, however, from a tight boot but from wearing one at all or walking before it was subdued. My best love to all. Write and believe me yours ever affectionately J. Yorke Scarlett.

No cover.

* * *

11

James Yorke Scarlett to Sarah Scarlett
8 Fitzwilliam Place, Dublin, 27 September 1842

8 Fitzwilliam Place, 27 September 1842
My dearest Sally, Not having much to write about I have held my peace of late.[91] We have just got into a very comfortable house and why we are going to leave it to roam off to the Highlands I don't know. Except that we said we would, as we purpose if all be right, and the wind and waves well balanced, to trust ourselves to them on the sixth to blow us over to Glasgow, thence to Kerrera and there to remain until the end of the month, when we hope Bank will be still standing to receive us and you too, if you will come.[92] Robert has promised himself. I am growing old, that's clear, for I would as soon be quiet here as go anywhere. Quiet, however, we are not, for we seldom dine at home. We are now going to dine at Lord Donnymore's and dined the other day at Lord Talbot's, and have some other engagements to last till we go.[93]

The weather has become cold and chilly and it is very good fun to sit by the fire and read nonsense of any kind. I believe that reading is a very idle amusement and prevents people acting. Some people travel in books. Some are charitable in books. Some are good and some are bad in books. We weep and we laugh in books. We live in an unreal world of imagination. Our doings are all imaginary. We grow fat on the toils, travels, danger and thirst of a polar expedition. Our fighting propensities expend themselves on the history of the Duke's campaigns without danger to our precious limbs.[94] We satisfy our charity in devising a remedy against poverty and reading the arguments in the *Times*. Depend upon it a very reading age is not a very brilliant one for exploits of any sort or kind. So if Jimmy proves an idle dog at school, as I think he will, we must hope he will be greater in performances of his own than in his knowledge of other men's deeds.[95]

We are never long without thinking of and talking of dear Lou. I am anxious to know what prospect she has before her and whether Hampton Court is likely to be obtained.[96] I should think it most desirable for her as a comfortable abode, not far from her relations and good for the education of her children. A thing to be thought of is the choice of a residence.

We hope to persuade you all to visit Dublin next spring, though we can't pretend to more than two spare beds here. Lord De Grey comes on Monday.[97] We are far from flourishing in Lancashire.[98] The cauldron has subsided but will bubble up again and the fire is not lit with my coal. Yours ever affectionately, J.Y. Scarlett.

Cover, The Honorable Mrs Scarlett, Abinger Hall, Dorking, Surrey. Postmark, 29 September 1842.

*   *   *

12

James Yorke Scarlett to Sarah, Lady Abinger
Burnley, 18 November 1845

Burnley, 18 November 1845

My dearest Sally, I have been so busy hunting and shooting since I saw you that I have had no time for letter writing. We came from Appleton yesterday and shall remain quietly till the end of next week, when we return to Stapleford, where I wish we were to meet you all again, though I fear you would get tired of so monotonous a life as you led there both your visits – unless you make up your mind that you are at home and do as you would do at home.[99] Few country houses afford much amusement, I think, for ladies; and 'at home' the arrangement of the house and other little interests give occupation which no other person's does. If, however, you can tolerate such a dearth of amusements, we shall, here at Stapleford or wherever we may be, hail your coming with delight. Robert talked of coming again. Tell him we shall be here till the end of next week and glad to see him and feed him a mutton broth and boiled mutton and turnips.

What have you done about Willy's entrance into the Guards?[100] I shall be in town for a day on the 3 December, or rather for as many hours as I am obliged to spend in the Military Board room at Whitehall discussing saddlery etc. With love to all your party, believe me ever affectionately yours, J. Yorke Scarlett.

Cover, The Lady Abinger, Abinger Hall, Dorking, Surrey. Postmark, 19 November 1845, Burnley; 20 November 1845, Dorking.

*   *   *

13

James Yorke Scarlett to Sarah, Lady Abinger
Stapleford, Nottinghamshire, 18 March 1846

Stapleford, 18 March 1846

Twenty-nine years in the army this day.[101]

My dearest Sally, My letter to Robert is of the greatest importance and requires an immediate answer.[102] It is to tell him that I have in my hands the resignation I have for some time expected of a lieutenant of the regiment, whose departure will make a vacancy; and, before I send it in, I wish to give him notice that, if he has any wish to obtain a cornetcy for Willy, he may make application forthwith.[103]

I cannot delay sending the resignation longer than by Saturday post. Lord Fitzroy will get it on Monday.[104] He holds a levee on every Tuesday; and, if Robert wishes to make an application, he must write a note to Lord Fitzroy on Monday, signifying his wish for an interview on Tuesday; or if he prefers making a written application he can do so. I shall give no advice on the subject but simply give you the option of preparing the request.

I hope to hear soon from Henrietta, who has been long silent and, as I thought, too much occupied in counting the waves at Brighton or something else to write. I have been and am very busy in various ways. We are sending twenty-four fine men to the 10th to fill their ranks for India.[105] I am doing my best to persuade them it is much better to leave me and go to the 10th after having spent much time and trouble hitherto in persuading them that to serve in the 5th Hussars was the *summum bonum* of a soldier's life.[106] Hurrah for expediency!

My headquarters march for York on Saturday. I shall be there on the twenty-fifth or twenty-sixth, but I shall not give up this house till the expiration of my lease on 1 May, and that will give me time to look for one at York. I think Charlotte will go with me on the twenty-fifth, but nothing fixed. Yours ever affectionately, J.Y. Scarlett.

Cover, The Lady Abinger, 4 New Street, Spring Gardens, London. Postmark, 19 March 1846.

*   *   *

14

James Yorke Scarlett to William Duckworth
York, 10 June 1846

My dear Sir, I am very glad to find that we are to have so excellent a recruit as your son to replace my nephew, who remained with us only long enough to provide himself with all his uniform before Prince Albert was so gracious as to offer him a commission in His Royal Highness's regiment, which it cost both the cornet and me much to accept; but there were several reasons which I thought ought to prevail and it is some consolation to me that I have him replaced so entirely to my wish, having heard such favourable accounts of Mr Duckworth and the name being long familiar to me and mine.[107]

As regards his horses, do what is most convenient. There is no objection to his joining without, as he certainly can procure them here better than in Hampshire, unless by some lucky accident. He will ride a trooper for his early drill and I shall be happy to give him my assistance in mounting himself. The earlier he joins the better – from six weeks to two months is the time usually granted by the Horse Guards – but, as this is the most favourable season for initiating him in his duties, I should be glad if he could make it convenient to join sooner. At the same time it is not exacted of him.

Any assistance or information I can afford you is at your service. I remain, my dear sir, yours faithfully, J. Yorke Scarlett.

*   *   *

15

James Yorke Scarlett to Sarah, Lady Abinger
York, 28 June 1846

York, Sunday, 28 June 1846

My dearest Sally, As I did not know how matters might turn out, I did not answer that part of your letter relating to Henrietta, though deeply interested in it, holding it wisest where I knew not what to say (not knowing the gentleman) to say nothing.[108] Your letter, however, to Charlotte putting the matter to rest, I have now only to congratulate you and say how truly I shall rejoice in Henrietta's happiness. From what you tell me of Mr Toler, I see every prospect of it.[109] And certainly he has fairly won the lady and will I think continue to think the prize well worth keeping.

Of course one would prefer that every husband should be exactly like the Apollo in shape and countenance, and every wife like the Venus de' Medici (though little ladies don't seem Mr Toler's taste). But, as that cannot always be, and the outward show is after all a very small ingredient in everyday home happiness if there is real love and kindness of heart, and *mutual respect*, I augur well for time to come with increase of affection. Without affection life is but a heavy affair – and with it the dark clouds cannot quite obscure the sun.

You must not let Henrietta see this, or I shall be out of favour for having hinted even (never having seen him) that Mr Toler has not the dignified mien of the Apollo and the manners *that* gentleman of marble would have perhaps if life had been breathed into the statue; not that it would have followed as a matter of course. For I have often wondered how in such fair forms of men as these men such vulgar souls of clay could dwell.

I hope Willy's love will be evanescent and that the fair lady is not deeply smitten.[110] However, I dare say Ireland would put all to rights and an 'unsophisticated salmon' charm away all his cares. I fear drill on a warm day will not be as beneficial, as it inclines to a lounge and idleness after.

What a nice mess the political world have got into. This mighty nation is put in jeopardy, and a mighty minister turned out, by a horse-racing, betting, bookmaking lord, not able to move one step beyond what he has already done.[111] A child may set a house on fire but it requires a clever man to put the fire out – and a Jew boy to be at the head of the English gentlemen!![112] I think Democritus would have split his sides; and, if to laugh at man's folly was a crime, he should have been punished by being now, when he could have killed himself with laughing.[113]

I am very curious to know what is to come next; who are to govern us and how. I cannot conceive how the Whig party is to rule. They may have themselves and the Irish and Radicals, but Peel still has a party. The Protectionists can't, after leaving Peel in the lurch for changing his opinion, themselves vote with the Whigs against him. However, whenever things get into a fix, something unexpected is sure to solve the matter and that I look for. Poor Campbell it seems is not at present to add to his list of lives for some future historian.[114]

Pray let me hear what you think and people say. The *Duke* I think made the oddest business of it.[115] He put the House of Lords into the condition of being unable to resist the Bill and then said don't fight against what you can't help.

Charlotte and I came from Richmond yesterday. I went on Thursday to see Lord Francis Gordon's Yeomanry, who performed very well.[116] I did not venture to ask him whether they would have Lord Ellesmere as their head next week.[117] He is a very excellent, honorable gentleman, whatever be his title. Love to all, ever your affectionate JYS.

* * *

15a

Charlotte Scarlett to Sarah, Lady Abinger

Accept a thousand thanks, dearest Sally, for your kind and *very interesting* letter, which I found on my return from Richmond yesterday.[118] Dear Henrietta has my warmest wishes for her happiness; and, whenever we hear from her that she has decided to reward her constant lover with her hand and heart, we shall send her our heartfelt congratulations, as everything I have heard of him both from you and Robert makes me think her prospects bright; and well she deserves every happiness which loving affection and fortune can give her. I have been very desirous for a letter from you ever since your last to Yorke, but did not like to write and ask questions.[119]

We spent a week very pleasantly at Swinburne Castle with the Cooksons.[120] It is an excellent house in a fine park, six miles from Hexham, and it was very nice being there in that hot weather, instead of York. We find our house comfortable and the situation convenient on some accounts, though we should both much have preferred a house in the country. We have been at the Minster this morning and I am going again this afternoon. Yorke is gone to the barracks and has left his letter for me to direct. Captain Blackburne and Mr Johnson dine with us today.[121]

I cannot tell you how sorry we were to lose Willie so soon, and so were all the officers he found at York. With kindest love to all at home, believe me your affectionate sister Charlotte A. Scarlett.

Cover, The Lady Abinger, 4 New Street, Spring Gardens, London. Postmark, 28 June 1846.

* * *

16

*James Yorke Scarlett to Sarah, Lady Abinger
York, 16 July 1846*

York, 16 July 1846
My dearest Sally, Charlotte received your letter this morning fixing the twenty-eighth as *the day*. We wish to be with you on the twenty-seventh. I have to attend a meeting at Burnley some day between 21 and 25 July, which cannot yet be fixed, about the inclosure of a tract of land.[122] I must be there to see that they don't come 'me cranking in' with some awkward arrangement or give us land without a road to it.

You have, I am sure, much demand on your mind and time just now, and I am about to add to your troubles by asking you to execute a commission for Charlotte and me, which we cannot do for ourselves because we are not in London; and we have been so long absent from it that we do not know what is now fashionable and appreciated in the way of ornaments by the gay world; *nor* do we know what Henrietta has or has not in her pearl box. Will you, who are in the habit of seeing what is pretty and have taste to chuse, fix on some ornament not exceeding £100 in value; or two things amounting together to the same sum, which we may give her as joint or separate presents as seems best and most convenient for her.

Charlotte is just going to run away from me and go for a day to Scarborough to see Eleanor.[123] The phaeton is at the door and I am going to drive her to the railway. With love to all, ever yours affectionately, J. Yorke Scarlett.

Cover, The Lady Abinger, 4 New Street, Spring Gardens, London. Postmark, York, 16 July 1846.

* * *

17

James Yorke Scarlett to Sarah, Lady Abinger
York, 6 October 1846

York, 6 October 1846

My dearest Sally, From the general dispersion of your family, it is difficult to know where to shoot at any of yours. To keep you all in recollection our thoughts must embrace Europe. I will, however, direct this to the *nest* as the most certain mode of hitting, I won't say the *old hen*, but the mother of the brood who generally clings to it with greater constancy than any other member of the said brood.

What are you doing? Are you in London or at Ashtead?[124] I think you might as well have been here with us; for, though I have been obliged to wander about a good deal, and Charlotte has gone to keep me company and avoid being left alone, we could have all gone together or you two might have stayed at home.

What signifies talking of what *might* have been? We have been expecting Robert and Fanny for the last fortnight and hoped to have had Fanny here for the Yeomanry and Hunt Balls.[125] The former is over, the latter takes place tomorrow, but we are ignorant of their intentions further than that they won't arrive, as I heard from Fanny last night that she knew nothing whatever of her father's motions. Among the minor disasters of life I consider their non-arrival leaves the spare bedroom and dressing room destined for them to be seized on by my good friend Sir Maxwell Wallace, who is sure to find out the vacancy.[126] However, for want of those I like better, he is welcome. Only he will attribute the 'good hit' to his own cleverness and not to my kindness. He was with us, self-invited, for the De Grey Ball and remained after we went to Harrogate on a Yeomanry inspection, congratulating himself aloud that, though *we* were going, the *house* was not, shewing plainly *what* the object of his friendship was.[127]

On the 15th Charlotte and I are going to Otterington for two days, near Northallerton; and on the twentieth to Brantingham – Richard Hawes; and think of going from thence till the end of the month to Burlington, but that will depend on the weather.[128] From the thirty-first I don't intend to move much from York till we finally take our departure, as I have no major in England at present.

If your rough scheme should not take effect, you now know as much of our plans as I do; and, though I say we have but a spare bed and dressing room (with a bed in it), we could manage to make a dressing room downstairs next my room. And we should not let Sir Maxwell take them from you.

I intend to squeeze out a day or two for shooting pheasants at Bank, so as to catch Willy going to or coming from Scotland, but I do not think I shall take servants etc over there to remain.[129] Willy sent me a letter from Toler to him, written in a very enviable *hand* and containing a good deal in a few words. I hope and trust he and Henrietta are spending the honeymoon so as not to exhaust its sweets. Have also heard from Peter, who seems in good spirits.[130] I fear Palmerston won't put him *first* for promotion on his list. I begin to think that we may have a trip to Portugal some fine morning after the marriages, should the Carlos party gain any strength and any interference take place on the part of France. Palmerston is so insolent by nature that he will get us into a quarrel if he can.[131] The Whigs have ever been great swaggerers; but when it comes to fighting and paying they have ever been found without any capacity for one or will for the other.[132]

We are all going to be ruined by the high price of wheat, oats and meat, in spite of Lord George.[133] It is a curious coincidence in Peel's favour. I never doubted Peel's wisdom but his manner of bringing about his plans I can't approve.[134]

Charlotte unites in best love to you and Aunt Fanny, who I conclude is with you.[135] We had the Dowager here for a day *en route* to Floors.[136] She seems to have no end of houses to visit. She was in high spirits and well. Ever your affectionate JYS.

Cover, The Lady Abinger, 4 New Street, Spring Gardens, London. Postmark, York, 6 October 1846.

*   *   *

Chapter 3

War with Russia

As colonel of the 5th Dragoon Guards, James Yorke Scarlett had shown himself a dedicated professional soldier. Taking immense pride in the standards the regiment had achieved under his command, he had made it outstanding in discipline, morale and performance. By the end of 1853, however, Scarlett had been an officer in the army for thirty-five years, serving only in England and Ireland, and had never faced an enemy. Although only fifty-four, he might well have thought that he had reached the peak of his career and have decided to retire to an extremely comfortable life in Burnley. Everything, however, was changed for him, and for the majority of the men in the British Army, by the outbreak of the Crimean War in March 1854.

After the defeat of Napoleon at Waterloo in 1815, the leading nations of Europe were at peace with one another for almost forty years. Britain, benefiting from its naval primacy won at Trafalgar, stood aside from continental involvement, reducing its army to a fraction of its wartime strength. On the Continent itself, Austria, Prussia and Russia made sure that France would not again disturb the peace. They also worked to counter threats of political or social revolution in their own territories.[1]

During these years three European countries, Russia, France and Britain, enlarged their empires. Russia, under the autocratic rule of Nicholas I from 1825 to 1855, expanded south. It seized the Caucasus from Persia in 1826–28 and, after defeating the Ottomans in the Russo-Turkish War of 1828–29, gained extensive shipping rights in the Black Sea. This southern expansion brought it uncomfortably close, from a British point of view, to northern India, as Russian naval power in the Black Sea seemed poised to extend through the Bosphorus to the Mediterranean, threatening Britain's line of communication to its eastern empire. The Russian navy, based at Sebastopol in the Crimea, might also be used to transport Russian troops anywhere around the Black Sea and to supply them there. This included the ability to land a Russian army on the Bosphorus and take Constantinople before any other power could mobilise.

With over a million men under arms, Russia had by far the largest army in Europe.[2] While its men looked superb on the parade ground, they were poorly equipped in terms of modern weaponry, lacked combat training and suffered from poor morale. Its generals were appointed for their political reliability rather than their military competence, while its officers and men, although brave, showed little initiative in battle. Russia was also handicapped by its vast size and poor infrastructure, making the movement of troops and equipment slow and inefficient. Its economic development, including its railway network, lagged far behind its western rivals. The only major railway which had been built in Russia by 1854 was that between St Petersburg and Moscow, opened in 1851. That there was no railway serving the Crimea was to prove a critical Russian weakness in the Crimean War.

Much of Russia's military strength reflected internal rather than international priorities, with Nicholas I ruling his state through his generals. Russia's militarism and its huge army were, however, seen as a threat by the other European states. As well as ruthlessly suppressing dissent inside Russia itself, Nicholas crushed a rebellion in Poland in 1831 and intervened to help the Habsburgs put down a nationalist uprising in Hungary in 1849. This made Nicholas, the 'Gendarme of Europe', hated and feared by liberals throughout Europe. Nicholas, however, lacked allies. Even the Habsburgs, who owed Nicholas a debt of gratitude for his intervention in the Hungarian crisis, were nervous of Russian encouragement of Slav aspirations in the Balkans. Nicholas was also mistakenly convinced that Britain, as a trading nation, would never go to war with Russia.

France, thwarted by defeat in the Napoleonic Wars in its ambition to dominate Europe, expanded elsewhere. Between 1830 and 1847 it fought a long and bitter campaign to establish control of Algeria, as the beginnings of a new empire in Africa. The large French army therefore had battle-hardened troops available in 1854. It was also professional in a way that the British Army was not, with officers promoted on merit rather than by purchase. The French navy, however, was less powerful than the Royal Navy.

Despite France's traditional status as a major power, Nicholas I held its rulers in contempt, referring to Louis-Philippe, who had replaced Charles X as king in 1830, as 'The Usurper'. After Louis-Philippe was deposed in the revolution of 1848, Napoleon I's nephew, Louis Napoleon, was elected president. Three years later Louis Napoleon consolidated his power by a coup, with the backing of the army. Following a plebiscite, he made himself emperor as Napoleon III in 1852. The Tsar, however, refused to recognise him as a fellow sovereign with the formal greeting 'Mon frère'. More substantially, Nicholas based his foreign policy on maintaining an anti-French coalition, relying on Austrian, British and Prussian distrust of France. Austria feared French interference in Italy, while the emergence of another Napoleon across the Channel reawakened the British nightmare of a French invasion. Prussia, intent on dominating Germany, knew that the French were opposed to German unification, especially under Prussian leadership. The Prussians had also been one of the worst sufferers under Napoleon I, losing half their pre-war territories by the treaty of Tilsit in 1807.

Napoleon III hoped to unite France by a programme of popular nationalism, working to rebuild French prestige and international influence. The principal aim of his foreign policy was to break up the grand alliance which had defeated Napoleon I. One obvious way of doing this was to exploit the widespread distrust and fear of Russia.

Britain, through the East India Company, increased its hold over India during the first half of the nineteenth century.[3] The small number of those in the British Army who had experience of fighting between 1815 and the outbreak of the Crimean War in 1854 had nearly all acquired it in the numerous small wars fought in India.[4] Smaller numbers of troops were stationed in Australia, Canada, New Zealand, South Africa, the West Indies and other British outposts, but Britain's army, which was less powerful than its navy, was only a tenth of the size of Russia's and spread thin. In 1846, out of a total of 100,600 men in its army, only 44,980 were stationed in Britain, with 23,000 in India and 32,650 in other parts of the empire.[5] Most of the British troops who served in the Crimean War, including James Scarlett and the Heavy Brigade, were drawn from its home forces and had never before been in battle. The small size of the army, and Britain's reliance on voluntary recruitment rather than conscription, made any losses hard to replace.

The most recent war Britain had fought, through the East India Company's army, was in Afghanistan between 1839 and 1842.[6] Its aim had been to exert British control over Afghanistan to prevent it from becoming a Russian satellite. This war had ended in total disaster in January 1842, when a winter retreat from Kabul led to the annihilation of the army. One of the very few British survivors, George Gleig, wrote that it was 'a war begun for no wise purpose, carried on with a strange mixture of rashness and timidity, brought to a close after suffering and disaster, without much glory attached either to the government which directed, or the great body of troops which waged it'.[7] Although the Crimean War ended in victory, British conduct of the war echoed a number of the failings of the earlier disaster.

Peace in Europe itself was broken in 1853 not by any direct conflict between the main European powers but because of the weakness of a neighbouring one, the Ottoman Empire. Much of the southern expansion of Russia's empire had been at Ottoman expense. Under Catherine the Great this had included the conquest of the Crimea in 1783, after which many of the native Tartars had been forced into exile. In the nineteenth century the Ottoman Empire had shrunk still further, losing control of Egypt and Syria. In Europe an independent monarchy replaced Turkish rule in Greece, while Serbia became an autonomous state inside the Ottoman Empire.

To many observers, including Nicholas I, it seemed that the Ottoman Empire was ripe for dissolution. Famously describing it as 'The Sick Man of Europe',[8] he was eager to come to an arrangement with Britain and the other European powers about its partition, although willing to keep it in being until this had been agreed. While the British had little sympathy with the Turks, they were strongly opposed to Russian domination or absorption of the empire, with its consequent threat to Britain's links to India. They regarded Turkey as an irreplaceable buffer between Russia and their own vital interests and were not tempted by the Tsar's proposal of Egypt and Crete as Britain's share of the spoils.

Britain had also recently greatly expanded its trade with Turkey and had no wish for this to be jeopardised. The British therefore preferred to preserve the status quo, in the hope that the Ottoman Empire would reform itself along western lines. Working through their long-term and influential ambassador in Constantinople, Lord Stratford de Redcliffe, Britain actively supported Turkish modernisers, notably Mustafa Reshid, who had been the Porte's ambassador to London.[9] France, which had invested heavily in Egypt and Syria, also had a strong interest in stopping Russian expansion. To Nicholas, however, the prospect of Britain or France controlling the Ottoman government was anathema. He was also riled by the British and French assumption that, while they could expand their own empires with impunity, any Russian expansion was seen as a threat to the peace of Europe.

Although earlier Turkish conflicts with Russia, including the war in 1828–29, had passed without outside intervention, a crisis began in the 1840s which escalated into the Crimean War. It started ostensibly with a bizarre conflict about the right to protect the Holy Places in Bethlehem and Jerusalem.[10] When the Catholic and Orthodox guardians of the Church of the Nativity fought over the possession of the keys of the shrine, the French provocatively claimed a right to intervene on behalf of the Catholics, even though French pilgrims to the Holy Land, mainly visiting as tourists, were dwarfed in number by the hordes of fervent Orthodox pilgrims. The claim, however, played well to French Catholic opinion and to liberals opposed to Russia.

Russia had long maintained the right to protect the interests of the Orthodox in the Holy Land, but now substantially widened its claims. In response to the French assertions, it demanded to be recognised as the formal

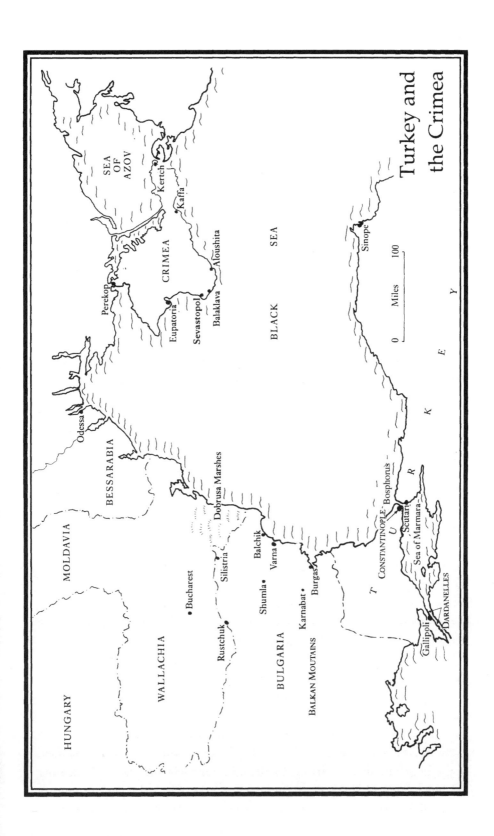

Turkey and the Crimea

HUNGARY

MOLDAVIA

BESSARABIA

Odessa

WALLACHIA

Bucharest

Rustchuk

Silistria

Dobrusa Marshes

BULGARIA

Shumla

Balchik

Varna

BALKAN MOUTAINS

Karnabat

Burgas

CONSTANTINOPLE

Bosphorus

Scutari

Sea of Marmara

T U R K E Y

Gallipoli

DARDANELLES

CRIMEA

Perekop

Eupatoria

Sevastopol

Balaklava

Aloushita

Kaffa

Kertch

SEA OF AZOV

BLACK SEA

Sinope

0   100
   Miles

protector of the Orthodox Church in eastern Europe as a whole, based on the treaty of Kutchuk-Kainarji of 1774. This, unlike the squabble in the Holy Land, had much wider implications, as the majority of Turkey's subjects in Europe were not Muslim but Christian. Russia's new claim, however, was strongly resisted by Napoleon III on the grounds of a prior treaty of 1740 between the French and Ottomans. Both countries then exerted pressure on the Turks, who had no wish to side with either claim and tried to defuse the tension by compromise. The escalation of the dispute was partly the result of Napoleon III's determination to increase French prestige by diplomacy and, if necessary, by war. Nicholas I seems also to have lost his habitual caution on a question that involved his religious obligations to the Orthodox Church and his position as the anointed head of Holy Russia.

To persuade the Turks to accept the Russian claim, Nicholas sent Prince Alexander Sergeyevitch Menshikov (1787–1869), later the Russian commander in the Crimea, on an embassy to Constantinople in February 1853 with instructions to force the Ottomans to accept the Russian terms.[11] When this failed, in July 1853 the Russians occupied Moldavia and Wallachia. Both were formally part of the Ottoman Empire but had an anomalous status under the treaty of Adrianople of 1829, by which they had virtual autonomy under Russian protection but with a reservation of a number of rights to Austria. As a deterrent, the British and French sent a naval force to Besika Bay, near the Dardanelles. Encouraged by this international support, when the Russians refused to retreat, the Turks declared war on the Russians on 4 October 1853, with the first shots being fired by a Turkish force which crossed the Danube to attack the Russians on 29 October.

The wholesale destruction of a Turkish fleet at Sinope by a more modern Russian force on 30 November 1853, although legitimate under the rules of war, was perceived as an outrage by the public in Britain and France, where Russia was seen as a barbarous autocracy.[12] It had been carried out in the face of the supposed deterrent of the Anglo-French naval force and, as such, was in explicit defiance of Britain and France.

Despite the opening of hostilities between the Russians and the Turks, all the parties involved hoped that the end of fighting and a peaceful solution to the problem might still be possible. Rounds of diplomatic exchanges between the European powers, brokered by Austria, resulted in the Vienna Note, an attempt to resolve the impasse. This proposed a solution acceptable to the Russians but unacceptable to the Turks, who had not been included in the negotiations until handed a demand for their acceptance. Following the breakdown of these talks, and after a joint Anglo-French ultimatum demanding that the Russians withdraw from Moldavia and Wallachia was ignored by the Tsar, Britain and France declared war on Russia on 28 March 1854.

Although the Crimean War takes its name from the peninsula in the Black Sea which became the main theatre of military operations in 1854–55, the war itself was fought over a far wider area. As befitted Britain, the premier naval power, its main plan was to attack the Russians in the Baltic. They hoped to capture and destroy Russia's principal naval base at Kronstadt, guarding St Petersburg. Despite sending a formidable fleet to the Baltic, Kronstadt was judged impregnable to attack from the sea (as later proved the case with Sebastopol). The threat of an attack near its capital meant, however, that the Russians kept large bodies of troops nearby. Naval operations also took place in the White Sea and as far away as the Pacific Ocean.[13] Of greater significance, the British and French imposed a blockade on Russian trade.

Because of the deteriorating situation in the East, the British coalition government, under Lord Aberdeen, had before the outbreak of war already put together an expeditionary force in alliance with France.[14] The British force, commanded by Fitzroy Somerset, Lord Raglan, who had for many years been Wellington's principal lieutenant, consisted of around 27,000 men, scraped together from the home establishment. As well as infantry and artillery, it comprised a division of cavalry, commanded by the Earl of Lucan.[15] Under him the Light Brigade was commanded by the Earl of Cardigan and the Heavy Brigade by James Yorke Scarlett.[16]

The appointments of Lucan and Cardigan were in many ways surprising.[17] Lucan had been on half-pay since 1837. He was out of touch with developments in the cavalry to the extent that he was unfamiliar with its current drill. Although energetic and intelligent, he lacked judgement and was quarrelsome. In his favour, he had some knowledge of fighting in eastern Europe, having been attached to the Russian army in their campaign against the Turks in the Russo-Turkish War of 1828–29. Cardigan, in contrast, was the most notorious man in the army, not only for bullying and duelling but for having been dismissed from his command of the 15th Hussars in 1833. Undeterred, two years later, he had bought the colonelcy of another regiment, the 11th Hussars, for £40,000. On top of this, Lucan and Cardigan, who were brothers-in-law, were at daggers drawn over Lucan's treatment of Cardigan's youngest sister, to whom he was married.[18] These appointments were made by the Commander in Chief, Lord Hardinge, without consulting the commander of the expeditionary force, Lord Raglan.[19] As Edward Hodge, the colonel of the 4th Dragoon Guards, wrote in his diary on 5 April 1854 before he left for the East, 'Lord Lucan commands the whole. He is brother-in-law to Lord Cardigan, and they do not speak. How this will answer on service I know not.'[20]

James Yorke Scarlett, in contrast, had an exemplary record as a dedicated and successful cavalry officer.[21] How much influence rather than competence was involved in his appointment is unclear. It is possible that his claims were supported by his long-term friend, the fourteenth Earl of Derby, who had been Prime Minister from February to December 1852, but Derby was the Leader of the Opposition rather than part of Lord Aberdeen's coalition government at the time of the appointment.

At first the plan was for the British troops to march through France to the Mediterranean, but in the event nearly all the troops went by ship the whole way. The fortunate ones went by the new steamships, which could reach the Dardanelles in two weeks. The less fortunate, and many of the horses, went by sailing ship, which sometimes took up to two months. The worst disaster to affect the Heavy Brigade occurred when the *Europa*, a sailing ship carrying a contingent of the 6th Dragoons (the Inniskillings), caught fire in the Bay of Biscay on 31 May and was lost with the deaths of nineteen men and one woman, as well as all the horses and equipment. Amongst those to perish was the colonel of the Inniskillings, Willoughby Moore.[22]

A number of senior officers, including Raglan, Cardigan and Scarlett, made their own way across France to Marseille.[23] Scarlett himself stayed with his regiment in Ireland until April before crossing to England. After a brief stay in London, he travelled with his brother, sister-in-law and niece through France, a trip recorded in his niece's diary. On their way down the Saône and Rhône, they twice ran across Scarlett's fellow brigadier.[24]

Many of the British infantry regiments first landed at Malta and spent a number of weeks there training. On their arrival in the East, with the exception of Sir George Brown's Light Division, most of the British force encamped on the eastern side of the Bosphorus, opposite Constantinople, being based at Scutari or nearby Koulali. In contrast, the first four regiments of heavy cavalry sailed directly to Varna, on the west coast of the Black Sea, calling only briefly at Malta and Constantinople. The French army totalled about 30,000 men, but had no cavalry. Commanded by Marshal Leroy de St-Arnaud, who had played a major part in the French coup of 1851, they landed initially at Gallipoli, at the mouth of the Dardanelles, as did the Light Division.

James Yorke Scarlett, despite starting after his regiment had sailed, spent well over a month at Constantinople, with the senior staff of the army, waiting for the other regiments of his brigade to arrive. A glimpse of him is provided in the memoirs of Henry Franks, when his old regiment, the 5th Dragoon Guards, passed through the Bosphorus without landing:

> Thus matters stood when we were anchored in the River Bosphorus on that quiet Sunday afternoon. I have stated how the men were having a view of the city, when a steam tender was seen approaching the *Himalaya*. There seemed to be a number of officers of high rank on board, and amongst them was soon recognised the familiar and beaming features of our old and tried friend, Brigadier General Scarlett. He had arrived in Turkey previous to us and was stationed at Scutari, with the headquarters staff, and some of the Light Brigade of cavalry, who had disembarked there before we arrived.
>
> As soon as he was seen, the men cried out, 'The General', and in a moment those on board seemed to come from all parts of the ship, crowding round the gangway, cheering, clapping their hands and acting in a very boisterous and somewhat unusual manner – more like a lot of schoolboys than soldiers.[25]

Despite the pleasure of seeing his old regiment, the campaign did not start happily for Scarlett. Left at Constantinople, when most of the army was at Varna, he was not taken into the inner counsels of the expedition and was treated dismissively by Lord Lucan, who was also left behind. According to William Forrest of the 4th Dragoon Guards:

> We have not much confidence in our cavalry general (Lord Lucan) and only hope he will allow the several brigadiers to move their own brigades. I much fear he will not do so and I think he will stick to the Heavies, for he and Cardigan would be sure to have a row directly. Lord Lucan and Scarlett are not upon the best of terms and the general feeling is that he has behaved ill to Scarlett. Lord Lucan is no doubt a clever sharp fellow but he had been so long on the shelf that he has no idea of moving cavalry, does not even know the words of command and is very self-willed about it, thinks himself right.[26]

Lucan was widely seen as a poor appointment:

> Lord Lucan is here and a rum one he seems to be. I hear his staff all wish themselves off it, he is so uncertain and difficult to get on with. Report says something disagreeable happened between him and Scarlett. The latter has gone to Devna and told me he found he was a nobody here. Lord Lucan had all reports made direct to himself.[27]

Writing prophetically, Forrest added, 'I trust Scarlett will be allowed to manoeuvre his own brigade and then all will go well with the Heavies – but I write this to you in order that if any mishap should occur to the cavalry, you may be able to form a correct idea how is happened. Do not say anything about Lord Lucan unless we come to grief.'[28] More succinctly, Frances Scarlett wrote to Mary Campbell, 'Lord Lucan is said to be the worst appointment in the army.'[29]

Apart from the predictable quarrel between Lucan and Cardigan, and the unnecessarily poor relations between Lucan and Scarlett, the campaign was strange in many ways from the start.[30] The British and French, after their long history of enmity, were now unexpected allies. (Lord Raglan, however, notoriously was apt to refer to the enemy as the French rather than the Russians.) They both saw their other ally, the Turks, as dirty and uncivilised, as well as of course Muslim, while their enemies were Christian. Although both agreed about the need to stop the Russians capturing Constantinople, the British and the French had different priorities. The British wished to destroy the power of the Russian navy, and its capacity to enter and intervene in the Mediterranean, and indeed the Black Sea, an aim of little interest to the French. The main French aim was to win a glorious victory against Russia on land, so as to build up French power and prestige in Europe. The Turks, although they had little choice in their allies, were wary of the danger of exchanging the Russian halter for that of Britain and France.

There was no unified command structure, despite an initial French attempt to assume overall command. This left the three allies under separate commanders, made worse in the British case by their navy, led by Sir James Dundas, being under separate command. The allies also had no settled strategy. Their initial aim was to form a defensive barrier west of the capital to protect Constantinople from Russian attack, the reason for the French initially landing their forces at Gallipoli and the British at Scutari.

At the request of the Turks, in May and June 1854, the allied forces moved by ship to Varna, a small port on the west coast of the Black Sea. This was to support the Turks, who were holding off the Russians at Silistria on the Danube, fifty-five miles to the north west of Varna.[31] Scarlett approved of the move:

> What we are to do when we all collect at Varna I don't know, but it is the place I have always pointed out as the proper one for anyone to occupy who meant to assist the Turks, as it would act on the Russian flank and rear in case of an advance by them. If they don't advance, shall we? At all events, whether for fighting or negotiation, I think we are rightly placed at Varna or the neighbourhood.[32]

The allies, however, were unable to bring any immediate armed assistance to the Turks because of a lack of supplies and transport. If, however, the expected defeat of the Turks at Silistria happened, the allies would be in an excellent position to prevent a Russian advance on Constantinople. In the event, before the allies were ready to advance, the Russians retreated back across the River Pruth, the border between Turkey and Russia. Not only had the Turks held out far longer than had been predicted, the Austrians, who had rights over the invaded provinces of Moldavia and Wallachia, had threatened to send troops to attack the Russians from the west. This persuaded the Russians to withdraw.

The Light Brigade and the 5th Dragoon Guards had already been at Varna for a month before they were joined by Scarlett. Three other regiments of the Heavy Brigade also arrived at Varna.[33] The officers and men of his old regiment were relieved to see him.[34] His nephew, William Scarlett, who reported on visiting him, also reflected on the uncertainty of as to where the army would go next:

> There appears no chance of a move. We hear Lord Raglan looks much at the maps of Circassia, and there is a report of our shortly starting for Trebizond.[35] It will soon be too late for any operations this year, and a winter campaign would involve great loss of life; but after all we shall be much stronger for next year and we shall have recruits at home to fill up our ranks as casualties occur. At present we have no reserve sufficient to give us much help on a great scale.
>
> The Uncle is up at Devna.[36] All his brigade has arrived except one transport. I staid with him for a couple of nights; he gave me a shake down in his tent.[37] He has not yet got into the full swing, and his servants are not quite handy, but a few days will put all that to rights. He is in robust health. We went down to bathe every morning at 6 a.m. The weather is very hot but tempered by heavy thunderstorms. We sit in the doors of our tents like prairie dogs above their holes, damning diplomacy and perspiring with heat. We are getting very much bored with doing nothing.[38]

Permission was given to the infantry to leave their beards uncut. Lord Lucan attempted unsuccessfully to prevent the cavalry from following suit. General Scarlett, however, himself grew a beard. According to Temple Godman, writing to his brother on 27 August 1854, 'There is a general order that *no one* need shave *at all* in Turkey, it is a great protection in heat and cold.'[39] G.M. Trevelyan identified the abandonment of shaving as one of the main long-term consequences of the Crimean War, making beards fashionable in later Victorian society. The other was the return to acceptability of smoking in polite society.[40]

While everyone agreed that the country was beautiful, and indeed good cavalry country, they also thought that Varna and the villages round it were dirty.[41] Unable to move or fight the Russians, the British and French troops lost many men to another enemy. In July 1854 cholera broke out, probably brought by a French ship from Marseille. At this time it was not understood that it was a water-borne disease. Mostly attributed to miasma, unhealthy vapour (from a Greek word meaning pollution), it could kill very rapidly. Many other causes were suspected. W.H. Russell, the *Times* correspondent, thought the cholera might be due to the cucumbers, which he described as 'deadly cylinders', eaten by the men.[42] According to William Cattell, of the 5th Dragoon Guards, 'The pest is popularly attributed to the indulgence in "kill-johns" (apricots) and red Tenedos wine, which our surgeon specially condemns, though several of us, myself included, regularly drank it as an agreeable change from the charcoal coffee, water being impossible.'[43] Cattell also reported an unlikely outbreak of piety amongst the troops, 'In the tents the men were reading their Bibles, an unusual sight. If seized they at once gave themselves up for lost and terror increased receptivity.'[44]

Although the troops moved camp numerous times, cholera inflicted many casualties. Indeed, during the Crimean campaign as a whole, cholera and other diseases, and infected wounds, killed many more men than the Russians. Scarlett did not avoid those stricken by cholera. According to William Cattell:

> Left with the sick and dying, and without rations which had been carried off in the flight, I went to General Scarlett for orders. He was quite calm and said, 'I am staying with the hospital and so do you.' In the evening Captain Duckworth came back, astonished to find only the hospital, my tent and the General's camp alone standing.[45]

There was, however, trouble with Scarlett's old regiment, the 5th Dragoon Guards. His replacement as its commander, Colonel Thomas Le Marchant, proved incompetent, uniting officers and men against him by misguided severity.[46] According to Henry Franks:

> We had not seen General Scarlett since we left Constantinople, and we wished many times that he was with us again; Colonel Le Marchant was so different in every respect. He very seldom made his appearance among us now unless when we were on parade, and then if he had anything to say to a man he had a most unfortunate way of finding fault

of the smallest matter, and if it was a non-commissioned officer that was at fault, he would say to him, 'I will break you, sir', or if a private, 'I will have you flogged, sir.'[47]

According to Cattell, the men were 'Harassed and worried by constant work from 4 a.m. till 8 p.m. under a sun hotter than they were used to, they know no rest, no regular hours of duty, and crimes were heavily punished. Stable duties were in the heat of the day – a new commanding officer had substituted irregularity and interference for the old routine under Scarlett.'[48]

Fortunately, Le Marchant solved the problems he himself caused by suddenly disappearing, probably from fear of cholera. According to Henry Franks:

> At length night came, and then it was found out that Colonel Le Marchant was gone. He had deserted his regiment in a mean and cowardly manner. Gamble, the servant, returned two days afterwards with waggon and oxen, and he produced a pass, signed by the colonel, giving him leave of absence for five days. Gamble stated that he had covered the colonel up in the waggon with grass, and had accompanied him to Varna, about forty miles distant from our camp. They had travelled all night, and when at Varna the colonel had gone on board one of the ships in the bay, but he did not know the name of the ship.
>
> This was the last time we ever saw Colonel Le Marchant, nor did we ever hear anything more of him. It is not often that we hear of a colonel of a regiment deserting, and of course it was a surprise to many people who had no knowledge of the man; but he was an exception to all the colonels I ever saw – he never seemed to take the slightest interest in the corps from the day he joined us at Ballincollig. I don't think he ever once visited the hospital tents, which were crowded with sick men, and they got it into their heads that he did not care whether they lived or died.[49]

Even with Le Marchant gone, the troubles of the 5th Dragoon Guards were not over. Their losses from cholera meant that they were commanded by Desart Burton, their senior captain. Following an inspection by Lucan and Raglan, they were put under the command of Colonel Hodge of the 4th Dragoon Guards. This was a fresh blow to General Scarlett. As he wrote later to the one-time colonel of the 4th Dragoon Guards:

> They had the misfortune to be highly disapproved by Lord Lucan, reported by him to Lord Raglan, who came at dusk in the evening to see them in their lines, and found them thin and the men dirty. And

having no field officers, and their senior captain dead, their surgeon dead and vet surgeon dead, and paymaster absent, his Lordship attached them to the 4th pro tem, for Hodge to give advice to Captain Burton in command, who was third captain and young in the service. I neither agree with Lord Lucan or Lord Raglan in their opinion ...[50]

Once it was realised that the Russians had retreated, the allied governments were left with a dilemma: whether to recall the force put together by Britain and France or to use it in another theatre. This decision was taken by the cabinet, at the proposal of the Duke of Newcastle, the Secretary of State for War, after an excellent and soporific dinner at Pembroke Lodge in Richmond Park.[51] The force was to sail to the Crimea and destroy the base of the Russian fleet at Sebastopol. Although this had always been one of the aims of the British expedition, it was only prioritised at a late point in the year. Little was known about the target and the allied commanders were without good maps of the Crimea or knowledge about the Russian strength there. When Raglan consulted one of his divisional commanders, Sir George Brown, on the wisdom of the plan, both agreed that their mentor, the Duke of Wellington, would have been against it. Brown, however, told Raglan that, if he refused to implement the plan, the British government would send out a more compliant general to replace him.

The result was that Raglan decided to go ahead with the invasion. Although Scarlett was a senior officer, he was not privy to the inner councils of the army.[52] For some time, it was unclear whether the Heavy Brigade would make up part of the initial invasion force. According to Temple Godman, writing on 27 August, 'Lord Raglan talking to Brigadier Scarlett yesterday told him he would embark with the Second Division; but whether he meant Scarlett or the 5th Dragoon Guards he could not say.'[53] On 8 September, he reported that 'Lord Raglan told Scarlett that as soon as they had landed they would send back ships for us.'[54] In the event, because of the shortage of suitable shipping, the Heavy Brigade stayed behind at Varna, although Lord Lucan and the Light Brigade sailed with the main force.

A massive armada of ships, carrying sixty thousand British, French and Turkish troops, set off for the Crimea, landing at Kalamita Bay on 14 September. While Scarlett and the Heavy Brigade waited near Varna, dramatic events took place in the Crimea. Following an unopposed landing, the Allied army marched south in full array towards Sebastopol. After crossing two rivers, they reached the third, the Alma. This was overlooked on the south by a ridge on which the Russians, commanded by Prince Menshikov, had been drawn up in a formidable defensive position.[55]

With the French on the right, nearer to the sea, and the British on the left, the allies succeeded in storming the Russian position, helped by a failure to guard what proved to be accessible paths up the steep slopes nearer the sea, which were taken by the French. The decisive event of the battle, however, was a frontal attack by the British infantry across the Alma, through the village of Bourliak, against the Great Redoubt and Kourgané Hill. At times in doubt, the discipline and high morale of the British troops, in which the Guards played a conspicuous part,[56] succeeded in routing the Russians, who retreated in disarray towards Sebastopol.

In all their plans, the allies had taken one thing for granted, based on their assessment of the Russian army. This was that, whenever it came to battle, the allies would win a quick and decisive victory. In a letter from Varna to his parents on 21 September 1854, Edward Fisher-Rowe of the 4th Dragoon Guards wrote, 'Hurrah for the Crimea, we are off tomorrow; fine country, people very friendly; take Sebastopol in a week or so, and then into winter quarters for the winter.'[57] Partly because of such questionable assumptions, the allies had allowed much of the year to pass without encountering a single Russian. While they were proved right by their initial victory at the Alma, they were wrong about its being immediately decisive. Their hopes of finishing the campaign quickly proved mistaken. When they reached the Crimea, it was already autumn and they were soon faced by another enemy, as deadly as the Russians, in the winter storms and weather, for which they were ill-equipped.

The allies failed to follow up their great victory immediately because of a disagreement between Raglan and St-Arnaud, with St-Arnaud insisting that his troops were not ready to advance, as they had left their packs behind them before the battle. Raglan was also wary of unleashing his only cavalry, the Light Brigade under Cardigan, to harry the fleeing Russians. Had the allies pursued the Russians vigorously after the battle, and had the Heavy Brigade been on hand, the Alma might indeed have been the only engagement of the war. Temple Godman wrote to his father on 30 September:

> They say if they had had cavalry at that engagement the other day, an immense number would have been made prisoners, or at all events prevented from entering Sebastopol. They certainly should have waited for the cavalry, for a few days could have made no difference as far as the weather goes.[58]

18

Frances Scarlett's Diary

5 April 1854

We returned home a week after Willy left us and, with the exception of one flying visit to London to see kind Jim, have been here remaining.[59] We have had a very nice letter from Willy, assuring us he has quite recovered and is enjoying himself very much. Like him, we must be happy whilst we can and cast as little as possible the shadow of uncertain evils.

Uncle Jim is Brigadier-General and commands the Heavy Brigade.[60] He will be off directly. How terrible will be the separation to Aunt Charlotte. What is our regret and anxiety compared to his! We talk very much of going abroad. Papa declares he is going to start immediately, as soon as ever he has settled certain businesses of Peter's.[61] I shall believe nothing till I am being sick on board the Folkestone packet, though I am forced to make a few silent preparations in the shape of gowns. I don't care much about going; though, possibly because I expect nothing, something agreeable will turn up. My mind refuses to make itself up, anything having been so often put off, and I *can't* realize the idea of 'dear abroad'. We shall see.

*　　*　　*

19

James Yorke Scarlett to Robert Scarlett, Lord Abinger
Ballincollig, 16 April 1854

Rosanna, Ballincollig, 16 April 1854

My dear Robert, It seems to me an age since we parted. I think you have not received a letter I wrote from hence directed to Abinger (I think) to ask what we should do with our jaunting car, which is built and paid for and has never yet been out of the maker's shop. Shall we sell it – or will you like to have it sent to Glasgow? It will, I fancy, be of no use in Turkey, though I am not quite sure, as it is a vehicle that overturns and gets righted again with less damage to self and owner than most other carriages. I think that the officers sent over to provide mules and horses report none are to be had for love or money in Turkey.[62] So I conclude I must get some mules from Spain.

I have been here almost since we parted in Town. Yesterday's *Gazette* gave me a new major. The loss of Balders, who has left us, is a great blow to the regiment at this crisis, as I also in some measure leave them and they are placed in new and unknown hands.[63] They feel this – and I feel it. For whatever my future reputation may turn up, my past is bound up in that of the 5th Dragoon Guards and, if they do not come up equal to the occasion, my labours have been in vain; but I hope they will, and am sure of it if they are properly handled.[64]

So much for the loss of my major. His replacement has a prestige to his name, Le Marchant.[65] One of the same name commanded the brigade of which the 5th formed part in the famous charge at Salamanca.[66] He was killed there.

Now for our plans. I linger here as long as I can be useful to the regiment, but as soon as Major Le Marchant joins I shall come to Town. The French march is quite given up. I believe the difficulties are on the other side of the water, but there has been much changing and doubt. I left the Palace last Wednesday week certain, as I thought, from the very highest possible authority that we were certain to go via Paris and Marseilles.[67] I conclude then that insurmountable difficulties have since occurred. In 1814 the 5th Dragoon Guards marched from Toulouse and embarked at Boulogne, through a *hostile* country, though not opposed by troops.

I hear every day from my Brigade Major, Conolly, who is in Town, and he will give me early notice of events.[68] If we, the cavalry, go by long sea it will not be necessary for me and my companions to be in so great a hurry, as by going overland or even by a steamer we shall be at Gallipoli or elsewhere long before them if we start a week after them.

One of my notions is to let my horses and baggage go by steam and go myself by Ostend, Bruxelles, Berlin, Vienna, Breslau, Trieste and then embark for Constantinople – or wherever we are to land; another to go via Venice and embark on the Adriatic. I must take Conolly and probably my ADC, Elliot, with me. I shall be very glad of Beatson's company and his advice too, for he is particularly well informed and very energetic.[69] I hope he will carry out his intention. Another way will be via Paris and Marseilles. Now if we can manage to unite with you, and Sally and Fanny, it will be so much the pleasanter and more satisfactory to me, but for a day or two I dare not make any plans, seeing that there is so much chance of change.

Conolly is looking out for a servant for me who can dress us and the dinner both – a difficult fellow to find and probably it will take two men to perform these offices. At present I have no one who could be of the least use to me as a personal servant abroad. All my present household will go to Bank with my poor dear wife, who behaves like herself but has been far from well since we came here, and she is peculiarly sensitive to any change of diet or water.

You will hardly have time to read to the end of this epistle, so I will only add that I have heard from Peter, who says they sometimes threaten him with Bulwer and sometimes with Normanby. Why don't they make him Minister at once?[70]

Ever yours affectionately, JYS.

*   *   *

20

Frances Scarlett's Diary

Saturday, 6 May
We are supposed to be off on Monday, but I feel as if something *must* come to stop our plans. For the last five months Papa has been always saying, 'One to prepare, two to make ready, one two, three and', but the 'away' has never come, nor can I believe that we can run the race. Our limbs are so stiffened and wearied with watching and waiting.

The family coach is ready, the courier is ready, we are ready. I have the feeling of a child. Will it never be Monday? Long suspense has made me impatient. Delay is irritating when there is no reasonable cause for delay, but my poor dear father has no decision and cannot the least enter into our feelings, who can and do judge promptly, and are ready to act promptly upon our judgement. I do not expect any great pleasure in our travels, knowing that to *expect* is to ensure disappointment and well I feel that clouds are lowering around us. We have hopes of travelling across France with our General.

Tuesday 9 May
Mama and I travelled in the morning up to the old town of Boulogne, which is very picturesque and thoroughly French – full of quaint forms, incidents and colour. What a tame affair an English town is compared with a continental one. In England we have expanses of wall, broken at regular distances by windows of a regulation size; people of taste indulge in some ornamental Greek work, but all is trig,[71] square, neat and ugly, well-glazed and coloured to resemble that description of marble of which, according to the American, London is built, and of which St George's Hospital is a good specimen.[72] Go into a French town – how the houses are piled one upon another, with thin, tall, pointed roofs. What a multitude of windows all how, no how, opening wide, and giving such delightful spots of deep shadow, what richness of colour on the weather-stained walls. And to complete the picture compare the figures which hang about the corners of French streets with our dowdy females and becoated and behatted men.

We went to the steamer in hopes of finding our General, but Lord Cardigan only appeared and could give us no tidings of his fellow Brigadier – he will probably turn up in Paris in a day or two.[73]

Leaving Boulogne at half past twelve, we got to Paris by seven. We travelled in the family coach, which is not nearly so amusing as going in the public carriages – it is diverting to hear the French people chatter to one another.[74] Here we have put up at the Hôtel des Deux Mondes, a new place where everything appears to be conducted in a very scrambling way.[75]

Wednesday 10 May
We were delighted with the appearance of the Colonel, who joined us according to agreement.[76] Papa doubted his coming, and thought he would slip off with his horses and staff, which sailed last Saturday. He is attended by his Brigade Major, Captain Conolly.[77]

Friday 12 May
We went down to Versailles and spent the afternoon touring round its stately galleries and stately gardens – truly a palace worthy of a king.[78] Exactly such an abode as one might fancy the *Grand Monarque* would build and delight in. Fortunately for us we had not time to go all over the palace, but saw the principal rooms containing the large historical pictures painted by order of Louis-Philippe.[79]

Uncle Jim was much pleased with our expedition, which he contributed largely to make pleasant. We all think of my poor dear Aunt with regret, wishing she were with us, but it would only have been for a few more days and then the parting must have come, and perhaps under more trying circumstances.

We got back to Paris late, dined at the Café de Paris, and retired to our respective dwellings to pack up, preparatory to a start tomorrow.

Saturday 13 May
We left Paris by the half past ten train and reached Chalon at nine.[80] We had half an hour's fever driving to the rail, thinking we were late. The Colonel and his aide de camp had arrived already, and we found Lord Cardigan with his aide de camp Lord Dupplin.[81] Our little quartette travelled in the family coach – one of the inconveniences of taking a carriage abroad is that on the railway you have your places for nothing, therefore to take advantage of it is only reasonable, but the public conveyances are much more comfortable and more amusing. Having twice before gone this road to Chalon, I did not feel much interest in the passage, with its one prevailing feature of poplars, poplars, poplars. There is about an hour of curious volcanic scenery before Dijon, which I had wholly forgotten.

Sunday 14 May

The steamer was by way of starting at five, but we loitered on the quay till six, watching the embarkation of a quantity of heavy baggage, and the polishing of Lord Cardigan's boots – this great man did not go till later, as the boat would not take his carriage. We left ours to follow with Müller.[82] The voyage down to Lyons is a dull business, the banks of the river quite flat, the cabin full of spitting Frenchmen and Frenchwomen too, and feeling ourselves as if one had got up a great many hours before the day was properly aired. At Lyons we left the Saône, and embarked upon the bosom of the Rhône. The Rhône vessels are better than those on the other river, though all are dirty and uncomfortable. We slept at Valence and found good accommodation at the Hôtel de la Poste.[83]

Monday 15 May

Before we started the Colonel (who has a most laudable wish to see everything he has time to see) and I rambled about Valence. The most amusing thing we saw was a number of little Frenchmen drilling, looking like so many insects in their red trousers. The diminutiveness of the French soldiers is quite astonishing; about five of them would go to make an average Grenadier.

After we had waited more than an hour, at half past ten our boat puffed up, and the first people we saw were Lord Cardigan and Lord Dupplin, rather triumphant at having come up with us, though we had stolen a march upon them.

The day was broiling and, when umbrellas and veils and uglies were of no more avail, I refuged myself in the cabin, leaving the hills and castles and vineyards to take care of themselves.[84] The Colonel was unremitting in his attention to Murray and the scenery.[85] It is quite edifying to see a person travel to such advantage!!

At Avignon, we had an hour to spare before the railway left for Marseilles, so my uncle, the Brigade Major and I, leaving the parents and couriers to creep about and look after the luggage, set off on a climb up to the papal palace to look at the lovely view from the eminence, quite unrivalled after its kind.[86] The evening sun shone upon the landscape, whilst a thunder cloud with falling rain gave just the proper amount of shade. My companions were most properly enthusiastic and said they would have travelled from England if it were only to see this view; a kind of sentiment I am always indulging in myself, but very rarely hear expressed by others.

We just took a glance into the cathedral and palace; and then, being seized with a sudden fright about the train, hurried through the streets of Avignon, threw ourselves into a bus, and found we had three-quarters of an hour to spare. We reached Marseilles at ten and, after much scrambling and wrangling, settled ourselves at the Hôtel de l'Orient and got a very bad supper.[87] Lord Dupplin joined our party. He looks bored with everything. What misery can equal the misery of living a life of bore!!

Tuesday 16 May
Whilst writing letters, in walked Gregorini from Florence.[88] It was pleasant to see the moonfaced familiar of the Signoria. He was on the look out for us by Peter's desire and just returning to him.

We all went out in a body first to a general storehouse of goods for the Eastern Army and then to make a *petit tour* of the town. At the storehouse the officers bought some things they did not want because they were cheap; and Captain Conolly went raving about, insisting that he could have saved £20 on his outfit, had he known of this source. In the inn yard we found Colonel Townley on his way to Constantinople and had ten minutes chat with him.[89] He told us the latest news from London, of fancy balls, elopements etc, asked if we were going to the East and offered to take anything to Willy for us.

At two we went down to the port and, taking a boat, round to the *Oronte*, the vessel which is to take the Colonel to Malta.[90] Lord Cardigan and Lord Dupplin passed us in the harbour on their way to their steamer; Colonel Townley in another boat, standing in a picturesque attitude, shouting last adieux.

L'Oronte was a good vessel, but all hopes of comfort for the poor travellers was destroyed by the fact of 130 filthy Arabs, in their filthy burnouses, being on board. These miserable animals, whom it is dangerous to touch even with the hem of our garments, were strewed about the deck in beautiful confusion, squalid, degraded, disgusting. So much for the romance of the desert.

We stayed a little time, chatting in the cabin; then came the signal for departure and we bid farewell to our dearest Colonel and descended into our boat; but still we lingered by the ship to see her till she was off. Captain Conolly came to the side, making absurd grimaces about the Arabs. Before long the wheels turned slowly and *L'Oronte* was on her way. We watched till the high ground hid her from our sight and we could no longer see the Colonel at the stern standing waving his handkerchief to us.

We were a very sad little party when we returned home; and, if we were sad at parting with the Colonel, what must his loss have been to poor Aunt Charlotte. Of that we all thought.

* * *

21

James Yorke Scarlett to Sarah, Lady Abinger
Malta, 25 May 1854

Malta, 25 May 1854

My dearest Sally, The *Valetta* having come in from Alexandria, and starting at once for Marseilles, I have just time to write a line to say we are off tonight by the French boat that came in yesterday from Marseilles.[91] I expect to be in Constantinople on 1 or 2 June. I hear they are meditating an early movement – advance toward Varna, I suppose.[92] My regiment is to come by the *Himalaya* and will be the first of the brigade to land, I believe.[93]

I hope to hear from you very often, as there are so many steamers now. Though I keep going farther off, my thoughts are still at Cannes and in England.[94] It is hard to bear the separation from me of one who was so long my constant companion and who so clung to me, but it does not do to think much.[95] Tell Robert his presents of books are most useful to me in keeping my mind engaged.[96]

There is plenty to look at in this beautiful little town, but it is all well described in the *Saturday Magazine*, no. 524, price 1d.[97] Both Conolly and I continue well.[98] The heat has increased but I have not found it too hot yet. I have bought four mules for £17 each, which is cheap at present; and I take out a cart, which would make a bedstead also. I think Fanny and Robert would be delighted with Malta. The rooms are cool enough and there is a shady side to most of the streets. I went last night to a party at the Governor's magnificent palace: no end of rooms, badly furnished (at least furniture), very old, badly lighted.[99] Not much to say for Maltese society. A great number of priests, Roman Catholic, in their robes present. No end of churches, bells and convents.[100]

Most of the French are gone to Athens.[101] We have five hundred on board for Gallipoli.[102] Mr and Mrs Drummond go out with us this evening, and many more who have been waiting here for a passage.[103] I found my major's wife here waiting for her lord.[104] She looks strong. That and wiry and hardy, and says she can shift for herself and is coming to Constantinople. I think *she* can manage it. Now best love to Robert and Fanny. Write to me as often as you can and believe me ever your affectionate JYS.

Cover, The Lady Abinger, Cannes, France, via Marseilles. Postmark, Malta, 25 May 1854; Paris, 30 May 1854; Cannes, 2 June 1854.

* * *

22

James Yorke Scarlett to Sarah, Lady Abinger,
Koulali, 20 June 1854

Koulali, 20 June 1854

My dearest Sally, Very many thanks to you and Robert for your most welcome letters.[105] I will not lose a post in answering them. I have heard from Charlotte to 2 June, at which time she was well and doing her best to live her best at Bank; and I trust she will find things go on smoothly.

Almost the whole world are gone to Varna or going today.[106] I am left till some more of my brigade arrive. The 5th went on in the *Himalaya* without disembarking. I went on board and was received with many a cheer.[107] They lost two horses and I have heard of their landing at Varna and marching off, much admired by the French, to the camp where I hope to join them.

Willy arrived there safe in *Simoom* and wrote a line to say so.[108] I have sent him your letter by a party of the 11th Hussars yesterday.[109] I am very sorry to have failed in getting him on my staff at present, as *all* the brigadiers applied and have all been refused an extra aide de camp. Willy was much disappointed, as was I, though I foresaw some evil as well as benefit that might have occurred from carrying out our wishes. So I console myself in the fact that whatever is, is best.

I am now very anxious to join him. This, though a beautiful situation, is a horrid hole and the sooner we quit it the better. The country is not unlike that about Ewhurst, Holmbury and Leith Hill; only, instead of heather read box, and put in the valleys melons, cherries, pines etc.[110] Still it has a green and well cultivated look. Roads there are for goats, sheep and mules, mere tracks: so much for Asia Minor. All the houses are made of wood painted red or yellow.

What we are to do when we all collect at Varna I don't know, but it is the place I have always pointed out as the proper one for anyone to occupy who meant to assist the Turks, as it would act on the Russian flank and rear in case of an advance by them.[111] If they don't advance, shall we? At all events, whether for fighting or negotiation, I think we are rightly placed at Varna or the neighbourhood.

The heat is becoming greater but has not become too great for me yet. Morning and evening are pleasant and there is a breeze on the hilltops. Give

1   General Sir James Yorke Scarlett (1799–1871).

2   James Scarlett, first Lord Abinger
(1769–1844), General Scarlett's father.

3   Sarah Scarlett, Lady Abinger (1803–1878),
General Scarlett's sister-in-law, by Edmund
Havell.

4   William Scarlett (1826–1892), General
Scarlett's nephew, aide de camp and heir.

5   Frances Scarlett (1828–1920), General
Scarlett's niece.

6 General Sir James Yorke Scarlett
(1799–1871).

7 Charlotte, Lady Scarlett, née Hargreaves
(1806–1888).

8 Lieutenant General the third Earl of Lucan
(1800–1888).

9 Major General the seventh Earl of Cardigan
(1797–1868).

10 Cattle Pier, Balaklava. This and the following photographs of the Crimea are by Roger Fenton (1819–1869), who was in the Crimea between March and June 1855. Sent out to the Crimea with a brief to present the war in a positive light, his photographs include no images of the wounded or dead.

11 Landing Wharf, Balaklava.

12   General Scarlett on horseback with
Colonel Alexander Lowe of the 4th Light
Dragoons.

13   Fitzroy Somerset, Lord Raglan
(1788–1855), Commander of the Forces in the
Crimea.

14   Lord George Paget (1811–1880), Colonel
of the 4th Light Dragoons, second-in-command
of the Light Brigade at Balaklava.

15   Captain Temple Godman (1833–1912), 5th
Dragoon Guards, with his camera-shy horse,
The Earl.

16 The 5th Dragoon Guards' camp, looking towards Kadikoi. Kadikoi, about a mile from Balaklava, was the main British camp. It was less exposed to the wind and less cold than the infantry and artillery lines on the heights outside Sebastopol.

17 Horse Artillery camp, with Major Brandling's troop, showing huts and bell tents. This was the troop that, by accurate fire, thwarted the Russian cavalry's attempts to reform after the Charge of the Heavy Brigade.

18   The 4th Dragoon Guards' camp. Entitled 'Convivial Party, French and English', it includes two Zouaves and the rare sight of a woman, Mrs Rogers, in the Crimea.

19   Officers of the 5th Dragoon Guards. From left to right (not all identified): Dr Cattell, Lieutenant Montgomery, Lieutenant Hampton, Lieutenant Ferguson, Major Inglis, Captain Godman, Major Burton, Lieutenant Burnand and Quartermaster Bewley.

20 Burnley Hustings, 15 November 1868. General Scarlett top right. This image is of a later date, as the Conservatives were on the left of the hustings, not the right, and women would not have made up part of the crowd.

21 Bank Hall, Burnley, General Scarlett's home from 1835–71.

my love to Robert and Fanny. The latter would have ample use for her pencil here.[112] I will write whenever I can. Ever yours affectionately, JYS.

Cover, The Lady Abinger, p.p. Londres, 3 Chester Square (Chez M. Sims, Cannes, Var, France crossed out), via Marseilles. Postmark, Cannes, 16 July 1854; other postmarks.

*   *   *

23

James Yorke Scarlett to Sarah, Lady Abinger, Scutari, 30 June 1854

Scutari, 30 June 1854

My dearest Sally, I shall write only a line to say I am still at Scutari waiting for my forces, which are slow coming, but I have passed on three ships of the Royals and wait for the last of two more, with which I proceed to Varna, according to orders. I hear a very bad report that the *Europa*, with Willoughby Moore and Headquarters Enniskillens, has been sunk in the Bay of Biscay and that the riding master and veterinary surgeon are drowned.[113] The horses of course destroyed; all other hands saved. I will hope it is false till confirmed.

The Russians have left Silistria and retreated.[114] Their direction is not so well known. Probably if Austria is in earnest, they are throwing back their right to Jassy and will occupy a line from thence to Galaty, with the Pruth and Bessarabia behind them, into which, if Austria joins us, they must retreat almost without a blow; but I daresay the newspapers through Varna and elsewhere give you quite as much and more that we know.[115]

Willy is well at Varna when I heard last from him and crying out for bacon and hams and tea, which I will take to him. Though we have missals to and fro daily, one hears very little of what one wishes to hear. I believe the 5th have gone to Devna and I shall have some trouble in getting my brigade together; but there seems no hurry or much for anyone to do as yet.[116] My mules from Malta arrived today and left my Maltese back at Gallipoli, for which I have thanked the captain most graciously.[117] We have had hot weather, 83 in the shade, but less relaxing than inland, and morning and evening very pleasant. I am perfectly well. If one walks slow, and keeps the shady side, one does pretty well. The Turks wear nothing but the eternal red fez, which would have been the worst protection against the sun that could be designed.

Our barracks rooms here have magnificent views. One window looks down the Sea of Marmora on the islands; Olympus is covered with snow.[118] The other on the Seraglio point and into the Golden Horn; the very best view of Constantinople, Galata and Pera.[119] I have been round the walls and in various directions at Therapia, Belgrade, in the forest, Byukdere etc.[120] (Several ladies are at Therapia and Byukdere.) I think myself, or rather

Charlotte, lucky in her not being here by herself, as the society at the *table d'hôte* is by no means what one would wish for one's wife and sisters; but it is certainly a beautiful spot; and, with a good family party and good house, which may be had, would be delightful. By herself I think she is far better at Bank. She writes in very fair spirits. I hear from others that she is doing well as I could wish and hope without me. I have had a very satisfactory letter from Eleanor and from my agent, Mr Helens.[121] All this cheers me, but it is a hole in one's life, which one feels more now that so much is expended, being separated from our friends.

I wonder if all my letters have reached you. We failed in getting Willy on the staff. Whether it is better or not I know not. We should both have much liked to be together, but it may be better delayed a little that he may see some service with his regiment.

Write to me very often, for any news from home and those I love is delightful to receive. I have now absolutely been a whole month in the Bosphorus and the novelty is quite worn off, and I pass Turks, dogs and storks without looking at them as strangers. Our horses do pretty well on barley and chopped straw, and would prefer good hay and oats I have no doubt. I think I hear the serjeant calling for letters, so, with best love to all, ever yours affectionately, JYS.

Cover, The Lady Abinger, Constantinople, 30 June 1854; via Marseilles, Cannes, Var, France; p.p. Londres, 3 Chester Square.

* * *

24

James Yorke Scarlett to Sarah, Lady Abinger
Camp Devna, 27 July 1854

Camp Devna, 27 July 1854

My dearest Sally, I suppose Chester Square will be the best direction for the line I am about to write, which is simply to say that I saw Willy yesterday and he was well, though he had a little overreached his strength by a hasty journey to Schumla with Ennismore and young Frank Gordon the other day.[122]

We are shifting our camp here to several other places in the neighbourhood, as cholera has broken out in the Light Division Infantry. We have lost a man of it in the 5th. We shall be somewhat altered, which is a bore.

There is nothing coming here to regret and one takes one's house on one's horse's back, if not snail-like on our own. Canvas agrees very well with me. I was never better in health and take a swim at six a.m. daily in a very clear basin, the source of the Devna lake.[123] That I shall miss. I go with the 5th to the village called Kotlubie and encamp at a spring.[124] The Royals go to another spot. The 4th and 6th are at Varna still, so that I cannot put my chicks together at all.[125]

I know not who may read my letters on the road, so I refrain from saying all that I feel inclined on our interim economy and management of matters, which sometimes makes me laugh. The newspapers I believe know a great deal more of us than we know, so I refer you to them, warning you not to believe *all* they say. I fancy the Russians are still in the west and I doubt their intention to cross the Pruth at present. An Austrian occupation seems an odd solution.[126] How will she behave if we attack Crimea?

I have heard very regularly from Charlotte and she seems to get on very well and just as I could wish, taking an interest in things and people about her. I am sure she is better off at Bank than she would be at Therapia. The climate has already told on a good number of officers. Dupplin, who came out with Cardigan you remember, is gone home sick; and several others and more will go no doubt.[127] All proclaim this mode of life as very dull, and I think nobody seems to appreciate the climate and beauties so justly set down in Murray's handbook.[128] Everybody's opinion seems to be 'twere well done', so 'twere done quickly', but things seem very slow, yet I don't see how they could go much faster.[129] We have by our advance here turned the Russian flank and thrown them back from Silistria to the Pruth. What next? Two months coming will probably open our eyes considerably; perhaps close the eyes of many too. Let us be content being under orders and do as we are bid.

Charlotte in her last said she was going to pay a visit at Appleton and Light Oaks – Richard Blackburne's.[130] I doubt her going to Inverlochy, as she will be rather out of the way of the post there.[131] She is very grateful to all her friends for their kindness. It seems to console her. I confess I shall hail with great joy the prosperous termination of this affair and a return to home, should such be my fate. I shall think I have done enough for my country and think of nothing but my own affairs and those who love me. I must now say goodbye and call the orderly. Love to Robert and Fanny, ever yours affectionately, JYS.

Cover, The Lady Abinger, 3 Chester Square, London. Postmark, British Army, 29 July 1854; DE 9 August 1854.

* * *

25

Frances Scarlett to Sarah, Lady Abinger
Bank Hall, Burnley, 29 July 1854

Dearest Mother, I am safely home with Aunt Charlotte, having left London at 9.15. She met me most kindly at Manchester, having come there by the train. I am happy to say that she is looking very well. Perhaps she may be a little excited with seeing me, but I think she really is well. I am agreeably disappointed with Bank, which is by no means so smoky and gloomy as I had been led to expect.... . Ever your affectionate child, Frances M. Scarlett.

*   *   *

26

Frances Scarlett to Mary Campbell
Bank Hall, Burnley, 9 August 1854

Bank Hall, 9 August 1854

Adorable Cat, I don't think you will ever get this letter, but still I will write because you were so good to me.[132] I received your precious letter this morning. How much *too* pleasant your tour seems to be. I long to be with you going about on the backs of mules and the soles of your feet. It gives me so much pleasure to hear that my young friends are enjoying themselves so much.[133] Aunt Stratheden sent me a letter of yours from Chamouni; otherwise I had nothing of your proceedings since you were not drowned and had just written to Cecie in a distracted state of mind for some news.[134]

It is a very wise plan your being picked up by the family at Cologne. You shall have another letter to greet you there, for Cecilia and Mama and I leave Bank next Tuesday, the fifteenth.[135] Papa goes tomorrow. I hope and believe our presence here has been a comfort to Aunt Charlotte. She is not at all in the way the Dowager would wish, but bears her trial, and it is a hard one, nobly, doing all she can to be well and cheerful for the sake of her absent husband.[136] We cannot prevail upon her to come south with us, which I am sorry for, as I am sure she frets very much when left to herself without any distractions except Eleanor.[137]

Give my best love to Burton.[138] We shall be delighted to see him at Torlundie whenever he comes.[139] An *enemy*, however, has already taken up an advantageous position on the ground: John Thursby goes up with us on the fifteenth, with every intention to kill, slay and exterminate.[140] I wish Hally could have had the first shine out of the muirs, but I shall have a private understanding with the keepers to see fair play and leave some of the grounds untouched for him; but, however, if there is anything like good sport this year, there would be plenty of fun for two guns without their ever crossing one another. I went out like old Mother Hubbard for a walk; and, when I came home, I found the whole matter settled between parents and Mr Thursby: trains, steamers and everything.

We have had capital letters from the Colonel and Willy. They have been encamped close to one another and seeing one another constantly. Both report well of their mutual healths. I fear some 'movements' are projected, which will make us very anxious. So long as the army was quiescent, grumbling, growling, swearing about beards and rations, we might be happy; but we must now expect some trouble.

Peter, I believe, is en route home and intends coming to Torlundie, which will be delightful. What he will do with the children remains to be proved.[141] He talks of bringing them to Torlundie, but this is impossible. He begs that we may 'knock up a deer for them' and provide two ponies for their riding. I long to see Peter in spite of all his naughty little ways.

This place is not cheerful, though I have been very quiet and happy with Aunt Charlotte. Smoke and chimnies are the features of the country; everything is black.[142] The roses are only to be looked at at a respectful distance and the strawberries taste of soot. Once upon a time, before the time of cotton mills, this has been a sweet land, but the grim hand of man has defaced it all cruelly; but I suppose we must have chemises, male and female, and it is very certain that the folks to whom the chimnies belong, and the folks who feed aforesaid chimnies with their coal, appear wonderfully indulgent to the nuisance.

It is impossible to stir outside the garden on account of the vagrant humans who err about. One day I made a trifling expedition by the side of a stream and began to think myself quite rural, when out rushed a number of men and boys in a state of nature to bathe in said stream. I fled and have not since attempted the rural. Aunt Charlotte and I, however, ride every day, which is very pleasant, though the roads are rather hard. John Thursby has lent me a nice quiet mare, which would be the thing for you, if he were disposed to sell; handsome thoroughbred and admirably quiet. I think his canter rough, but he declares it is the hard roads. I shall just throw out a few feelers on your behalf. I shall never have a horse under me for pace like Parkhurst, and you sold him for £34.[143] What a pity he was insane. You ought to have sold him to a mad doctor.

Meantime, I was forgetting that you will never receive this and I might spare myself the trouble of writing all this rubbish. Greet Hally with affection from me. I shall hear all about you from him. I have not been angry with you for not writing, dear, because I know how difficult it is to combine correspondence and rapid travelling. How I wish you were coming to the Highlands with Hally. Haven't you had travelling enough for this bout? Remember your health. Ever your attached friend.

*   *   *

27

James Yorke Scarlett to William Duckworth
Varna, 23 August 1854

Camp on Adrianople Road near Varna, 23 August 1854

My dear Sir, It is with very great pain that I feel called on to inform you that your son, Captain Duckworth, has had an attack of cholera and that at present he is in a very weak and precarious state, though I am far from despairing of his recovery.[144] At present he is on board the *Bombay* transport in the harbour of Varna, having been removed there from our former camp at Kotlubie by one of the ambulance carriages. He is under good medical treatment and I trust that by the aid of sea air, which is recommended, he may recover and live to do honour to his family and his country. He is much esteemed by officers and men in the regiment, and his services can be ill spared at present. We have lost one senior serjeant and very many men from cholera, which has been fatal to every regiment in some degree in whatever situation, and also in the navy – the French still more. I will keep this open till the last moment that I may give you the latest intelligence. I think it will be absolutely necessary for your son to return to England to recruit, should he overcome the attack.

24 August

It is with the deepest regret that I now inform you that I have received a note from the medical officer on board the *Bombay* to announce the demise of your son, Captain Duckworth, who expired at 3 a.m. He was sensible to the last and expired without any pain. The state of weakness to which he was reduced by the disease, and the inability to take any nourishment, appear to have been the immediate cause of death. I cannot express the grief felt by myself and by his brother officers to whom he was justly dear. Preparations are making to bury him on shore and he will be attended to the grave by the regiment.

May God support you under this affliction. I remain yours faithfully, J. Yorke Scarlett, Brigadier General.

I will write again by the earliest opportunity. JYS.

Addressed to George Duckworth Esq., Beechwood, Southampton.

* * *

28

James Yorke Scarlett to Sarah, Lady Abinger, Varna, 24 August 1854

Camp at Adrianople Road near Varna, 23 August 1854
My dearest Sally, Many thanks for yours received the twenty-first inst. I am glad to find you arrived safely in old England and no doubt this will find you at Torlundy. The same post brought me a nice letter from Fanny. I will answer it by the next post, if possible.

Willy and I are now near neighbours in sight of each other's camp. He removed from his last camp the same day we left ours and we arrived here the same day. August has been a fatal month for our forces, for none more than the poor 5th Regiment, who have lost one officer, Dr Pitcairn, and thirty-two men by cholera.[145] All regiments have suffered, the French more than us, and the navy have lost many.[146] Probably a battle fought would not have been as fatal to us. I need not dwell on this distressing theme. I trust it is all over.

Willy and I are quite well. He had another slight attack of ague but is all right now and dined with me today.[147] Poor Captain Duckworth and Mr Fisher, regimental surgeon, and Colonel Le Marchant are all ill, the two first I fear dangerously so.[148] Duckworth is on board a vessel, the *Bombay*, in the harbour and Fisher in the general hospital.

Now there seems to be a prospect of some movement. Various are the conjectures, but probably, ere you receive this, some event of a decisive kind will have taken place, which I cannot tell because I don't know; and, if I did, I suppose I should be wrong to tell. You must therefore look to the newspapers, which generally know what *has* been done, though they have been very incorrect of late. I believe nothing less than the taking of Sevastopol will satisfy John Bull, but whether he will be indulged in it is another question.[149]

The evacuation of the principalities by Russia and their occupation by Austria will enable the Russians to direct a larger force to Odessa or the Crimea, so that I don't know that we gain anything by the retreat from Silistria and the evacuation of the principalities if we intend to make an attack elsewhere in the Euxine.[150] Time will tell.

We have had a great change in the weather. It is now cool and cloudy, a great relief from the blazing sun. I have suffered from nothing but a scorched nose and cheeks, and my hands are like a Red Indian's or not quite so fair. The Guards and infantry have leave to wear moustaches and hair ad libitum.[151] Willy sports a respectable crop on upper lip and chin, which becomes him. We talk together of home and home friends whom we shall be most glad to see again – and to talk with them instead of them.

I forget whether I mentioned that Varna had been set on fire by the Greeks and a great part of it is still smouldering in ruins.[152] Many stores, French and English, have been consumed and the loss of them is felt very much. I hear our friends the French made somewhat free with the food saved from the flames and added a few Greeks most deservedly to the burning items to quench the flames. The fortifications are not injured and the fire has been, so far as destroying the town is concerned, a benefit. The cholera will be smoked out and a better town built probably, if we or the French undertake it. If the Greeks were to renew it, it will be no better than the old one.

The sudden and violent attack upon the 5th Regiment by the cholera prevented our running on to Schumla and Silistria, which I regret as I wished to *see* the waters of the Danube, even though it be not our destiny to cross them this season.[153]

I believe no one is in love with this country for campaigning. Though beautiful to see, it is by no means pleasant to dwell in. It might be made with industry and good government a garden or extensive park. There are not any large towns, but the country is covered with low brushwood and divided into hill and valley, and otherwise extensive plains which undulate – and if cultivated would be rich in produce and in beauty – but most unwholesome to an Englishman. I believe the plain of Devna and Kotlubie, where we were last encamped, are notoriously unhealthy.[154] There is a marsh at the head of the Devna, a lake from which no doubt miasma arises. The banks are filthy when the lake is low during summer heats.

The weather has now become much colder with the change of moon, as foretold by the natives, and I begin to think that we shall cry out about cold instead of heat in another fortnight. If we *are* to do anything this year, we should not delay too long. I suppose we may say our trip to Varna and advance to Devna has not been in vain, since it assisted to raise the siege of Silistria and to free the principalities from the Russians. They could not have advanced whilst we held Varna and the mouths of the Danube and navigation of the Black Sea.

If Nicholas is wise, he will now try to stop further proceedings.[155] The difficulty will be to get him to gulp down the dose and pay something towards the war, which will be better for him than the loss of Sebastopol and his fleet. I fancy whatever happens that our ally the Sultan will be something like the horse which unwarily let the man mount him to hunt for the stag.[156] The French will ride him if we don't and probably he will have to carry double.

I think that Lucan has done all he could for poor Mrs W. Moore.[157] I know she was attached to her husband, but as they lived so much apart probably she will bear it better than many might. He behaved very nobly. He might have been saved but for the cowardly behaviour of the crew, who, when they got on board the Prussian brig, cut away the boat lest they should be sent back to the burning vessel, which they expected would blow up. I heard a good deal from a Dr McGrigor and a young cornet, who escaped.[158]

I must finish this scrawl with my best love to my Lord and Fanny. I hope you had a pleasant visit at Bank. I am sure Charlotte would be delighted to see you and do all she could to make you at home. Love, my dearest Sally, your affectionate JYS.

Cover, The Lady Abinger, Torlundy, Fort William, North Britain.[159] Postmark, Army, 24 August 1854; Fort William, 10 September 1854.

*   *   *

29

Frances Scarlett to Mary Campbell
Inverlochy, 13 September 1854

Inverlochy, 13 September 1854
We expect Peter this week (the end).[160] We sent him a letter from Aunt
Stratheden to Bank to him.[161] Young Sims comes tomorrow. Hally and I had
a scheme of inveigling Peter up to the Northern Meeting, but I don't think
I wish to go now: we are so anxious about our soldiers, now perhaps in the
midst of battle, that the idea of *balls* is rather revolting.[162] Yesterday we heard
from Willy, on the eve of embarking for Sebastopol. He says he feels not
for himself but for his father's anxieties and his mother's tears.[163] If they are
properly led, success cannot be doubtful, and his next letter will probably be
from the field of victory. These are solemn words! God protect our dear ones!
The pestilence of the night season has spared them. May they now be saved
from the arrow which flieth by daytime.[164] They are not likely ever to be in
greater hazard than they have been from cholera. The 5th Dragoon Guards
has been so cut up that it is now incorporated in the 4th Dragoons.[165] This
must be a blow to Uncle Jim at the very moment of action, when the laurels
they so long looked forward to seem within their grasp: his own regiment,
in which he took such pride, has ceased to exist, mowed down ingloriously
by cruel disease. Captain Duckworth is dead, besides two other officers;
two sent home on sick leave, one being Major Weatherley in command; and
several others incapacitated.[166] Uncle Jim himself is quite well. So is Willy.
Lord Lucan is said to be the worst appointment in the army.[167]

I shall write again directly we have farther news; and, considering the
length of time all the movements have hitherto taken, very great expedition
is not to be expected. But as the season is so far advanced, something must
be done now or not at all. Hally sends you all sorts of love. He has given me
a small cow. I have long wished for a match for Ena's *cat*.[168] Now I have got it.
My very best love to you all. I was very sorry to see the death of Cecie's friend
Flora Perry in the papers.[169] Ever your friend Frances M. Scarlett.

* * *

30

Charlotte Scarlett to Frances Scarlett
Bank, Burnley, 13 September 1854

Bank, 13 September 1854

My dearest Fanny, I return the two letters you so kindly sent me to read, and which I need not say were most interesting and I was very glad to see the handwriting, as I always am, of those two so dear to us, for I can in truth say that, next to my husband, Willie's health and happiness are now my chief anxiety, and they are united in my prayers that they may be protected in the time of danger and season of sickness and return to us safe.[170]

I heard from your uncle of a later date and make some extracts for you:

Camp, Adrianople Road, Varna, Monday night, 28 August

I have need of your letters, for I am in no great spirits, having seen so many friends, and so many of the poor men, carried off by cholera; but it has, I trust, ceased its ravages. It is not true that Doyle is dead; he is gone to England.[171] So broken up are we by this month's disasters that the 4th Dragoons and 5th Dragoons are for the present united under Colonel Hodge,[172] as the 5th have no commanding officer, Le Marchant being sick at Therapia and not likely to join; no surgeon, no paymaster, no vet surgeon.[173] They have lost three officers, thirty-nine men; a great loss in so small a body. Other regiments have suffered much, but not so much in proportion. Our horses are now too many for our men. I need not tell you how grieved I am.

The Guards have received orders to embark tomorrow. We suppose the Crimea is the point they tend to; the others are to follow. Willy came to tell me this tonight, the order having only just arrived. This campaign must soon terminate, as the weather will not permit much longer active operations. Probably before this reaches you, much will have been decided and my conjectures rendered useless.

Last night we had a regular gale, which tried the strength of my tent poles and pegs, and raised a hurricane in the tent, but I managed to keep sheltered in bed. If it grows colder, I have another tent lining to put up. Hitherto I have not suffered in health, but am on the contrary stronger than in the relaxing climate of Ireland. Nevertheless, I have seen enough of Turkey and care not how soon I leave it.

Tuesday 29 August

The Guards marched down this morn at 5.30 to embark. They go to Balchik Bay probably.[174] I am still of opinion no attack will be made and some settlement will be effected from all I hear, but it is well to be prepared for what may happen. The Heavy Brigade will certainly not go till vessels return for them; and the infantry must land first.[175]

The weather has become much cooler from a northerly wind blowing fresh. It is still hot in the sun and the dust is annoying, and I fear the invalids will not benefit much as yet from the change. Lord de Ros and his ADC are both gone to Therapia and probably will go to England.[176] A great number of officers are gone or going home on sick leave. Burnand, Ferguson and McNeil go on board a transport for a short time.[177] I hope they will soon be fit for work again. MacNeil suffers from asthma, Burnand from liver, Ferguson from fever, but none are dangerously ill. Poor Swinfen has ague, but that will get well.[178] Elliot and Conolly are neither of them strong; and I was yesterday very near being at a brigade marching order without any staff. Elliot, however, did rally and come out.

If I continue as well as I have been, you need not fear for me. I now hope things are coming to a crisis and that whatever course they take it will bring me nearer home in the end. As yet you will see that to make any plan would be premature, so many things may occur to overthrow it. Write to me as usual: British Army in Turkey. All letters so directed are sent out in one bag. I fear the regularity with which we have hitherto received our letters may be interrupted, but do not omit to write and number your letters; and if you do not get mine as regularly as hitherto, you must attribute it to my being more employed and not having the convenience for writing.

I hope that the Inverlochy party will pay you a visit as they return. My horses are pretty well; not too fat certainly. You must not let your spirits sink but look to happier days when we shall never lose sight of each other to make up for this separation.

Dear Fanny, I have scribbled this out of a long letter full of kindness and consolation, and the rest is about trifling matters at home, which shows me how he thinks of my comfort, and expressions of the greatest kindness to myself, which I will not copy.

Poor Mr Fisher died the same day as Captain Duckworth.[179] I think the next mail will arrive in two or three days. I have not heard from Peter, what day he will be here, but I hope he will not stay long in London, from whence the accounts of cholera are so dreadful.[180] Give my best love to your party and believe me your ever affectionate aunt, CAS.

* * *

31

Frances Scarlett to Mary Campbell
Bank Hall, Burnley, 13 October 1854

Bank Hall, 13 October 1854

Dearest Friend, I thought my letter from Torlundie would just catch you at Paris, and yet not be stale, but you made more haste than I gave you credit for. By this time you have it, with Peter's part enclosure, which will satisfy your mind as to the way Hally and I are conducting ourselves. This morning arrived your two letters: yours to me forwarded from Torlundie; Hally's I read as soon as I perceived that crafty title 'or FMS' in the corner. I have sent it to him to Hartrigge with yours to me.[181] Of course he won't set off for Paris, because it would be absurd. I had no idea you would be home so soon. It is a pleasure to think that you will be in England in a day or two, though we shall not meet at present any the more for that.

We have no fresh news from Willy since the glorious letters of the 21st and 22nd, of which I gave you an account.[182] We were made *so happy* that we have almost forgotten that we must be as anxious as ever again. I hear all the wounded Fusiliers are doing well, except Colonel Haygarth, whose case is a bad one.[183] Sir Charles Hamilton brought us a message from Willy that he was 'quite well and flourishing on the 24th'.[184] Colonel Moncrieffe said he had 'behaved bravely'.[185] The same regiments are not twice running in front, which is a comfort. Peace! Peace, when shall we have peace? I am sick with horror when I read the details of that cruel battle – and yet the men do not suffer half as much as the women. What is a wound compared to dying away by slow degrees of care and anxiety!

We were quite shocked to find the change that two months had worked in poor Aunt Charlotte. She has fretted herself to a shadow, neither eats nor sleeps; she is just the person to fade away with no complaint that admits of doctoring. How can you minister to a *mind* diseased?[186] She has received no news of the landing of the Heavy Brigade in the Crimea and news of nothing but storms.[187] A letter from the Colonel would relieve her immensely, but then would come the dangers of the war. I cannot help fearing that her life depends on how long this state of things continues, but do not tell this to *anyone*. I would not be one to cast the shadow of uncertain evils. Mama and I are resolved not to leave her till something is settled and she can have some peace. For she is certainly much the better for our being with her. We shall try to persuade her to come to Abinger; but, when she gets into a very low, nervous state, it is very difficult to induce her to move.

I want to go out to the East to nurse our brave soldiers.[188] Here *is* the opportunity we have *talked* about so much and so often. Will you go? How can we manage it? I am not joking but cannot see my way through a mass of difficulties. I have always upheld the doctrine that women were no use in the East, and worse than useless. *Now* we could be ministering angels. Oh, Polly, if you knew how I *craved* for something *to do*.[189] I *feel* as if I were ready to encounter any fate, but fear all the time it may be only a passing enthusiastic frenzy. We know not what we can do till we are tried is true in two senses. Papa has been talking of his yacht all the summer, but now, when I tell him I am ready to go, I suspect he will declare the scheme impossible …

With tender love to you all, ever your attached Friend.

* * *

32

Frances Scarlett to Henrietta Graham-Toler
Bank Hall, Burnley, 16 October 1854

Bank Hall, 16 October 1854

My dearest Henrietta, We arrived here this evening, when I received your letter.[190] I do not see why people should trouble themselves to yell and scream because we fulfilled our original plan of remaining a certain time in Scotland. It is giving themselves very unnecessary fatigue; and the Duchess of Gloucester may go into fits if she pleases.[191] In order to appease *your* astonishment, I may state that we were not kept in suspense longer than anyone else, only we got our news a day later. The telegram about dear Willy came to Bank on Monday afternoon. We got the official list of the killed on Monday and of the wounded on Tuesday, which had been telegraphed to Glasgow direct and came up to Fort William.

But do you not know of a *dread* so horrible that you do not wish to learn anything? And a feeling that an agony of suspense is better than the possibility of a terrible certainty: that bad news ever travels fast enough; and that every hour that it is delayed is an hour of grace? If you have ever felt this, you will see why it did not occur to us to fly south as soon as we heard of the Battle of the Alma. We did entertain the idea of so doing for a short time, thinking the change might be a relief to Mama, but the dread of meeting disastrous tidings on the journey decided us to await our fate where we were. We should, moreover, have missed Willy's glorious letters from the battlefield, which naturally came to Torlundie, where he expected us to be.

Now, my love, you understand how absurd are the groans of a multitude, who know nothing of the motives which influence the actions of others; and when Dowagers, and Duchesses egged on by Dowagers, go into fits you will perceive that their emotions are all wasted.[192] I will not, however, say a word against the Dowager, who has been very kind and sent us all the information she could with much sympathy; but she does love abusing her friends. That's a fact.

It is a great comfort of course being here, and to get 'today's paper'; but I believe the satisfaction to be more ideal than real. It is not as if we could act on any information received. I am sick with horror at this war. My sense of *glory* is drowned in my compassion for the brave men who have lost their lives; for the wounded, suffering in agony; and still more for the sorrowing friends of those who have fallen – had it been our fate to mourn for our gallant brother!

Is not the bubble reputation dearly bought by the broken hearts? Is not the state of warfare a state of unchristian barbarity to be tolerated only because in this sinful world force must be met with force? Give peace in our time, O Lord.[193] How many, many years we have *said* this prayer, but it is only now that we have learnt to *pray* for the blessing.

I want to go out and nurse those poor soldiers at Scutari.[194] They may not be so badly off as the *Times* represents; but it is not probable that they are very well attended to.[195] We know they have no nurses. Ask Jane and Georgie (West) what they think, but they are not strong enough for the business.[196] Mama scorns the idea of my being a hospital nurse, for the other day I was assisting at putting on some leeches on Papa, when I fainted almost dead away, and had to be recovered; but, with a little practice, one would soon get the better of that weakness.[197] Would Polly go? Couldn't we get the Dowager to lead us? For the first time, I think that women might do good at Constantinople. The French have sent out five hundred Sisters of Mercy.[198] Why can't we do the same? I am quite serious, though of course you think me raving.*

We left Inverlochy on Friday at four p.m. and reached Oban at seven, where we dined and slept. The voyage was rough and made me feel sick, and I have felt unwell in consequence for the last two days. There was a poor lady in the cabin with three small children who bothered and shrieked incessantly. Saturday the swift boat, the last of the season, picked us up at Oban at seven a.m. and brought us to Glasgow. We found Lord Ranelagh on board.[199] He is looking decidedly ten years older than when I danced my first 'come out' quadrille with him. Sunday was spent at Glasgow: church in the morning and a walk about the town with Peter in the afternoon. It was not unpleasant.

We all fancied we were going to have the cholera.[200] I was so bad that I had to confide in Hally, being afraid to tell my parents for fear of affrighting them. (I am quite right now.) This morning we started at nine and got in at five. Peter and Hally went off to Edinburgh. Aunt Charlotte is looking very much thinner than when we left and is depressed in spirits – who can wonder? I hope we shall do her good. Write very soon and largely. Ever your attached sister.

* * *

---

* French nursing in the Crimea, mainly provided by nuns from the order of St Vincent de Paul, was far superior to that of the British early in the war. Five members of the Irish Sisters of Mercy, founded in Dublin in 1831 and with a house in Bermondsey, set off for the Crimea before Florence Nightingale. Russian nurses from the Community of the Holy Cross, founded by the Grand Duchess Elena Pavlovna, the sister-in-law of Nicholas I, were also active in the Crimea. The Russians claim Dasha Sevastopolskaia, who cared for those wounded at the Alma, as a precursor of Florence Nightingale.

Chapter 4

Balaklava

At the Alma on 20 September 1854 the British and French won a resounding victory but, by not pursuing the retreating Russians immediately afterwards, they failed to capitalise on it. Although the Russian army had been defeated, it had not been destroyed. Four days later, on 24 September, when the allies finally reached Sebastopol, they missed the opportunity to capture the city, at this point lightly defended, from the north. Instead, considering such an attack hazardous and likely to be unacceptably costly in lives, they marched around the city to reach the ports of Balaklava and Kamiesh to its south. Given the choice by the French, Raglan chose the picturesque but problematic inlet of Balaklava as the British supply base.[1]

Even after they had established themselves to the south of Sebastopol, the allies continued to waste valuable time. The British artillery expert, General Sir John Burgoyne, advised against any immediate attempt to storm the city, again on the grounds of likely casualties. This resulted in the inevitability of a formal siege. The allies, however, had insufficient numbers to invest the city, which allowed the defenders to bring in reinforcements and supplies from the north throughout the following year. The delay also gave the Russians time to strengthen the city's defences, directed by a highly talented military engineer, Eduard Todleben.

Balaklava proved to be the Achilles heel of the British Army, especially once it became clear that the campaign would be prolonged. As opposed to Sebastopol itself, a large and superb natural harbour, or even Kamiesh, which was several times its size, Balaklava, no more than a poor fishing village when the British arrived, was both desperately cramped and difficult to enter from the sea.[2] The inadequate dockside space meant that supplies piled up, were damaged or even rotted.[3] These physical limitations, when added to the extraordinary complications of the British Commissariat, meant that the men of the British Army often went short not only of essential clothing and equipment but even of food.

Just how unpleasant Balaklava soon became was recorded by Fanny Duberly in December 1854:

If anybody should ever wish to erect a 'Model Balaklava' in England, I will tell him the ingredients necessary. Take a village of ruined houses and hovels in the extremest state of all imaginable dirt; allow the rain to pour into them, until the whole place is a swamp of filth ankle-deep; catch about, on an average, a thousand Turks with the plague, and cram them into the houses indiscriminately; kill about a hundred a day and bury them so as to be scarcely covered with earth, leaving them to rot at leisure – taking care to keep up the supply.[4]

Because it was impossible for all the supply ships to enter the harbour immediately, many were forced to ride at anchor outside it.[5] This resulted in the disaster of the storm of 14 November 1854, when numerous ships were sunk or damaged. Much of the army's stock of winter clothing went down in the *Prince*.

Apart from its inadequacies as a port, Balaklava was a problem because of its position. It was six miles from Sebastopol and over five miles from the British lines. To reach the latter entailed a lengthy climb without adequate means of transport.[6] Although there was a metalled road on the top of the ridge above the port, as well as a rough track nearer the sea leading up via the Col to the Sapouné Heights, the army was extremely short of mules. All the heavy equipment required, including the siege guns, had to be dragged up laboriously, often manually, to outside Sebastopol. Conversely, Balaklava was at least two hours' march away from the main lines of the British infantry encamped outside the besieged city.

The plain between Balaklava and Sebastopol was divided by a low ridge, the Causeway Heights, into north and south valleys. Along the top of the ridge ran the Woronzow Road. Those in either valley could not see what was happening in the other valley or what was happening on much of the ridge. While the British commander, Lord Raglan, on the Sapouné Heights, above the plain and nearer to the British lines besieging the city, had a panoramic view over what became the battlefield of Balaklava, he was dependent on aides de camp on horseback to deliver orders. These contrasting sightlines, and the difficulty of clear and timely communication, had a critical impact on the battle.

The first regiment of the Heavy Brigade to arrive in the Crimea was the Scots Greys, landing at the River Katcha on 24 September, four days after the battle of the Alma. They had only left England at the end of July. After spending seven weeks at Koulali, opposite Constantinople, they arrived in the Crimea without going to Varna. Of the regiments of the Heavy Brigade, only the Greys took part in the Flank March around Sebastopol. The other four regiments of the brigade, which had been left behind at Varna, sailed to the Crimea two days later. William Cattell, of the 5th Dragoon Guards, complained about conditions aboard the *Jason*:

> On the 26th we, with Scarlett and staff, left in *Jason* and the 4th Dragoon Guards in the *Trent*, each towing a transport with Inniskillings and Royals. After the liberal treatment on the *Himalaya*, the screw company did not win our confidence. There was no table liquor. Anyone wanting a glass of sherry had to order a bottle which stood amongst others with your name attached, on a shelf overhead.[7]

Scarlett and the 4th and 5th Dragoon Guards arrived unscathed at Balaklava.[8] William Scarlett, the General's nephew, reported to his mother on 2 October: 'The Brigadier has arrived and I dined on board ship with him yesterday. He is naturally much disappointed at having missed the action where he was so much required. They are landing the Heavy Brigade fast and he will soon be at work. He is looking the picture of health'.[9]

Meanwhile the troops not on the steam ships suffered far more than a restriction on their officers' consumption of sherry.[10] Soon after leaving Varna on the evening of 26 September, with the steamers towing the sailing ships, a storm forced the tow ropes to be cut, scattering the fleet.[11] According to Serjeant Major Cruse of the Royals:

> If I live for a century I shall never forget the terrible sights … The *Jason*, finding she could not tow us longer with safety to herself, cut us adrift without notice at midnight, and the ship, being left all at once to the mercy of the raging of the Black Sea, soon became in an awful plight. The whole of the stabling on deck broke adrift and the officers' horses were dashed from one side to the other.[12]

The Royals lost almost a hundred horses, more than at Waterloo, while one of the Inniskillings' transports, the *Warcloud*, had to return to Varna, having thrown seventy-five horses overboard. The latter regiment finally arrived at Balaklava with only six of their horses.[13] Altogether the brigade lost 226 horses, a loss only partially made up by seventy-five horses transferred from the Light Brigade.[14] If a similar storm had caught the main allied invasion force, two weeks earlier, the history of the Crimean campaign might have been very different.

By early October, nevertheless, the cavalry division, including the Heavy Brigade, were together for the first time in the war. The brigade consisted of five regiments, each comprising two squadrons:

1st Dragoons, The Royals, Lieutenant Colonel John Yorke

2nd Dragoons, The Scots Greys, Lieutenant Colonel Henry Darby Griffith

4th Dragoon Guards, The Royal Irish, Lieutenant Colonel Edward Hodge

5th Dragoon Guards, Princess Charlotte of Wales's, Captain Desart Burton

6th Dragoons, The Inniskillings, Lieutenant Colonel Henry White

Although the brigade numbered around 1300 men, with 945 horses, by no means all of them were available to fight. Due to the shortcomings of the Commissariat, over three hundred men of the brigade were involved daily in foraging, while others were sick or on picquet duty. The total strength of the brigade at the battle of Balaklava, including its officers, was under eight hundred and perhaps as few as seven hundred.[15]

Because of its distance from the bulk of the allied forces, Balaklava was not only highly inconvenient but also a serious liability in terms of defence. As the allies had an inadequate number of men to prosecute the siege, they had few men to spare to provide a secure defence of Balaklava. Kamiesh, in contrast, far nearer to the French and indeed the British lines, was safe from Russian attack.[16] With priority given to conducting the siege of Sebastopol, the defence of Balaklava was improvised and inadequate. Six redoubts formed an outer ring of defence. One was on Canrobert's Hill, a separate hill to the east of the others on the Causeway Heights, but all were hurriedly constructed and of little strength.[17] The first four were occupied by Turkish infantrymen with a handful of British cannon and artillerymen.

Between the Sapouné Heights and the port was the large British encampment at Kadikoi. The defence of Kadikoi and Balaklava was under the command of Major General Sir Colin Campbell. Although his force amounted to over four thousand men, half of these were the inexperienced Turks manning the redoubts.[18] The only fully trained infantry in Campbell's main force was a single regiment, the 93rd Highlanders, with 550 men stationed just to the north of Kadikoi. With them were the four nine-pounder field guns and two twenty-four pounder howitzers of W Field Battery of the Royal Artillery. There were another 180 men of the 93rd on Mount Hiblak above Balaklava, where there were also five batteries, with twenty-three guns, manned by 1200 Royal Marines. These, however, were intended to defend against an attack from the north from the direction of Kamara.

In extremis, Campbell could also summon a hundred convalescents, able to bear arms, from Balaklava.[19]

The other force guarding Balaklava, in conjunction with Campbell's force but under the command of the Earl of Lucan, was the British cavalry division, consisting of the Light and Heavy Brigades. Cavalry, of little or no use in a siege, could move much faster than infantry. Both brigades were encamped in the south valley to the west of Kadikoi. Because of their mobility, they were ready to meet a Russian attack from whatever quarter, an unusual role for cavalry to add to its usual ones of scouting, foraging, skirmishing and providing picquets and vedettes. The cavalry was not, however, intended to act on its own but to act with Campbell's force to delay any attack and, by doing so, to buy time until the infantry could deploy.

Lucan's position was an uncomfortable one. He was senior in rank to Campbell and, in normal circumstances, would have expected to have been in overall command of the defence of Balaklava. He had, however, forfeited the trust of Lord Raglan, following his protracted wrangling with Cardigan and after disagreements over the use of the cavalry at the Bulganek and the Alma. It had not helped when the cavalry took the wrong path during the Flank March, exposing Raglan himself to the Russians. Raglan had indeed stopped inviting Lucan to conferences attended by the other lieutenant generals. He had also given Campbell command of the immediate defences of Balaklava, independent of Lucan. All this undermined Lucan's position and almost certainly contributed to his decision to follow Raglan's fatal fourth order without question later in the day.[20]

Well before the Heavy Brigade landed in the Crimea, Lucan had lost the confidence of his senior officers. Colonel John Yorke of the Royals, writing to his sister from Devna on 20 July, told her:

> We are disappointed with Lord Lucan. He is an excitable man, without system, finds fault at every moment, is very energetic at times, but takes up something new before he has carried out his former view. He is also muddle-headed (I understand) in the field and, instead of bringing the cavalry together for his own practice, he remains doing nothing at the landing place.[21]

Three days before Balaklava, Yorke predicted that Lucan was likely to cause a disaster:

> Our next misfortune is Lord Lucan. When there is the least appearance of alarm he becomes excited to madness and abuses everybody and in the most uncourteous manner. The other night he sent round an ADC to

say we were to remain stationary during the night and, as if he doubted our obedience to his orders, his message added (in the presence of the men) that he would send any officer home under arrest who left his post, as well as the commanding officer who permitted it. Poor General Scarlett can do nothing for his brigade. Lord Lucan by nature opposes everything he does not think of himself and we are consequently fearing his want of temper and judgement should anything serious occur. He is sure to do wrong and then throw the blame on others. He is a very unfit man to command such a brigade: a hot-headed Irishman.[22]

Although defeated at the Alma, the bulk of the Russian army had survived. The delay in attacking Sebastopol meant that the Russians were not only able to strengthen the garrison of the city but could keep their main army outside it. In early October this army was reinforced by the arrival of another twenty thousand men, many from Bessarabia, including cavalry and artillery. In addition, two more divisions, the tenth and eleventh, were nearing the Crimea. This would bring the overall strength of the Russian forces to between 85,000 and 90,000, giving the Russians a superiority in numbers over the allies of as much as ten thousand men.[23]

It was not difficult for the Russian commanders to identify the lengthy British supply line from Balaklava to the troops besieging the city as a critical weakness. The British were also only too aware of the likelihood of an attack on it. Indeed, before the battle of Balaklava they had responded to what looked like attacks on several occasions, most recently on 20 October. As Lord George Paget of the 11th Hussars observed on 12 October:

We are now regularly turned out about midnight, and I shall soon wake at the regular time, but we always turn in again in half an hour. Every fool at the outposts, who fancies he hears something, has only to make a row, and there we all are, generals and all. Well, I suppose five hundred false alarms are better than one surprise, so there is no help for it.[24]

Wary of another false alarm, when a spy on 24 October reported that the Russians were going to attack on the following day, Raglan dismissed the information. He told Lord Lucan's son, who had brought the message, 'Let me know if there is anything new.'[25]

The rumour of an attack turned out to be true.[26] Early on the morning of 25 October, having gathered over several days at the village of Chorngun, a substantial force of Russian troops, commanded by Lieutenant General Pavel Liprandi, crossed the Tchernaya, the river flowing into the harbour of Sebastopol. The Russians may have numbered as many as 25,000 men overall, including thirty-four squadrons of cavalry and seventy-eight guns.[27] After moving into their positions from 4 a.m., the Russians began a three-pronged attack, with 14,000 infantry and thirty-six artillery pieces, at 6 a.m.

The aim of the attack was to cut the British supply line and, if possible, capture not only the redoubts on Canrobert's Hill and the Causeway Heights but also Kadikoi and Balaklava itself. Although Russian accounts of the operation are opaque, with a number of their generals issuing self-glorifying or self-exculpating accounts of the battle, both to the Tsar at the time and in their later memoirs, there can be little doubt that the capture of Balaklava was the final aim of the operation.[28] Two accounts based on Russian sources agree. 'There is little doubt that Menshikov's intention, according to the widely accepted Russian view at the time, was to capture Balaclava';[29] and 'A swift strike against the redoubts was certain of success, after which they could turn their attention to Balaklava itself.'[30]

The Russian attack began when their left-hand column, under Major General Gribbe, moved west, crossing the Tchernaya by the Baidar bridge and taking the village of Kamara, from which the Russian artillery commanded Canrobert's Hill and the eastern end of the Causeway Heights, before attacking No. 1 Redoubt. The Turks defending it put up a stout resistance but were overcome by greatly superior numbers. As Lord George Paget noted:

> A great deal was made of the behaviour of the Turks in their abandonment of these redoubts, and by none more than ourselves (the cavalry), but the truth is, they were placed in very trying circumstances. The bravest troops in the world never should have been placed in charge of those redoubts, *en l'air*, and unsupported as they were, or rather at such a distance from all supports.[31]

The failure of their allies to support the Turks in their redoubts set an unhappy precedent on a day when both brigades of the cavalry division later had cause to complain of an absence of support.[32]

The centre column under Major General Semiakin, after crossing the Tchernaya at a ford, captured Redoubt No. 2 without difficulty. The third column, under Colonel Skiuderi, using the road from the Traktir bridge to Balaklava, took Redoubts Nos. 3 and 4.[33]

Suffering heavy casualties, the Turks defending the redoubts fled back towards Balaklava, having lost nearly all cohesion. During this early stage of the battle the British cavalry division had advanced to near the first redoubt in the south valley within the range of cannon fire.[34] Once the redoubts had fallen, however, the division was forced to retreat to the west of Kadikoi by Russian fire from Canrobert's Hill and the Causeway Heights.

As soon as it was confirmed that the Russian attack was in earnest, Raglan had sent messengers to two of his infantry divisions, ordering them to march down to the plain. The nearest was the 4th Division, commanded by Sir George Cathcart, who told Captain Ewart, the aide de camp bringing the message, that there was no possibility of his men moving immediately:

> Lord Raglan on observing the flight of the Turks called me, and desired that I would immediately proceed to Sir George Cathcart, and request him to move his division, as quickly as possible, to the assistance of Sir Colin Campbell at Balaklava. I was just starting with this order, when General Airey came up, and said, 'Remember, you are on no account to conduct the division by the Woronzoff road.' I then galloped off as hard as I could go, and on reaching the camp of the Fourth Division found Sir George Cathcart dressed, and seated in his tent. I at once delivered my orders, upon which Sir George replied, 'It is quite impossible, sir, for the Fourth Division to move.' I then stated that my orders were very positive, and that the Russians were advancing on Balaklava. He replied, 'I cannot help that, sir; my division cannot move, as the greater portion of the men have only just come from the trenches.' For the third time I repeated my orders, stating that I had myself seen the Turks flying from their redoubts towards Balaklava, and that every moment was of consequence, as Sir Colin had only the 93rd to depend upon besides the cavalry. Sir George then said, 'Well, sir, you may return to Lord Raglan, and tell him, that I cannot move my division.'[35]

Although the Duke of Cambridge's First Division was quicker to get moving, it was further away from Balaklava. Because, however, of the instruction not to use the Woronzow Road, both divisions came via the Col, with further delay caused by a bottleneck made worse by French infantry and cavalry also using the same route.[36] In the event, the British and French infantry were so long in reaching the plain that neither took part in the fighting, though the French light cavalry, the Chasseurs d'Afrique, arrived in time to play an important part in the aftermath of the Charge of the Light Brigade. This delay in the deployment of the allied infantry, caused by muddled orders and the refusal of Sir George Cathcart to move his troops immediately, was the essential background to everything that happened on 25 October, turning the Battle of Balaklava into a cavalry battle. This was something that Lord Raglan had neither planned nor foreseen.

At about 8.30, on the Sapouné Heights above the battlefield, Raglan issued the first of his orders to the cavalry: 'Cavalry to take ground to the left of the second line of redoubts occupied by the Turks.'[37] Although the intent of the order was almost certainly to remove the cavalry from danger until the infantry arrived, its wording was ambiguous and in part incomprehensible. As left and right depend on the position of the viewer, it was unclear whether 'left' in the order referred to Raglan's own position or that of Lucan and the cavalry. There was no second line of redoubts, so it was impossible for the Turks to be occupying it. Lucan sought clarification from Captain Wetherall, the aide de camp who had brought the message. This resulted in Wetherall leading the two brigades back to a position between Redoubt No. 6 and the foot of the Sapouné escarpment.[38]

While Russian infantry and artillery captured Canrobert's Hill and the Causeway Heights redoubts, a force of around five thousand men under Major General Zhabokritsky occupied the Fedoukine Heights, adjoining Sebastopol and overlooking the north valley, to protect the Russians' right flank.[39] Soon after 8.30 a strong body of cavalry, under General Ivan Ryzhov, crossed the Fedoukine Heights into the north valley.[40] This force must have crossed into the north valley rapidly, as they would have been easily visible to Lord Raglan on the Sapouné Heights as soon as they entered the valley, yet his second order was made without reference to it. That no British scouts were posted on the Causeway Heights was an extraordinary oversight for which Lord Lucan, and perhaps his brigade commanders, must take the formal blame.[41] Part of this force, perhaps four hundred men, split off and, crossing the Causeway Heights, advanced towards Kadikoi. There they were confronted by Sir Colin Campbell and the 93rd Foot.[42] Much has been made of the encounter that followed, with the 93rd being credited as the Thin Red Line that stood between the Russians and Balaklava, though this was not the original term used by William Henry Russell of the *Times*.[43] The truth of it seems to be that the Russians failed to engage, perhaps fearing a trap, and retreated.[44]

Despite the failure of this cavalry detachment to engage Campbell's force, up to this point of the day the Russian plan had gone extremely well. They had achieved an improbable surprise, due to Raglan's failure to heed the warning of an imminent attack, and had captured all four of the manned redoubts and their guns, establishing their artillery on Canrobert's Hill and on the Causeway Heights and forcing the British cavalry to retire. Before advancing further, however, they needed to make sure that their infantry and artillery were not caught in the flank by allied forces as they descended into the south valley. Here again the Russians were more than fortunate.

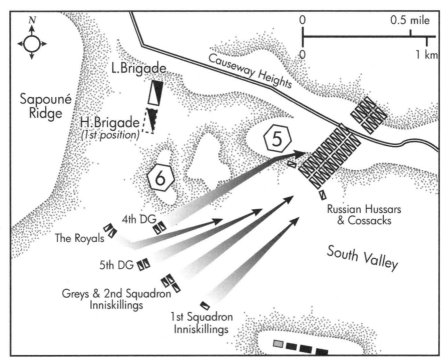

The Charge of the Heavy Brigade.

The slow deployment of the allied infantry, and the distance they had to travel from their lines outside Sebastopol, meant that they would not be in a position to affect the outcome of the battle for another two hours.

If the Russians deployed their infantry and artillery in the south valley and advanced towards Kadikoi and Balaklava, only the British cavalry remained as a threat to them. It was therefore General Ryzhov's task to engage and, if possible, defeat the British cavalry division, so as to clear the way for the planned Russian advance without endangering their exposed flank. Once again fortune favoured the Russians. Their main body of cavalry managed to cross both the Fedoukine Hills and the north valley, before climbing to the top of the Causeway Heights, without the British cavalry being alerted.

Because of the attack on the redoubts, and the threat to Balaklava, Raglan had issued a second order to Lucan, very soon after the first one: 'Eight squadrons of the Heavy Brigade to be detached towards Balaklava to support the Turks who are wavering.'[45] Why eight squadrons, rather than all ten, of the Heavy Brigade were specified is unclear. Moreover, the order both split the Heavy Brigade and moved these squadrons away from the infantry that was due to arrive. Finally, although the squadrons would reinforce

Campbell's force, it was too late in the day to support the Turks, who had already abandoned all four redoubts.[46] Lucan perversely also ordered Scarlett to advance in columns rather than lines, which made it much harder for the eight squadrons to ready themselves for action.[47] Scarlett clearly disagreed with Lucan's instructions. 'From the manner in which the squadrons were scattered about, no regular shipshape movement could be made to get them into the position, and they got back anyhow, the best way they could, to my exceeding disquiet.'[48]

Soon after the eight squadrons began to move towards Balaklava, while still passing the remnants of the Light Brigade camp and a vineyard, and spread out over a considerable distance, the main body of enemy cavalry suddenly appeared on the ridge above them.[49] The first sign of the presence of the Russians was the sight of their lances coming over the top of the Causeway Heights[50] This was noticed by Alexander Elliot, Scarlett's aide de camp, who brought it to Scarlett's attention.

The Russian cavalry under Ryzhov seem, oddly, to have been equally surprised to find itself above the Heavy Brigade. The Russians, despite their numerical supremacy and the advantage of higher ground, having advanced at a trot, halted and started to realign, pushing out horns on either side of their leading body so as to form a pincer formation. Lord George Paget saw 'the Russians halt, look about, and appear bewildered, as if they were at a loss to know what next to do'.[51]

The exact number of the Russian cavalry commanded by Ryzhov is uncertain, being reported very differently by observers at the time and by later historians. Counting a large body of cavalry in a short time, either from a distance or with only a partial view available, was always bound to be approximate. Temple Godman, of the 5th Dragoon Guards, thought there were 1500 to 2000, while Scarlett himself later estimated them at 3000.[52]

Whatever their number, the constituent elements of the Russian cavalry force were eight squadrons of the 11th Kievsky Hussars, six squadrons of the 12th Ingerlandsky Hussars and six squadrons of the 1st Ural Cossacks.[53] They certainly greatly outnumbered the Heavy Brigade. Ryzhov also had the 12th Light Horse Battery and the No. 3 Battery of the Don Cossacks with him, each with eight guns. An estimate of the number confronting Scarlett, made from the likely numbers of the Russian formations, has been calculated at 2000.[54]

The uniforms of the Russians made a clear contrast to those of the British. 'The Russians, as far as they could be seen in this particular body, had black horses, wore a black oilskin cover, over a very broad-topped old-fashioned shako, and a dark grey overcoat. They were altogether a black-looking mass.'[55]

> The dress of the Russians was a red broad-topped stiff felt chaco, with brass double-headed eagle in front, and an oilskin cover over all. Underneath their greatcoats they wore a dark green jacket, with coarse orange worsted lace; trowsers of sky blue, with red piping down the seams; and a narrow strapping of leather from the fork to the bottom. Their horses were in good condition; they used layers of felt, or some soft substance sewn together, under the saddle, and a blue shabraque with red edging, and their emperor's (or some other) initials in red at the corners.[56]

The men of the Heavy Brigade stood out vividly, in contrast, in their red uniforms and blue trousers on their powerful horses. Particularly easy to recognise, even from the distance of the Sapouné Heights, were the Scots Greys with their bearskins and grey horses. The two Dragoon Guard regiments wore brass helmets, while the Royals wore silver-gilt ones.[57]

Controlling cavalry was a difficult business. While the Russian cavalry was adept at parade ground manoeuvres, they had little experience of reacting and adjusting to unforeseen circumstances on the battlefield. In the view of an experienced cavalry officer:

> Anyone with experience in *bona fide* mustering of cavalry by actually counting the men (and not trusting to the states) will know that squadrons of eighty men are not on parade every day, and that to manoeuvre twenty-five of such squadrons in one close or quarter-distance column, at a rattling good pace such as these men were moved at that day, is all but impossible, as the men in the centre are crushed out of all shape and dressing. The intervals between their squadrons must have been very slight, so slight, indeed, as not to be observed from the ground where C Troop saw them at their nearest, about 450 yards distant, before the collision. The column could in no way be seen through from front to rear, as would be the case in a similarly-formed body of English cavalry at the present day, with their twelve yards intervals.[58]

While the Russians were halted, Scarlett acted decisively. Superior training and professionalism now paid dividends. Having dressed the squadrons nearest to him, consisting of two squadrons of the Scots Greys and one squadron of the Inniskillings, three hundred men in all, he moved them to their right to allow the 5th Dragoon Guards to get clear of the nearby vineyard and the remains of the Light Brigade's camp. He then ordered his men to charge uphill at the Russians, putting himself well in front, followed by Alexander Elliot. Behind the two men came the brigade trumpeter, Thomas Monks, and Scarlett's orderly, James Shegog. Scarlett's brigade major, James Conolly, had been sent back with an order to the second squadron of Inniskillings with whom he then charged.

There are many accounts of the Charge of the Heavy Brigade.[59] Alexander Elliot himself, the second man to disappear into the Russians, told the Duke of Manchester his version of what happened six years later:

> They had scarcely changed their front when Elliot pointed out to Sir James Scarlett that Russian cavalry was coming over the hill to the north. Scarlett doubted it at first but with the glass saw it was so.[60] The column of Russians trotted down upon them. Scarlett then formed the Greys and one squadron of the Enniskillens and led them towards the enemy who had paused for a moment but were then deploying on the move.
>
> It was a race between the English and Russians who should be ready first. Scarlett went forward. Elliot remarked to him that they were too far in front of the line. Scarlett admitted it and waited hollering for them to come on. He and Elliot rode in among them and were separated in the crowd. When Elliot found himself surrounded by the enemy he backed out to the Greys. He struck a man and cut down a dismounted man when one of them gave him a bad cut across the back of the head. Scarlett went round to his right among the Russians and so back to his men.[61]

Temple Godman, an officer in Scarlett's old regiment, wrote to his father on the day after Balaklava:

> At this time a large mass of cavalry came over the hill in front of our camp, and would in a few minutes have been in our lines, and have cut down the few men left, when we got the order to advance.
>
> The Greys and Inniskillings went first, then we came in support of the Greys. Their (the enemy's) front must have been composed of three regiments, and a very strong column in their rear, in all I suppose about 1500 or 2000, while we were not more than 800. However, the charge sounded and at them went the first line; Scarlett and his ADC well in front. The enemy seemed quite astonished and drew into a walk and then a halt. As soon as they met, all I saw was swords in the air in every direction, the pistols going off, and everyone hacking away right and left. In a moment the Greys were surrounded and hemmed

completely in; there they were fighting back to back in the middle, the great bearskin caps high above the enemy.

This was the work of a moment. As soon as we saw it, the 5th advanced and in they charged, yelling and shouting as hard as they could split. The row was tremendous, and for five minutes neither would give way, and their column was so deep we could not cut through it. At length they turned, and well they might, and the whole ran as hard as they could pelt back up the hill, our men after them all broken up, and cutting them down right and left. We pursued about 300 yards, and then called off with much difficulty. The gunners then opened on them and gave them a fine peppering. It took some little time to get the men to fall in again. They were all mixed up together of course, all the regiments in one mass.[62]

A week later, Temple Godman wrote to his brother:

I had hardly time to put in my glasses when a cloud of Cossacks came towards us, spearing the retreating Turks, who kept firing at them; with them came a very large body of regular cavalry, supposed to be over 2000. We advanced, formed line, and by this time they were close to our camp and would soon have cut down our servants. The Greys and half the Inniskillings charged first, but they were so close to our old camp, we (the first line) could not get up any pace to the charge, so they met nearly at a walk.

The Greys and Inniskillings were immediately surrounded, which we seeing the 5th and the rest of the Inniskillings went in with a shout and a yell, and for about five minutes we were all hacking away at each other, pistols discharging, and the devil's own row, then they turned and ran up the hill again as hard as they could go, and we after them. Having called off and formed again, a matter of some trouble, for all the regiments were mixed, we had time to look about; there were over forty lying dead and dying in pools of blood, with most fearful cuts. We lost a corporal, quite hacked to pieces, and one man shot; another must die, his lungs came through his back. We lost this day two officers wounded, two men killed, nine wounded, gone to Scutari; five men were slightly wounded, seventeen horses killed, two officers' chargers missing and twelve horses wounded.[63]

William Forrest, of the 4th Dragoon Guards, described what it felt like during the charge:

I did think of my wife when we were in the act of charging ... When once in amongst them I scarcely saw anybody, that is to recognise them. One could not look about much until the Russians began to run ... My own attention was occupied by the hussar who cut at my head. I cut again at him, but do not believe that I hurt him more than he hurt me. I got a cut on the shoulder, but the edge must have been very badly delivered, for it has only cut me a rent and slightly bruised my shoulder. I did not attempt to use my revolver, for I had determined to keep that undercharged and in reserve in case of being wounded or dismounted.[64]

While Elliot, Forrest and Godman all took part in the charge, the men of C Troop of the Royal Horse Artillery observed it from close by. Unlike Raglan and Russell, watching from the Sapouné Heights, Captain John Brandling and C Troop were near at hand. The account by an unnamed observer provides valuable evidence on a number of matters:

It may be remarked that no one in the inner plain had a better view of the Heavy Cavalry charge before, during and after its execution than the men of C Troop. They were not occupied with any dressing, and had merely to look to their front, and to their left while passing by the rear of the Heavies, to see all; and the ground is such that while passing by the rear they saw, over the heads of their own cavalry (except a very few yards just in front of the latter), the clear ground right up to the enemy's horses' feet.[65]

To these accounts, and to the many others, we can now add Scarlett's own.[66] This was in a letter written to Colonel James Chatterton, the former commander of the 4th Dragoon Guards, six weeks after Balaklava.[67] That it was meant to be private is clear, 'You will see that some of this is for your eyes only.' Apart from its intrinsic interest in being written by the leader of the Charge of the Heavy Brigade, it brings out a number of significant points.[*]

---

[*] It is likely that Alexander Kinglake, the author of *The Invasion of the Crimea*, saw this letter in 1876. He wrote to the General's niece on 10 July 1876 from 28 Hyde Park Place, London: 'Dear Mrs Sidney Smith, I feel greatly obliged to you for your kind compliance with my request. My lengthened communications with General Scarlett gave me the advantage of being able to draw from him by careful questions much more than he, with his modest disregard of self, would have *volunteered* to tell, and there were happily officers serving under him who were able and willing to make the glorious truth known; but still it is interesting and satisfactory to me to have the succinct narrative (written from the Heavy Cavalry camp) which you have been so good as to send me. It is so modest and soldierlike; so modest because almost veiling the part the writer had taken; and so soldierlike because treating one of the most magnificent exploits that history treasures as if it were a matter of course! Believe, dear Mrs Sidney Smith, most truly yours, A.W. Kinglake.'

It confirms the poor relations between Scarlett and Lucan, traced back in the letter to Lucan's putting the 5th Dragoon Guards under the command of the colonel of 4th Dragoon Guards at Kotlubie. To this Scarlett adds his disquiet before the charge at Lucan's insistence that the eight regiments 'stand in contiguous columns, but with wide intervals of squadrons. He told me he disapproved of lines and everything was to be done by squadrons!!'[68] In lines regiments were placed alongside each other, while in columns they were strung out over a considerably greater distance.[69] He confirms that his order to move his squadrons to the right before the charge was to allow the 5th Dragoon Guards to get clear of a vineyard. In contradiction to Lucan's later claim, Scarlett states that he himself ordered the charge. He also says that he got into a gallop and met the Russians before they had made any further advance:

> I ordered the advance. The ground was bad, uphill and some of the picket ropes of the Light Brigade camp interfered, but we got into a trot and gallop and went right at them before they had time to deploy, which they were in the act of doing. They did not advance to meet us but stood still and we were soon hand to hand and deep into them in regular mill.[70]

Finally, he puts a number on those killed in the charge: one officer, Grey Neville, of the 5th Dragoon Guards, who died later of his wounds, and two men killed from each of his regiments, as against forty-five Russians 'on the ground dead or wounded'.[71]

The Charge of the Heavy Brigade was in fact not a single charge but a multiple one. The 5th Dragoon Guards followed behind the Scots Greys and the first squadron of Inniskillings, while the second squadron of the Inniskillings, from slightly further east, met the left wing of the Russians at an angle. Colonel Edward Hodge then led the 4th Dragoon Guards in an attack on the Russian right. Finally, the Royals, who had been left behind with the Light Brigade by Raglan's second order, charged into the Russians' right-hand flank. Under Colonel John Yorke, they came to the aid of the other regiments of their brigade on their own initiative.

After the charge, Lucan tried to claim the credit for setting the 4th Dragoon Guards in motion, something deeply resented by their colonel. Hodge wrote to his mother on 6 December 1854, 'I do think that Lord Lucan might as well have given me the credit of our flank charge, and not to have told such a falsehood about it saying that he ordered it, when he never gave any orders to us at all.' In a later letter, on 10 April 1855, he told her that the flank charge 'was quite my own idea'.[72]

Which regiment charged when, and on whose authority, caused some dispute and jealousy between the regiments of the Heavy Brigade, all of whom wanted their own contribution to be recognised, if necessary at the expense of others. Temple Godman, of the 5th Dragoon Guards wrote:

> The *Illustrated News* account is a very bad one, they put in the Royal Dragoons as having charged. They were not in the fight. All the men they lost were hit afterwards, when we got under the batteries in support of the Light. The 4th Dragoons were hardly in it, they executed a flank movement. The Greys got most spoken of, being so easily distinguished by their bearskin hats and their horses. They and the Inniskillings and the 5th Dragoon Guards were the only regiments in the thick of it.[73]

Edward Fisher-Rowe, of the 4th Dragoon Guards, however, disagreed, crediting his own regiment with coming up at a critical moment when the Scots Greys had been retreating:

> It is rather annoying that the Scots Greys should monopolise all the credit of the Heavy Cavalry charge at Balaklava, and it is curious no officer should have thought it worthwhile to contradict it. The only credit they had was that they happened to make the first charge, in which they failed to rout the Russians, who outflanked and would have surrounded them had not the 4th and 5th come to their assistance, and so great was the confusion that they broke our line as they came full speed in the opposite direction. Men who were looking on from the hills around speak much more strongly on the subject than I do here.[74]

After dining with the General a year after the battle, Edward Hodge made a very reasonable comment: 'Breakfasted with Scarlett and discussed the Battle of Balaklava. His account and mine do not quite agree. I am sure that, in an affair of that sort, we only know what is taking place immediately about us.'[75] Hodge, however, retained a suspicion that Scarlett was unwilling to give the 4th Dragoon Guards their due. 'He has always been jealous of us, since Lord Lucan said in his speech that, by our charge in flank, the Russian column was defeated – also the 5th being put under my command at Varna.'[76]

The pace of the horsemen when they reached the Russian line varied, but some at least got up a considerable speed.[77] General Scarlett himself describes going at a trot and then a gallop. As seen by C Troop:

> A squadron of Heavy Cavalry, which had in some way been detached to the right, now passed at a good distance in front of C Troop, and at a

splendid pace, the men sitting well down, and in good dressing; in this form they tore in on the left flank of the Russians, and catching them, as they did obliquely, and on the bridle arm, unhorsed whole troops of them.[78]

Lord George Paget from a distance saw part, but not all, of the brigade encumbered by the vineyard, to avoid which Scarlett had dressed his men to the right:

> This has been called a charge! How inapt the word! The Russian cavalry certainly came at a smart pace up to the edge of the vineyard, but the pace of the Heavy Brigade never could have exceeded eight miles an hour during their short advance across the vineyard. They had the appearance (to me) of just scrambling over and picking their way through the broken ground of the vineyard. Their direct advance across the vineyard could not have exceeded eighty or one hundred yards.[79]

An observer on the Sapouné Heights told Colonel Hodge's mother, 'the 4th came up at a very slow trot, till close to, when they charged them in flank at a gallop', though his second-in-command, William Forrest, described the pace as 'little better than a trot'.[80]

The result of the joint charges was a mêlée in which few men were killed on either side.[81] According to Major Thornhill, who took part in the charge, 'It was just like a mêlée coming in or out of a crowded theatre, jostling horse against horse, violent language, hacking and pushing, till suddenly the Russians gave way.'[82] There was a low number of casualties for a number of reasons. Although both sides carried firearms, these were little used, or at least had little effect and caused few injuries. The swords of both sides seem to have been remarkably blunt, while the thick overcoats of the Russians and the helmets of the British deflected many blows. A number of British cavalrymen suffered multiple wounds, none of which proved serious. Scarlett himself was wounded five times, while his aide de camp, Alexander Elliot, received no less than fourteen wounds.[83]

The larger horses of the British gave them a local advantage against the shorter, poorly mounted Russians:

> Our troops had the mastery in strength of men, and power of horse, of which they gave grand proof in unhorsing the enemy right and left, and it was thought, that if it had been possible to have taken the Russians in rear, or right rear, the whole mass would have thrown down their arms, or at any rate that great numbers of their dismounted men would have been driven into our position and made prisoners of war.[84]

The tight formation of the Russians also prevented them from making full use of their great numerical superiority, so that many members of the Russian cavalry, especially in their second main line, never engaged the British cavalry: 'there was a formidable body of them (certainly one half) that had never been reached or touched by our people; for when all the squadrons of the Heavies had executed the charge at the front, and partially on the flanks near the front, their strength may be said to have been expended.'[85]

The cutting and hacking was only carried on about as far as the fifth rank from the Russian front, and about as far inwards as the breadth of twelve horsemen on their flanks near the front. On the left flank, which was in full view of C Troop, certainly two-thirds of the flank nearest the rear was quite untouched: the remaining third next the front would be rather more than the breadth of front of the detached squadron which charged in that way, and which landed its left on the left of the Russian front rank. Probably on the Russian right flank, the attack may have extended farther towards the rear, but the same rule holds good: only a certain number of horses standing sideways could have been ridden down or destroyed at the first crash, and the horses inside these would hardly feel it, or suffer inconvenience from it.[86]

The Russian ranks also seem to have opened to allow their attackers to pass into or through them, rather than forming a solid block which might have stopped the British charge in its tracks. According to Kinglake:

in describing the supposed issue of conflicts in which a mass of continental soldiers was assailed by English troops extended in line, it used to be said of the foreigners that they 'accepted the files'. This meant, it seems, that instead of opposing his body to that of the islander with such rigid determination as to necessitate a front-to-front clash, and a front-to-front trial of weight and power, the foreigner who might be steadfast enough to keep his place in the foremost rank of the assailed mass would still be so far yielding as to let the intruder thrust past him and drive a way into the column.[87]

Finally, there can be little doubt that the British morale was superior and that members of the brigade showed far more individual initiative than their opponents.

After a number of minutes of uncertainty, the Russians began to retreat. They were followed for a few hundred yards by the British, who with fine professionalism then came to a halt and reformed before they came into the range of the Russian artillery on the Causeway Heights. The Russians also attempted to reform but were thwarted by the accurate fire of C Battery of the Royal Horse Artillery:

> The Russians, however, halted short of the ridge, and their officers could be seen holding their swords up and endeavouring to rally them, and get them into order, which they very soon would have done, but C Troop now came into action, and fired forty-nine shot and shell at them, at a range between 700 and 800 yards, with admirable results, the 24-pounder howitzers making splendid practice. This effectually prevented the Russians rallying, and they quickly retired, keeping a little inside the crest of the ridge, and thence over into the outer plain.[88]

While C Troop, under Brandling, played a decisive role in preventing the Russians reforming, another nearby British formation played no part at all in the Charge of Heavy Brigade, failing to provide support at a critical moment. At the head of the south valley, Lord Cardigan and the Light Brigade, not more than 500 yards from the scene of the unfolding action, did nothing.[89] According to Lucan, he had told Cardigan:

> I am going to leave you. Well, you'll remember you are placed here by Lord Raglan for the defence of this position. My instructions to you are to attack anything and everything that shall come within reach, but you will be careful of columns or squares of infantry.[90]

After the event Lucan was adamant that Cardigan should have come to the aid of the Heavy Brigade. Cardigan, however, remembered Lucan's order very differently:

> I had been ordered into a particular position by Lieutenant General the Earl of Lucan, my superior officer, with orders on no account to leave it, and to defend it against any attack of the Russians; they did not however approach the position.[91]

When asked by one of his officers, Captain William Morris of the 17th Lancers, to allow him to go to support the Heavy Brigade, Cardigan expressly forbade Morris from doing so and muttered enviously, 'Damn those Heavies – they've the laugh on us today.'[92]

The Charge of the Heavy Brigade was by no means the end of the day for General Scarlett and his brigade, although in its immediate aftermath those who had won a great victory against daunting odds were proud of their achievement. The atmosphere, and what happened next, was described by John Yorke, the colonel of the Royals:

After this there was a good deal of merriment, and we thought we might get to breakfast. I put sticking plaster on old Scarlett's hand, as he had a slight sword cut, when to my surprise the Royals and Greys were ordered to advance under one of the redoubts which had been abandoned but not taken by the Russians.[93]

After seeing the Heavy Brigade's success, Raglan had turned his mind to the recovery of the redoubts, issuing a third order at about 9.30:

Cavalry to advance and take advantage of any opportunity to recover the Heights. They will be supported by infantry which have been ordered to advance on two fronts.[94]

Lucan inevitably found this order puzzling. The meaning of the 'two fronts' was unclear and no opportunity to recover the Heights was in any way obvious. This, however, did not matter for the time being, as any advance was to be supported by infantry 'which have been ordered to advance on two fronts'. Lucan took the order therefore as an instruction to wait for the infantry to arrive. He merely moved the Light Brigade to the west end of the north valley and awaited developments.[95]

Over an hour later, Raglan, having seen the Russians removing cannon from the redoubts they had captured, issued his fourth and fatal order at about 10.55. This was taken down by the Quartermaster General, Richard Airey:

Lord Raglan wishes the cavalry to advance rapidly to the front. Follow the enemy and try to prevent the enemy carrying away the guns. Troop Horse Artillery may accompany. French cavalry is on your left. R. Airey. Immediate.[96]

Delivered by Captain Louis Nolan to Lord Lucan, who relayed the order to Lord Cardigan, this led to the Charge of the Light Brigade a quarter of an hour later.[97] The causes of the disaster and the meaning of the order have been endlessly debated. Interpreting it as an order to attack the Russian battery at the other end of the north valley, and unable to see the captured guns in the redoubts on the Causeway Heights, Lucan sent Cardigan and the Light Brigade to ride a mile and a quarter through an enfilade of artillery fire from both sides of the valley and into the direct fire of the Don Cossack No. 3 battery.[98] Not unexpectedly, the brigade, and above all its first line, suffered heavy casualties in reaching the battery at the end of the valley.

Whatever its target, Raglan's order explicitly instructed the cavalry, not just the Light Brigade, to advance rapidly. In accordance with the order, the Heavy Brigade moved forward in three lines behind the Light Brigade. Following the Greys and Royals were the 4th Dragoon Guards. Their major, William Forrest, wrote that 'We, the Heavies, were taken down the valley as support to the Light Brigade and we had batteries playing upon us, upon both flanks.' They soon came into the range of fire of the Russian batteries on both sides of the north valley, suffering considerably more casualties than they had during their earlier uphill charge. According to John Yorke:

> Just as I passed under it, the magazine blew up and covered me with sand; and, as soon as this cleared off, I found myself in this now termed valley of death, and the Light Brigade just in front advancing at a more rapid pace than ourselves. The rest of the Heavy Brigade, tho' stated to be likewise here in Lord Lucan's report, were safe in the rear, showing how inaccurate are those reports. For it was only Royals and Greys this time, and in a few moments we were in the hottest fire that was probably ever witnessed. The regiments were beautifully steady. I never had a better line in a field day. The only swerving was to let through the ranks the wounded and dead men and horses of the Light Brigade, which were even then thickly scattered over the plain. It was a fearful sight I assure you, and the appearance of all who retired was as if they had passed through a heavy shower of blood, positively dripping and saturated, and shattered arms blowing back like empty sleeves, as the poor fellows ran to the rear.
>
> During all this time there was a constant squibbing noise around me, proving even in these improved days of gunnery what numbers of shot do not take effect. However, another moment and my horse was shot on the right flank. A few fatal paces further and my left leg was shattered in this fearful manner you know.[99]

The brigade were already advancing, with Scarlett and his aide de camp William Beatson well in front of the Greys and Royals,[100] followed by a trumpeter and orderly, when Lucan ordered them to halt, without first telling or consulting Scarlett. Before giving the order to halt, Lucan had remarked to Lord William Paulet, the Assistant Adjutant General, 'They have sacrificed the Light Brigade. They shall not have the Heavy, if I can help it.' Lucan's phrasing neatly pre-empted any accusation of personal responsibility.[101]

Nine years later, Scarlett described the circumstances in a letter to Lord Cardigan, having just read an affidavit by Lord Lucan:

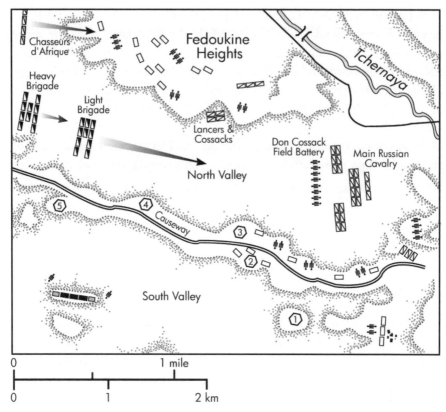

Chasseurs
d'Afrique

Fedoukine
Heights

Tchernaya

Heavy
Brigade

Light
Brigade

Lancers &
Cossacks

Don Cossack
Field Battery

Main Russian
Cavalry

North Valley

⑤   ④
Causeway
③
②
①

South Valley

0   1 mile

0   1   2 km

The Charge of the Light Brigade.

Certainly it differs considerably from mine on the same subject; but
I am still convinced that my version is the correct one. The facts are
imprinted on my memory from the following circumstances. Whilst
riding some distance in front of my brigade towards the enemy, with
Colonel Beatson, my acting aide de camp, the trumpeter and an
orderly, Colonel Beatson looked back and told me my brigade was
retiring. Not having given an order myself, I was naturally surprised
and annoyed.[102]

If Beatson had to look back to see that the brigade had been halted, Lucan
must have been behind rather than in front of Scarlett and his staff, in
contradiction to Lucan's claim that he rode between the two brigades during
their advance.[103] Although the Heavy Brigade retired out of the artillery
crossfire, they were able to cover the retreat of the remnants of the Light
Brigade as they made their way back from the Russian battery they had
attacked. By refusing to allow the Heavy Brigade to follow Cardigan and the

Light Brigade, Lucan had returned to Cardigan in full measure the latter's own failure to come to the aid of the Heavy Brigade earlier in the day.*

According to Scarlett, after being halted by Lucan, 'We then regained the crest of the hill and remained there till dark night, when we withdrew to our camp, having been out from six a.m. to eleven p.m.'[104] There is a final glimpse of Scarlett on what had been a very long day, recorded in the history of C Troop:

> As night set in, the whole of the troops withdrew out of the plain. As long as there was any light the Russian cavalry could be seen extended in long lines right across the bottom of the outer plain. When it was dark, General Scarlett came to C Troop, then near the ridge, and said, 'Artillery, try to light fires with this long dry grass, so as to make the Russians believe we are staying here all night.'[105]

The Battle of Balaklava, on 25 October 1854, has eclipsed all other actions during the Crimean War and has been written about ever since, mainly because of the Charge of the Light Brigade. Seeing it, however, from the viewpoint of General Scarlett and the Heavy Brigade adds an unusual angle, allowing the two charges by the cavalry division, and the battle as a whole, to be seen in a new perspective.[106]

Balaklava was an extremely odd battle for a number of reasons. Almost uniquely in modern warfare, it was a cavalry battle in which the infantry was scarcely involved.[107] In it the British cavalry, whose main purpose was to scout ahead of an army, to charge only at the climax of a battle and to pursue a defeated enemy, was turned into a defensive force. Its deployment alone, without significant infantry and artillery support, was also highly unusual.[108] This was particularly so given Raglan's previous careful husbandry of his cavalry. He had explicitly prevented the Light Brigade, prior to the Alma, from advancing against the Russians at the River Bulganek; and had also not allowed Lucan and Cardigan to pursue the defeated Russians after the Alma. This had led to the accusation that Raglan was keeping his cavalry 'in

---

* One of Lord George Paget's later criticisms of Lord Cardigan's conduct during the Charge of the Light Brigade was that he had *not* looked back. 'It was well known that he never looked back from the moment he first put spurs to his horse, and for anything that he could know to the contrary, the advance of those regiments *might* have been countermanded by the lieutenant general; or their onward course might have been impeded or turned aside by some eventuality unknown to him, in this unusual contest.' Paget, *The Light Cavalry Brigade in the Crimea*, p. 213.

a band box'. This caution was then replaced in his fourth order, which told the whole of the cavalry to advance rapidly, laying it open to heavy casualties.

Although famous for its two charges, making it in popular imagination a byword for extreme bravery and heavy loss in the face of impossible odds, in reality Balaklava was a relatively, even remarkably, bloodless battle. Far greater losses were sustained on both sides at the Alma and Inkerman, let alone Waterloo or the Somme. While no definitive count is possible, the Russians may have suffered 238 deaths and 312 wounded, against overall losses by the British of 360.[109] Turkish losses are also uncertain but were less than either.

Against the axiom that cavalry should, wherever possible, charge downhill, the Heavy Brigade won a remarkable victory against a greatly superior force of Russian cavalry while attacking from below. To the anxious watchers of what was an extraordinary spectacle seen from the Sapouné Heights, the Heavy Brigade's success, when it seemed threatened with imminent destruction, was astonishing. 'It was a terrible moment. "God help them! They are lost!" was the exclamation of more than one man, and the thought of many' was the reaction of William Russell of the *Times*. He continued:

With unabated fire the noble hearts dashed at their enemy. It was a fight of heroes. The first line of Russians, which had been smashed utterly by our charge, and had fled off at one flank and towards the centre, was coming back to swallow up our handful of men. By sheer steel and sheer courage Enniskillener and Scot were winning their desperate way right through the enemy's squadrons, and already grey horses and red coats had appeared right at the rear of the second mass, when, with irresistible force, like one bolt from a bow, the 1st Royals, the 4th Dragoon Guards and the 5th Dragoon Guards rushed at the remnants of the first line of the enemy, went through it as though it were made of pasteboard, and, dashing on the second body of Russians as they were still disordered by the terrible assault of the Greys and their companions, put them to utter rout.

This Russian horse in less than five minutes after it met our dragoons was flying with all its speed before a force certainly not half its strength. A cheer burst from every lip – in the enthusiasm, officers and men took off their caps and shouted with delight, and thus keeping up the scenic character of their position, they clapped their hands again and again. Lord Raglan at once despatched Lieutenant Curzon, aide de camp, to convey his congratulations to Brigadier General Scarlett, and to say 'Well done.' The gallant old officer's face beamed with pleasure when he received the message. 'I beg to thank his Lordship very sincerely', was his reply.[110]

Later in the day, Raglan visited Scarlett and complimented him in the hearing of C Troop. '"Now tell me all about yourself." Scarlett replied, "When the Russian column were moving down on me, Sir, I began by sending first a squadron of the Greys at them, and" – but at the word "and" his Lordship struck in, saying, "And they knocked them over like the devil." He then turned his horse away, as if he did not need to hear any more.'[111]

Balaklava is also famous for the confusion caused by unclear orders which were then misinterpreted. As has been seen, the four orders issued by Lord Raglan to Lord Lucan and the cavalry division on 25 October were all ambiguous. With the exception of the second order, which divided the Heavy Brigade, these orders also contained a fundamental ambivalence in that they referred simply to 'the cavalry', rather than any particular element of it. Although the Light Brigade was already placed at the head of the north valley, and the Heavy Brigade had already been engaged that day, Lucan could have ordered Scarlett rather than Cardigan to lead the charge up the Valley of Death.

Instructed by Raglan to act together in three of his orders, the cavalry division failed to do so at two critical points in the day. Despite its presence nearby, the Light Brigade did not to come to the Heavy Brigade's assistance at the time of the latter's charge. The Charge of the Light Brigade also saw a failure of one half of the cavalry division to support the other, even though the order from Lord Raglan which set it in motion referred to all the cavalry. 'Lord Raglan wishes the cavalry to advance rapidly to the front – follow the enemy and try to prevent the enemy carrying away the guns.'[112] Lucan did not question the order and dispatched his hated brother-in-law, the Earl of Cardigan, and the Light Brigade down the valley. Following Raglan's order the Heavy Brigade was lined up, ready to support them, and was already advancing under fire when halted by Lucan. Only at this point did Lucan finally question Raglan's order, cancelling the Heavy Brigade's advance without first informing Scarlett.

It has been argued that, had Lucan not countermanded the order, the Heavy Brigade might have helped the Light Brigade win a signal victory, as the Russian forces were in disarray.[113] Not only had the Light Brigade silenced the guns of the Don Cossack battery which were their target, they had ridden beyond it and, despite their very small numbers, had induced something like panic in the Russian cavalry behind the guns. The Heavy Brigade, which was drawn up in three lines, with Scarlett again ahead of the front line, would therefore not have been facing the Don Cossack battery. The battery on the Fedoukine Heights had also just been forced to retreat by a timely and highly effective charge by the Chasseurs d'Afrique. The arrival of the Heavy Brigade, in good order and at almost full strength, in support of the Light Brigade might have led to an unexpected and improbable victory.

The men of the Light Brigade reasonably claimed that they received little or no support. There was no sign of the infantry promised in Lord Raglan's third order or the troop of horse artillery mentioned in his fourth. When the Light Brigade advanced, they certainly expected to be followed by the Heavy Brigade, which was lined up behind them as they started towards the Russian battery. As Lord George Paget, who commanded the 4th Light Dragoons in the charge, complained on reaching the battery: 'Well, at last we got up to their guns and cavalry, and took the former (nine I counted), sabred some of the drivers, and, to our horror, then found that we were not supported!'[114] Due to last-minute reordering by Cardigan, the Light Brigade had charged in three lines, not two. The first line, with the 17th Lancers on the left and the 13th Light Dragoons on the right, was followed by the 11th Hussars. Paget commanded the third line, leading the 4th Light Dragoons on the left with the 8th Hussars to his right. The *only* support that Paget and the third line of the Light Brigade can have expected was that of the Heavy Brigade.[115]

This was not only a cause of dismay but was also ironic. Just before the charge, Cardigan had ridden over to him to say:

'Lord George, we are ordered to make an attack to the front. You will take command of the second line, and I expect your best support, *mind, your best support*', this last sentence being repeated more than once, and perhaps with rather a marked emphasis, as I thought, though it was probably more the result of excitement than anything else. But it caused me to answer with equal emphasis, 'Of course, my Lord, you shall have my best support.'[116]

Even during the Charge of the Light Brigade, and after the third line had passed the silenced guns of the Don Cossack battery, there seemed grounds for optimism. Colonel John Douglas of the 11th Hussars, whose regiment had reached the guns relatively unscathed, had no hesitation in advancing beyond them:

We then came up to the guns, my right squadron going through the right of the battery, and here a Russian officer decorated with several orders surrendered to me. But I was obliged to leave him to his fate. I here saw a body of Russian cavalry to my left front, and on the impulse of the moment I determined to attack them; my reasons were, that I thought I could do it with *very* great advantage, being under the impression that I should *jam* them into the gorge of the valley, here forming a sort of cul-de-sac from which there would be difficulty in escaping, as the aqueduct and the River Tchernaya barred any hasty egress. I, strange to say, was all along impressed with the idea that we were being supported, and that shortly both infantry and fresh cavalry would come up. Well, I determined to attack this body of cavalry; they appeared as if they had been in support of their guns, retiring some, and as we came upon them they got into confusion and very loose order. My men got greatly excited, and we pursued at our best pace, they sweeping round the base of the hills to our left front, forming the end of the valley.[117]

Nevertheless, even if they had routed the Russian cavalry and brought back the guns of the Cossack Don battery, the joint charge of the Light Brigade and the Heavy Brigade would have been a tactical rather than a strategic success, with little impact on the outcome of the siege or the war. Such a victory would, however, have greatly changed the later perception of the Battle of Balaklava. If the combined charge of the cavalry division had snatched victory from the jaws of defeat, it would undoubtedly have lessened the notoriety of the Charge of the Light Brigade. It would also have led to very different verdicts on those involved.[118] Raglan would have been praised for ordering of the charge. Nolan would have received credit for having clarified Raglan's order and for pointing Lucan in the right direction; and his famous view that cavalry could succeed in attacking artillery would also have been posthumously vindicated. Lucan, Cardigan and Scarlett would have shared the glory of a joint victory, won by collaboration and professionalism. The casualties suffered by the Light Brigade would have been judged acceptable, given the success of the operation. The Battle of Balaklava, however, might have attracted less future interest from being a well-earned victory rather than a heroic failure. Finally, Tennyson might have found it difficult to write as successful a poem about 'The Charge of the British Cavalry Division' as he did about 'The Charge of the Light Brigade'.[119]

While the combined forces of the British cavalry division might have won a memorable tactical victory by following up the Charge of the Light Brigade, what has not been previously observed is the strategic importance of the Charge of the Heavy Brigade. Although there were few casualties, especially on the British side, during the eight or ten minutes of the Heavy Brigade's charge, there is no doubt that it checked and drove back a large and mobile Russian force. A more probable outcome of the encounter would have been for the superior Russian force to have swept the Heavy Brigade aside, inflicting numerous casualties. Whether the Light Brigade would at this point have joined the fray or (still obeying what Cardigan claimed were his orders) it had retreated towards the British lines, the likelihood is that the Russian cavalry would have been left in command of the field and of the south valley.

When confronting the Heavy Brigade, however, as not unusually in the Crimean War as a whole, the Russians failed to show initiative or to take advantage of a highly favourable situation. Their commander, General Ryzhov, acted indecisively and was unable to finish the realignment of his force before the Heavy Brigade was ready to charge. By bringing his troops to a halt, and then allowing them to be attacked when static, he handed the initiative to his opponents.

Ryzhov's own account of the battle, published in 1870, is incompatible with what was widely observed at the time:

> One could not help being amazed as the enemy, superior in numbers, allowed us the freedom to ascend the height and, it may be said, gave me the time to draw up my units right in front of his nose and send them to indicated points. But that is the way it was: the enemy stood calmly and waited as by agreement. The silence on each side was surprising; only the Cossacks were shouting, but that was far off and no one paid them any attention. Only an enemy battery's heavy fire from the direction of Kadikoi reminded us where we were and why we had come. Finally my entire line flew quickly at the enemy's front …With God's help, the end was glorious for us.[120]

The minutes preceding the Charge of the Heavy Brigade were critical not only to the result of the battle of Balaklava but to the outcome of the war. Ryzhov failed to take advantage of an unparalleled opportunity, where victory might have given the Russians control of the British supply line. According to Mark Adkin:

> Afterwards, with hindsight, the military historian can often see the critical few moments in an action when resounding victory or devastating defeat hang perilously in the balance, when a slight push by somebody, somewhere, on either side is all that is required to tip the scales. Such a moment was when Rijov's leading squadrons pulled up the slope towards the Causeway crossroads.[121]

While the timings involved are not exact, the enemy attack had begun at 6 a.m., with all four redoubts captured by 7.30.[122] The Russian cavalry were in the north valley by 8.30 and by 9 had crossed the Causeway Heights at two points. The stand-off between Campbell's 93rd Highlanders and the detachment of Russian cavalry took place just before 9, while the Charge of the Heavy Brigade itself was over by 9.10. The British First Division, however, only reached the plain at 10, when they would have still been over an hour away from Balaklava. The 4th Division only reached No. 6 Redoubt at 11. If the Russian cavalry had swept the Heavy Brigade away, it would have dominated the south valley for at least two hours. Its success would also have allowed the Russian infantry and artillery on Canrobert's Hill and the Causeway Heights to descend into the south valley to make a concerted attack on Kadikoi and on Balaklava itself.

With the British infantry absent, the British camp at Kadikoi and Balaklava itself would both have lain open with little to defend them. Although the gallantry of the 93rd Foot under Sir Colin Campbell has been much vaunted, it is likely that, faced by the full strength of the Russian forces, including artillery and infantry, they would also have been swept away, after which it is hardly probable that the pensioners, Turkish remnants and artillery high above the port would have saved Balaklava.

Even if they had only captured Kadikoi and Balaklava briefly, the Russians could have inflicted incalculable damage on the British. Burning the ships and piled up supplies in Balaklava would have crippled the British Army and probably have made it impossible for it to continue the siege. If the Russians had established command of the British supply line, it would have put the British in an impossible position. The British and the French had insufficient troops to continue the investment of Sebastopol and to mount a major attack on a well-entrenched Russian position defending Balaklava at the same time. Any large withdrawal of the forces outside Sebastopol would have been met by a Russian sortie from within the city which would have had a good chance of capturing and destroying the allied siege works and of raising the siege. The small numbers of both Russians and British killed during the Charge of the Heavy Brigade therefore give a false idea of its importance in the outcome of the Battle of Balaklava and in the Crimean campaign as a whole.

In the event, the Russians of course failed to capture Balaklava or to break the British supply line. Nevertheless, they claimed Balaklava as a victory. It was celebrated immediately by peals of bells in Sebastopol. The captured cannons were presented by Menshikov to the Tsar as trophies. Kozhukov claimed it did more than anything else to bolster Russian morale:

General Liprandi's battle brought no tangible benefits, but nevertheless it was extremely important for the entire Crimean army and greatly influenced the course of the whole campaign. It was not important that we took a position, almost completely wiped out the English cavalry that day and took away nine guns. What was important was that the success of 25 October revived the army's depressed spirits, convinced it of its powers of resistance and prepared it for those efforts and sacrifices which the heroic defenders of Sevastopol would endure for eleven months. In this regard, the battle of 25 October was so important that hardly any other event of the Crimean War can compare with it, including even the repulse of the assault.[123]

That Balaklava had encouraged the Russians was demonstrated the day after the battle, when they made an attack on the right of the allied siege lines in an action known as Little Inkerman. In the event, they were driven back without difficulty by the British Second Division.

To a degree, British accounts agree, not claiming Balaklava as a victory and concentrating on the glorious failure of the Charge of the Light Brigade. Looked at, however, from another angle, Balaklava represented a major Russian failure in not taking advantage of their best hope of overall victory. The remarkable initial success of the Russians in mounting a surprise attack in force, then capturing the redoubts on Canrobert's Hill and the Causeway Heights, was combined with the woefully slow reaction of the allies and a series of blunders by Raglan. This presented the Russians with an opportunity not just for a moral victory, but for the capture of the British supply line and indeed the capture of Balaklava itself.

Part of the reason for the Russian failure to capitalise on this opportunity can be put down to the poor quality of their conscript troops, including their cavalry, which had signally failed to have an impact at the Alma, and to their indecisive leadership and low morale.[124] Part of it ought, however, to be put down to the remarkable victory for professionalism and high morale achieved by General Scarlett and the Heavy Brigade. As Lord George Paget, who himself took part in the Charge of the Light Brigade, wrote:

It was a mighty affair and, considering the difficulties under which the Heavy Brigade laboured, and the disparity of numbers, a feat of arms which, if it ever had its equal, was certainly never surpassed in the annals of cavalry warfare, and the importance of which in its results can never be known.[125]

In the wake of the Charge of the Heavy Brigade, Lucan tried to take the credit for Scarlett's success, claiming that he had ordered the charge:

> The Heavy Brigade had soon to return to the support of the troops defending Balaklava and was fortunate enough in being at hand when a large force of Russian cavalry was descending the hill. I immediately ordered Brigadier General Scarlett to attack with the Scots Greys and Enniskillen Dragoons, and had his attack supported in second line by the 5th Dragoon Guards, and by a flank attack of the 4th Dragoon Guards.[126]

This claim Scarlett's letter to Colonel Chatterton explicitly refutes.[127] It was also refuted by what Alexander Elliot later told the Duke of Manchester. 'Elliot asserts positively that Lucan was in the rear of the Heavy Cavalry – and gave them no orders. The whole thing was done by Scarlett.'[128] While Lucan was close at hand during the charge, and may indeed have issued orders, including getting Henry Joy, his divisional trumpeter, twice to sound the charge, the decisions taken and the orders that were obeyed were Scarlett's, not Lucan's. Conversely, in his own report Scarlett does not mention Lucan in connection with either of the charges of the day.[129] Scarlett's later correspondence with Cardigan on the matter adds an interesting perspective on the charges of both the Heavy and Light Brigades.[130]

Lucan then failed to endorse Scarlett's recommendations for awards, leaving the latter to discover this from a *Times* report almost a month later. Scarlett wrote to Raglan's military secretary to clear himself from the charge of not having recommended Elliot and Beatson:

> I am aware that it would be presumptuous in me to dictate in any way what names the lieutenant general commanding the division thinks proper to submit for the approval of the commander of the forces, but I am anxious to relieve myself from the imputation of having done injustice to the merits of two officers from whom I received the greatest assistance on the day alluded to.[131]

Much has been written about the antipathy between the Earls of Lucan and Cardigan. Far less has been made of the very poor relations between Lucan and Scarlett. Lucan had treated Scarlett's old regiment, the 5th Dragoon Guards, badly at Kotlubie.[132] On the day of Balaklava, Lucan ordered the eight squadrons of the Heavy Brigade to march 'in contiguous columns, but with wide intervals of squadrons. He told me he disapproved of lines and everything was to be done by squadrons!!', clearly disagreeing with Scarlett's own preference.[133] Then, during the Charge of the Light Brigade, Lucan cancelled the Heavy Brigade's advance without consulting or even telling Scarlett. Although it is not clear at what exact point this happened, in a letter two days after Balaklava William Forrest, of the 4th Dragoon Guards, records that 'Lord Lucan blew up Scarlett as Lord Cardigan used to blow up a captain with about as much reason.'[134]

The recriminations about the Charge of the Light Brigade, which began immediately after it took place seldom involved Scarlett. Lucan and Cardigan, however, continued to dispute about it for years. Scarlett was involved as a witness in a libel case in 1863 brought by the Earl of Cardigan against Colonel Somerset Calthorpe, a nephew of Lord Raglan, for statements made by Calthorpe in his book, *Letters from Head-Quarters: or The Realities of the War in the Crimea* (1856). While there were a number of passages in the book to which Cardigan objected, his chief complaint was about the accusation that he had retreated prematurely, owing to his horse taking fright, swerving and galloping to the rear after reaching the Russian guns which were the target of the Charge of the Light Brigade. This had left the brigade without a commander at a critical point.[135]

One issue to do with General Scarlett can now be resolved: what he was wearing during the charge. It is uncontested that he wore a blue coat over his uniform.[136] The authenticity of the helmet, however, now on display in the Royal Dragoon Guards Museum in York, which has two sizeable dents in it, has been questioned.[137] Fortunately, there is clear evidence to hand. Temple Godman, of the 5th Dragoon Guards, writing to his father on 26 October 1854, the day after the battle, told him, 'Scarlett was wounded in the bridle hand, but not much. He and Elliot were in the thickest, and his helmet was battered in, and the skirt of his frock-coat sliced down.'

Godman repeated the information about the helmet when writing to his brother a week later, on 2 November 1854, 'Our Brigadier behaved most pluckily, went right in, got his helmet smashed, hand cut, clothes cut through, and horse much cut, and a spent ball on the arm, he is all right.'[138] That Scarlett was wearing his 5th Dragoon Guards helmet during the Charge of the Heavy Brigade may have persuaded the Russians that his aide de camp, Alexander Elliot, was the leader of the attack. Earlier in the day Scarlett had told Elliot that he should wear his staff officer's cocked hat. Although both survived, Elliot suffered fourteen wounds to Scarlett's five.

The damage done to Scarlett's helmet is corroborated by an unpublished letter from the General's nephew, William Scarlett, to his sister on 2 November 1854.

I hear everybody praising Uncle Jim's gallantry and boldness. Colonel Beatson says they ought to make him a KCB. He charged in at the head of the Greys. He has a slight wound on his bridle hand, a spent ball struck his wrist merely bruising him a little, and his clothes and helmet show severe signs of the fray. He unhorsed a couple of scoundrels himself.[139]

To discount these accounts, from an officer of the 5th Dragoon Guards who took part in the Charge and General Scarlett's nephew, who became his ADC immediately after Balaklava, would require both Elliot and William Scarlett to be mistaken or lying; or for someone to have dented the helmet deliberately in the immediate aftermath of the battle.[140]

There is also later evidence, provided in the memoirs of the General's great nephew, Sidney Scarlett Smith. 'Sarah, Lady Abinger, the Dowager, was a great feature of our lives. After Abinger Hall was sold by my Uncle Willy, she returned to London, to 30 Queen's Gate Terrace. General Sir James Scarlett's helmet was in the drawing room and we used to hold it to the light to see the Russian sabre cuts.'[141] The General also gave his sister-in-law a glove which he had worn at Balaklava marked with blood.[142]

The Balaklava helmet clearly stayed with William Scarlett, later third Lord Abinger, the General's heir, in London and was then at Inverlochy, the castle William Scarlett built near Fort William, being inherited by subsequent Lords Abinger before being given by the ninth Lord Abinger to the nation in 2004, together with his medals, in mitigation of death duties.[143] While two other helmets now at Towneley Hall also once belonged to the General, neither of them was worn by him at Balaklava.

A second question, less capable of resolution, is the identity of the horse Scarlett rode at Balaklava. All that can be said for definite is that, according to Kinglake, Scarlett rode a 'thoroughbred bay, standing fully, it seemed, sixteen hands'.[144] Although in his letters, Scarlett refers to his horses on several occasions, the only horse he names is Silvertail.[145] As bay horses can have silver tails, it is possibly that Silvertail was the horse he rode in the charge.[146]

A final question of interest is why Scarlett was not awarded the Victoria Cross.[147] To charge uphill alone, up to fifty yards ahead of his staff and even further ahead of the first troops of his brigade, against an enemy force numbering thousands, was an act of conspicuous and outstanding gallantry. That it took place at the critical moment of a battle, when both his brigade and the whole British Army were in jeopardy, adds to its significance. Scarlett's display of decisive personal leadership against overwhelming odds must have inspired the men who followed him to what proved to be a complete and unexpected victory.

To modern eyes, Scarlett and indeed Cardigan seem obvious candidates for the Victoria Cross. Both led charges ahead of their brigades, plunging into the enemy first. Although the award was not officially instituted until 1856, and its first presentation was not until 1857, a number of those who had fought at the Alma, Balaklava and Inkerman were amongst its earliest recipients.

The problem was that the early, and indeed lasting, definition of the Victoria Cross was that it was for lower ranks of the navy and army, not for commanding officers.[148] This was made explicit in a letter from General Sir Charles Yorke in reply to a query over a claim in July 1860:

> the only question is whether the VC should be awarded to a commanding officer who gallantly leads his regiment in some very desperate service. Nothing could be more conspicuously gallant than the conduct of Lieutenant Colonel Forbes … and the only reason why HRH did not recommend him as well as the officers for the VC was, I believe, that he thought the Order of the Bath was the proper distinction for the commanding officer, and that had been granted to Lieutenant Colonel Forbes.[149]

The Duke of Cambridge commented on this:

> I concur with Yorke's opinion that Forbes' conduct … was admirable, but I think that the Bath to a superior officer stands in the place of the VC and I feel that if you depart from the rule, you will get into great difficulties. The fact is that the Bath can only be given to officers of a certain rank in the service, whereas the VC is open to all, even the private, and I have always understood that this was one of the objects for establishing this order.[150]

This attitude lasted a long time. In July 1900, 'With regard to Colonel Ian Hamilton, I am to observe that the act for which he was recommended was performed when he was commanding a brigade. The VC has never been conferred upon an officer of so high in rank.'[151] Hamilton (1853–1947) was twice recommended for the Victoria Cross. Both recommendations were disallowed; the first on the grounds that he was too junior and the second on the grounds that he was too senior. No VC was awarded to a brigadier general until 1917.[152]

Early recipients of the Victoria Cross were selected after nomination by the commanding officers of their regiments. Although 111 VCs were awarded for exceptional bravery during the Crimean War, all went to relatively junior ranks. Of seven VCs awarded after the Alma, two went to captains, four to sergeants and one to a private. Of the twelve given after Balaklava, one went to a lieutenant, two to surgeons, six to sergeants, two to corporals and one to a private. The three awarded to members of the Heavy Brigade were to Serjeant Major Henry Ramage, Serjeant John Grieve, both of the Scots Greys, and the surgeon James Mouat, though Mouat's award was given for his actions during the Charge of the Light Brigade rather than that of the Heavy Brigade. Scarlett recommended Beatson and Elliot for the VC, but Lucan failed to endorse the recommendation.

This did not mean that Scarlett's bravery went unnoticed. As William Scarlett wrote home, 'Colonel Beatson says they ought to make him a KCB.'[153] The knighthood of the Bath, not the Victoria Cross, was at the time the traditional award for acts of conspicuous courage by senior officers. This indeed is what Scarlett received, being knighted in the Crimea by Lord Stratford de Redcliffe. Only later did the Victoria Cross become the unrivalled award for supreme bravery.

James Yorke Scarlett was also promoted to major general. As William Scarlett reported on 28 December 1854 to his sister, 'So we are to have our medals and clasps. This is very satisfactory and the General is made major general, which is also a good thing as it will put him up on the list and will probably lead to his getting a good appointment at home, when the war is over.'[154] On promotion to major general James Yorke Scarlett forfeited his whole earlier investment in his career. As Temple Godman told his mother, 'The Brigadier we hear is made a major general, at all events he is sure to get it soon. This is one step without purchase. He will lose nearly £15,000, but this I don't suppose he cares about.'[155]

33

Frances Scarlett to Henrietta Graham-Toler
Bank Hall, Burnley, 3 November 1854

My dear Henrietta, You will be very glad to hear that Aunt Charlotte has had a capital letter from Uncle Jim this morning, safely landed at Balaclava.[156] He had met with a severe gale, which has separated the transport from the steamer, and he was then anxiously looking for their arrival. He has seen Willy the 3rd of October, who was in high glee over the victory and very flourishing.[157]

Aunt Charlotte was made very happy with this news, which she has been waiting for for three weeks, and looks many degrees better this morning than she did yesterday. I send you dear Willy's letters of 21 and 22 September, the last ones. Do not show them to anyone. We all agree that they contain expressions which might injure him if made public.[158] You will see what I mean. You can read them to Aunt Fanny.[159] I have heaps of letters from everyone about Willy. Yours most lovingly, FMS.

*   *   *

34

James Yorke Scarlett to Lord Raglan
Camp Sebastopol, 27 October 1854

Camp Sebastopol, 27 October 1854
My Lord, I have the honour to report to you for the information of Lieutenant General the Earl of Lucan, commanding the Cavalry Division, that the brigade of cavalry under my command, consisting of the troops named in the margin, were as usual under arms an hour before daylight on 25 October.[160]

Shortly after daylight, a report was brought from the advance pickets that a force of the enemy, consisting of cavalry and infantry, were advancing to the attack of the force held by the Turkish Regiment.[161]

My brigade with the Light Brigade was advanced towards the ridge of high ground, on which they were situated, and halted by the lieutenant general's order in rear of No. 1 Fort, facing the road from Balaklava to Kamara village; the Second Dragoons (Scots Greys) having one squadron in advance, supported by its Second Squadron [and] the Enniskillens at a short distance on the right in the same order, the remainder of the brigade being placed by his Lordship's order in support.[162]

In a short time the Turks having been attacked in front in their entrenched position gave way, and the hill was quickly crowned by the enemy. Having remained till the Turks made good their retreat (though in great disorder) and finding the advanced squadrons within the range of the enemy's rifles and artillery from the hill, the brigade was ordered to fall back and subsequently to take up a position with the Light Brigade, immediately in rear of the hill ridge.

Whilst in this position, I received an order to proceed with four regiments to the right rear, in support of the body of Turkish infantry. Whilst in no position to execute this movement, the enemy's cavalry appeared on the left flank over the hill in considerable numbers and very near us.

The Scots Greys, Enniskillens and 5th Dragoon Guards having wheeled to the left, the enemy was immediately charged by the Scots Greys (the other regiments coming up in echelon) and were entirely defeated and driven back over the ridge; the Horse Artillery coming up at the same time fired several shots into the retreating body.

The Light Brigade at a later period of the day being ordered to advance over the ridge, and down the valley towards the Blackwater, the brigade under my command followed in support, advancing for some time under a very heavy fire from both sides of the valley.[163]

The Light Brigade having suffered so severely from fire of musketry and artillery as to necessitate its retreat, the brigade under my command was halted till it had rallied in our rear, and then slowly retired to the crest of the hill, where it remained till withdrawn after dark.

The loss through the day, from the fire of artillery and rifles, has been much greater than for the charge against cavalry; I have the honour to forward the returns.

In conclusion, I beg to express my satisfaction at the manner in which the charge was made, and at the cool and collected manner in which every individual behaved, under a very severe fire.

Lieutenant Colonel Hodge, Commanding 4th Dragoon Guards, Captain Burton, Commanding 5th Dragoon Guards, together with the Commanding Officers of the other corps, viz Colonel Griffith, Yorke and White, did all that could be wished for. Major Shute of the Enniskillens acted with great promptness in wheeling his squadron outward to protect our right flank in the charge.[164]

My best thanks are due to Brigade Major Captain Conolly, to Lieutenant Elliot my aide de camp, severely wounded, who afforded me every assistance, and also to Colonel Beatson of the Honorable East India Company's Service, who is attached to my staff as a volunteer.[165] I have the honour to be &, &, J. Yorke Scarlett, Brigadier General.

* * *

35

James Yorke Scarlett to Colonel Thomas Steele
November 1854

Sir, Having read in the *Times* newspaper of the eighteenth instant a copy of a supplementary despatch, from Lieutenant General the Earl of Lucan to Lord Raglan, Commanding the Forces in the Crimea, in which no mention is made of the services of my aide de camp Lieutenant Elliot, or of my extra aide de camp Colonel Beatson of the Honourable East India Company's service, who by my Lord Raglan's permission was attached to my staff on 25 October last in the affair near Balaklava, I am induced to forward to you an extract from the dispatch I submitted to Lord Lucan by his order on that occasion.[166]

I am aware that it would be presumptuous in me to dictate in any way what names the lieutenant general commanding the division thinks proper to submit for the approval of the Commander of the Forces, but I am anxious to relieve myself from the imputation of having done injustice to the merits of two officers from whom I received the greatest assistance on the day alluded to.

Lieutenant Elliot, till severely wounded, was by my side in the charge, and previously displayed the greatest coolness and courage. Colonel Beatson also gave me all the assistance his experience and well known gallantry enabled him to do through the day.

Having so far relieved myself of any injustice to the merits of these officers, I have the honour to be, &, &., J. Yorke Scarlett.

*   *   *

36

Frances Scarlett to Henrietta Graham-Toler
Bank Hall, Burnley, 3 November 1854

I hope to see you before long, for we leave this the beginning of next week. We should have staid a week longer, but Mama is so poorly with suffocations and palpitations that I much want to get her under Bright's care as soon as possible.[167] I am sure too that the air or something about this place is not wholesome, for she is always having pains in her stomach; for that matter, so am I, and so is Aunt Charlotte. We have tried all we could to get Aunt Charlotte to come with us, but she is as firm as a rock. We regret leaving her very much, but we cannot stay on here for ever, and Mama should not delay getting some advice. As at present advised, we shall be in town on Tuesday. Hally is here.[168] Your affectionate sister.

*   *   *

37

Frances Scarlett to Mary Campbell
Bank Hall, Burnley, 9 November 1854

Dearest Friend, I hope we shall be in London on Saturday. Hester has very kindly lent us her house in Portman Square for the time we remain.[169] I do not propose myself to you, though sure of your never-failing welcome, because I wish to be with Mama, who is ailing both in mind and body. I look forward to great things from Bright, and also from the change from this most gloomy and depressing place. It is too much for her to have to support Aunt Charlotte's low spirits as well as her own anxieties.

Aunt Charlotte is in a very alarming state, her courage and her mind have completely given way. She passes the day in sighs and moans, and is perfectly impracticable to advice. She is a complete wreck, it is a most heart-breaking case; and the more distressing from her refusing to take any means to help herself.

I thought of staying a few days longer here, but I do not know that it will do much good, and I am most unwilling to trust the dear mother out of my sight. I shall most probably go to town with her. Could you not look me up on Saturday evening? How glad I shall be to see my exemplary Cat![170] It seems five hundred years since the beginning of May. Within the memory of man, there has never been so long a year as this, or one so brimful of care and troubles. Ever thine own.

P.S. 10 November. I shall certainly go to town tomorrow, as Mama says she cannot do without me.

* * *

38

James Yorke Scarlett to Frances Scarlett
Camp Kadikoi, Crimea, 10–12 November 1854

Camp Sebastopol, Crimea, 10 November 1854

My dear Fanny, Willy is my pro-tem extra ADC (my own, Elliot, being wounded with a sabre cut on the head and a scratch on the nose; neither dangerous), and is now busy poring over an old newspaper, wrapped in a *grego*, which means a very warm, comfortable kind of native cloak with a hood to come over the head.[171] I hope (having got him here) to retain him with me, as he thereby escapes the work of the siege, which is wearing and not without danger if a shell intrudes into the trenches. Thank God our casualties have comparatively been few from the compliments sent to us from Sebastopol.[172]

I think Willy has written since the last affair, an attack of the Russians on the right of our line which was repulsed very completely and with very great loss of life to the Russians, but not without a lamentable loss of life on our part and especially among the officers.[173] It was a dear victory.

The taking of Sebastopol does not seem so easy a task as some anticipated. I wish I could say we had made great progress, but the exchange of shot and shell goes on daily and nightly too. On the 5 November affair Willy was mounted with me and, as the cavalry could not act on the ground on which action was fought, we were not exposed to any shot.[174] He probably has been saved by being with me, as few officers escaped untouched. Among the number, not dangerously, is poor Hugh Drummond. The ball might have gone through him [had it not had] the complaisance to go round him, which singular as it seems is not uncommon.[175]

As yet it is impossible to say where our winter quarters are to be. I shall come home, if possible, during the winter.[176] I am very grateful to you and Sally for your kindness to dear Charlotte, and I hope this will still find you at Bank.[177] I fear you will not find it affords you any amusement beyond some books and good fires, which are two things not to be despised. I should like to be of your party, I can assure you.

Here we have hitherto had fine weather, though this 10 November is a rainy day. As long as the wind is south, it will do; but we have had a hint what it can do when the wind comes from the north on two occasions. By the time this reaches England, I feel the joys for the triumph of the Alma will have been somewhat tempered by late events and the slow progress we have made, the slowness of which has given time for considerable Russian reinforcements to arrive.[178] We both, cavalry and infantry, are in great need of them. Our calculations seem to have been made upon false principles; and the supposition that man and horse can endure for ever in spite of Turkish heats and Russian lead and steel.

I see there is great excitement about the care of our wounded; and, while some say nothing can be worse than the attendance and appliances, Dr Smith writes enumerating the superabundant supply of medicines, men and stores.[179] I believe there were sent out abundance of both, but medical men, like others, will get sick and there seems a great mismanagement of the stores, which are always somewhere but not where they are wanted; but I hope that will be remedied. The whole scene is a new one to most of those engaged in it and many mistakes will occur amongst the actors, which I hope will be diminished with experience. We entirely depend upon the ships and sea for our existence here. What we possess in the Crimea, and the supplies we can draw from it, would not feed ten rabbits.

Many officers have found their way home or are candidates for it. Among these I hear Lord George Paget is selling out.[180] What would not the old Lord Anglesea say, if he could rise from the grave![181] Few there are here who would not throw up their hats into the air if assured that *with honour* they could eat their Christmas pie in merry England; and none more glad than myself. I daresay our excellent French allies would prefer the old style of campaign of Louis Quatorze, which sent them all to Paris in the winter to their friends and to the admiration of their loves.[182]

The stupid old Turks, after seeing them race from their entrenchment before Balaklava, I cannot count as allies; and I consider any point they occupy as taken the moment it is attacked.[183] They are of no use but to dig trenches and bury the dead. The Turks who behaved so well at Silistria were not Turks but Egyptians and Osmanlis.[184] This will not go for two days, so I shall leave space.

12 November

As the mail goes tomorrow, I will finish this rambling epistle through which I fear you will have some difficulty in finding your way: a tent, especially on a windy day, is not the most convenient library to compose one's epistles. If we could get the gardener's cottage at Abinger, we should think ourselves housed in a palace.[185] Willy is sitting in his *grego*, which seems a second skin, scribbling away. It is very consolatory to have him near me and I hope to keep him, even after Elliot's return.

I hope you will not only answer this, but write to me very often, as letters from home are invaluable to us Crimeans. All now, I fear, looks like a winter residence in the Crimea, but I will not make up my mind that *that* is to be till I cannot help it. Evident it is that we are not masters of Sebastopol. I fancy the British Lion will growl not a little at all this delay of his hopes. Love, best love to you all, ever your affectionate J. Yorke Scarlett.

*   *   *

22   *The Departure of the 4th Dragoon Guards from Kingstown in 1854*, painting by H. Quinton.

23   General Sir James Yorke Scarlett (1799–1871).

24   Robert Scarlett, second Lord Abinger (1794–1861), the General's brother.

25   Abinger Hall, Surrey, the country house bought by the General's father in 1810.

26   William Simpson, *Balaklava Harbour.* Simpson (1823–1899) was in the Crimea from November 1854 until after the end of the siege of Sebastopol in September 1855. He arrived too late to witness the cavalry charges at the Battle of Balaklava. Eighty of his water-colour images of war in the Crimea were published in *The Seat of War in the East* in 1855.

27   William Simpson, *Cavalry Camp.*

28 Alexander Elliot, *Crimean Hut*, 1855: left to right, James Conolly, Alexander Elliot, William Scarlett, James Booth (servant) and James Yorke Scarlett.

29 William Simpson, *General Scarlett and his Staff*. The General is the fourth from the left in the group of officers.

30   Alexander Elliot, *The Charge of the Heavy Brigade, 1855*. Elliot (1825–1909), a talented artist, was General Scarlett's aide de camp and, wearing a cocked hat, was the second man into the Russian ranks during the Charge of the Heavy Brigade. The fourteen wounds Elliot received during the charge, none of them serious, prevented him from taking part in the Heavy Brigade's advance in support of the Light Brigade.

31   William Simpson, *The Charge of the Heavy Brigade*. Simpson and Elliot both show the obstruction to the charge caused by the remnants of the Light Brigade camp. If the two leading British horsemen are meant to be Scarlett and Elliot, they are not wearing what it is known they wore on their heads.

32   William Simpson, *The Charge of the Light Brigade*. Simpson shows no sign of the Heavy Brigade in his depiction of the charge, despite the brigade having advanced to where it came under heavy fire from the Russian guns before being halted by the Earl of Lucan.

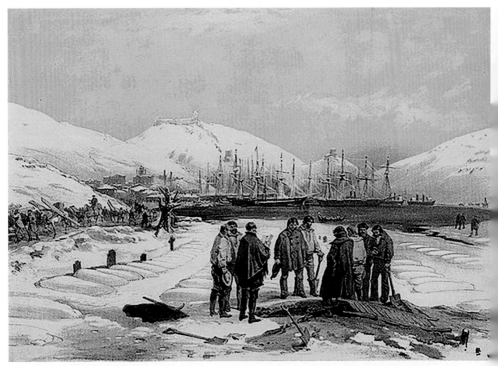

33   William Simpson, *Winter in the Crimea*. Graves at the head of Balaklava Harbour.

34   Sir Francis Grant (1803–1878), *General Scarlett*. The identity of the horse in the portrait, and indeed that of the horse the General rode at Balaklava, is uncertain.

35   Scarlett's Balaklava helmet (front).

36   Scarlett's Balaklava helmet (back).

37 The Battle of Balaklava on
the base of a silver centrepiece
given by General Scarlett to his old
regiment, the 5th Dragoon Guards.

38 The silver centrepiece, with the figures of
two mounted soldiers on the top, has depictions
in silver of Balaklava, Inkerman, Lierena and
Salamanca, notable battles in the regiment's
history. The inscription reads: 'Presented to the
5th Princess Charlotte of Wales Dragoon Guards
by Major General the Honorable Sir James
Yorke Scarlett, Knight Commander of the Bath
and Commander of the Legion of Honour as a
token of his affection for the regiment to whose
discipline at home and gallantry before the enemy
he owes his reputation as a soldier.' It was given
by the General to the regiment at a dinner at
Aldershot in 1859.

39 Bank Hall,
the General's
home in Burnley
and two of his
horses.

39

Mary Campbell to Louisa Spranger White
London, 14 November 1854

Stratheden House, 14 November 1854

Dearest Lou, We are in a state of tremendous excitement about the war.[186] We expected the *Gazette* to be out on Saturday, but it was not out till Sunday evening.[187] I was at St Paul's with the Wests when Henry came in and, at a pause in the service, told us that George Cadogan, their cousin, was safe and General Scarlett slightly wounded.[188] You may fancy what an agony I was in for further news and directly after tea I rushed home and found they had just got the *Gazette* and we all assembled to read it; and the passage in Lord Raglan's dispatch about *our* General and his brilliant charge of cavalry we read a dozen times over![189]

There is a splendid account of the whole thing in a letter from the *Times* correspondent this morning.[190] I tried reading it aloud this morning at breakfast, but when I got to the 'Bravo, Highlanders, well done!', I had to give up the paper and Peter began reading; but he could get no further than the first trumpet sounding for the cavalry to charge, and then we made Cecie read while we sat by crying.[191]

There is a letter from the General. His wound is a sabre cut on his hand, but nothing of importance.[192] Willie was all right up to the twentieth, but now we know of this other battle, on 5 November, and everybody's anxiety begins afresh.[193]

Aunt Abinger and Fanny come up to Portman Square (the Frasers' house, which is lent to them) on Saturday and are to stay a week or so.[194] Aunt Abinger suffers from palpitations of the heart and a feeling of suffocation, particularly when she is agitated, which of course she must be constantly in these times; and she has seen Dr Bright, who however is comforting.[195] Aunt Lou and Mary Augusta came up to Gloucester House on Monday (yesterday), and, as the Duchess is not well, they dined with us, as did Aunt Abinger and Fanny and Peter, who has been staying here.[196] He is gone today and takes his children for a week to Bournemouth.[197]

This is our first rainy day and rather puts me out. Fanny came to luncheon and I gave her your amber bottle, which she likes very much. She is gone now and Aunt Lou and Mary Augusta are come. Mary Augusta is sitting by the fire reading Willie's letters about the Battle of Alma. He has written to them by every post, that is every five days.[198]

The Mintos and Aldersons dined with us on Saturday.[199] Lotty and Harriet look blooming. They are anxious of course about their brother Gilbert, who is in the Crimea.[200] Nothing but the war is talked of and, if people get for a moment onto any other subject, they fall back immediately to the all absorbing topic. We shan't get the details about this Battle of Sebastopol for a week, I fear.[201]

Mama bids me thank you much for the basket, which arrived today, containing woodcocks, chickens and eggs, and is very acceptable. The woodcocks are to be eaten by sixteen lawyers at dinner tomorrow.[202]

I have begun *the* letter to you but seldom get composed moments enough to write anything but this sort of scrawl. I send you a letter from Hensie, which I have answered; so burn it.[203] I wish you would look at your Dresden cases and tell me about them, because Augusta has written to me and I want to answer her and tell her whether you have got them safe. Ever dearest your most affectionate MSC.

* * *

40

Frances Scarlett to Mary Campbell
Abinger, 6 December 1854

Abinger, 6 December 1854

Dearest Polly, The Stratheden House subscription is gorgeous.[204] I have given immediate orders for three dozen more waistcoats. Tell Charles Pepys that his good friends are to keep their good works for the present and that farther information will be sent in due time.[205]

I am sitting at my writing table with Dante gazing mildly at me and the two bronze lodges, one on each side, holding piles of papers.[206] They are *immensely* useful. After immense consideration I chose three which stand by their own strength. Cally shall have the pendant ones when she returns to Parkhurst.[207]

I rode my new horse Velvet (the name it was bought with) and think we shall be great friends. It is nearly thoroughbred and, when in condition, will be as lively as a kitten. I hope it will carry my weight, but as old Mrs Brigstock once said to me when she was sitting before me at a concert, 'I am aware of my dimensions.'[208] Powells dined here last night.[209] We gave them some little presents and they were highly delighted.

Thanks for Willy's letter. I had a long one from our General this morning. They write in small spirits I fear. God help them: it seems as if men could and would not.

I have no thoughts of going up to town again. I am going to *try* and settle. It does me good to sit once more in the 'Parson's Chair' and take counsel with my old friend Jeremy Taylor, who tells me in his quaint way that we must not be passionate as children, and carried away with transports of *sense* and mistaken interests.[210] Young Sims comes to us tomorrow.[211] Georgie Sumner pays me a visit next week.[212] With much love from thine Friend.

*   *   *

41

*James Yorke Scarlett to Colonel James Chatterton
Camp Kadikoi, 7 December 1854*

My dear Chatterton, It is very late to redeem my promise of writing to you and not till you have jogged my memory, but it is difficult to write under a tent, and we have been, until today, under canvas since we landed in June; horses exposed to the heat and cold, rain and mud.[213]

Many thanks for your kind congratulations – more than I deserve is the merit accorded to me by my friends, but I do hope that at Balaklava the Heavies lost no fame but added another leaf to their laurels.[214] It was just in time, for our horses were then tolerably fresh; much indeed are they reduced now from want of food and exposure.

The Light Brigade exists no more, forming barely a regiment. My own corps suffered horribly at Kotlubie in Bulgaria by cholera, losing forty-five men and three officers, and having since sent seventy to hospital when they marched from Kotlubie to the camp over Varna.[215] Starved on the march, and with so great a deficit in hands, they were paraded in watering order without saddles next morning after arrival. They had the misfortune to be highly disapproved by Lord Lucan, reported by him to Lord Raglan, who came at dusk in the evening to see them in their lines, and found them thin and the men dirty.[216] And having no field officers, and their senior captain dead, their surgeon dead and vet surgeon dead, and paymaster absent, his Lordship attached them to the 4th pro. temp, for Hodge to give advice to Captain Burton in command, who was third captain and young in the service.[217] I neither agree with Lord Lucan or Lord Raglan in their opinion, but of that no matter, at least here.

Now for Balaklava. We were in the usual morning parade an hour before sunrise in that morning of 25 October. We were just turning in to breakfast when a report was brought that the Russians were seen advancing to attack the forts entrusted to the Turks on a line of hills which separates the plain of Balaklava from the valley of the Blackwater, which plain has also some eminences, through which a gorge, so that troops in that plain cannot be distinctly numbered and many may be hid from view.[218]

My brigade was ordered to the back of the further fort, which was the strongest and had a heavy gun: my orders to give a support to the Turks and to charge any cavalry that appeared round it and opposite to where I was placed.[219] The no buono Johnnies fired their big guns lustily; but, as soon as a body of Russian infantry swarmed up the height and got near their trench, they fired a volley in the air and bolted down the hill towards us – double quick. We covered their *run away*, but they began to fire from the redoubt and we were obliged to retire out of Minié distance.[220] The first hint that I got of it was the fall of one of the horses of the Greys, and my orderly's mare being shot through the thigh.

We crept a few yards back and waited to see if the cavalry would come on. None came then. At this time I had the Greys and Enniskillens in front, the 4th, 5th and Royals in support.[221] Lord Lucan would have them stand in contiguous columns, but with wide intervals of squadrons.[222] He told me he disapproved of lines and everything was to be done by squadrons!! Shortly afterwards, we received an order to join the Light Brigade in our rear and take up with them in a position to watch a gully through the curtain, which as I have said separates the plains.[223]

From the manner in which the squadrons were scattered about, no regular shipshape movement could be made to get them into the position, and they got back anyhow, the best way they could, to my exceeding disquiet. They had scarcely scrambled to the position, and some had not arrived, when I received an order from Lord Raglan to [send] four regiments of the brigade back to the Turks and 93rd,[224] who had been charged and repulsed a charge of Russian Lancers;[225] the Turks bolting into Balaklava, some bolting into boats and calling, 'Ship Johnnie'. The sailors gave them a whopping with their sheathed cutlasses and drove them back.[226]

Just as I got the Greys and 5th into motion, we saw some Russian cavalry crown the hill on our left and advance down the slope, as if to come into the plain.[227] As soon as we could clear a vineyard, and get opposite to them, the Greys and 5th wheeled left into line.[228] The Enniskillens came up in sight of the Greys, with one squadron; the other a little in echelon, as there was no time to be lost.[229]

I ordered the advance.[230] The ground was bad, uphill and some of the picket ropes of the Light Brigade camp interfered, but we got into a trot and gallop and went right at them before they had time to deploy, which they were in the act of doing.[231] They did not advance to meet us but stood still and we were soon hand to hand and deep into them in regular mill.[232]

The Greys were a little in advance, and their flanks got surrounded, but the 5th and Enniskillens came up, got upon the flank and backs of the Russians, and the whole mass gave way before us after a short struggle and ran.[233] The 4th, who had only then with the Royals come up, rattled in and completed the affair. A troop of Horse Artillery crowned the ridge and pelted the flying mass till they rallied behind the infantry.[234]

In this affair we had a few officers wounded and, odd enough, I believe each regiment lost two men killed.[235] Neville of the 5th was wounded and died of his wounds at Scutari.[236] Our loss was trifling in the charge. Some forty-five Russians lay on the ground dead or wounded. Many more fell in the valley, from the shot of the artillery, or dropped from wounds received.[237]

So much for 25 October, and so far we had nothing to regret. For some time we remained stationary and I imagined we were waiting for our infantry to arrive and retake the forts. The Heavy Brigade dismounted pretty close together. After the lapse of an hour and a half an aide de camp, Captain Nolan, came with a written order from General Airey, written by Lord Raglan's desire, to order Lucan to advance the cavalry to pressure the enemy and try and prevent their carrying off the guns.[238]

Lucan saw no enemy running away with guns; neither did Cardigan, and so the latter remonstrated. But, as Lucan considered the order to advance imperative, he ordered Cardigan to advance. Down the valley they went, and we in support, under a cross-fire from both hills on the flanks and fire from a battery of guns in front.[239] The shot and shell reached us. The Lights started into a gallop and ran headlong, on the battery in front, into a regular horseshoe of fire. They fell fast in the advance; many reached the guns and cut down the gunners. Cardigan rode between the muzzles of two guns as they exploded, but no man or horse could [stay] there, and they came back in the best manner they could, breaking through some Lancers, who had closed to their rear.[240]

We halted as soon as they commenced to retreat and remained till the shattered remains had got into our rear. The French Chasseurs d'Afrique were on our left in rear; we had Royals and Greys in front; 4th, 5th, 6th in support.[241] Yorke was wounded and leg broken, of the Royals, and many horses killed; and the 5th lost nineteen horses killed.[242] The total you have seen.

We then regained the crest of the hill and remained there till dark night, when we withdrew to our camp, having been out from six a.m. to eleven p.m. The Russians may claim that they kept the fort they gained, and they have kept it till this morning. Now I believe they have all retreated and joined the force at Inkerman.

I have not, at this moment, time to send you the *states*, but my five regiments cannot turn out eight hundred effective men and horses. We lost sixty horses in eight days from exposure and low diet. I must now beg you give my regards to Mrs Chatterton and to believe me ever, yours faithfully, J. Yorke Scarlett.

You will see that some of this is for your eye only. The 4th Dragoons behaved well, as indeed did *all*, under most trying circumstances.[243]

* * *

42

Sir James Yorke Scarlett to the Earl of Cardigan
Horse Guards, 23 January 1863

My dear Lord Cardigan, With reference to our conversation and the questions you put to me I will now endeavour as far as I am able to give you my reminiscences in writing.

After having put my brigade in motion, accompanied by Lord Lucan, and having proceeded some distance down the valley, I perceived Captain Nolan's body under my horse's feet, and very shortly after I perceived a great number of men and horses of your brigade disabled who must have fallen in the advance. The next thing which attracted my observation was the first line which had charged, but which had been hidden from my view by the dense smoke, returning broken and in detached parties. And subsequently I perceived a compact body of the Light Brigade trotting slowly under the Fedoukine heights and making for our left rear; it was subsequent to this that you rode up and spoke to me. My brigade had been halted after retiring a short distance and I was somewhat in advance of them. I remain yours faithfully J. Yorke Scarlett.[244]

*   *   *

43

Sir James Yorke Scarlett's Affidavit in the Queen's Bench
Re the Earl of Cardigan, 15 April 1863

I, James Yorke Scarlett of the Horse Guards and of No. 29 Princes Terrace, Knightsbridge, in the County of Middlesex, Lieutenant General in the Army and Adjutant General in Her Majesty's Forces, make oath and say as follows:

1. I was in command of the Heavy Brigade of Cavalry at the Battle of Balaclava and at the time when the Light Brigade was charging the Russian battery the Heavy Brigade was drawn up about halfway between the Russian battery charged by the Light Brigade and the place from which the Light Brigade commenced their charge and was advanced to support the Light Brigade. The Heavy Brigade did not charge the Russian battery having been ordered by Lord Lucan to retire after they had made an advance in support of the Light Brigade.

2. At the instant when the first line of the Light Brigade charged into the battery it was almost impossible from the dense smoke and confusion to discern what took place. But a few moments afterwards, I observed the remnant of the Light Brigade as well as the remains of the second line retreating towards the ground which they had occupied immediately before the charge while dismounted men and horses without riders were scattered over the space which the brigade had traversed.

3. A few moments after this Lord Cardigan coming as far as I could see from the direction of the battery and with the retreating troops rode up to Lord Lucan and myself and commenced exclamations against the sad mistake which had arisen in consequence of Captain Nolan having given the order to advance, until I informed his Lordship that, in advancing to support the Light Brigade, I had nearly ridden over Captain Nolan's dead body. At this time the Heavy Brigade had been halted after retiring a short distance and I was somewhat in advance of them. I remember on this occasion pointing out to Lord Cardigan the broken remnant of his line as they were retreating up the hill, and I consider that the whole affair from the time when the Light Brigade moved off to charge until Lord Cardigan came up and spoke to myself and Lord Lucan did not last above twenty minutes.

4. I firmly believe from the information I received both at the time of engagement and afterwards that Lord Cardigan was the first to charge into and through the Russian battery and that he was amongst the last, if not the last, to return from behind the guns.

Sworn 15 April 1863[245]

*   *   *

44

Sir James Yorke Scarlett to the Earl of Cardigan
Horse Guards, 5 June 1863

Dear Lord Cardigan, I return you the copy of Lord Lucan's affidavit. Certainly it differs considerably from mine on the same subject; but I am still convinced that my version is the correct one.

The facts are imprinted on my memory from the following circumstances. Whilst riding some distance in front of my brigade towards the enemy, with Colonel Beatson, my acting aide de camp, the trumpeter, and an orderly, Colonel Beatson looked back and told me my brigade was retiring.

Not having given an order myself, I was naturally surprised and annoyed. I halted myself, with Colonel Beatson, and sent the trumpeter to sound the halt. The brigade, at the sound, halted and fronted. On riding up to them, Lord Lucan told me they had retired by his orders. We had a few moments' conversation as to what should be done, whether advance again or not. We remained halted, the propriety of which was determined in my mind by seeing what I believed to be the second line of the Light Brigade coming out of action. It was whilst we were thus situated that you rode up and I told you I had seen Nolan's dead body, having nearly ridden over it. You then left the spot and rode in the direction of your brigade, who were making their way to the rear on our left flank. Believe me yours faithfully, J. Yorke Scarlett.[246]

Lieutenant General the Earl of Cardigan, KCB, 42 Portman Square.

Chapter 5

The Crimea

The Battle of Balaklava, despite the heroics of the cavalry division, left the Russians with a strategic advantage: the control of the Woronzow Road, the obvious communication and supply route between Balaklava and the allied forces besieging Sebastopol.[1] Two weeks later, on 5 November, the Russians made another attempt to defeat the allies. A renewed advance across the Tchernaya led to a bloody infantry battle at Inkerman, with hand-to-hand fighting and severe casualties, before the Russians were repelled. It extracted a heavy toll on the Guards officers, but William Scarlett was not involved, having become his uncle's aide de camp after Balaklava, replacing the injured Alexander Elliot. At Inkerman the cavalry was mounted and to hand, but the terrain and course of the engagement meant that they were not deployed.[2]

Only a week after Inkerman, the British suffered a major blow at the hands of the weather rather than the Russians. A storm on 14 November caused havoc in the harbour of Balaklava itself and sank a number of ships anchored outside it, including the *Prince*, which was carrying much of the winter clothing needed by the troops. The loss of this clothing, and the many failings of the Commissariat, led to major problems in the winter for both men and horses. The cavalry horses, on inadequate fodder, were reduced to carrying supplies up to the British lines around Sebastopol. Although General Scarlett established his base in a hut in the main camp at Kadikoi, shared by his nephew and other officers, the army suffered terribly, with horses which had survived the charges of both the Light and the Heavy Brigades dying in great numbers.

Temple Godman, of the 5th Dragoon Guards, described the position on 8 January 1855:

Take for instance our cavalry: we lost about a third from mismanagement in the field, and for the last six weeks we have been doing the duty of Ambulance and Commissariat. Of course we have lost many horses through this extra work which is severe, and often when the men come in half-starved with cold and disgusted with such usage, one hears them say they wish they had been shot and put out of the way at once.

If they had not been doing the Commissariat duty, we should long ago have had our horses under cover, and perhaps men too. We and other regiments have got the glanders, from bad and short feeding, hard work and exposure. We have only ninety-nine horses left, and some of these I hope we may save, as we have got some sheds nearly ready for them. We have had Turkish clothing for about ten days, but this gets wet and freezes on their backs as hard as a board. No wonder they die.[3]

On 2 March 1855 the position had become so bad that, according to Lord George Paget, 'The Light Brigade today mustered forty-four horses, of which about twelve are serviceable. Scarlett, I believe, has told Lord Raglan that he had better send home the Light Cavalry Brigade.'[4]

Scarlett saw little prospect of the early capture of Sebastopol, which grew stronger rather than weaker as reinforcements and supplies poured in during the winter.[5] Even if Sebastopol was taken, there was no guarantee that this would end the war even in the Crimea.[6] As he sensibly observed, the whole campaign had suffered from unclear objectives, inadequate forces and a divided command.[7] In common with many others, he also pointed out the shortcomings of the Commissariat.[8]

Whatever his worries about the course of the campaign, and the heavy losses suffered by the men and horses of the Heavy Brigade in the winter, this was overshadowed by constant worry about his wife, Charlotte, who, despite the best efforts of her family, remained deeply depressed:

The fact remains that whether she is right or wrong not to take more courage, she has not done it; and if sorrow preys upon her it is because she cannot help it. This makes me very miserable and I pray for peace as a solution of the difficulty. I cannot allow her to be the sacrifice to ambition. If she is in danger, I must come to her rescue. I wait very anxiously for the next accounts.[9]

As he concluded: 'Nothing in the shape of honours can repay me for any injury done to her, which God prevent.'[10]

On 17 February 1855 Lord Lucan left the Crimea, having been recalled because of his inability to work with Lord Raglan, due to their differences over the responsibility for the Charge of the Light Brigade.[11] General Scarlett took his place as the commander of the cavalry division. Edward Hodge became the commander of the Heavy Brigade and Lord George Paget of the Light Brigade.[12] In early April, however, very anxious about his wife, Scarlett returned home. During his absence, the cavalry division was commanded by William Parlby, the colonel of the 10th Hussars.

On his return to England, Scarlett was welcomed as a celebrity. On a visit to Burnley, where he arrived on 19 April, he was received by cheering crowds and presented with a sword. At a banquet there in his honour, on 2 May, he spoke about the Charge of the Heavy Brigade.[13]

In London Scarlett was treated as a social lion. As described by his niece, Frances Scarlett,

> The General came and was the *lion* of the evening. Young ladies rushed up to me. 'Will you just point out General Scarlett to me?'; and all that kind of thing. He stood in the centre of a circle and happy were those who had a right to go up and claim acquaintance. He was very kind to Jane West, and she delighted. I conveyed them both home in my brougham. I thought it a pretty arrangement, as it will be *nuts* to Jane to say that she has been three in a brougham with General Scarlett.[14]

None of this made up for the General's misery about Charlotte. Frances Scarlett described a meeting with him after his return to England. 'He seemed *very much* out of spirits. We asked, "How is Aunt Charlotte?" He answered, "As bad as possible. Nothing can be worse." He was hardly able to speak about her and turned away as if he could not bear the subject.'[15] He had been to see both a leading medical specialist and the Commander in Chief, and had come away dismayed from both interviews.[16] He was pressed to return to the Crimea by Lord Hardinge.[17] As his niece, Frances Scarlett, reported to her mother, Lady Abinger, the General, in the end, agreed, putting duty before his personal feelings.[18] He returned to the Crimea in June 1855 and stayed there until the end of November.[19]

The history of the cavalry in the Crimea in 1855 was very different to that of the previous year. After the heavy losses of horses during the autumn and winter of 1854–55, in battle, to disease and to the weather, the division began to recover its strength. It was also steadily reinforced, reaching a strength of over four thousand towards the end of the 1855. Many of the new recruits, however, were almost untrained and quickly succumbed to disease. The horses were also often of poor quality. Captain Shakespear of the 4th Light Dragoons described a draft of horses:

> If you can picture … a very inferior 'bus' horse (not a cab horse mind, but a 'bus' horse), having been driven for six years between Hammersmith and Brentford, and then drafted into a Light Cavalry regiment as a trooper, you have the nearest description I could give you of a draft sent out to us in the steamship *Arabia*.[20]

Not all the drafts, however, were as bad. Two additional trained regiments, the 10th Hussars and the 12th Lancers, arrived in April and May from India, and the 6th Dragoon Guards, the Carabiniers, between June and August, followed by the King's Dragoon Guards. Reflecting the increased strength of the cavalry division, it was divided into three brigades. These were the Heavies under John Lawrenson, the Light Brigade under Lord George Paget and the Hussars under William Parlby. James Yorke Scarlett was promoted to lieutenant general.[21]

While the increase in strength of the division was gratifying, there was little opportunity for the cavalry to prove its worth in combat, or to do more than train and perform routine tasks. It had no specific role in the siege of Sebastopol, which occupied the first nine months of 1855. Had the first main attempt on the city on 18 June succeeded, this might have led to a war of movement. In the end, Sebastopol fell on 9 September, but this was not followed by an advance into the Crimea. During both of the attempts to take the city, the cavalry acted out of sight of the city to control sightseers.

At the final battle of the war, at the Tcherneya on 16 August, the cavalry was mounted and nearby but was not brought into action. In a battle directed by the French, there was, however, a danger that the cavalry might once again be ordered into a reckless charge against a strong enemy position.[22] According to Lord George Paget, commanding the Light Brigade, this involved an unsupported advance under heavy fire across two difficult obstacles, the aqueduct supplying water to Sebastopol and then the ford over the River Tchernaya:

> About 7 o'clock an aide de camp came from General Scarlett to inform me that an advance of the cavalry across the river was intended – a somewhat startling announcement, in truth, and one which, had it been carried out, would in every sense have completed the affair of 25 October; for not only would the results have been disastrous (as I will show later), but, oddly enough, we should have commenced this advance from the very point from whence we were driven back on that day.[23]

The projected advance, which would have been made with the Chasseurs d'Afrique, was halted at the last minute:

> About three or four troops of the 12th Lancers had broken into open column and were advancing at a trot, when a French staff officer galloped up to me, *ventre à terre*, and holding up his hand, begged that I would halt at once, as 'On a changé d'intention', General Pélissier having ordered that the movement should be given up.[24]

In September a squadron of the 10th Hussars was sent to Kertch, where on an expedition with the Chasseurs d'Afrique it had to fight its way out of a difficult position.[25] Then in early October the Light Brigade, under Lord George Paget, was sent to join a French and Turkish force at Eupatoria. Although faced by a large Russian army in the interior of the Crimea, there were no more than skirmishes between the two sides. On 24 November General Scarlett arrived there on HMS *Valorous*. 'To our surprise, *Valorous* has brought Scarlett, but only on a lark, to have a look at us, and he returns tomorrow to Balaklava.'[26] In the event, Scarlett was unable to land due to the wind until 26 November, when 'Scarlett landed today, and I have been lionising him, and he and d'Allonville lunched with me.'[27]

Towards the end of the year, the division went into winter quarters at Scutari, with the prospect of renewed action in the Crimea in 1856. As late as 20 December 1855, Temple Godman was still expecting a campaign the following year: 'We hear much of peace, but we have done ever since the commencement of the war, and the papers don't seem to think much of it. Scarlett went home a few days ago; he told me he hoped to see us here again in March, before we start to take the field.'[28] There was, however, no renewed campaign, as the war was brought to an end by the treaty of Paris in March 1856.

There can be no doubt about the popularity of General Scarlett as the commander of the cavalry division, despite the frustration caused by the inability of the cavalry division to play a significant part in the campaign. He was universally liked. According to Edward Hodge, writing on 16 February:

> You ask about General Scarlett, and say you never see his name mentioned in the papers. Pray do not suppose that those who are mentioned in the papers are the only people who work. Scarlett is very active. He is constantly riding through our lines, and looks well after his brigade.[29]

After Lord Lucan was recalled, Hodge wrote, 'We all like the change from Lucan to Scarlett. The latter is most active. He does his work like a gentleman, and gives no unnecessary trouble.'[30]

When Scarlett left the Crimea on 31 March 1855, Hodge wrote:

> I regret to say that General Scarlett is going home today. Mrs Scarlett's health is so precarious that he is obliged to go. I consider him a very great loss to us at this moment. This will give Lord George Paget the command of the division pro tem. and Shewell the 1st Brigade. I hope that Scarlett will soon return.[31]

A few days later, on 12 April, Temple Godman wrote to his sister, 'Should you hear of General Scarlett, let me know. I am so sorry he is gone. We lose the services of the best man in the division. I fear poor Mrs S. is too ill for him to return, though he would much wish to do so.'[32]

The most intimate report of the General's activities at the end of 1854 and in 1855 comes from the letters of his nephew, William Scarlett, who for some of the time was his aide de camp. Writing to his mother in November 1854, William describes their joint housing:

> The General and I are sitting side by side and he has opened the wrong ink pot. I wish you gave a better account of yourself: there is no use fidgeting about what can't be helped and you only make yourself ill for nothing.
>
> We are pretty cold, as you may suppose, but very healthy. I wear two shirts and two pair of trousers, then my red coat, then a blue regimental coat I bought at a sale, then a shooting jacket and that with a great coat and cloak and gloves keep me going by day, and plaid and blankets help at night.
>
> The Turks are going to Eupatoria tomorrow. They are knowing fellows and have built themselves into holes. The General has given £25 for wood vacated by one regiment. Some will do for ourselves and horses, and the rest will serve as firewood. We inspect our property tomorrow.[33]

This proved very satisfactory:

> I am still with the General. We have left our tents and have burrowed into the ground. The General bought a quantity of wood, collected by the Turks and sold by their pasha for his own benefit, when the regiment left for Eupatoria. With the assistance of a party of French Zouaves, we have constructed a cabin,* very like those I know so well in Scotland.[34] We have a chimney in one corner and it is warm enough. We shall therefore not suffer from wet or cold. The General and I both get fat, and living so much in the open air seems to suit us well.[35]

---

* A drawing of their cabin was made by Alexander Elliot. 'I enclose a sketch done by Elliot of the excitement consequent on the arrival of eight parcels per *Arabia*. Booth is holding the candle, the other figures you can easily recognize. Send the drawing on to Aunt Charlotte when you have laughed at it yourselves.' William Scarlett to Robert, Lord Abinger, 16 March 1855. See plate 28.

There were, however, limits to their comfort. On 18 January 1855, Edward Hodge reported:

> Dined with General Scarlett. He gave a very nice dinner, but still there was an air of much discomfort about his room. They all dined with their greatcoats and caps on. It was very hard work finding my way thro' the snow this evening. Really dining out here is beyond a joke.[36]

William Scarlett also wrote to the General while the latter was on leave in May 1855 with practical advice for his return and news of a cavalry field day:

> Should you come out, I recommend you bring a good strong Whitechapel cart on high wheels and harness for two cobs or mules. We never can march for any distance in the Crimea and a cart can travel well over the steppes. This morning all the cavalry turned out for a field day, which was successful. I believe we have now about 1600 sabres in case of need.[37]

After the General's return to the Crimea, William Scarlett again became his uncle's aide de camp: 'It is very jolly being with the General, not because one can eat and drink like a Christian with one's legs under a table, but because it is so nice being with him. I never thought I should be able to rejoin him, but he is to have the rank of lieutenant general, which will give him two paid aides de camps, one of which I am to be.'[38]

On August 27 James Yorke Scarlett was knighted by Lord Stratford de Redcliffe. 'Today our dear General was invested with the collar of KCB and knighted. He looked the most soldierlike and handsomest man of the whole bunch. Péllisier was there; he looked a snob.'[39] Seven months earlier, William had noted, 'They have given him £100 a year for his distinguished services, which to a man who possesses thousands is no reward. If they don't make him a KCB, I shall say they have the happy knack of giving the wrong rewards to the wrong people. Many a poor devil would have preferred the £100 per annum to the KCBship!!'[40]

Many of William Scarlett's letters refer to his uncle's health, nearly always reporting favourably on it. In October 1855, however, the General had an attack of dysentery, the only illness he had throughout the entire Crimean campaign. 'Our dear General has not been well, but I am happy to say he is now all right again; the fever and dysentery have left him completely and in a few days he will regain all his strength.'[41] A week later he declared himself cured: 'The General came up to my tent the day before yesterday for a change of air; I think it did him good; he has promised to come up again, though he now votes himself quite well.'[42]

The first anniversary of the Battle of Balaklava was celebrated by a parade. According to Edward Hodge:

> Anniversary of my first cavalry action: Balaklava. General Scarlett had out the cavalry and horse artillery, and a very good show we made. The 4th mounted 201 horses. The marching past was good, also the trotting past. The rest I thought very indifferent. I fear that Scarlett cannot handle a large body of troops, and I think he is very wrong for not having his division out oftener. This is the second time only that we have been out.[43]

Whatever Scarlett's shortcomings in handling large bodies of troops, the men of the division celebrated in their traditional manner. 'Much singing in the men's huts and of course much drunkenness.'[44]

After leaving the Crimea on 29 November, General Scarlett spent over three weeks at Scutari, where the cavalry division had gone into winter quarters, before leaving for home on 27 December 1855.

45

James Yorke Scarlett to Sarah, Lady Abinger
Camp Kadikoi, Crimea, 11 December 1854

Camp Kadikoi, 11 December 1854
My dearest Sally, Many thanks for yours; and may I thank Robert for his kind letter.[45] The good opinions of our relations and friends is what I am most ambitious of, next to the consciousness of having done as much as I could to do what is right. I am overpaid by the praises I have received for the acts performed; but, as one works a long time in the dark and obscurity without notice, perhaps one should consider the payment for the present as partly for the past – the feeling I have strongly implanted in my mind, which is the satisfaction which any distinction I may gain would have given to my dear father, who set a high value on reputation and distinction.[46]

However, our Balaklava affair has been succeeded by one yet more glorious for the British Army, though accompanied with sad losses and on the whole probably has retarded our operations by the loss in officers and men.[47] The loss of the Russians was numerous. I could not ride a few steps without treading on the dead. Four thousand and more were faced by us. The cavalry had no immediate place in the fight, though we were mounted and close at hand. The ground did not admit the action of cavalry. Willy was mounted at my side as extra aide de camp and thus perhaps escaped the fate of many a Guardsman.[48] On the whole it was an unexpected attack and somewhat hastily opposed, as the troops could turn out. A picket had been seized and carried off and guns brought up unknown to us; and, without any warning but a shell bursting in the camp, some fifty thousand Russians appeared on the right flank to the attack. However, they got a proper drubbing and have kept quiet since.

As to Sevastopol, there it is in status quo, or rather better able to stand an assault than it was. I leave those who have the management to work out that affair but scarcely hope to dine in Sevastopol on Xmas Day. Take it I suppose we must and shall, but how and why I don't quite see. Heavier guns may do something and are being put in position, but I don't understand taking a town by pelting it, with its gates open and supplies allowed to enter and all who wish go in and out.[49] If we can lead another army to the north, we may do something. What people wish they report, and we hear all sorts of tales one day to be contradicted the next.

Cardigan has gone home on medical certificate and was nothing grieved to go.[50] We, i.e. Willy, Conolly, Elliot and I, are now housed in comparative comfort after being blown out of our tents; and the cavalry, having nearly perished with cold and short commons, are now come down for food and shelter near to Balaklava where they are better off and still near enough if wanted.[51] The Light Brigade is no more, being reduced to a regiment in number.[52] The brigade cannot mount more than six hundred horses, so much from the incidental losses besides shot and steel.[53] I am very glad to have Willy with me, as it keeps him out of the trenches and cold. We sleep in the same room and are capital friends; and he is really very useful to me, taking his full share of the trouble of our little establishment.

Your box of provisions and meat came most opportunely.[54] We depend entirely on the ships for anything beyond salt beef and pork, and indeed on them for that only. The portion of the Russian territory in our power at present would not feed many rabbits. The abundant supplies brought in by natives, fertile valleys, delicious fruits, flocks and herds are also a fable. Children and women are things we have heard of; none exist within the reach of our visual organs. To be sure, I have a picture of the Tzar in my room, and a quantity of church ornaments and pictures taken from a church opposite which is converted into a hospital.[55] We preserve them to be replaced when we depart. Our roads are in a sad state but are being mended and the weather is now mild as milk and dry, if it will but last.

You must not let your anxiety, which is natural, make you forget that no fears will mend matters and that it is, you say and feel, in God's hands alone that our lives are held! We may escape all these dangers. We might have been cut off at home by accident or disease. Be of good heart then, my dear Sally, since it is the best chance for our all meeting again and talking over the past in comfort and happiness. I am somewhat anxious for the periodicals from England to see what impression politically the non-taking of Sevastopol and the affair of the fifth produce. It will either lower our tone or excite the greatest impressment to send us reinforcements. It is a crisis in this affair. The post has not come and Lord Raglan has his letters etc.[56] We are aware he is made a field marshal and we are anxious to see what others may have gained.[57] The French are more prompt in the distribution of their honours; and more of ours will be posthumous, since Inkerman took some of the Heroes of the Alma.

I have written a hasty, illegible scrawl, but I have many letters to answer. May God bless you, and with love to Robert, believe me yours ever affectionately JYS.

* * *

46

James Yorke Scarlett to the Earl of Lucan
Camp Kadikoi, 22 December 1854

Camp Kadikoi, 22 December 1854
My Lord, I have with regret the honour to call your attention to the number of sick horses and the daily deaths of from four to five horses in the regiments of my brigade.[58]

This decrease of effective horses is so rapid that some of the regiments will be unable to furnish the required number of pack-horses and draw their own forage when it becomes their turn to give the picket.

The improvement which had taken place since the horses came to a more sheltered spot has within the last twelve days ceased to be visible. Many are becoming affected with diseases of the lungs, etc, which end in glanders. The cavalry when they came down here were in a state that required care and grooming to renovate and restore them to condition.

They are now employed six hours *per diem* in carrying provisions or forage, which leaves the men few hours of daylight to groom and clean arms and appointments in such weather as this, and leaves no possibility of proceeding with hutting or building stables.

It is for your Lordship to consider whether the cavalry can perform their present duties and retain any chance of doing effective service in the field when called on now or at any future period. It may be for the good of the service generally that they should perform their present duties, but it can scarcely be relied on that they will also be effective as cavalry at a future period.

There has been latterly no deficiency of forage, but many horses are off their feed from debility and low fever, contracted from long exposure, and are unfit for work in consequence.

I wish lastly to advert to the want of veterinary medicines, for which applications have been sent in. I have the honour etc, J. Yorke Scarlett, Brigadier General.

*   *   *

47

James Yorke Scarlett to Dudley Campbell
Camp Kadikoi, 25 December 1854

Camp Kadikoi, Xmas Day, 25 December 1854
A merry Xmas to you, my dear Dudley, and happy New Year; and, whether it may be your fate to pass them as a soldier or a lawyer, may you have many of them and prosperous.

It is a very difficult thing to give advice as to the choice of a profession. There is little doubt but that your father could, if he wished it, procure you a commission in the 5th Dragoon Guards or some other Dragoon regiment, even at your *mature* years.[59] Whether it would be prudent and lead to your ultimate advancement and happiness in life is another matter. A soldier's trade is a very poor one and to live in it he must have a fortune independent of his profession. I never recommend any young man to enter the cavalry with a less capital than £20,000. I don't mean to say that all have it and that it may not, by very great prudence and economy, be possible to do with less; but, before you get a lieutenant colonelcy and command a regiment, you will have had to pay at least £10,000 for commissions, which will only produce you a life income of £400 per annum with some deductions for necessary regimental expenses. You will see therefore that he who makes up his mind to be a soldier makes up his mind to pursue an expensive and unprofitable profession in money matters. With your prospects, as the son of the Chief Justice, I think the law holds out much more prospect of acquiring a fortune – and with it acquiring the means of establishing yourself as a married man and useful member of society.

Promotion in the army is slow, as I can testify, as I have served thirty-six years and at the *wrong* side of fifty find myself only a brigadier general, when perhaps I ought more properly to seek retirement and rest. Certainly there is much to gratify one in military fame – it comes rapidly at the moment. From comparative obscurity one's name may blaze out like a meteor for the moment, but it is to be considered that lookers on, though they can see and admire the brilliant light, have not been cognizant of the dull and tedious darkness which has preceded. The brilliant actions of a campaign strike all the world, but they do not see the many inconveniences, sufferings and privations of a campaign.

Think well then, my dear Dudley, before you encounter all the hardships of a military life and do not be dazzled by the bright side of the picture so much as not to see what is portrayed on the dark side. Weigh all things and then make your choice. I think in Horace you will find an observation which is a true one for *all* professions, viz. he that would carry off the prize 'multa sudavit et alsit' etc.* I assure you Willy and I have found it very hot all summer and are sitting without a fire on Xmas Day – and it is deuced cold I can tell you.

Now, my dear Dudley, having like a good uncle said all there is to say on the subject of a profession, I must thank you for your letter and tell you what little news there is here. At present we are sending up daily large guns and mortars to batter the Sevastopolites into submission. It is evident those guns we have, at the distance we can place them, have not been sufficiently powerful, proving that the force of cannon balls diminishes in increasing ratio with the distance. We hoped to have ate our Xmas dinner in the town, in place of which we are blowing our fingers outside and hope to be in by New Year's Day, but that hope may fail also.

In the meantime the cold is killing our cavalry very fast, as we have no villages which afford shelter for them and our horses cannot stand the exposure to the cold whilst standing in a sea of mud, as all the country becomes in rainy weather. Today we have a sharp frost and the return of dead horses in my brigade alone last night is twenty-six. The wooden houses, warm clothing etc are very pleasant to hear of, but as yet only a portion of the former has come out and none of the latter; and when we get them landed there will be some difficulty with our present means of transport to get them to the lines on the hill occupied by the troops.

I have had a letter from Hally telling me that he has bought my horse from Major Bolton.[60] He has got him very cheap, as I would not have taken double the sum knowing the habits and qualities of the animal, but he requires a very steady rider; and from being of a most timid disposition (and the most dangerous of all horses are timid horses, as when alarmed they will rush into all sorts of scrapes and behave very like vicious horses; and generally the ignorance and brutality of grooms render them so in the end), Hally's horse requires the gentlest treatment and a soothing course. He is a very trained Irish hunter, but not trained yet to flying leaps over hedges and timber.

Willy sends his love with mine to all our dear relations at Stratheden House.[61] It is a consolation to us not be forgotten by them in our banishment. Ever, my dear Dudley, yours affectionately J. Yorke Scarlett.

* * *

---

* Horace, *Ars Poetica*, lines 412–14,'Qui studet optatam cursu contingere metam, multa tulit fecitque puer, sudavit et alsit, abstinuit Venere et vino.' 'He who in the race-course craves to reach the longed for goal, has borne much and done much as a boy, has sweated and shivered, has kept aloof from women and wine.'

48

Sir James Yorke Scarlett to Robert, Lord Abinger
Camp Kadikoi, Crimea, 4 January 1855

Camp Kadikoi, Crimea, 4 January 1855

My dear Robert, though I have nothing new to add to my last, yet, as I have time and opportunity to write, I think you will be glad to hear from me. In my last I mentioned, I think, how much we felt your kind and affectionate anxiety about us and our thankfulness for the things come and coming. One or two boxes have been delivered containing some warm socks, jerseys, drawers, two famous plaids and gloves; all of which will be most useful; also a box from Fortnum and Mason.[62]

We hear too that on board *Manilla*, *Charité*, *Arabia* etc there are other packages for us, but that such is the mode of stowage that we cannot yet come at them.[63] However, we have at this moment all we need as we have a good roof over our heads, a fireplace and fuel, so that we can keep ourselves warm enough and have plenty to eat, all well and have no bodily ailments of which to complain and no duty at present to perform which keeps us out in the cold. Intense cold we have had none, though the ground is now covered with snow and it snows still. For those on the heights in tents it is a much harder trial and on their account I am very anxious. Our horses are without any protection but horsehair clothing as yet, but the process of making huts goes slowly on for want of men to work at them, and I fear we shall have few horses to stable by the end of this month. My own horses are under cover and tolerably well.

I think I mentioned the Commissariat, Transport and the Ambulance had so failed as to necessitate our regiment's horses doing their duty carrying provisions to the infantry and bringing away invalids to hospital.[64] As this entails daily a march of some ten to fourteen miles (*daily* at least), on horses much weakened and impoverished, and keeps men and horses from their camp six hours per diem, loading and unloading and the journey, little time remains for grooming, cleaning opportunities etc. The consequence is that the cavalry cannot recover their strength and appearance. I have represented it in vain and wash my hands of it. I will *not* be responsible. There seems some strange notions in the Quartermaster General's department about cavalry and their uses. What may come from England I don't know. None will be left here of this lot for any spring campaign, I fear. In my brigade we have lost something more than one half the horses and still more in the Light. Ten died last night, and if they go on at that rate they will soon come to nothing. The Russian cavalry, I am *told*, have left the Crimea, not as a certainty but possibly more and more probably.[65] They are dispersed among the villages.

I can give no guess as to the time for taking the town, as I see no reason why we should be more able now than hitherto, unless we rely on subduing their fire by our heavier guns, making our batteries nearer the walls and the wearing out of Russian patience, courage and powder. The latter must be diminishing fast.

Lord John's speech on the twelfth has somewhat surprised me as to the *good* we are to obtain by the Austrian treaty, which seems to me to amount to nil.[66] She is to go to war if the Emperor refuses the four conditions, but he has I understand accepted them; so that, if we are not content, she is in no way bound to assist us. It would almost seem that age had obscured Lord John's intellect, for a weaker speech I never read, whether we look to his reasons for sending the army to the Crimea; or the hopes he discerns from his treaty; or the prospects he holds out. We are told in that situation that we *must* have peace; or he must prosecute the war with all the force England and France can put forth; and we have no time if it is war to come.

I imagine that, when the snow is hard in Russia, the Emperor will be able to collect great forces and great supplies at or near Perekop that we shall find a very superior army to oppose us in the spring. We also, if we exert ourselves and can take the town, must also have time to bring up troops and supplies by sea into Sevastopol, which would serve as a pretty secure base of operations during the summer. But it is no use sending out reinforcements by hundreds when we send away sick by thousands; and we must expect to lose many combatants by next April from sickness. Neither huts nor a complete supply of warm clothing is yet given to the men. The delay in unloading transports and getting things carried to the front is lamentable. Could better despatch have been made, the cargo of the *Prince* would have been saved.[67]

The French have been great helps to us making roads and carrying shot for us, each two men carrying a shell on a pole. The Turks are very little use in any way and are very sickly and die fast. The roads are in a bad state, for wheels and all loads are better carried on pack animals or by men. All our men, both cavalry and infantry, ought to be furnished with waterproof boots and waterproof leggings to cover the trousers from knee downwards to keep off the horrible clay mud which clings to men and horses, and everything it comes in contact with.

All *tight* clothing for body or legs is utterly unfit for soldiers on service, except perhaps on the calf of the leg to admit a boot to pull over it. I have ordered Mr Martin, my bootmaker, to send me out some pantaloons and boots; in the meantime I have got some Turkish thin shoes over which I put some Turkish boots which open with a hinge and are very good to ride in but too heavy and clumsy for pedestrians. Now that we have got rid of clothing colonels, I hope we shall be able to get our men conveniently as well as handsomely dressed. Their present tight dresses were entirely unfit for the heat of summer and quite as unfit for winter. The consequence is they are dressed in a most motley fashion.

Not so the French, who are here pretty much as they are in Paris. The Chasseurs d'Afrique, with their little Arab horses, are to my mind the perfection of *light* cavalry – not as ours fit to charge anything and everything – but better able to endure fatigue and short commons and do real light cavalry work.[68] The French horses have not had so severe a trial yet as ours, having gone from Varna to Bourgas and come here first from thence; but they are falling off and will not stand this exposure.[69] Our small peace establishment forced us to send out ten regiments, mustering about the war complement of three; so that actually regiments will be almost wiped out and nothing left but the name and the depôt troops at home.

5 January

We have a bright day but snow on the ground with a north wind. We individually, being housed, suffer at present no hardship; but for those in tents and trenches I dread the cold. Nineteen horses died last night in the brigade and I fear there will be an increase in the numbers of men in hospital. If the ministers have not better reasons for undertaking this expedition than those assurances by Lord John, viz the fear of disappointing the country and the army by leaving it inactive in Constantinople, they have much to answer for.

They should be guided now in their negotiations – or it should be well considered – by what resources they have to fall back on to recruit this army. My idea of war is that there should be a *definite* object in view; that sufficient means according to all human calculation should be provided to obtain it; and that, when gained, it should be of that nature that it will serve as a basis for peace or for further operations. Now if we gain Sevastopol, it does not follow that we shall gain peace; nor does it follow that we shall gain the Crimea; nor, having gained both Sevastopol and the Crimea, does it follow that we can come to any satisfactory arrangements about keeping it. However, we must leave it to you at home, these considerations. The present weather I imagine is favourable to the Russians in enabling them on sledges to forward troops and ammunition and food over the Steppes and Perekop, though I do not think they will undertake any attack on us at present. The contractor for a rail road from Balaklava to our lines is here and laying down levels for it.[70] The road over the plain is not difficult but has the defect of being too near the enemy; that more within our lines is difficult from steep hills and narrow gorges.

I have heard from Charlotte regularly but she never says anything about her own health and does not tell me, what I fear from Thursby and Eleanor, that she has taken some medicine ordered by their doctor Todd.[71] He is a clever man but I know Charlotte hates medicine and puts no faith in doctors. I confess I am very uneasy about her. Her mind is so constituted that she cannot throw aside any impression which seizes it, and she dwells on it incessantly to the exclusion of other subjects which might direct her mind from the one idea. I said all I could to encourage her to pay you a visit to Abinger, but I see she has not the resolution to undertake the journey and she feels that the exertion is too much for her.[72] Nothing in the shape of honours can repay me for any injury done to her, which God prevent. I hope to hear again today or tomorrow from her.

Willy is well as could be wished and in good spirits. He sleeps in my room and on my bed. I have a sofa belonging to the house. We never undress but make our toilet after daylight when all is light. Our best love to Sally and Fanny.[73] I have received the latter's letter and will write to her when the things arrive. Your ever affectionate JYS.

Cover, The Lord Abinger, Abinger Hall, Dorking, Surrey. Postmark, TS 24 January 1855; Dorking 24 January 1855.

* * *

49

Frances Scarlett to Sarah, Lady Abinger
Ormerod Hall, Burnley, 19 January 1855

Ormerod, Burnley, 11 o'clock in my bedroom, 19 January 1855. Private.
Dearest Mother, To begin at the beginning.[74] We had a coldish journey up
to London but a warm welcome and dinner at Stratheden House.[75] It looked
dismally cold this morning when we started at half past eight with the daily
hardly aired,[76] but having judiciously clothed my feet and hands, and having
a fan heat in the carriage and lots of wrappers, I was perfectly warm all the
way and, instead of being very wretched, as we expected, we are a very cosy
little party.

John Thursby has a very bad cold and sneezed and coughed and complained
of pains here and pains there, but I don't think he was very bad.[77] I felt quite
funny when I found myself amongst the chimney-pots of Burnley again and
smelt that very smoky smell.

The Thursbys were expecting us and received us very kindly of course. I
wondered what Aunt Charlotte would say, and Mrs Thursby herself seemed
doubtful how she would take our coming. I was taken immediately to my
room to dress, and in the morning Aunt Charlotte came in and met me with
her old *kindness*, much more subdued but less nervous than she was; but I was
not so much struck as I expected.

She spoke to me quite naturally and kindly about my journey, asked after
you, Henrietta and the children, and in the evening she talked to us, not
much certainly, but still in her old way; but I noticed a wild, strange look in
her face, quite unnatural to her when she was silent.[78] She spoke sharply to
Mr Thursby, who wanted her to come near the fire, and seemed *sullen*.

I have had but one moment's conversation with Mrs Thursby, when Aunt
Charlotte went upstairs after dinner. Mrs Thursby said she was behaving
very differently from what she did when they were by themselves and would
probably keep herself up for a day or two in order to deceive us as to her real
state. She wanted to go off to Bank when she heard we were coming, but
was dissuaded partly from not being able to make up her mind whether she
would have a single or a double fly.

She brought down her work after dinner, a thing she has not done for
weeks. The Thursbys are very much obliged to us for coming, and are
evidently relieved by our presence. We ourselves are entirely satisfied that

we have done the right thing. It has caused no breach in the family, and the lie being broken, Aunt Charlotte will not wish to fly from us. Her feeling seems to be [uncertain word] at showing the state she is in.[79]

Mr Thursby talked to Peter.[80] He thinks very seriously about her health bodily and mentally. I do not think it possible to conceal that her existence is only hanging by a thread. She has a bad hacking cough, which must wear her out.

I shall be able to tell you more about her in a day or two, and if there is a faint chance of bringing her up. Aunt Charlotte came into my room when we went to bed and talked quite nicely how you had written to her about coming up; and she had never answered; and were you not surprised; and how she never wrote to anyone now.

I said all the kind little things I could; only little about her having refused to come, throwing in the cold weather, but just said how happy you would be to see her again. She did not say to *me* that she would not come, though I have no doubt that her own mind is made up not to move. We shall see. I shall write you at length all I observe. I see no hope except in some happy accident. It is a melancholy prospect. I rejoice much that we came and came at once without delay or notice. No harm has been done so far is good; and I am sure the relief we must be to the poor folks here is alone a sufficient reason and reward for our journey.

Things go on here much as they did. The dogs walk about the room. Michael sits and does nothing and is pleased to be noticed.[81] I feel a compassion for him because he is snubbed. William looks delicate and hectic.[82] We talked parishes and riddles together. John and I played at backgammon and made little jokes.

I hope you and Papa are pretty comfortable together. I was very sorry to leave you, but we were right to come. Yours ever most affectionately, Frances M. Scarlett.

* * *

50

Orders to 5th Dragoon Guards
25 January 1855

Regimental Orders, 25 January 1855

Her Majesty having been graciously pleased to promote Brigadier General Scarlett to the rank of major general, the tie which bound him to the 5th Dragoon Guards is broken.[83] His name no longer appears in the roll of the regiment as their lieutenant colonel. Though this promotion is most flattering to the major general as a reward for his services performed in the field, he cannot see the connection which has so long existed between him and the regiment he has had the honour and pleasure to command dissolved without feelings of pain and regret. It has during his command been the pride and delight of his life to have received from every General Officer who has inspected the 5th Dragoon Guards their full approbation of the regiment, and to have been able to place on their records the special approbation of the greatest soldier of the day, the late Duke of Wellington.

From the time he joined the 5th Dragoon Guards as major in 1830 until he relinquished the immediate command at Ballincollig in 1854, the regiment was in the highest state of discipline. No corps of cavalry landed at Varna in more splendid order. Since that period sickness and death have made terrible ravages in the ranks, disasters which could not wholly be avoided, but which perhaps greater experience in campaigning might have diminished.

Weakened in numbers and in health, the regiment notwithstanding proved by their gallant conduct on the 25 October at Balaklava that they are inspired in battle with the same spirit by which their predecessors won an undying reputation for the corps in the Peninsula. It is a source of pride and satisfaction to the major general that he should owe his promotion to the gallantry of the 5th Dragoon Guards. The interest he has so long taken in their welfare and honour will only cease with his life.

*   *   *

51

Frances Scarlett to Henrietta Graham-Toler
Abinger, 4 February 1855

My dear Henrietta, Peter and I returned from Ormerod on Thursday. Our visit was unsuccessful in as much as we could not persuade Aunt Charlotte to accompany us, but still we did good by making a little cheerfulness during the time we staid. The Thursbys were very kind and glad to see us, so our journey was not fruitless. I never expected Aunt Charlotte would move. Her state of melancholy apathy is very sad. We had a doctor over to see her, but she would not consult him properly, and I doubt if she will take his medicine.

We staid a day in London and came down yesterday. Fred is condescendingly to pay us, or I should rather say Mama, a visit and is behaving quite rationally.[84] What an increased crisis there is in the political world! What will turn up? Perhaps you or I shall be sent for ...

The Amateur Exhibition is going on rapidly.[85] I hear the Queen is going to contribute, but that is a secret known to everyone. I collected £130 for tobacco. W. Evelyn sent me £3 with the prettiest note imaginable. He is not at all nervous on paper. He must propose in a little decidedly.[86] My dear child, you must be very dull alone. It seems horridly selfish of me not to go to you, but in this naughty world we think of nothing but ourselves. Yours ever affectionately, Fan.

*   *   *

52

Frances Scarlett to Henrietta Graham–Toler
Stratheden House, 16 February 1855

My dearest Henrietta, We are head over ears in flannels and calico, as usual, and send off a parcel next week through Lady Stratford to Miss Stanley at the Koulali Hospital.[87] The Campbells are making up a box to send to Willy, if you want to send anything.

The Amateur Exhibition is getting on grandly. I hear of numerous contributions. How funny it will be when it opens, and how glad I shall be when it is over! I have written to Aunt Charlotte to lend me my picture of Glen Nevis for exhibition, as it is my most creditable performance. I think I shall get Aunt Fanny to let me sell that picture of Leith Hill.[88] She don't care about it. I am doing besides some Italian sketches. So much for my contribution. Ever your affectionate sister, Frances M. Scarlett.

*   *   *

53

Sir James Yorke Scarlett to Frances Scarlett
Sevastopol, Kadikoi, 5 March 1855

My dear Fanny, I must not let another post go without telling you how greatly I feel your kindness in having gone to Ormerod to cheer up poor Charlotte; and I am sure your presence did her good and that, if she would have accompanied you back to Abinger, it would have had a good effect on her; but she is like Rachel, who, having lost what she loved most, would not be comforted.[89] How much I wish she would think with your song that 'behind the cloud the sun is shining'; but all this is vain. The fact remains that whether she is right or wrong not to take more courage, she has not done it; and if sorrow preys upon her it is because she cannot help it. This makes me very miserable and I pray for peace as a solution of the difficulty. I cannot allow her to be the sacrifice to ambition. If she is in danger, I must come to her rescue. I wait very anxiously for the next accounts.

I have not a brilliant command here in the cavalry. The horses are so much reduced that I almost despair of their being brought round, though they have left off the daily trick of dying, and hobble about a little more firmly on three legs. If Charlotte can endure it, I feel it right to remain here yet a little longer. If not, I must let Lord Raglan seek for some other commandant for the cavalry.[90] Many better there are to take my place, but none but me can help poor Charlotte.

I have written a long letter to your Dad and shall add nothing more to this than to announce the arrival and distribution of the tobacco to the cavalry; and of the arrival, though not delivery, of the warm clothing for the 5th, which is not even now too late. I wrote to Felix the thanks for the tobacco and repeat them here to you, who most of all deserve to have them.[91]

The warm weather and winter departure are at hand, and no doubt we shall all wonderfully revive here till the very hot weather returns. What is in store for us God only knows and in Him we must put our trust. I think the management of affairs will be improved. What we want now are *numbers*. We began this with too small a force and without proper reserves. The ministry have much to answer for in not casting their thoughts forward. War is best conducted by a dictator. One mind should be responsible for and direct the whole; but there should be subordinates innumerable to carry out his behests.

Give my best love to Sally and Peter.[92] We expect today or tomorrow mails which are due. Tell him I have not yet recovered my silver watch. Charlotte has got my gold one. Ever, my dearest Fanny, your affectionate Uncle Jim.

Sebastopol where it was; no nearer. Billy all right.

*   *   *

54

Frances Scarlett to Sarah, Lady Abinger
Stratheden House, 13 March 1855

To Lady Abinger, Ormerod House, Burnley
Dearest Mother, Many thanks for your letter. I appreciate very much the kind and tender spirit in which you have written. Your account of Aunt Charlotte is very sad. What does she say about the General's return? Does not that prospect rouse her?

Peter and I went to the play last night. It was sufficiently amusing as things go. We had the children and Alice Jenkins, who is a very well behaved young person.[93] Cally will not have Peter at Parkhurst and has written to him to say that she must remind him 'that every man's house is his castle', and many other things to the like effect, all owing to Peter's having written to Mrs Carter to say he was coming without having gone through the previous farce of *adoring* Caroline.[94] Of course they would quarrel as soon as they came to business.

Peter will go to Abinger on Monday and, unless anything occurs to make me change my mind, I shall go with him. Mrs Carrick called this morning and I gave her five shillings for which she evinced becoming gratitude. I made her sit down and tell me all her history: a sad little tale of love and sorrow. She said she could not do needlework because, when she sat still, she wore herself out with thinking, and so took to charring.

Mary and I have been to the Soldiers' Lodging House. I gave Mrs Douglas 10s. in your name for rent.[95] There were several widows since my last visit; and when I asked what they wanted it was 'a scrap of mourning for the poor children'. One woman received us coldly, saying 'He's dead'. I thought her unfeeling, but a few words thawed her and with tears streaming down her face, she said 'she should never know what it was to be happy again. He were the best of husbands.' Certainly married life is seen in its most attractive form in the Victoria Lodging House, for the soldiers' wives, when you speak to them of their husbands, be they dead or alive, immediately burst into tears, declare the said husbands never spoke a cross word to them, were together the best of men, sober and devoted, and they the happiest of women. Now as we must be morally certain that half our brave soldiers are drunk three times a week, and that they all beat their wives from time to time, when they deserve it, there must be some fascination about soldier husbands, as *all* the wives unite in a common system of duplicity. Yours ever, FMS.

* * *

55

Sir James Yorke Scarlett to Frances Scarlett
Camp Kadikoi, Crimea, 16 March 1855

Kadikoi, 16 March 1855

My dear Fanny, I am now able to tell you that the nephews and nieces' box has arrived and most warmly do the remains of the 5th Dragoon Guards thank their kind countrywomen for their recollection of them.[96] Many a gallant heart that stepped out of the *Himalaya* on the shore at Varna is laid low by a disease which no care or caution seemed able to check.[97] We lost comparatively few in action. Those who remain are looking well now and have become seasoned soldiers.

The great event which took place on the second of March I trust may turn out favourable for the peace of the world.[98] You will not wonder that I am most anxious that it should do so for private reasons, for I confess I would give much now to be at Bank and try to raise poor Charlotte's drooping head. The last accounts I have from Eleanor, though not worse, are far from satisfactory and I shall be guided by the next, which I expect on Monday, what course to take. God grant that the event which he has brought about may bring a solution of my individual difficulties by setting me free.

I cannot write a long letter at present as it is late and I must try to get some sleep, as I have been wakeful rather at night lately. I quite approve of your efforts in favour of the dear old church at Abinger and I send you £50 to assist in your designs. I have long thought that we were wanting in not having placed in the church some record of our affection for one whose memory is dear to us all and to whom we owe so much.[99] You may consider me a partner in all you wish to do in this matter; and, if you bear a debt, I will be responsible for you.

We have by *Peninsula* packet received two beds and bedding, but have not opened them yet as we are not at present in want of them.[100] You at home have left us nothing to want, having clothed and fed us superlatively. All things here are getting into better order and we are high and dry now out of the mud, men and horses improving daily, but we want great reinforcements to make us a fighting army and advance.

They have sent two gentlemen, Colonel Tulloch and Sir J. McNeill, who never saw a campaign and know nothing about me, to take notes of the state of the army and set us to rights.[101] They had better *learn* by spending a night or two in the trenches the whys and the wherefores; or we could accommodate them with three horses each to ride and groom.

Pray thank all the contributors to the 5th Dragoons' box in their name when you have the opportunity and, with best love to all at Abinger, believe me most affectionately J. Yorke Scarlett.

*   *   *

56

Frances Scarlett to Sarah, Lady Abinger
3 Chester Square, 19 March 1855

To Lady Abinger, Ormerod, Burnley
Dearest Mother, I shall be very glad to have my parents back on Monday.
I shall go home by an early and see that the house is victualled etc, etc.[102]
Thank Papa for his kind letter. The Stratheden House party started yesterday
for Torquay. They left at nine. The house was so intensely melancholy when
they were gone that I made all the haste out of it I could; not even Fred's
offer to come home *every day* to dinner, if I would stop, could charm me to
stay a moment longer than was necessary to lock up my boxes. Aunt Fanny
received me very kindly; though very nervous at first, is quite happy now she
finds I am not *determined* to make all the noise, I can and don't wish to play
upon the piano, and am content to sit quietly in the back room.[103] It is very
sad to see her neck in a yoke, which galls her so terribly and makes her last
days miserable, when they might be cheerful.

I had Aunt Stratheden's brougham yesterday and took Peter and the
children to Wylde's Globe.[104] It was much too instructive, but we liked the
lecture on the model of Sebastopol, because the lecturer talked about the
gallant General Scarlett. In the evening I dined with Peter, quite a *small*
party. He had Madame Jeannin and Alice, young Sims, John Campbell,
Coutts Arbuthnot, a friend of Coutts he had asked to bring – so like him:
a man with awful moustaches who lived in Ceylon and was in the habit of
shooting elephants.[105] We had music after dinner and everything went off
very glibly. Madame Jeannin improves upon me. There is an affectation of
brusquerie about her manner at first which is repelling, but which passes off.
She is not so immensely clever as Peter represents. Nobody can see the two
together and imagine they are anything but the most correct friends. She
speaks enthusiastically of his kindness to her. She spoke of Florence society
and said everybody was so nasty there that Peter was the only person she
liked and she was the only person he cared for. These things are not said
where there is any *arrière pensée*.

Polly, Cecie and I went to one of Ella's concerts on Thursday.[106] The
music was very good. I met Algie West and had a long talk with him about
Sebastopol.[107] He gave me a very clever, amusing account of 'Life in Camp'
and how they did nothing but eat and never washed, except their hands

sometimes, not for want of appliances but from having got used to dirt. He described Willy as handsomer than ever, and was quite charmed with General Scarlett and all his kindness. Algie said the most gallant soldier in the army was Hughie Drummond: not only brave in battle, that they all were, but cheery under all circumstances, making light of everything, a soldier to the backbone. Young Sims tells me there is a print of a fight with Captain Drummond killing three Russians.[108] He is going to get it for me, if it is not more than eighteen pence.

I asked Dudley to come to Abinger, if he wanted a home in the absence of his people, but I have not heard from him. I also asked Fred (in order not to be behindhand in civility), but he cannot expose the British Empire to jeopardy by leaving his post at present.[109]

I hear that wretch Lord Fitzhardinge is dead.[110] I am very glad because Georgie will now be happy and Captain Berkeley's constancy be rewarded.[111] With much love, your ever affectionate child, Frances M. Scarlett.

I am just going to take Jane West out driving in the Stratheden House brougham, which is at my disposal as long as I remain in town.[112]

*   *   *

57

Frances Scarlett to Sarah, Lady Abinger
26 Montpellier Square, London, 28 April 1855

To Lady Abinger, Abinger Hall, Dorking
Half past nine a.m., 28 April 1855
Dearest Mother, Uncle Campbell had an interesting communication with Lord Hardinge in the House of Lords last night, which he related to us at dinner, *in confidence*.[113] Lord Hardinge desired him to write to the General to come up,[114] as soon as possible, as the authorities wished to take his advice about sending out cavalry; that *all* concurred in wishing him to go out as commander of the Cavalry Division; that Lord Cardigan was as obnoxious as Lord Lucan, and it was desirable to prevent his having the command.[115] The General's appointment had been submitted to the Queen, who approved. Lord Hardinge urged that it would be a very fine command, as the cavalry was to be largely reinforced, and said many handsome things of our General. His resignation could not be accepted, as he could not be spared. He should have leave till the end of May; that is he must be at his post by that time, as the campaign would open then.

Uncle Campbell wrote off instantly to the General, telling him all this, and urging him to come up immediately.[116] He told us he had been telling him all his mind. He did not say *what* he had been saying, but he told us that he *ought* to make a sacrifice of his wife, even of her life, to his country. I wonder if he would judge so sternly and uprightly if Aunt Stratheden's life was in his hands! I think not.[117]

I know you will tear your wig at all this, which will place Uncle Jim in a very hard position. He is not a man to be moved by worldly honour, and he will consign himself to oblivion if he thinks he sees that that is his duty. He may be moved by the cry 'the country needs you', but he is too modest about himself to think he is absolutely necessary.

Taking her with him is the only way of solving the difficulty. Lord Cardigan said to Aunt Stratheden, 'Why does he not take Mrs Scarlett with him? She might live with him in his hut at Kadikoi.'[118] I can't imagine this possible, however. Don't put about this. *He* will be a grander and more heroic man if he sees all this distinction pass away from him than if he was smothered in glory and honour, and we must hope and believe that England has 'many knights as good as he'. Still, it *chafes* one's spirit. Mary is furious and says she shall cut the whole family and turn hermit if he does not go.[119] She is like her father: self-sacrifice to the backbone, even to the extent of sacrificing your own flesh and blood. I feel sure that the General will judge better than any of us what is right and best. Lord Panmure has resigned on account of illness.[120]

I am very snug with Peter.[121] He treats me very well and I have plenty of hot and cold water, the only little comforts without which I begin to count the days when my visit will end. My deafness is decidedly better. Papa turned up at Stratheden House and dines here today with Dudley and the Jeannins. Dudley appeared unexpectedly from Paris yesterday to see his family. We were much pleased to see one another. Uncle Campbell thinks that nothing will be done at Sebastopol and that the bombardment is all a farce and only to please the French.

Just received your letter. I can't think what are the *sentiments* Willy reproves. I have always made it a rule to write only facts to *him*, because he has *no* sentiments himself. I suppose, for lack of something to say, I have allowed my feelings to run away with me.

Cecie is coming for me and we are going to walk to the Exhibition together.[122] I lunch at Stratheden House to meet the Wests. I am very glad your cold is better. Your ever affectionate child, Frances M. Scarlett.

Cover, The Lady Abinger, Abinger Hall, Dorking, Surrey. Postmark, London, 29 April 1855. Crest FMS on seal of envelope.

* * *

58

Frances Scarlett to Sarah, Lady Abinger
26 Montpellier Square, London, 1 May 1855

Montpellier Square, 1 May 1855
Dearest Mother, Peter and I drove up to the St George's Hotel yesterday, at the moment that the General arrived in his cab from the station.[123] He seemed *very much* out of spirits. We asked, 'How is Aunt Charlotte?' He answered, 'As bad as possible. Nothing can be worse.' He was hardly able to speak about her and turned away as if he could not bear the subject.

He immediately spoke of something else. He has not mentioned her since and we of course could not question him. He is looking very well, rather redder and a little fatter in the face, but he is much depressed evidently. We only talked a few minutes then, and he went off after contrivances of his own and was coming to dinner.

Hally and Dudley dined with us, and nothing could be more interesting than the General's conversation, we four putting him questions, which he answered in the most charming way.[124] It was delightful to listen to him. His old blythe manner seemed to come back to him as he talked of the charge and all the doings in the Crimea.[125] He said that, previous to the charge, Lord Lucan had ridden up to him and all the orders he gave were, 'Do what you like.' He occasionally made some allusion to 'if he went back'.

About tea we adjourned to Stratheden House (where we did not dine, as some judges were being entertained) and had more talk.[126] Uncle Campbell and the General went off to have a private talk.

I have just come back this morning from Stratheden House. All Uncle Campbell would let out was that the General had said he was the only person who could induce Aunt Charlotte to take any means to restore her health, and he considered it his duty to stay with her, unless he should be able to take her with him. The General was to see Lord Hardinge this morning.[127] We expect him presently and I will not close my letter in case I have anything to add. He said the hospital at Scutari was beautiful. He was introduced to Miss Nightingale, who he averred to be sixty.

Cover, To Lady Abinger, Abinger Hall, Dorking.

* * *

58a

Dearest Mother, I had no time to finish my letter to you this morning, so go on with my story now.[128] The General came about two and we had a deeply interesting conversation about his position. He had been to Dr Ferguson (about Aunt Charlotte) and to Lord Hardinge.[129] He said both interviews were very unsatisfactory.

Dr Ferguson had a bad opinion of the case, as far as he could judge from description. About Lord Hardinge, he said, 'They are very hard to me. They say I must go out, though I tell them it would be to condemn my wife to insanity.' He spoke most feelingly about it, saying:

> To leave her now would be to consign her to a madhouse, to plunge a knife into her heart with my own hands. If she were really mad, I could do no good, and should leave her to others, who could look after her as well as I could. If she were merely ill, others would reside here; but I am the only person who has a chance of recovering her. She is no longer rational on some points. The first blow towards insanity has been struck.

From these last expressions, she must evidently be much worse. From his description, she goes on in the same old way she did, wringing her hands, walking up and down the room, moaning, 'too late, too late'. He gets her to go out, but with difficulty, and has to stand over her to get her to put on her boots and things. She follows him about like a dog and is restless if he leaves the room. She eats and sleeps better and will at times talk quite like herself; her memory of everything is quite perfect, but she has never asked anything about the Crimea.

He offered last Sunday to read to her the service, but she threw away the prayer books, saying they were of no use. He seemed much shocked at this, as an instance of change in her. He did not say how she received him, and we did not like to question him on so painful a subject. He seemed to dread her taking a *dislike* to him, as a natural phase of her disorder. I should think Ferguson put this into his head.

Of course we talked about her going out with him.[130] He said he did not think it possible she should; but afterwards we discussed the plan. 'Supposing her to bear the journey', he said, 'how could I leave her alone with foreigners and Turkish servants?' I said, 'She need not be *alone*, though you cannot be with her always.' He looked pleased and said, 'I know you will do what is kind towards me.' As to her going to the Crimea, that seemed out of the question; to leave her at Therapia the only plan, if she were recovered so far as to bear the journey and endure the separation.[131]

In the midst of all this conversation, in walked Coutts Arbuthnot![132] I immediately took the General down to lunch and we had more talk. He thinks the authorities treat him very harshly and ought not to put the alternative before him of insisting on 'his walking over his wife's grave'. He evidently considers them all not only cruel but needless. I again said, 'in all the plans, count on our assistance'. He said, 'I do and know all your offers are sincere.'

Presently, Mary, Hally and Dudley called for me and we walked to the New Water-Colour Exhibition.[133] Hally begged I would walk with him because my gown was smarter than Mary's. We had a nice walk and enjoyed our exhibition. ...

There is a dim chain of reasoning in my mind that, if Uncle Jim goes out again, he will take Aunt Charlotte with him; and that we *must* go too; that Uncle Jim ought to go for the sake of his country, if possible; and that we shall serve our country somehow by going. The dim chain grows dimmer still here, and I cannot see anything beyond it. The future is a chaos over which some spirit sits brooding sternly.

Having seen the General, I imagined I would return home to you; but now I think I will not. I could not bear to be away whilst anything was under discussion. Poor Mother! You may well say, with Peter, that I am 'intolerably selfish', but I feel as if I should do you little good by going home at present and you still less.

2 May

I perceive by your letter that *you* are prepared to go abroad. There is a very nice apartment in this square, No. 20, which I could take for you if you like to come up. If you don't go to the hotel, as you propose, I think it would be a very good plan. There is only one sitting room, so Papa would not lodge there. It would be too uncomfortable for you to have his meals about at all hours. The rent is two guineas a week: drawing room and bedroom, and room for the maid; and man too at a small additional charge; a respectable woman in the house who would do the cooking; use of the kitchen for 2s. 6d. per week. You cater for yourself. It is quite genteel and nicely furnished, and on the same side as us.

I took it into my head that it would be a good thing for you to come up to a lodging, which is so far cheaper than an hotel, and have been looking at shoals of apartments. None answered but this. I advise (if you do not go to the hotel with Aunt Charlotte) that you write to me by return of post to take the lodgings for you, and come up on Friday or Saturday.[134] You can be independent of Papa, who can do whatever he is accustomed to. You might have Sam and the horse and hire a brougham, as Peter does.[135] This, with Thomas, would make you quite independent. Ever your affectionate child, Frances M. Scarlett.

*   *   *

59

The Return of Major General Scarlett: Presentation of a Sword and Grand Banquet, 2 May 1855

Burnley Advertiser, 5 May 1855

The return of Major General Scarlett from the Crimea has been made the occasion of considerable rejoicings in Burnley during the past fortnight.[136] The gallant General has been received by his fellow-townsmen with a hearty British welcome, not however unmingled with the deepest regret as to the cause of his return: the serious illness of the Hon. Mrs Scarlett. We trust the health of Mrs Scarlett may speedily be restored and that the General may be soon enabled to resume his place at the head of that brave cavalry he has so bravely led. That his services are valued by the army will be evident from the following extract from the *Times* Correspondent.

> Major General the Hon. J. Yorke Scarlett, commanding the cavalry division, left Balaklava on 2 April, attended by Captain Elliot, aide de camp, by the *City of London* for London, whither he was summoned on account of the serious illness of his wife. It is hoped by every one under his command that his absence will be short, for he has gained the confidence and regard of officers and men in the cavalry division. His place will be taken by Lord George Paget, and Colonel Shewell will act as brigadier of the Light Cavalry Brigade.

Major General Scarlett arrived at the Holme Station, near Holme Chapel, at five o'clock on Thursday afternoon, the 19th ult. It was generally rumoured that he would arrive early in the morning, and the church bells began ringing before six o'clock. Flags were also exhibited in various parts of the town. Nothing, however, could be ascertained with certainty until about three o'clock in the afternoon, when a telegraphic message was received, stating that the General would be at the Holme Station at the hour above named.

As soon as this message became known, a guard of honour, consisting of Captain Brereton's company of the 5th Royal Lancashire Militia, with the band and colours, under the command of Lieutenant Colonel Towneley, proceeded to the station to receive the General. There was a considerable assemblage of the townspeople and of the inhabitants of the neighbourhood.

The train arrived at its time and, on the General alighting, he was received by the military with the salute due to his rank, and three times three cheers were given by the crowd around. The gallant General looked remarkably well and was evidently surprised by the hearty reception he met with. He bowed repeatedly in acknowledgement and, after thanking Colonel Towneley and several gentlemen that he recognised, he drove off to Ormerod House, where the Hon. Mrs Scarlett has for some time been staying.

On Friday the 20th ult., a deputation consisting of Lieutenant Colonel Towneley, J. Moore, B. Chaffer and R. Shaw Esquires, waited on General Scarlett at Ormerod House requesting his attendance at a banquet, when he would be presented with a sword as a token of the esteem in which he is held by his friends in Burnley, and to ascertain the day most convenient to him. The General complied with the request and named Wednesday the second of May.

The committee at once entered into the necessary arrangements and two of their number were despatched to London to select a sword suited to the purpose. The subscription opened to defray the cost has been responded to by gentlemen representing all shades of politics, and the total subscriptions amount to nearly £200, including sums from 2d. up to £10 10s.

To a stranger it would be evident that Wednesday last was no ordinary day in Burnley. The streets toward evening were thronged by an immense concourse, and flags and banners were suspended from the church tower and from many a window. Streamers were stretched across Bridge Street and St James's Street bearing the words 'Honour the Brave' and 'Scarlett for Ever'. From the Bull Hotel a flag was suspended bearing the inscription 'Well Done Scarlett' and on the reverse 'Balaklava'.

The Presentation

The presentation of the sword took place at the Court House, half past six being the hour fixed upon. The admission was confined to subscribers, the galleries being reserved for the ladies. The day was beautifully fine and the streets leading to the Court House were lined by an immense concourse of persons, who greeted the gallant General on his appearance with the heartiest enthusiasm

On alighting at the gates of the Court House, he was received by Lieutenant Colonel Towneley and nearly all the officers of the 5th Royal Lancashire Militia in full dress uniform; Lieutenant Mansel, Third Light Dragoons; Le Gendre N. Starkie Esq., MP, and several officers of the Lancashire Yeomanry Cavalry also in uniform; Lord Abinger; the Venerable Archdeacon Master, T.H. Whitaker, the Reverend W. Thursby, George Stansfield, J. Moore, J. Roberts, J. Heelis, W. Hopwood, J. Spenser, R. Shaw, B. Chaffer, J. Holgate Esquires, etc, etc.

The General having taken his seat, and silence being restored, the chair was taken by Lieutenant Colonel Towneley, who, on rising to present the sword, observed that they had met that day to shew that the neighbourhood was not backward in doing honour to British valour as exhibited by the brave forces who had fought the battles of their country. They had been enabled to trace the progress of the army; they had seen it decimated by sickness in the Crimea; and they had witnessed the noble spirit with which it rose from the bed of sickness the moment it was called to face the enemy. They saw it when it met the Russian forces on the heights of the Alma. The enemy had boasted he could hold the position for three weeks; his forces were dislodged and dispersed in four hours (cheers). In the moment of victory the British Army did not forget that humane conduct which ever distinguishes all the really brave.

They passed onward to Balaklava. It was there their friend and neighbour General Scarlett had led on the brave men under his command to victory (rounds of cheering). The heavy cavalry had to meet a force ten times their number and in four or five minutes that force was put to flight. They followed the progress of the army to Inkerman, where 14,000 put to flight an immense Russian army led on by the sons of the Emperor.

They had met on that occasion to do honour to the bravest army that had ever left the shores of their country, through one who was their neighbour. That neighbourhood had supplied the brave man to whose noble conduct they had met to testify (prolonged cheering).

In former days the Militia of that part were commanded by the father-in-law of General Scarlett. Before he became a general he had raised his division of the service to the highest reputation. They all knew what his conduct had been as a gentleman and a neighbour; they knew what that conduct was as a general. They had seen him lead brave men on to victory in defence of their country. They need never fear for their country while they had such men.

General Scarlett had received the public thanks of the Queen and the British Parliament, and shortly he would bear on his breast a medal for Balaklava. They would all unite in giving him a permanent record of their sense of his services. Colonel Towneley concluded by presenting the sword to the gallant officer, saying 'General Scarlett, I hope you will accept this sword as a mark of esteem and regard for your noble public conduct' (immense cheering).[137]

General Scarlett on presenting himself was received with the most enthusiastic applause. He referred to honours received on former occasions, when he had felt it necessary to claim the indulgence of those to whom he had to speak, but his embarrassment on the occasion before him, when the matter was personal to himself, rendered it much more necessary for him to pray for their indulgence. To receive the thanks of his sovereign, of the House of Peers and of the British people in the House of Commons was what any man might be proud of. He had never dreamt that such honour would have fallen to his lot. But when he came home amongst his neighbours and friends, and found them gathering around him, prepared thus to honour him, it came much nearer his feelings and he had great difficulty in finding words to express himself adequately on the occasion. He accepted, with proud satisfaction, the gift they had honoured him with; he would preserve it and he trusted that it would never be disgraced in his hands.

The meeting would be mistaken if they attributed the success of the charge at Balaklava to him personally. Whatever honour he might have acquired, he owed it to the brave and gallant men who followed him on that occasion; and, however silent he might properly be about his own services, he would say that they could not cherish too much the deeds and memory of the gallant men who on that day followed him into the ranks of the Russian army (great cheering). They had been reduced by sickness, but the spirit in their bosoms was unconquerable. They were the same men who had left the shores of Britain with high hope and warlike enthusiasm.

In describing the approach of the Russians on the morning of the battle, the General said he was sorry to say the Turks under cover of the Heavy Brigade had deserted the forts. They were not, however, much to blame; they retired before an enemy twenty times their number. Shortly after this they saw an immense dark mass of Russians approaching. They were in the presence of the enemy in a moment. They experienced some difficulty from the nature of the ground, but the men lost no time; not one of them disobeyed the order to charge. In an instant they were engaged hand to hand with the Russians (cheers). The brigade numbered from 700 to 800; the Russians somewhere about 3000. It was with great satisfaction that, after five or six minutes, they saw them melt away before them and vanish down the valley.

These men, who had shewn such a high state of discipline under the fire of the enemy were not less attentive to what they were ordered to do in the pursuit. After the flight of the Russians, he was soon enabled to get them in order. If they had gone forth in the pursuit they would soon have been under the fire of the enemy's guns.

Speaking of the Light Cavalry charge at Balaklava, the General remarked that it was fruitless in some respects, but as long as history was written and remained it would be recorded that six hundred British cavalry charged into the very centre of the Russian army. When the remainder of that heroic band returned they cheered as they passed the Heavy Brigade, which had been ordered to their support. He thought, without reference to himself, that they might justly be proud of the men who had fought their battles in the Crimea.

The infantry at Inkerman were equally deserving their admiration. Inkerman was entirely a British soldiers' fight in which their valour predominated – a fight in which every man played a conspicuous part (cheers).

In concluding, the General said he had referred to these things as he thought they would not be unwilling to hear of them from one who had been present. He would preserve the sword they had presented to him; he had no son, to whom it would descend, but it should pass to one as dear to him – his nephew, the eldest son of Lord Abinger; one who would be found worthy of any distinction the country could bestow on him. He assured them that mark of their esteem would be as highly valued as any distinction that could be bestowed upon him (loud and prolonged cheering).

Major General Scarlett left the Court House at about half past seven in an open carriage, accompanied by his brother, Lord Abinger; his brother-in-law, the Reverend W. Thursby; and Lieutenant Colonel Towneley, and drove at a slow pace to the Church of England Literary Institution, where the banquet was held. The streets were if possible still more crowded than before and in his progress the General repeatedly acknowledged the hearty greetings of the multitude.

*   *   *

60

William Scarlett to James Yorke Scarlett
Crimea, 18 May 1855

Crimea, 18 May 1855

My dear General, People here are much pleased with the reception you have met with at home, but after all one's own conscience gives more satisfaction than the shouts of a thousand voices, who would condemn with as little penetration as they praise.

Should you come out, I recommend you bring a good strong Whitechapel cart on high wheels and harness for two cobs or mules. We never can march for any distance in the Crimea and a cart can travel well over the steppes. This morning all the cavalry turned out for a field day, which was successful. I believe we have now about 1600 sabres in case of need,

I should, of course, like to return as your aide de camp but I don't quite see how it can be done. It would hardly be the correct thing as lieutenant colonel to be extra aide de camp and, independent of Elliot having the best claim, he is a much better man in cavalry than I can ever hope to be; and I could hardly serve under a man so much my junior in rank, though not in service. I have not so much a personal feeling about it, for the pleasure of being with you would far outweigh that, if it existed, but one must look a little to what folks might say and think. The command of a company of Guards is not a bad one, is agreeable without too much responsibility; and, if I rise, I am gaining experience in my proper branch of the service. Besides I flatter myself I can command a company of Guards, and being up to one's work is always satisfactory.

The news of the place is next to nil. The Sardinians are arriving fast and to my mind are certainly much finer, smarter men than the French.[138] Their officers are younger and are as a whole more gentlemanlike, fewer rising from the ranks. Some of my old Sardinian friends are to arrive in a few days. I quite incline now to your opinion as to the necessity of investing the town before taking it. We are certainly increasing our batteries most formidably, both in weight of metal, closeness and number of guns, but the Ruski is not idle.

The weather is getting tremendously hot but the men improve in health and spirits. If we could only get rid of this siege, how we should chaw them up in the open!

Give my best love to Aunt Charlotte. Make her your first thought.

*   *   *

61

Frances Scarlett to Sarah, Lady Abinger
3 Chester Square, London, 24 May 1855

Chester Square, London, 24 May 1855
My dearest Mother, You will not see me till Saturday; that is unless the fancy takes me to go home, which is not improbable, as I never feel in the same mind for two minutes together. Aunt Fanny and I went out in the carriage and did business together; and, after a quiet dinner, I went off to Stratheden House in order to get the maid there to dress me. Hally drove up to the door at the same time with me, having just returned from Epsom. We had tea together and talked till the evening party was well assembled.

The General came and was the *lion* of the evening.[139] Young ladies rushed up to me. 'Will you just point out General Scarlett to me?'; and all that kind of thing. He stood in the centre of a circle and happy were those who had a right to go up and claim acquaintance. He was very kind to Jane West, and she delighted.[140] I conveyed them both home in my brougham. I thought it a pretty arrangement, as it will be *nuts* to Jane to be able to say that she had been three in a brougham with General Scarlett.

Everybody seemed to me to be grown very old; probably they thought the same of me. There was Mrs Carew, once rather pretty, grown into a wizen little witch; Lady Dowrich faded and passée.[141] The world looked dim, haggard and covered with hair. Lady Mary Williams asked me to a ball, which I thought good natured, and Lady Alderson to a hop.[142] I talked to a number of people and thought them all a nuisance.

The General said Aunt Charlotte had been out with him in his brougham. Earl, the Stratheden House maid, knows of a travelling maid who has lived seven years with Mrs Bathurst.

Your candles came yesterday. I will bring them down. Tell Mrs Moore I have thrown out feelers about Scutari Hospital.[143] The Richardsons are going to write immediately to Miss Stanley to know what opening there is.[144] When I said I knew a lady who wanted to go out as superintendent, Helen cried, 'How odd that a day, no two days ago, I was applied to for just such a person, and I answered I was not the least likely to hear anything of anyone to suit.' She had forgotten the *name* of the applicant, but was going to find out, somehow or another, all about it. So I hope to have something to tell when I come down.

The children have come to dine. I am going to take them to see a light of some kind, and afterwards I dine at Stratheden House. Aunt Fanny is rather disordered – the prawns of course.[145] I wish I were at home. I always wish I was where I am not. I should like to go to Stratheden House, only I cannot leave Aunt Fanny, who is very glad I stay with her, unless I go to Peter, and to move is a bother.

I wish we were on our road to Constantinople. I don't tell a creature of the plan of our going. All the speculations of what is to become of 'poor Miss Scarlett' amuse me. The family of course know of it. Hally is longing to join the party and have a berth in the yacht. If he could only make out to his own and everybody else's satisfaction the immense use he could be to us all, he would settle his affairs and be ready for a start tomorrow. He and I made lovely plans how *we* would manage *you* all; and, when you were all safe in your inn, we should go out and amuse ourselves together. We talked of one plan till it seemed the most natural thing in the world. My best love to Mrs Moore.[146] Don't tell her any of my nonsense. I hope you are pretty well, ever yours affectionately, FMS.

Cover, The Lady Abinger, Abinger Hall, Dorking, Surrey. Postmark, Dorking, 25 May 1855.

*   *   *

62

Sir James Yorke Scarlett to Frances Scarlett
Crimea, 3 August 1855

Crimea, 3 August 1855

My dear Fanny, Sir James sends you his most affectionate thanks for your congratulations and, if he lives to see your smiling face again, will be very happy to show you the fine decorations which at present he has not got. My honours are quite equal to my deserts, and far beyond them, but there is a note out of tune that makes discord of the whole.[147] My lofty aspirations are brought down when I reflect on *what price* I have paid for them.

I do not know if Willy by last post informed you that his dignity has come into collision with his inclinations, and that he had, as field officer, been required to give up his appointment as ADC and return to his regimental duties.[148] We fought about it with his colonel, Lord Rokeby, a little; but, the dignity of the Guards being concerned, we could not succeed.[149] Thus, with one ADC married and can't come, another sick by the way, and one too big to be useful except in the Guards, I am left with Conolly for my sole companion, and our happy family entirely dwindled into us two.[150] We shall fill up the blanks soon, but we don't fancy a new set quite.[151]

We are digging away like other moles to undermine this weary town, which will finish by making fresh works behind those we destroy. In fact, until we can shut the back door, I believe we shall never get into the front. No one seems to have the power to adopt the only course. I have nothing to do with the matter: it is an infantry, artillery and engineers affair entirely.

I have just had an interview with General Markham,[152] who has arrived from England to put all things to rights; but, like other remedies, he disagrees with some; and Lord Rokeby became indignant that Markham should have a division and he only a brigade of Guards; so to smooth matters they have made the brigade of Guards into a division, which makes all right.[153] How much in a name!

My forces are daily increasing by men and horses dropping in from various steamers. I am now nearly up to four thousand; but half of them untrained and hardly able to get on a horse; and quite unable to keep on him without a little more practice.[154] Poor old Bull is paying for his economy, in former days, by paying double now and having a bad article.

Lord Raglan is a great loss.[155] The present general is a very gentlemanlike man, and I like him, but we know nothing of him in the field and he has a command for the first time.[156] We rather talk about the fifteenth as a day for something to be done.[157]

What are your plans? Will you go to the sea with the Erlwood family?[158] Louise writes comparatively good accounts of poor Charlotte. That she is not worse is very clear – but to those who were not so much with her as I was. So that I am not so much struck with the improvement and consider that, as she is better known, she appears to more advantage and more like her former self. However, that her health is better, and that she takes more air and exercise, and does not shut herself up, is much gained. I trust all will yet come right. I hope that poor Addy's little child may do her good by interesting and attracting her.[159] If she takes an interest in anything, it is so much gained.

What are your plans? There is a letter from your mother to Willy which I think he will come for today. If not, I shall send it this evening to his camp. All London will now, I conclude, be going out of town to shoot grouse; and the war will be left to its own legs to trudge on as well, or as ill, as it can. I see that Roebuck's motion has ended in a majority for ministers.[160] If they stay in town, and keep Parliament sitting till the war is over, they will die in their places, for I see no termination to it.

Suppose Sebastopol is taken, the war is not over.[161] Suppose the Crimea is occupied; the war is not over. I see no probable event to finish it. You may put a child in the corner but can't make it say it will be good if it is obstinate; and if you keep it in the corner you must stay and watch it, or it will come out and be naughty again; and, if it is as big as yourself, it may come out in spite of you.

Well, goodbye Fanny. Give my love to My Lord and Lady, to both of whom I shall write by next post. I have not heard from Peter and don't write because I don't know that my letter will reach him.[162] Ever your affectionate Uncle Jim.

* * *

63

Sir James Yorke Scarlett to Frances Scarlett
Crimea, 29 September 1855

My dearest Fanny, I think this will find you *facing* your nerves under the shadow of Ben Nevis.[163] I have nothing in particular to say of things here except that Willy and I are both well and leading lazy lives.[164] Not to hear the thundering of cannon is the only novelty: a little, however, still goes on between the north and south sides of the harbour; and the town is too much commanded from the north for any groups to stand chatting in any exposed place. A poor soldier, who thought he was cooking in a very secure spot, was surprised and killed by the splinter of a shell.[165]

I do not anticipate any advance. The position of the Russians on the north side is not attackable in front, and to separate our army and land a portion at Eupatoria would lay us open to an attack on Kamiesh and Balaklava with a diminished force to resist it; and, whilst we were kicking up a row at Eupatoria, we might find our base of operations at Balaklava and Kamiesh cut off from us.[166] Consequently, what the *Times* may write notwithstanding, I think we will hear of no more battles this year.[167]

The 10th Hussars, that is a squadron sent to Kertch with a squadron of Chasseurs d'Afrique, got beyond their depth the other day, to cut off some arabas, and a troop of the 10th got surrounded by some two thousand Cossacks.* They cut their way through but the 10th lost about fifteen men

---

* This action, on 21 September 1855, was reported in many British newspapers. See, for instance, the *Liverpool Standard and General Commercial Advertiser*, 23 October 1855. 'The detachments of Chasseurs d'Afrique and of the 10th Hussars went out for a reconnaissance, the former as first column, the second in support. The Chasseurs d'Afrique, being as much as ten or twelve miles ahead, fell in with a body of Russian cavalry numbering nigh 600 men and, not being able to encounter them with such odds, being only a troop of scarcely more than 100 men, they sent back to the place where the Hussars were stationed to get reinforcements. The commander of the latter, unwilling to leave the position which was to insure a safe retreat unprotected, left one troop there, and advanced with the other; but, as the distance was considerable and it was essential not to fatigue the horses, he could only arrive at nightfall at the appointed spot. The French Chasseurs, in the meantime, had found means of retiring, and when the morning broke the troop of Hussars found itself alone, and its retreat cut off by the Russian cavalry, which, in following the French, had come into the rear. So nothing remained but to break a way through the enemy's squadrons, and this was done most gallantly, with the loss of only sixteen men – a new proof the Russian cavalry has not the least chance, even with such great odds in its favour, in encountering English cavalry, whether Dragoons or Hussars, light or heavy; but it is likewise a slight memento of the often-experienced, one might say, stale truth, that divided command is just as bad, if not worse, for cavalry than for infantry, and that it does not answer better in field than in siege operations.'

and the Chasseurs d'Afrique eight. How many Cossacks suffered I don't yet know. They acted imprudently but very gallantly to ride on themselves. The 10th were commanded by Captain Fitzclarence, a son of my old friend George Fitzclarence, Earl of Munster.[168]

The weather is getting somewhat Ben Nevisish of a morning and evening – 'bracing' – but the sun is powerful in the midday. Quarters for the cavalry are being prepared on the Bosphorus. I hope to get home by December at latest, but nothing is certain in these times. I hear not worse accounts of my dear wife from Louise, who writes to me so kindly by every post.[169] In some things Charlotte seems quite herself, but she wants the spring of hope. She will not be comforted etc. Exactly what is the dark cloud on her mind I am uncertain. She cannot sit down to write to me. She directs sometimes a newspaper, selecting those she thinks will interest me most, and I believe that I am in her thoughts constantly; but what she thinks or wishes I am in the dark about. It is very queer, as there is no bright star for me to look forward to, though I do not despair and see a glimmering of light.

I am afraid the grouse will find you long walks to look for them this year, as I imagine them not to be plentiful. Willy dined with me yesterday and we discussed home matters. He is getting stout and a walk on the Lochy's banks would do him good.[170] I hope he will be able to get home this winter. I confess I do not see *Peace* anywhere. Now we have got Sevastopol and destroyed the fleet, or made the Russians do it, we are just as far off as ever from any definite object. As long as Russia has a bomber, she will resist and give us a dance here, there and everywhere.

The corporal is come for the letters. Therefore I must terminate in haste, with love to all around you who care for me, your affectionate uncle, J. Yorke Scarlett.

Chapter 6

Aldershot

In line with his deserved reputation and his abilities. General Scarlett had a distinguished career in the army after his return from the Crimea. After three years commanding the southern division of the army, while acting as Governor of Portsmouth, he became Adjutant General for five years. As Adjutant General he was a key figure at the centre of the army, based at the Horse Guards.[1] His final post, from 1865 to 1869, was to what was considered the plum appointment as Commandant of Aldershot. He retired from the army on 1 November 1869, when he was promoted to the rank of full general.

As well as rank, he received many awards and honours. Knighted in the Crimea in 1855, he was promoted to the Grand Cross of the Order of the Bath in 1869. Although he was not awarded the Victoria Cross, he was given the Sardinian Al Valore Militare and the Turkish Order of Medjidieh (second class).

His portrait was commissioned by the officers of the 5th Dragoon Guards, with engravings of it advertised by the *Morning Post* in July 1857:

> Major-General Sir J.Y. Scarlett on his favourite Charger, in command of the Brigade of Heavy Cavalry at Balaklava; painted for the officers of the 5th Dragoon Guards, by Francis Grant, RA, now exhibiting at the Royal Academy. A Highly-Finished Mezzotint ENGRAVING by Mr F. Bromley, size 27 inches by 21 high, is in progress, for which subscribers' names are received by the publishers, Messrs Froes, 41 Piccadilly, London W.[2]

He, in turn, presented to his old regiment, of which he was the colonel, a magnificent silver centrepiece, on which the side of the base showed scenes of the battles in which the regiment had been involved, including Balaklava, where the lead horseman, wearing his regimental helmet, is presumably the General himself.

He attended at least some Balaklava dinners, including one at the London Tavern in 1857 where the Earl of Lucan was also present:

Yesterday being the anniversary of the battle of Balaklava, the officers engaged on that occasion dined together at the London Tavern. Covers were laid for fifty. The chair was taken by General Sir James Scarlett, who was supported by the Earl of Lucan, Lord G. Paget, CB, Colonels Douglas, Hodge, CB, Conolly, Lowe, Mayow, Wardlaw, Shute and Hartopp, Majors Jenyns, Brown, and Manley; Captains George, Sandeman, Glynn and Hunt; Sir George Wombwell, Bart., &c.[3]

Scarlett, continuing the traditional stance of Wellington, which was to be continued by George, Duke of Cambridge as the Commander in Chief of the army, was not a reformer. He took, however, a keen interest in the Volunteer movement and was the honorary colonel of several regiments, including two in Burnley and in Lancashire, often inspecting them.

While there are very many official letters from General Scarlett during these years, and even more orders issued under his authority as Adjutant General, there are few personal letters. Charlotte Scarlett seems to have made a good recovery in the years after the Crimean War. In June 1860, for instance, she attended a state ball.[4] The Queen took an interest in her and asked after her health. There are a number of references to the General in her diaries. On 7 February 1856, after he dined at Windsor, she wrote: 'Sir J. Scarlett is a most amiable sensible man, and an excellent officer. He told us many interesting things.' Subsequently, he is mentioned frequently as a dinner guest at Osborne, particularly while he was Governor of Portsmouth.

His final posting at Aldershot came at a time when the camp was changing from a makeshift training area to the centre of the main military area in England.

64

Sir James Yorke Scarlett to Frances Scarlett
Windsor, 8 February 1856

Windsor Castle, 5.30 p.m.
My dear Fanny, I owe you a letter and, as I have been a long time in debt, I will at least remedy the neglect in some measure by writing you an epistle from a great house. As you will perceive from my date, I have but just arrived here and have been ushered into a snug little sitting-room about fourteen feet square, a good fire, a picture of William III on horseback or Prince Rupert – it may be either; a zebra, a red deer, a camel leopard or giraffe; and a portrait of Mather Brown.[5] Who he was when alive I am obliged to confess ignorance, but he was a good-looking fellow with a green velvet gown and black beard, for I take it from his costume he is not alive now and did not live yesterday. There is also a chest of drawers, commode and I write at a capital library table with right royal pens. And here I am in this grand castle till Friday – ain't it awful?[6]

The good man who ushered me in looks very good natured and will come to me a little before eight, he says, and shew me the way to the drawing room. Isn't he a good fellow? How would I ever have got there without him? I don't think there will be more than two miles of passages to walk, judging from appearances in the dark, as I seem quite at one end of the great court. However, that will give me an appetite for dinner and exercise, having had none today owing to the rain.

Out of this room is my bedroom with a French tent bed; and beyond that a small dressing room for washing. A great transition from the Crimea, whose mercies I suppose I may thank for my present position. But, on my honour, I don't know whether what I am about to encounter is not as formidable as the Russian line at Balaklava; but, as that danger vanished by opposing it, I shall hope to get through somehow; more especially as I retain a lovely recollection of Her Majesty's sweet smile and gracious manner at Buckingham Palace on two former occasions.

I have not the least notice who is here or to be here, but that will burst upon me ere long no doubt. In the meantime, I will tell you that I really will not obey your cruel behest to kill all my relations at one blow at Brighton, though I felt the greatest inclination to commit the wholesale slaughter.[7] But having to run up to Town three times, and really thinking my being with Charlotte seemed a comfort to her, I have not yet liked to leave her when I could avoid it; and I live in hopes of seeing you with a heart more at ease soon. I think we have improved and, though by no means well, that progress is made towards a more settled and comfortable state of mind. To a stranger, except that she is taciturn, there is nothing remarkable about her; and on common topics and people her judgement and opinions are sound and correct, her memory perfect on all subjects. The monomania is her distress about some imaginary evil that she cannot or will not name, some illness for which she will find no name, of which she will describe no symptom, for which she will see no medical man or seeing will not speak to him; some evil which she cannot name which haunts her perpetually and for which she conceives all kindness vain. I hope that this will vanish by keeping her in as good state of health as we can and by calming her nerves as much as possible; but no one can tell how trying it is to see her real distress without the ability to alleviate it. For, whether for real or imaginary evil, she certainly does grieve sadly and feels pain of mind.

I shall finish this when I come to bed and tell you my adventures.

11.30 p.m. According to my promise, I now bid you good night, my dear Fanny, having very little more to say than when I laid down my pen at eight and was ushered along the long passages; and, after a dire amount of walking, arrived at a fireplace with a lot of red collars and a few ladies of the household. After shaking hands with a few whom I knew, as Bouverie, Bowater, and some whose faces I knew but forgot their names, I accompanied the only guests into the drawing room: viz Colonel Gordon, Lord Aberdeen's son, and Mrs Gordon.[8] The others waited for the Queen and Prince, and preceded them into the drawing room, where both shook hands with Mrs Gordon and the Prince with me. And then all went to dinner. Very grand and good feeding.

After dinner we returned to the same drawing room. I had the honour of a conversation with Her Majesty and after with the Prince. Then came a host of violins and other instruments and played three pieces of music admirably. Then Her Majesty and her ladies sat at a table and drank tea; and the gentlemen stood anywhere and some played whist. At eleven the party broke up by the Queen and Prince's departure and I found my good man waiting to bring me here again with a promise at 9 a.m. (rather early) to come and take me to prayers and breakfast.

The remainder you shall have some other opportunity. I was decked out very fine, with star and red ribbon and medal clasps *selon les règles*.

Love to all Abinger, Père, Mère, Willy. Peter, I hear, is in London.[9] Ever, my dear Fanny, yours affectionately, J. Yorke Scarlett.

Cover, The Honourable Fanny Scarlett, Abinger Hall, Dorking (crossed out and 3 Chester Square). Postmark, Windsor, 9 February 1856.

*　*　*

65

Sir James Yorke Scarlett to Frances Scarlett
Erlwood, 4 June 1856

Erlwood, 4 June 1856

My dear Fanny, I was much pleased this morning to be greeted with a bulletin so favourable to my skill in pharmacy. Depend upon it that my medicine was that which cured you. Take it only when sick and it will prove a friend like other poisons, which all medicines are more or less. Besides the relief to my mind as to your health, which, as you properly observe, should have been worse only for the brandy, your letter is a great addition to my country interests, especially as the pleasing anxiety of ascertaining the advent of another egg is suddenly wrested from me by the deplorable fact, but one of which you duly warned me, that the bantam having filled her nest has most pertinaciously planted herself upon it, considering her egg-laying mission to be completed.

But I have since your departure some additional interests, not to console me for that want, for that is impossible, but to divert my mind in the acquisition of a brown puppy of the Windsor breed of spaniel, which though no bigger than my hand and only six weeks old has the talents of a much more advanced dog and licks the blacking off my shoes and does other puppy acts with great energy.

I have also got here my Crimean baggage and my horse Silvertail, the best of my stud of six horses and four mules, the remainder having been sold for very fair prices at Scutari.[10] The public not knowing his merits allowed him (Silvertail) to be bought for £59, whereas I value him more than those that sold for £95 and £91, between which prices all the others were sold. Of course I have lost on the whole, as I gave from £71 to £120 for them, but not more than the insurance on their safe voyage over would have come to. I miss my beating at chess every evening and have got deep into *China* by Mr Huc, a French missionary, which is not *so* interesting.[11]

We had a splendid day for the Wellington College.[12] Mary, Louisette and I, and Elly on horseback, went.[13] We drove up to the staircase of the compartment or block where our seats were without trouble and had a capital view of all the cortège at the stone laying; and, by a very short walk, gained the terrace from which we saw the review, which was good: the ground not favourable for manoeuvring but in shape etc like the valley of the Tchernaya on a small scale that the battle of the sixteenth of August might have been acted there – our terrace being taken for the French lines and our troops for Russians.[14]

The weather is still beautiful to an eastern degree and I think you would, in spite of London's charms and dissipation, be well placed at Erlwood or Abinger on such a day. We are going to drive and after that I shall take a small ride. I can give nothing new with reference to that which is my chief concern, except that Charlotte appeared in her new gown this morning, but it has not prevented the morning being spent as usual in lamentation and sighs, which rend the heart of her husband the more that he can offer no remedy to a grief unexplained. Would she but say what grief real or imaginary excited her mind, one might attempt a remedy. She has this moment got up to shut the window because I sneezed as if I had got a cold. What a mixture of care for others with a determination to do nothing for herself. Love to those who value it. Ever your affectionate J. Yorke Scarlett.

Cover, The Honorable Fanny Scarlett, Stratheden House, Knightsbridge, London. Postmark, Farnborough Station, 4 June 1856.

*   *   *

66

Sir James Yorke Scarlett to Frances Scarlett
Portsmouth, 9 October 1857

My dearest Fanny, You do not overrate the deep interest I take in all that concerns you.[15] There is no station of life which in my estimation would have been too splendid for you to fill with grace. But it is neither splendour nor riches which confer happiness; and a competency with a sensible, well principled gentleman capable of exciting and retaining your affection, and still more your esteem and respect, is in my opinion a happy lot; and what more can one ask for?

I agree with every word you have written, though I should no doubt have given you, had I the power, in addition to all the qualities which in a husband would have rendered you happy, both rank and wealth. Yet would I prefer seeing you married to a moderate income and a gentleman to all that rank and wealth could bestow without those qualities in your husband without which a wife learns quickly to become indifferent to or despise her husband; or even though loving, unable to respect and honour him.

If therefore you have found in Mr Sidney Smith one whom you can love and esteem, marry him; and don't delay. At your age and with your good sense you are well able to judge for yourself, and I recommend as little delay as possible. As the wife of a clergyman you will not be called on for great expence and I have no doubt, with prudence at present, will get on very happily.

I have not time for more at present. I may venture to tell Charlotte because I can perfectly depend upon her never opening her lips on the subject, till duly promulgated, if I tell her not. She is no worse and I think Ryde has done good, but it remains to be proved whether she will remain here with me or go to Erlwood next Tuesday. I proposed to Louise to remain here with me for a time at least, but she is anxious to get back to Erlwood, and though content to have Charlotte there does not like to be here with her – alas![16]

Ever, my dearest Fanny, your most affectionate J. Yorke Scarlett.

*   *   *

67

Sir James Yorke Scarlett to Frances Smith
Government House, Portsmouth, 4 February 1858

Government House, Portsmouth, 4 February 1858

My dear Fanny, 'I promised to send you a lock of my hair'. That seems like the beginning of a ballad, but I have not time even if I *had* the *intention* to continue it; but I do intend that you shall answer this and tell me how Mrs Sidney Smith progresses.[17] Whether she comports herself like a respectable matron and has already convinced her husband that she is at least worth five shillings or a crown. I have long entertained a notion you would make a most capital wife and I have very little fear of being ever obliged to confess to an error of judgement. I know you can talk and be silent, read, ride, walk, be cheerful, look good humoured and are discreet. What more can a man want?

But I will come someday to Brampton Ash and ask *Mr* Smith about it. Only just inform him that he must not make you forget your dutiful uncle – I flatter myself Peter and I are his most formidable rivals.[18]

I have no news to tell you. We have had so many proper princes here that we begin to look blue. The last, however (not the least, for there was upwards of two yards of him) left today and will no doubt be very sick crossing to France this evening. Now with best regards to your spouse and everlasting love to yourself, believe me your very affectionate J. Yorke Scarlett.

I have heard from Willy from New Orleans. He will be home by the first of next month because he can't help it.[19]

Cover, The Honorable Mrs Sidney Smith, Brampton Ash, Market Harboro'. Postmark, Portsmouth, 4 February 1858; Market Harborough, 4 February 1858.

*   *   *

68

Sir James Yorke Scarlett to Frances Smith
Portsmouth, 24 December 1858

Portsmouth, 24 December 1858
My dear Fanny, Most welcome was your letter, for, through my sins of correspondence or rather non-correspondence I have very few letters to tell me how the family world joys, and there is no part of it I am more interested in than yourself. I need not say how pleased I am to hear that all is *couleur de rose* with you and the purple light of love still sheds its soft radiance over you.[20] Long may it do so. Good sense, good humour, forbearance are the materials of a cage to keep the young vagrant, and it don't so much signify whether the bars be gold or copper so that the above are employed in its structure: when once thoroughly domesticated in his cage it requires a good deal of shaking to make him fly out and entirely away.

I trust you and your spouse will have a happy Xmas and many happy new years. I can't say much for my own merriment as we shall be quite alone, my staff flying off to be merry elsewhere; but every dog has his day and I must not grumble if, after years of happiness, many desires and aspirations granted, I find myself not without troubles in my latter days. I certainly should like to join an extensive Xmas party at Abinger if there is to be, as there ought to be, one; but there is no chance of it even if asked. I have not heard from my Lord for some time. Pedro is you see refixed at Florence, only hung on a Naples peg, but because not so high as at Rio what he formerly would have jumped up to with glee he now gets up to somewhat unwillingly and hardly thanks his stars for shining on him.[21]

I hear the dressing bell ring so will finish this tomorrow.

I think, to continue my thoughts of yesterday, that as far as Bina is concerned the advantage of being at Florence depends greatly on who Peter is able to put about her.[22] The society generally there is very bad and hers should be selected more carefully than a single man sometimes selects; yet notwithstanding all *your* experience, matrimony is a great lottery and one I should not urge Peter to enter into, though I should be glad if I *could secure* him a *good* wife. It would be a novelty to him, poor fellow. One may make a guess, but one cannot positively pronounce on wines without trying them – and that is not allowable, I believe.

I had a very kind invitation from Willy's regiment to go and dance in the Tower:[23] the idea of *dancing* in the Tower seems singular or seeing others dance, at least on terra firma. Axes, bowls of poison, daggers, a gentleman in rusty armour smothering tender babes seem more natural associations with the place than fiddles and crinolines. I should expect a strong taste of Malmsey in all the drinkables and the atmosphere must be of a *confined* nature in Julius' Tower. I am sure if I went there I should come away to dream I had seen all the beheaded heroes dancing with their heads under their arms with Beefeaters and crown jewels in red morocco and velvet cases in one quadrille.

I know nothing of your progenitors or their whereabouts but conjecture they must be at Abinger by this time. Next month the new rail – to London from hence is two hours – will be opened and pass through Gomshall, which will place me within an hour of Abinger; and I shall be caught at my old tricks of poaching no doubt some day my Lord's or his neighbour's partridges and surprising Sally at luncheon.[24]

Peter, Willy and I talk of a shooting partnership below hill, but whether it will come off or not I don't know. I am willing, for I don't know that I can spend money on two people I like more, though I should not expect to derive great benefit from it myself. It might possibly give Willy a reason for being more at Abinger. He talks of asking my Lord to make over to his care the farms and rents of them. I doubt his doing so, but he would be wise to do so as it would attach Willy to the place and give him some satisfaction and put an end to money matters between them.

Short accounts make long friendships they say, but I say no accounts at all make much longer and more secure ones. Let all your money transactions be with strangers whom it is lawful to hate and detest and then perhaps you won't so honour them.

Now, my dear Fanny, wishing to you and your husband a merry Xmas and happy new year and each succeeding happier still, believe me your very affectionate uncle, J. Yorke Scarlett.

I can't read this over so excuse repetition, if any.

Cover, The Hon. Mrs Sidney Smith, Brampton Ash, Market Harboro'. Postmark, Portsmouth, 24 December 1858; Market Harborough, 26 December 1858.

*   *   *

69

Sir James Yorke Scarlett to Sidney Lidderdale Smith
Horse Guards, 24 June 1861

Horse Guards, 24 June 1861
My dear Sidney, I am grieved to tell you that I have just heard of Lord Abinger's death, which took place this morning not more than ten minutes after I had left the house from the bursting of some internal vessel in the stomach.[25] Sir H. Holland has brought me this sad intelligence.[26] Poor Fanny begged me before I left this morning to write to you by post, lest you should not receive her telegram asking you to come to her. The sooner you can do the better, and the longer you can stay. This and the Chancellor's death are heavy afflictions.[27] Believe me yours affectionately, J. Yorke Scarlett.

*   *   *

70

Sir James Yorke Scarlett to Sidney Lidderdale Smith
London, 17 August 1861

25 Princes Terrace, 17 August 1861

My dear Sydney, I congratulate you on Fanny's safety and the possession of another arrow to your quiver.[28] A girl might have been a prettier plaything, but the boy is more fitted to meet the realities of life and I trust the newcomer will have all the requisites for the race. I daresay Master Harold will welcome his playmate with open arms.

I have not heard from Willy since he started for Scotland. He was somewhat annoyed that he could not be released from the forfeiture entailed by the will.[29] I was very willing to give such release, as I feel sure that, knowing Robert's real intentions and knowing the restriction placed on Willy was chiefly to satisfy Peter and myself, I think we might have stretched the point and that the spirit of the will was carried out; but, as I am the least concerned in the matter of any party, I did not think it right to persuade them to act as I did; not from the expense in law [which] must be incurred, and we shall be bound not by the testator's wishes but by the law's interpretation of them.

However, I see no reason for doubting that all and each will have their due and all disputes, if not all expence, will be avoided. With love to Fanny and the family, believe me yours affectionately, James Yorke Scarlett.

*   *   *

71

Note by Frances Smith

The cavalry returned in April 1856 and the General went at once to Erlwood to take charge of Aunt Charlotte, setting Aunt Lou (Lady Currey) free for a much needed rest. I spent some weeks in May at Erlwood. A short letter to my sister will give my impressions:

> Aunt Charlotte is worse than no companion to Uncle Jim. I read all the morning and, when we do not drive, I walk in the afternoons and he and I play chess all the evening. It is wonderful how unsatisfactory this sort of life is. The General is a charming companion and the best man that ever lived. My heart has preached to me a very good sermon ever since I have been here. It is a lesson to see how *he* bears his trial. I have never heard him say if such things had been done, or left undone, this would not have happened.

Uncle Jim was invariably cheerful and had a happy way of interesting himself in everyday things. A large aviary of pigeons were a constant source of amusement. Very often he drove Aunt Charlotte and me in his smart phaeton. He was at all hours of the day an interesting companion and liked recounting his Crimean experiences. Our battles at chess beguiled evenings which might have seemed long; but, as in style we were fairly matched, to win was a pleasant triumph to either; to be beaten made the next game additionally exciting. Aunt Charlotte would sit silently beside us. She was never averse to me, only moody. That visit to Erlwood was one of the good things in my life.

In the summer the General moved to Portsmouth, of which place he had been made Governor, and took Aunt Charlotte with him. In 1859 he was appointed Adjutant General and bought an excellent house in Ennismore Gardens, where they went to reside.[30] Gradually his continued attention and encouragement worked an improvement on Aunt Charlotte, though it was yet several years before she quite regained her normal state; but by degrees she emerged from her reclusion and made no objection to the family and intimate friends coming to the house.[31] Whenever I went to London I went to see her and marked the improvement. On one occasion we were sitting in the window of the drawing room, looking up Ennismore Gardens, and she saw Sidney walking up and down; he was waiting for me. 'Who is that man?'

– she knew really quite well. 'It is Sidney, my husband.' 'The next time you come, you may bring him in.' That was all, but I knew all it meant: awakened kindness, curiosity and interest. We soon called and Sidney was graciously received. To my surprise, she presented me one day with a beautiful locket and chain, green chrysolite with pearls and rubies. The General was jubilant about that locket. By such acts to him and many others did she show her return to *herself*, ever the kindest and most considerate and generous of human beings.

In 1865 she offered to be godmother to Bob and sent him £50.[32] I forget at what date the General persuaded her to get on horseback again. She had ridden all her life constantly. Once again, magnificently mounted, she rode daily with him to the War Office. She told me that as soon as she was in the saddle she felt as much at home as if she had ridden only the day before.

The complete resumption of her social position may be marked by her presentations at Court. The *Morning Post* records her brave attire in 1867:

> The Honourable Lady Scarlett, train of magnificent mauve broché satin lined with white glacé and bordered with rouleaux of mauve velvet and edged with white satin; skirt of the richest white satin with garniture of tuile, and festoons and bows of Irish lace. Tiara, stomacher etc, etc of diamonds; headdress floral and lappets.

The Queen was always much interested in Lady Scarlett and, whenever the General met her, asked after her most particularly. Her womanly heart understood how great the trouble had been, and how loyal the General had shown himself both to Queen and wife.

There were two especially pleasant events in these years that I would like to record. One was a visit in the winter of 1867, when Sidney and I spent the New Year's Day and a week afterwards at Bank Hall, Burnley, with Uncle Jim and Aunt Charlotte. The house was full: a gay and lively party; the host and hostess delightful and doing all they could to make their guests at home and happy. The men had capital shooting, in spite of snow. No one could be cold indoors, for there were blazing fires in every room, including bedrooms, all day long, and general cheerfulness prevailed.

The other pleasant event was a visit of a few days we paid later on to Aldershot. The General was there commanding. He had a charming house, Forest Lodge, on the outskirts of the camp. We saw reviews, which Aunt Charlotte attended on Champion, her sixteen-hand splendid chestnut.[33] We had dinner parties at which the military element largely prevailed and went to the military chapel.

One feature, charmingly characteristic of the General, I will not omit. He had in the garden a very large cage of guinea-pigs, and a daily visit to these most uninteresting of animals was part of the programme. The Duke of Cambridge and all his glittering staff came one day after an inspection or review to lunch at Forest Lodge and royalty caused no agitation to Aunt Charlotte.

Chapter 7

Burnley

Although often absent on duty, General Scarlett was the most prominent man in Burnley, his home for thirty-six years.[1] Due to his marriage to Charlotte Hargreaves, he was also the wealthiest man in Burnley and the highest ratepayer. He was active in promoting many charitable causes in the town, notably those to do with church extension and education. He was also active in public matters and had almost stood in 1852 as a Conservative in the county election for North Lancashire, only to withdraw his name just before the contest. His national reputation, allied to his high moral standing, generosity and affability, ensured that he was held in high esteem by the inhabitants of Burnley.

His local reputation and influence were, however, exposed to a severe test in 1868, the year of the first election under the Second Reform Act, passed by Disraeli's Conservative government in 1867.[2] Under the Act Burnley, as a rapidly growing manufacturing town, had become a constituency for the first time.[3] The question the election raised was whether the newly-enfranchised borough, where a much broader range of electors had been given the vote for the first time, would back the traditional rulers of the country in the Conservative gamble of widening the franchise; or would support the Liberals, strongly entrenched in Lancashire's rapidly expanding industrial towns.

The Second Reform Act had settled a long-standing and highly contentious issue which had divided both parties. A cautious extension of the franchise, proposed in 1866 by the Liberal Prime Minister, Earl Russell,[4] had split the Liberals and resulted in a minority Conservative government. This was led by the Earl of Derby, as Prime Minister in the Lords, and Benjamin Disraeli, as Chancellor of the Exchequer, in the Commons.[5] In February 1867 Disraeli introduced a Conservative Reform Bill. Against a background of popular unrest, including major demonstrations organised by the Reform League,[6] the Conservative Bill ended up being considerably more radical than the Liberal Bill of the previous year. In the process of its passage through Parliament, the Liberal leader William Gladstone and Disraeli himself both introduced and accepted amendments which dramatically extended the franchise to include all men who paid rates in urban areas.[7]

The Act also made substantial changes to the constituencies. Four boroughs were disenfranchised for corruption and many smaller boroughs had their representation reduced from two MPs to one. Nine boroughs, however, nearly all in the north of England, became entitled to return an MP for the first time.[8] Amongst these was Burnley, previously part of the county seat of North Lancashire. With a population of 45,000, its new electorate numbered over 6000. By drawing the constituency boundaries close to those of the borough, the Act made the county seat safer for the Conservatives by the subtraction of Burnley, but in doing so excluded potential Conservative voters living in areas near to but outside the borough.

The first general election under the new Act was held in November 1868. The Liberals had lobbied strongly for Burnley to be enfranchised. As the Burnley Reform Association 'for the advancement of political and social economy and retrenchment in local and imperial taxation', they had petitioned for Parliamentary Reform.[9] Their candidate in the 1868 election was Richard Shaw, a local factory owner.

The Conservatives responded in early 1868 by forming the Burnley Constitutional Club, aimed at defending the constitution and church. As they needed a strong candidate if they were to have any chance of defeating Shaw, they approached General Scarlett, as the leading local Conservative, to ask him to stand as the Tory candidate. Scarlett was not the originator of the suggestion that he should stand but agreed to do so out of a sense of duty. How far he did so out of personal loyalty to his long-term friend, the Earl of Derby, is uncertain.

The Liberals recognised the threat that the General's candidacy was to them:

> It is quite clear that the Tories had but one card to play and that card was General Scarlett. No other name was ever mentioned, so far as we can learn, as that of Tory candidate for Burnley. And why? Was he not a soldier? Did he not employ a large number of persons to get and sell his coal for him? And were not these people proverbial for their little knowledge of public affairs, most easily imposed upon, humbugged and coerced?[10]

For the first fifty-five years of the General's life, the evidence for his activities and views is often sparse. The election campaign of 1868 in Burnley, however, was extensively covered by the two local newspapers in Burnley, supporting opposing sides. The *Burnley Advertiser* supported the Conservatives, while the *Burnley Gazette* supported the Liberals. Both reported the election at great length, disagreeing with each other about the merits and views of the two candidates, and about their likelihood of success.[11]

Because of the uncertainty about the consequences of the Reform Act as a whole, and in particular about its effects in the industrial north, the election was hard fought. In Burnley, as elsewhere, the contest involved both national and local issues. These included the traditional dividing lines between the Conservatives and Liberals: the cost of government, the control of education and the position of the established church. Both sides sought to take the credit for past reforms, including the Abolition of Slavery, the Repeal of the Corn Laws and the extension of the franchise itself.[12]

A particular issue was the question of the endowment of the Church of Ireland, which enjoyed most of church income in Ireland but only represented some of the Protestant minority there (excluding both Catholics and Protestant nonconformists). Gladstone threatened to disestablish the Church of Ireland and to redistribute its income. This was a policy strongly attacked by the General in his speeches, as representing the thin end of a wedge which would lead in turn to the disestablishment of the Church of England and to a wholesale attack on property rights.

> I do not care for calling the Irish Church a part of the Church of the United Kingdoms of Great Britain and Ireland. I say it is the Church of the United Kingdom, and I do object to that little 's' in the United Kingdoms of Great Britain and Ireland. I say it is one kingdom, and must be so. From the relative situation of England and Ireland in the nature of things it must be so. If Ireland was three thousand miles away, it might be different; but, as it is close to us, it must be united to us. The county of Dublin should be as much part of it as the county of Surrey, or the county of Hampshire, and it will ultimately be so.[13]

The General based his campaign on tradition and on the virtues of the British constitution, with the monarch presiding over two Houses of Parliament.

> I am no orator; I pretend not to eloquence, but in a few words I will tell you that I am a supporter of the Throne and of the British Constitution. I consider that our constitution, our limited monarchy, our House of Peers, and our House of Commons ensures to the people of England as perfect a freedom, and infinitely more, than any republic that ever yet existed. Our limited monarchy has advantages that no republic gives and it is free from its vices. Our limited monarchy is such that it must be governed, it must be ruled, by public opinion. Her Majesty the

Queen reigns over this country by her ministers. These ministers are responsible to the House of Peers and to the House of Commons, and the House of Commons is elected by the people and public opinion, and after it has been properly discussed, after the wheat has been winnowed from the chaff, that public opinion will invariably prevail.[14]

Local and personal issues were also raised. The *Burnley Gazette* questioned the General's record as an employer and queried his military record. The paper accused him of keeping the price of coal in Burnley artificially high and of preventing the establishment of a town cemetery because it was near Bank Hall. It also reminded Liberals of the active part played by the General's father in the prosecution of the Chartists in Lancashire.[15]

General Sir James Yorke Scarlett professes the Toryism of an ultra school. His politics are the politics of a dragoon, and he drives them fast and far. He has been fifty years in the army; his civilian recollections date from the era of blanketeering expeditions and Peterloo massacres, when his father, the Sir James Scarlett of those days, the Lord Abinger of ours, acted as the official prosecutor of miserable men, whom famine and bad government had driven to the verge of rebellion.[16]

As an election in a new seat at a time of uncertainty, held before the introduction of the ballot box, there was a good deal of rough behaviour, each side accusing the other of intimidation and dirty tricks. Both sides held mass rallies, heckled by their opponents. Both sides also sought to influence opinion, with the Liberals bringing in a Radical professor from Oxford and the Anglican clergy urging their congregations to support Scarlett.[17]

After an eventful campaign, a poll was called for after a contested hustings. The final result was announced on Wednesday 18 November. Out of a registered electorate of 6817, Richard Shaw had 2620 votes to General Scarlett's 2238, giving Shaw a majority of 382. Burnley continued to return Liberals throughout the rest of the nineteenth century, but twice returned Conservatives between 1900 and the First World War. A number of Conservatives were, however, returned in Lancashire in 1868, including at Blackburn. As the General wrote, after his defeat, in a letter to his supporters:

Though your efforts to return a Conservative Member to Parliament have not on this occasion been crowned with success, do not be discouraged by temporary defeat. The election has been carried by about the number who, on being canvassed, declined to give their sentiment. The fact has been elicited that there exists in this large population of working men a strong body who will support the Throne and Protestant institutions which have rendered England the home of freedom and liberty of conscience.[18]

Overall, the general election of 1868 produced a large majority for the Liberals. The result was not, however, without hope for the future for the Conservatives, by demonstrating the existence of a strong working-class Tory vote. In subsequent general elections between 1868 and 1905, the Conservatives, helped by a split in the Liberals over Irish Home Rule, were mainly victorious nationally.

Scarlett had, however, fought a gallant campaign. In recognition of this, he and his wife were honoured by Conservative presentations in the following year. On Thursday, 4 February 1869, Lady Scarlett was presented with a vase by the 'Conservative Ladies of Burnley':

Thursday was quite a gala day with the Conservatives of Burnley, especially with the ladies, who had fixed on that day for the presentation of a magnificent vase, of the value of £360, to Lady Scarlett, in grateful recognition of the services which Lieutenant General the Hon. Sir James Yorke Scarlett had rendered at the recent election by contesting the borough on Constitutional principles.[19]

In August 1869, again reported at length in the two local newspapers, the General himself was presented with two vases by the Conservative Working Men of Burnley on an occasion attended by thousands of supporters in the grounds of Bank Hall:

The strength of this attachment was evidenced by the presentation, on 14 August 1869, of two very handsome vases in the Italian style with very rich *repousée* ornaments; their general form being an oval resting on a tripod, producing a novel and striking effect. On the cover was a figure of Fame, appropriately holding in her hands emblems of the various industries of Burnley; on the space between the two handles were shields, carrying in high relief on one side a representation of the charge of the Heavy Brigade at Balaklava; and on the other the Battle of Brunnanburgh,[20] while in the centre of the tripod was a carefully executed model of the general on horseback in his full uniform.

In the afternoon there was one of the finest processions ever organised in Burnley, no fewer than 10,000 taking part in it. Subsequently 8500 were provided with tea and 300 ladies and gentlemen partook of luncheon in a marquee erected in Bank Hall meadow. Major (now Sir John) Thursby presided,[21] and the presentation was made by Mr Thomas Whittam who stated that the vases, which had cost £300, had been subscribed for chiefly by workmen, the number being 4137. Each of the vases bore the inscription:

> Presented to Lieutenant General the Honourable Sir James Yorke Scarlett, GCB, by the Conservative Working Men of Burnley as a token of the profound esteem with which they regard him, not only as a soldier of long and distinguished service and honourable merit, and as a private gentleman whose Christian virtue and great benevolence has endeared him to the various ranks of society, but especially for the noble spirit of self-sacrifice with which he contested this borough in the Conservative interest.

> A beautifully illuminated address accompanied the vases, in a prominent position being an excellent photograph of the General surrounded by cherubims, with a wreath of laurel above, and at the foot a sleeping lion with the motto, 'He shines with unstained honours.'[22]

72

Burnley Gazette, 18 May 1868

Reasons Why Mr R. Shaw Should Represent Burnley in Parliament

1 Mr Shaw is a native of Burnley, and a man of the people.
2 Mr Shaw is well acquainted with the wants of the town and could therefore forward our interests in Parliament.
3 Mr Shaw is commercial and manufacturing man, therefore a fit and proper person to represent our commercial and manufacturing community.
4 Mr Shaw is a sound Liberal and strongly in favour of economy and retrenchment in the expenditure.
5 Mr Shaw would vote in the interests of the working men.

Reasons Why General Scarlett Should Not Represent Burnley in Parliament

1 General Scarlett is not a native of Burnley and not a man of the people.
2 General Scarlett knows nothing of the wants of our town and could not therefore forward our interests in Parliament.
3 General Scarlett is not a commercial or manufacturing man, and therefore is not a fit and proper person to represent the commercial and manufacturing interests of the town.
4 General Scarlett is a Tory, and being a military man would naturally be in favour of a large and extravagant expenditure on the army and navy.
5 General Scarlett would vote in the interests of the aristocracy and not in the interests of the working man. The Tories have not waited for an answer from General Scarlett, but have at once formed themselves into election committee in his behalf. The Liberals have done so for Mr Shaw, and hence both parties have committed themselves to the contest.

*   *   *

73

General Scarlett's Adoption
Burnley Advertiser, 14 November 1868

On Monday night, General Scarlett met his friends and supporters in Mr Newsome's Circus. The platform – the boxes of the circus – was principally devoted to the ladies, a large number being present. Other portions of it, and the balcony and promenade, were occupied by the principal supporters of the candidate. The ring had been supplied with seats, so that every portion of the large building was made available for the comfortable accommodation of the audience, which numbered about four thousand. The sight was one of the most imposing character, every part being crowded with anxious listeners.

The entrance of Sir James Scarlett was the signal for taking up the cheering that had been heard outside when his carriage drove up to the doors; and heartier cheering and more enthusiastic waving of hats and handkerchiefs could never be. Mr Greenwood presided.[23] The chairman, after the greeting his rising called forth had subsided, said the great event that would decide who was to be first member for Burnley was near at hand. He referred to the abuse that had been heaped upon General Scarlett by the supporters of his rival candidate. General Scarlett had been a liberal benefactor to the town; but what had Mr Shaw done for it? He professed himself to be a sincere member of the Established Church. If they might judge of a man by the company he kept, Mr Shaw would have some difficulty convincing them of this. Who were his friends? His principal supporters had for their object the separation of Church and State. They cared nothing for the Irish Church, but in so far as it was a stepping stone for the attack on the English Church. They must judge of a man not by his words but by what he did. (Cheers.)

General Sir J.Y. Scarlett, who was received with great cheering, said:

I am glad to meet you on this occasion. It is impossible for me to see all of you individually at your own homes to explain the grounds on which I solicit your suffrages. I am glad also on this occasion to see that we are honoured with the presence of some ladies, because I know that, wherever they appear, they shed grace and geniality over the assembly (applause), and I am sure that neither by word or deed will any Conservative or Liberal in this place betray the confidence they have placed in us. (Hear, hear.)

I believe I may say that on this occasion I address more particularly the district of Trinity and Wood Top. There was no room in that district which would hold so large an assembly, and therefore we have assembled here tonight. The last time I had the honour of addressing an assembly at Trinity and Wood Top was upon the occasion of Lady Scarlett laying the first stone of the Wood Top School (hear, hear), and I am very glad to find that the Wood Top School is now opened, and that it is in full work and prospering. (Hear, hear.)[24] Upon the occasion of laying the foundation stone, I believe Mr Shaw was a generous subscriber, and I was in hopes to have met him that day, and that he would have honoured the proceedings by his presence, but it so happened he was out grouse shooting, I believe (laughter), that day and could not attend. I have no doubt that was the case, but I never dreamt at that moment that he and I should be placed as opponents for the suffrages of the electors of Burnley, though, perhaps, with his acute mind, coming events might have cast their shadows before, and so, perhaps, he did not wish to meet me on that occasion. (Hear, hear.)

I should have been glad to meet him because I had a great regard for him. I had known not him alone, but his father before him – and if I mention the dead, and those who have passed away, it is not to injure their memories but to praise them. (Cheers.) Mr Shaw's father was a solicitor, and a great friend of my late father-in-law, Colonel Hargreaves. He was trusted by the Colonel, and he was a faithful friend to the Colonel, and was, moreover, a most excellent Conservative. (Cheers.) I lamented exceedingly when he was taken from us; and the goodwill and friendship which I felt for him was inherited by his son; and, as a proof of that – though he may have forgotten it – when there was some little difficulty about his succeeding to his father's place in the office of Shaw and Artindale, Mr Thursby and I exerted ourselves to smooth any little difficulty there was in the way. I do not know what influence we had, but Mr Shaw succeeded not only to the office of his father, but he succeeded as our solicitor; and during the time he was so employed I must give him the credit to say that he acted in a most honourable and upright manner and that I had every reason to respect him. (Cheers.)

Nor, gentlemen, do I blame, or find the least fault with him, that he is my opponent on this occasion. If everything is conducted as it should be between gentlemen, there will be no reason why, because we differ in politics, there should any personal ill-feeling between us. (Cheers.) Between me and Mr Shaw there is none, because I do not believe for a moment that he would be party to the abuse and the scurrilous language that has been employed with regard to myself (hear, hear), but at the same time I must say that I was a little surprised to find that he had brought a prophet into this land in the shape of one Mr Rogers. (Laughter.)[25] Like Balak of old, perhaps he wanted a prophet to curse me. (Laughter.)[26] Whether he went to a high or low place I do not know, but he did go to some place, and got one to curse me – one who, not content with cursing me, even intruded on the grave of my father; he was not content with abusing me as a soldier, but he must rake up the ashes of the dead. (Shame.)

Now I do not condescend to enter into the defence of the late Lord Abinger – it is not necessary to do so – but I was reading only yesterday a very interesting work which I take in, called *Notes and Queries*, and there I met with an epitaph upon the late Lord Scarbrough in very nervous language,[27] such as they used in that day, but I think it so apposite to the late Lord Abinger that I venture to quote it:

> In courts lived devoid of slavish fear,
> Nor lost the Briton in the British peer,
> Honoured and loved all the world beside,
> One man accused him, and that base one lied. (Loud cheers.)

Now I do not wish for a better epitaph for the late Lord Abinger, and there I leave that subject. I will only say this that Mr Shaw would not have used that language, because Mr Shaw knew Lord Abinger well, and knew me well, and my career as well, and would not personally have made use of that language; but it surprised me that he should stand by and that at the end of Mr Rogers' speech he should thank Mr Rogers for what he had said. (A voice: 'Shame on him'.)

An honest man may see a thief commit robbery, and yet not be an accomplice, but if he consents to that robbery, if he thanks the thief, and expects that some benefit will accrue to him from the robbery, then how stands the case? Is he an accomplice or is he not? (Cries of 'Yes'.) I have no more to say upon that point.

Mr Shaw opposes me not personally but upon principle: he opposes upon the principle of Liberalism. Very well, I have no objection to that; but in what respect is Liberalism better than Conservatism? Is Liberalism more loyal to the Queen, to the throne of this kingdom? (No.) Is Liberalism more devoted to the Protestant institutions of this country – to the Church and State? (No.) Is it more eager than Conservatism that public opinion should be filtered through the House of Commons, discussed in the House of Lords, and when found to be correct it shall be carried into law? No, gentlemen, not so. What then does Liberalism claim to itself? Did the Liberals pass the Catholic Emancipation?[28] No, it was the Duke of Wellington. Did the Liberals repeal the Corporation and Test Acts?[29] No, it was Lord Derby. Were the slaves in the West Indies manumitted by the Liberals? No, Lord

Derby was the person who did it. Did the Liberals give you the repeal of Corn Laws? No, it was Sir Robert Peel. (Cheers.)[30] Did the Liberals give you that Reform in Parliament which now sends these men to be spoken to by me tonight? No, it was the Conservatives. (Loud cheers.)

Well, you will say, but it was consequence of the agitation of the Liberals; it was because the Liberals constantly agitated, and they drove the Conservatives to pass these laws. They drove the Conservatives but the Conservatives would have gone there themselves – they only waited to see the subjects properly discussed; and, when the proper time arrived, public opinion prevailed and these laws were carried. Therefore, if the Liberals do so well as agitators in opposition, all I can say is let them remain there (hear, hear, and cheers); but I have no objection occasionally to give them a turn at the helm, because without they do not know the difficulty of navigation. (Hear, hear.)

Now during the time they have been in power what great benefit have we derived from the Liberals? (A voice: 'None'.) I will not answer that myself; I will leave those who are on the side of the Liberals to answer the question for themselves. (A voice: 'The New Poor Law Act'.) I address here gentlemen who are connected with our manufactures as operatives and therefore whose interests it is the duty of the legislature to study. Now I could read to you nineteen Acts brought by the Conservatives for the purpose of bettering the condition of the operatives in mines and in factories; and I can tell you that most of these measures were opposed by the Liberals, and more especially by Mr Bright.[31] (Hear, hear.)

Now Mr Bright I believe to be an exceedingly clever man, and he has that about him which would have made a good lawyer too, because he knows where to put the strong point and keep back the weak one. (Laughter). He tells you in a speech the other day how Cobden carried the repeal of the Corn Laws, and what benefits have accrued to us.[32] He says look at the quantity of corn imported into this country before the repeal of the Corn Laws, so much; now look after the repeal of the Corn Laws, and see how much greater it is. Then, he says, because the rich could not eat more than they did, therefore all that has come in must have gone to the poor, and thus what benefit it must be to the poor. But he forgot say that the rich have increased as well as the poor. The population has increased in all ranks. And then he forgot to say that many a sack of flour has gone into a mill that does not make bread. I am told that a great deal of that flour which has been brought over from foreign ports has been used in our manufactures and was not exactly made into bread. I do not find any fault with it, but do not let him tell us that the poor get more bread because the quantity of corn imported has been increased; still, I hope that under no circumstances shall we ever repent the repeal of these Corn Laws. (Hear, hear.)

Well then, the Liberals are very good in opposition, as they generally bring things forward for us to discuss, and they have now brought forward one which requires serious discussion – that is the disestablishment and disendowment of the Irish Church. I cannot help thinking that either Mr Gladstone himself, or those who prompt him and support him, are not bad generals – as I think Mr Bright would not make a bad lawyer – because they see the Church of England is very strong in England, and they could not attack her front; so they try a manoeuvre on the flank to destroy the Church of Ireland, before they commence with the Church of England. (Cheers.)

Now, why at this particular moment was it necessary to bring forward that momentous question of the Church of Ireland? There is no doubt a great difficulty about that question because the Protestants of Ireland have not increased to that degree in Ireland that we had hoped for. No one can venture to say that it is the church of the majority; we must own too that the revenues are unequally distributed in proportion to the labour to be done; all that wants reform and very grave consideration. (Hear, hear.) Mr Shaw says that here I have made a base insinuation against Mr Gladstone, but what I did say I repeat: that, when Mr Gladstone was in power, he never did bring forward that reform; and, now that he is out of power, he takes it up as a war cry with which to unite his party, and so regain his seat on the Treasury benches. (Cheers.)

Aye, it is his *cheval de bataille*, it is the war horse on which he means to ride into power. (Hear, hear.) When he was in power he went to look at the steeds in the stable. He looked at the Irish Church, but he put it aside; he looked at this and the other, but they did not suit; then he looked at Reform, which he thought was the best horse to mount, but what did he do? He careered about with it and then was upset. (Laughter). And then the Conservatives were obliged to coax him up and put him in his saddle, but he could not guide the steed, and then the Conservatives were obliged to carry reform themselves, which they have done. (Cheers.) But I say, Mr Gladstone has united the party, and the question of the disestablishment of the Irish Church has become a serious one.

I am not particular about names. If you say the Irish Church is the church of the minority, I do not care for calling the Irish Church a part of the Church of the United Kingdoms of Great Britain and Ireland. I say it is the Church of the United Kingdom, and I do object to that little 's' in the United Kingdoms of Great Britain and Ireland. I say it is one kingdom, and must be so. From the relative situation of England and Ireland in the nature of things it must be so. If Ireland was three thousand miles away, it might be different; but, as it is close to us, it must be united to us. (Hear, hear.) The county of Dublin should be as much part of it as the county of Surrey, or the county of Hampshire, and it will ultimately be so. (Hear, hear.) But there is a struggle now going on, and perhaps it is better to be decided on the point; and if our government and ministers would pluck up their courage and say 'Ireland, you must be England', we should have the dispute sooner settled. (Cheers.)

I do not see that the disestablishment of the Irish Church will lead at all towards that very desirable end – the firm union of England and Ireland. On the contrary, it is my belief that it will create a greater separation. (Hear, hear.) I believe you must have in every state an established religion. I say this without the slightest reflection upon any body of dissenters. I do not argue the point whether the Church of England or whether any particular Protestant sect of dissenters may be the best. That is not necessary tonight, but I do say, if you mean to have freedom of conscience, if you mean to live in peace and quiet, there must be one state religion which dominates, not improperly, but leaves freedom of religion to all, and which we can look to as the religion of the state. (Cheers.)

Without that it appears to me that a struggle must take place between every sect for priority, till perhaps we are merged in one; which will be the Roman Catholic religion.[33] (Hear, hear.) Now, I have the greatest respect for the Roman Catholic gentry of England, and I do not believe that there is any Roman Catholic gentleman in England who, if asked the question or if he had the power, would wish to alter our laws, and to introduce the Popish religion into England, and to place the Queen and her successors under the dominion of the Pope. I believe that the Roman Catholic gentlemen of England, who adhere to the faith of their fathers, are loyal at heart and would not wish to alter the position in which England stands. (Hear, hear.)

But I do not say that of the lower orders in Ireland, or of the Roman Catholic world universally. Therefore, I say, that if you do away with the Established Church in Ireland, which will but precede the attempt to do away with the Protestant Church in England, you will open the road to all sorts of troubles, and freedom of conscience and freedom action will disappear from this land of England. (Cheers.) I will not trouble you further on that subject. You have all read the arguments on the other side and have made up your minds on the point. All I begin with and end with is this: that you must have a state church for the United Kingdom, and I say you must have it for Ireland as well as for England, though I do not wish to harass them with a name, as affecting any kind of supremacy over it. The Irish people do not pay to the Protestant Church, the landlords pay for it almost entirely. A very few

Catholic landlords pay, perhaps one-ninth of the whole, and they are perfectly willing to continue it. Therefore the Irish have no reason to complain of that church, except that they object to the name of the thing.

There are other subjects on which you might like to know my opinion, and one very serious one is education. (Hear, hear.) Now, I am sure everyone who hears me tonight will agree with me that day after day we find that it is absolutely necessary to educate every child that is brought into the world. If we do not educate it in some way it will become little better than a wild field. I know I am not singular in my love for education. There is a very general feeling in its favour, and there are various modes proposed, every one wishing to do the best. Some are in favour of secular and compulsory education: that people should be obliged to send their children to some school; and to meet all wishes and scots. They say do not let us have any religion taught in the school, but let the education given be merely secular education. That seems very plausible at first, but it has been tried in a place to which many of our Liberal friends are very fond of referring – it has been tried in America.

I have been looking over some papers about secular education in America, and I have made one or two little extracts that I thought might not be inappropriate at this time. One of the greatest men, and one whom the Americans almost worship, said, on his deathbed, 'Never sever education from religion.' (Hear hear.) Then comes another well-known character, who, whatever our political opinions may be, we all look to as one of the greatest men of England – I mean the Duke of Wellington. He said, 'Education without religion renders men clever devils.' (Cheers.)[34] Ex-Governor Clifford, an American, gave a general impression derived from long familiarity with the prosecution of criminals, both as a district attorney and attorney general, and he says:

> The merely intellectual education of our schools, in the absence of moral culture and discipline, which in my opinion ought to be an essential part of every system of school education, furnishes but a feeble barrier to the assaults of temptation and the prevalence of crime. Indeed, I am by no means certain that the mere cultivation of the intellect does not increase the exposure to crime by enlarging the sphere of man's capacity, and through its agency ministering to his sensual and corrupt desires.[35]

The Reverend Mr Townley of Toronto quotes from an educational journal and says everybody knows that the most depraved beings in our country are among those upon whom most is expended for education, also that 'thieves, incendiaries and assassins have come from our schools by thousands'.[36]

These are the schools where no religion is inculcated – schools for secular education. (Hear hear.) Another man says he insists 'that a great change must be adopted in our system of education, for in the midst of our schools depravity is growing up'. He says also that in his official capacity he is brought into contact with five or six hundred teachers who were morally unfit for their work, and that under the present training of American youth there was not one out of ten teachers in New England to whom he would trust the moral training of his child. (Applause.)

Then Professor Greenlove thought he must put more moral instruction into his system, for two of his scholars had been executed for murder, and two others had rushed to self-destruction. (Hear, hear.)[37] All this is very sad, and before we put on a compulsory rate, we should consider a little first, and know whether we cannot get a religious instruction first, and when the children get to a certain age they may take any secular instruction you like; but, unless a child is grounded in his duty to God and his neighbour, the chances are the education he receives, and the knowledge he gains, will make him what the Duke of Wellington said, not a good man but a clever devil. (Cheers.) This is very difficult question; I do not pretend to lay down any law upon the subject, but whether I am in Parliament or not, it is one that will always interest me and engage my particular attention. (Hear.)

Another subject has been placed before me and that is trades unions. I have before stated, as I state now, that I have no objection to trades unions – to the combination of the workmen and the combination of masters each for protection and, if they can manage it, for arbitration; but I do beg that you will consider that both sides must be consulted, and that people must not be led or rather misled by paid lecturers: people who go about to excite them, whose knowledge is not very extensive and who are not aware of the injury they are doing. The trade of England is the staple of England. Our great glory consists in our trade; our position depends upon our trade; but if, by insisting upon extremely high wages, we drive capital and trade away from England to Belgium, France, Prussia and other nations, the trade which has rendered us great and wealthy will desert us, and then we shall repent too late perhaps our own avarice on both sides. (Hear, hear.)

Therefore this is a matter to be subjected to cool and impartial reasoning, and in which we must not be carried away at the instigation of any demagogues, because I am sorry to say there are men who when troublesome times occur are always ready to come and excite the operatives to have resort to violent means. We have seen what atrocious mean things were done in one town to which I will not further allude. (Hear, hear.) When I say I am not

222 General Sir James Scarlett

averse to trades unions, you must remember that they must be carried out by just and lawful means, and not by the operation of intimidation. (Cheers.)

Another subject brought before us is that licensing of beer houses and public houses.[38] Now I must say that the beer houses, which were extremely well meant to give the lower orders cheap beer in their own houses, have run into great abuse; and that houses are established which no man, not even the men who frequent them, will conscientiously say are any credit to society and ought to be kept up. Many of these houses that have been refused licences by the magistrates get licences from the excise, and I should be anxious to come to some arrangement by which the magistrates, and not the excise, should alone have the power of granting licences to these houses. (Cheers.) No man is more unwilling than I am to curtail the comforts, amusements and pleasures of the working man; very far from it. I would do everything possible, and if a plan was designed for erecting houses and places where he might be raised in the scale of society, and where he might enjoy himself in a rational manner, I should be the first to subscribe to support such a system. (Cheers.) The Permissive Bill for which I have been asked to vote for I agree with in principle entirely, because it is designed to have houses of entertainment for the sale of liquor only in places where they are really required – but I do not think the machinery of that Bill as set forth in the paper sent me will have the desired effect, and therefore I shall not pledge myself to vote for it in its present form; but, as far as the principle goes of giving every inducement to men to abstain from intoxication and to resort to rational amusement, that shall have my best and firmest support. (Cheers.)

There is another subject which touches us all most nearly, and that is the taxation of the country. There is no doubt that the taxation of the country has become enormous – but I do not say enormous for the extent of the empire. We must not alone think of such towns as Burnley, Birmingham and London, but we must recollect that the British dominions extend over the whole globe; that the sun never sets upon them; and that our money is spent in India, Australia, New Zealand, Canada and a variety of places, all of which places are part of the British Empire. Therefore we must not expect to keep up so large house on a very small sum; but, as every good housekeeper knows, by looking sharply after the expenditure of the house, he may keep down the annual outgoing of money. (Hear, hear.) Now that is the duty of every Member of Parliament, and I assure you that, if I should have a seat in the House, that will be one of my particular missions. (Cheers.)

I am myself somewhat acquainted with the army, having served for many years, and having held high position in it. I know that the working part of the army are not over paid, and I know that the real combatant part of the army is not the most expensive part of it. If we have £15,000,000 to pay for the army this year, we have only £8,000,000 to pay for the combatant part of the army. A vast number of excrescences have grown up – I do not say they are unnecessary, nor do I say you will make any reduction. Mr Shaw will tell you that the moment he goes into Parliament you will have no taxation to pay whatever. (Laughter and cheers.) I am afraid Mr Shaw will be disappointed; and, if you elect him, you will be disappointed too. (Hear, hear.)

Certain expenses must be paid, and it is always difficult to know what certain people pay. Now there is a certain Captain Sherard Osborn, who was quoted by Mr Shaw the other day.[39] Captain Sherard Osborn says, 'I will reduce your expenditure by £5,000,000 directly I am in power!' I hope he may. (Laughter.) I recollect a very gallant friend of mine, who commands the Mediterranean fleet, Lord Fitzclarence Paget, who said, when out of power, he would save a very large sum indeed; but he was made Secretary of the Admiralty after that, and we heard nothing more of saving (laughter), and he confessed that what he had before said was a mare's nest he had found; and so he never fulfilled the hope he had excited.[40]

I am only afraid that those who now talk of reducing the estimates are only deceiving themselves or attempting to deceive you. But I do believe that the estimates may be reduced, and I am happy to tell you that there is an attempt being made at the War Office to reduce the expenses of the army, and I do hope that next year, with the lower estimates then passed, Mr Disraeli, if in power, will have the credit for it; and, if Mr Disraeli is turned out by Mr Gladstone, and the Liberals come into power, that, although the Liberals may claim the credit for the reduced estimates, you will give the credit where the credit is due to the Conservative Party. (Cheers and applause.) Be that as it may, I shall glad to see them reduced so far as is consistent with the efficiency the services of this great and extended empire. (Cheers.)

I do not know that there is any other subject that so occupies the public mind at this moment. If any gentleman wishes to ask a question, I shall be most happy to reply. (Cheers.)

No questions being put, General Sir J.Y. Scarlett said:

Perhaps I may presume that you agree with my sentiments. It is my desire and inclination to consult the wishes of all, and to do the best I can for you; and, if you send me to Parliament, I certainly shall do my best to serve the town of Burnley, and not only the town of Burnley but the country in general. (Cheers.) Believe me, gentlemen, it is from no wish of my own that I am placed in this position, which I am told I am unfit for in a variety of ways. (Laughter.) I am a soldier, that is one reason; I am this, and that, and the other reason; but what when the ladies are present I most object to is being told I am too old. (Laughter.) Now I do confess I wish a younger man was in place, and you may depend upon it that, if a younger man had come forward and asked for your votes as the Conservative candidate, I should have been very happy indeed to have supported him and have placed myself in the background; and, as soon as you find a young man who will come forward more acceptable to yourselves and to the ladies (laughter and cheers) if entrusted with the honour of being your representative, I shall most willingly resign it into his hand. (Loud cheers.)

Mr Folds briefly moved, and Mr B. Chaffer, in a most telling speech, seconded the resolution that Sir James Yorke Scarlett, KCB, was a fit and proper person to represent the borough of Burnley.[41] The motion was carried unanimously and with long continued cheering. On the motion of Major Thursby, seconded by General Scarlett, a hearty and enthusiastic vote thanks was given to the chairman.

*   *   *

74

History of the Burnley Election
Burnley Gazette, 21 November 1868

In May 1867 the Tories of Burnley began to see that its political enfranchisement could not be much longer delayed, and began to think about securing its representation by electing General Scarlett as its first Member. Accordingly, a requisition was got up and, after a very long delay, with the view of making it as long as possible, they presented it to him. He was in no hurry to give them an answer, and when he did give one it was of the most evasive and uncertain character. He neither said yea nor nay, but put off his final decision on the ground of the election being so remote; a valid objection, which should have prevented the requisition being got up to him until months after it was presented.

It was the Tories who first disturbed the even tenor of our lives in this matter, and commenced a controversy which for length, heat and asperity is without parallel in any newly-enfranchised borough. Of course, the Liberals saw that if the Tories took the field they must take it too, and a requisition was got up and presented to Mr Shaw, and he also, on the plea of the election being so far distant, did not give a final and definite answer.

It is quite clear that the Tories had but one card to play and that card was General Scarlett. No other name was ever mentioned, so far as we can learn, as that of Tory candidate for Burnley. And why? Was he not a soldier? Did he not employ a large number of persons to get and sell his coal for him? And were not these people proverbial for their little knowledge of public affairs, most easily imposed upon, humbugged, and coerced? Of course the facts were so, and then, when we add to the fact that he lived two or three weeks in the year within few yards of Bank Top railway station, and Mr Shaw lived about a mile further off 'all the year round', was it not clear to the Tory mind that Mr Shaw was not fit to represent Burnley?

At length the Tory Reform Bill, so transformed by Liberal agency that its very parents did not know or could say what part or parts of it belonged to them, passed, and Mr Shaw issued his address. From the very day that address was issued the flood-gates of electoral license were opened, and a stream of falsehood was sent forth which continued with little intermission until the close of the poll, and will be, doubtless, carried on by the able (!) and conscientious (!) writers on our contemporary for some time to come.

The Tories were wise selecting General Scarlett for their candidate: no man would have stood half the chance he did and, had he not consented to stand, it is morally certain there would have been no contest. Other names were mentioned on the Liberal side than that of Mr Shaw, but they met with so little favour that no action was taken on their behalf. Misrepresentations enough to form a volume have appeared in our contemporary, and there never has been the slightest retraction or apology for any one of them, and we don't suppose there ever will, for 'Sinners that grow old in sin are hardened in their crime.'

But these were nothing to the lies of canvassers and election agents. It would be easier to state the things they have not charged Mr Shaw with than those they have, and among other things that he was responsible for the articles, leaders and management of the *Burnley Gazette*. All we care to say about this is that Mr Shaw has never sent to us any attack on General Scarlett – never sent us any defence of himself against the falsehoods of the Tory scribes concerning him nor anything of the kind. Once he accidentally heard that a letter had been sent to us on the ground that General Scarlett was the representative of the principles and policy of his intensely Tory father, Judge Abinger, and therefore unfit to represent Burnley, and he sent a particular request to us – not a command, for which he had no authority – not to insert it; and, although it was put in type, it was not inserted.

Has General Scarlett done anything of the kind for Mr Shaw in the columns of the *Burnley Advertiser*? If so, we shall be glad hear of it. Articles of considerable asperity have appeared in this paper, but none of them have been inspired by Mr Shaw. They were called forth by what we must call the villainous articles of our contemporary, and not from the pen of one writer but of many. We have said in this and other journals that the Tory element is strong in the working classes, especially among those who, from defective education and tippling indulgence, are most easily deceived, corrupted and coerced, and the electoral result has proved it not only in Burnley but in other towns of radical Lancashire. Take away from the number who polled for General Scarlett all those who have been deceived by falsehood, all those who have been corrupted by promises of future benefit, and all those who have been coerced by fear of loss of employment and business, and there is still a residuum of comparative moral and social respectability, but happily too small to injure our future Member.

The election meetings in Burnley have done much towards the political enlightenment of its people; have made 'Those think who never thought before, and those who thought to think the more.' The lectures in the Literary Institute have failed to win the election.[42] The eight column committee have failed to win it. The '*Tiser* with all its falsehood and venom has failed to win.[43] The lavish expenditure of money in election expenses has failed to win it. The Church in Danger and the No Popery cry have failed to win it. The false pretence that the Tories were political and financial reformers has failed to win it. The majority in favour of the Liberal candidate is large and satisfactory, of undeceived, unbought and uncoerced votes. What can Liberals desire more?

The Tories of Burnley have no longer a majority in the Town Council, and all the Tory officials of the town will have to behave themselves as they ought to do, yea from the highest to the lowest. Henceforth there must be no cliquerie or Creekerie. Even martial Harry can do nothing more than lead the forlorn hope, for where Sir James Scarlett failed he is not very likely to succeed.[44] He may be a captain of the 'reds' as well as the 'blues', but he is only a captain after all, and shares the *general* – confound that pun how it will poke in – defeat.

The Burnley Balaclava has turned out a huge and disastrous blunder. The meetings in favour of Mr Shaw grew in number and zeal almost every time they were called. The meetings in favour of Scarlett were large and frequent; many Liberals went to them for the fun of the thing and they were not disappointed. General Scarlett did not see through the hollowness of his meetings and he persevered, as a soldier should do, to the end. He did the best he could, his friends did the best they could for him, and the result is a crushing defeat. We are assured, however, that he will win 'next time'; but the chances are that his next time will never come.

Farewell, a long farewell to all thy expected greatness, General Scarlett. KCB thou mayest be; an MP for Burnley – never. As thou art so anxious to promote our interests, we hope thou wilt find out a way to do it, albeit we have declined to put our trust in the party to which thou dost belong and which contains many worse men than thee, but which as a party under the old watchwords must pass away. We never heard but one Liberal doubt the result of the election, and he only feared intimidation. How well the Liberal canvassers did their work, how faithfully they recorded its results, the poll on Tuesday abundantly testifies.

*   *   *

75

The Burnley Election: Nomination of Candidates
Burnley Advertiser, 21 November 1868

The nomination of the candidates for the representation of the borough of Burnley in Parliament took place on Monday. The hustings were erected at the upper end of the Cattle Market, the best site in the town for the purpose. The ground for the reception of the two parties in the contest, it was stated on the authority of the borough surveyor, was equally divided between them, the side on the left of the hustings being appropriated to the Conservatives and that on the right to the Liberals. From the centre of the hustings, leaving sufficient space for each side to get to the hustings, ran a passage nine feet wide down to within a few yards of the back of Newsome's Circus, branching off right and left towards the two entrances to the market. In this passage and the entrances were stationed about two hundred of the county constabulary, under the direction and command of Superintendent Alexander.[45] Along this passage the candidates and numbers of their committees passed to the hustings, the principal members of each occupying the front. A space of a few yards between these was railed off in which were the Mayor, the Town Clerk and the reporters. Above these were the other members of the committees and supporters of the rival candidates. The hustings held about four hundred, the accommodation being equally divided between the parties.

The supporters of the two candidates began to assemble early; and, long before the time fixed for the commencement of the proceedings – eleven o'clock – the ground on both sides near the hustings was closely packed, the Liberals at first considerably outnumbering the Conservatives. Mr Shaw, the chairman and vice-chairman of his committee, and other members, entered the market about ten minutes before eleven o'clock and made their way to the hustings amidst the cheering of their supporters and hooting from the opposition. The principal members of the Conservative committee on proceeding to the hustings were cheered in a similar way by their friends, and hooted by the other side. The Mayor and Town Clerk appeared in their official robes.[46] About 11 o'clock, a moving mass down Parker Lane indicated the approach of General Scarlett, who shortly entered the ground on horseback and dismounted at the entrance to the fenced off passage. He was loudly cheered as he proceeded to his place on the hustings. Some thousands rushed in after him, and the Conservative side was filled from the hustings to Parker Lane. The numbers on both sides were estimated at 15,000 and upwards.

The bellman having called silence in the usual way, the writ was read by the Town Clerk. The Mayor then said he should feel obliged if they would be silent, or at least as silent as they possibly could during the whole of the proceedings. The men of Burnley had then a privilege which they had never been allowed to have until that election; and he hoped that the election would be conducted as the men of Burnley generally did conduct public business. He was sure of one thing, and he had lived in Burnley forty or fifty years, that if the people of Burnley were left to themselves they would generally do as they would like to be done by. (Hear, hear.) He would not take up their time by any remarks he might make; that devolved upon the proposers of the candidates. It was for them to instruct the vast assemblage before him. He would call upon any gentleman who had a candidate to propose to do so at once; only he besought them to hear both sides patiently and quietly; and, they might depend upon it, they would never have reason to regret it. He then called upon any gentleman who had a candidate to propose to do so at once. (Cheers from both parties.)

Alderman Coultate, who was loudly cheered by his own party, said he considered it was an honour, which had happened the first time, in being called upon to propose the first Member for the borough of Burnley.[47] (Hear, hear.) He had called him the first Member, although he ought more correctly to have called him the first candidate, but he had no doubt himself as to the result of the election. They were now for the first time in possession of the franchise; and although some of them had lived there fifty years, yet they had never given a vote. And to whom were they indebted for that privilege? (Cries of 'Tories', 'Liberals', and cheers.) He remembered many years back (confusion for a considerable time, groaning on the left of the hustings answered by cheers on the right) attending various meetings for the purpose of advocating Parliamentary Reform, and for the purpose of obtaining the franchise for Burnley, and he could only say that on all those occasions the gentlemen on the other side of the platform were conspicuous by their absence. (Hear, hear, laughter, cheers.) The Tories pretended to have carried Reform and all the great and good measures. (Hear, hear, from the Conservative side.) He denied that *in toto*. (A voice, 'Pill box', and cheers.)

He begged to thank Mr Chaffer for the first insult offered on that platform. (Loud cheers from the Liberals.) He hoped that the individuals in the crowd there (pointing to General Scarlett's supporters) would not take an example of the behaviour set before them on that platform. (Hear, hear, and cheers.) It was well known that the Tory Party had done exactly what they were sent to Parliament not to do, and then they claimed the victory to themselves. It was well known that when the late measure of Reform was brought in there were so many checks upon that it was worth nothing; and now, by the efforts the Liberal Party, it was its present state, and they were in the enjoyment of the franchise. (Hear, hear.) The measure itself was so large, so successful, that they were almost alarmed with their own tremendous success. (Cheers.) A Conservative Party objected to the £6 franchise as being the introduction of democracy and the destruction of their institutions, and then they had brought in household suffrage and called it a Conservative measure. The measure which the Conservatives had passed was without exception the most democratic measure which had been passed during the last century. ('Cut it short.')

Of the two candidates before them one of them had always supported Parliamentary Reform (hear, hear), whilst the other had not. He said he did not wish to make any personal observations, or say anything offensive to the high personal character of General Scarlett, who was well known to all of them. (Cheers from the Conservatives.) They all admitted that he was an excellent gentleman (hear, hear, and cheers); they all admitted that he was a most benevolent neighbour; they all admitted that he was lavish almost in his expenditure for benevolent purposes. But at the same time he begged to tell them that the high personal character of General Scarlett was the 'stock-in-trade' of his claims to represent them in Parliament.

They were there that day for the purpose of electing a representative in Parliament of their opinions (hear, hear) and therefore, however high the personal character of the candidate might be, the question was, 'Does he represent our opinions?' Were his (General Scarlett's) views on the Irish Church the same and theirs? No. Were his view on the ballot the same as theirs? No. If, therefore, they were simply asked to vote for a gentleman because of his personal character, when his political views were opposed to theirs, his character was not sufficient. But Mr Shaw represented the views of the majority of the electors of Burnley. (Hear, hear, cries of 'No'.) They therefore asked those electors to show their hands when the time was called in favour of Mr Shaw as the first Member for Burnley. He concluded by nominating Mr Shaw as a fit and proper person to represent the borough of Burnley in the next Parliament. (Cheers.)

John Massey Esq. seconded the nomination.[48] He remarked that, next to the honour of being elected the representative of that large and increasing town in Parliament, was the honour of being called upon to move or second the nomination of any gentleman to fill that post. (Hear, hear.) It was a post to which he never dreamt to attain, for in years past their struggles for Reform and the enfranchisement of that large town had been so uniformly put aside from one cause or another that he had begun to despair of a Member ever being given Burnley during his (Mr Massey's) lifetime. He concurred in the remarks of Mr Coultate in reference to the high personal character of General Scarlett. He should be sorry if anyone said a word against it. (A voice: 'You said it.') Of all the men whom the Conservatives could have brought forward, there was no man who fitted them as the champion of their cause as General Scarlett did. (Cheers from the Conservatives.) It was a credit to the Conservatives, and was also a credit to the Liberals to have an opponent worth calling one (loud cheers); for, had the Conservatives brought forward a second or third-rate man, the victory of the Liberals would have been little to boast of when they had, as he believed they would do, placed Mr Shaw at the head of the poll. (Cheers, and cries of 'Oh! oh!') He had nothing further to say, except that, whilst General Scarlett was a veteran soldier, he was only a recruit in the ranks of Reform. (Hear, hear, and cheers.) But whilst Mr Shaw was comparatively a young man, he was a veteran in the cause of Reform. (Hear, hear, and applause.) And when he had won the victory, they would have more glory and honour. They wanted to send a gentleman to Parliament from Burnley who was well acquainted with the trade and commerce of the district. (Hear, hear.) It was by trade and commerce that the town had been enlarged, and to the right management of this they had to look as their great hope in the future. He concluded by seconding the nomination. (Loud applause.)

James Roberts Esq., JP, was received with loud applause from the Conservatives.[49] He remarked that, like the gentleman on the other side, he felt it a great honour to propose such a gentleman as General Scarlett. (Cheers.) Mr Coultate had said that the gentlemen on that side of the platform had always been conspicuous for being opposed to Parliamentary Reform. (Cries of Hear, hear, and 'No no!') He said they had always been on the side of Reform. (A voice: 'What does ta want there, then?' and laughter.)

His object in rising was mainly to answer the objections which had been made against General Scarlett being their representative. They had been told that they ought to have a man of business to represent them. (A voice: 'We ought to have.') Well, General Scarlett had shown himself a man of business ever since he (Mr Roberts) knew anything of him. He had had control almost of the management of an army; and they could not for a moment suppose that a man in that position could be anything but a man of business. (A voice: 'He's a soldier.') He dared say General Scarlett would know very little about the inside of a cotton mill; he would perhaps not know what a cotton spinning machine is, or a mule; he would be more at home as a civil engineer than a cotton spinner.

Many objections had been raised because General Scarlett was a soldier; but it was taken for granted because men were soldiers they liked fighting. They, of all men, were the men most likely to avoid it. What was there in being a man of war? (Here a commotion took place, in consequence of a pigeon being sent off from General Scarlett's side, with a piece of blue ribbon attached to it.) Mr Roberts, continuing, said that the Duke of Wellington, on being asked if he could describe a victory, said he knew nothing so dreadful except a defeat. (A voice: 'That's what you are going to get.') General Scarlett was one of the most likely men to prevent a war. In the first place none of them liked to have the income tax doubled; and if there was a war the first thing that would be done would be to double the income tax, and General Scarlett would be one of the largest payers. In addition to that, he would have to take his part in the front of the battle. He had done that once, and he (Mr Roberts) was sure there was nothing in fighting for a man of General Scarlett's temper, as he was one of the mildest men he knew. He concluded by nominating Sir James Yorke Scarlett as being a fit and proper person to represent the borough of Burnley in Parliament. (Loud cheers.)

James Folds Esq., JP, seconded the nomination. He expressed the pleasure and pride he felt at having the honour conferred upon him. He had no doubt they all knew how Sir James Yorke Scarlett had served his Queen and his country; and, if they sent him to Parliament, he would represent them as faithfully in Parliament as he discharged his duties in the army. (Applause.)

The Mayor said: Has any other gentleman another candidate to propose? If not, the candidates will now address the electors. No one rising.

Mr Shaw rose to address the electors and was loudly cheered by his supporters. After congratulating the electors on their first assemblage at the hustings, and expressing the pleasure he had in Mr Lomas, their respected townsman, presiding over their proceedings, he said he was sure that Mr Coultate and Mr Massey would ever look with feelings of pride on moving and seconding the first Liberal candidate for Burnley. (Cheers). He then proceeded to remind them that the day after they would be called upon to discharge one of the most sacred duties of citizenship (cheers); and he sincerely hoped that, whatever the result the election might be (a voice: 'No. 2'.), they would all so demean themselves that they would be entitled to the good opinion and confidence of all Englishman. (Hear, hear.)

The issue of that election was not the one which the friends of his honourable opponent persisted in putting forward; it was not a personal question. If it were, he would be on the other side of the platform. It was a political question; it was a question involving the best interests of our country, and he said the man who sacrificed the interests of his country for his personal feelings was a traitor to his country. (Hear, hear, and loud cheers.) He would speak unkindly of no man, but when he saw Mr James Roberts get up and tell them they had in Sir James a complete man of business, it brought to his recollection a time when Mr James Roberts solemnly moved that Sir James Scarlett was not a fit and proper person to represent North Lancashire. (Loud and continued cheers.) If Mr James Roberts could satisfy his conduct on that occasion to his conscience, he (Mr Shaw) would be perfectly satisfied. (A voice: 'He cannot.')

But the issue they had to decide was whether they wished to have the principles of Liberalism, or the old, effete, worn out principles of Toryism. (Hear, hear, and applause.) General Scarlett entertained the highest opinion of what Toryism had done for the people in the past (hear, hear), and he looked hopefully to it in the future. General Scarlett told his audience in the circus that the passing of the Test and Corporation Act was brought about by the agency of Lord Derby. If General Scarlett would read history, he would find that that measure was passed by a Liberal Government (cheers) and that, instead of being introduced by Lord Derby, it was introduced by Lord John Russell. (Applause.) General Scarlett also claimed for the Tory Party the emancipation of the Roman Catholics, but history told them that the Duke of Wellington declared that he proposed that measure not because he liked or approved of it on principle, but from fear. (Hear, hear.) General Scarlett also told them in the circus that the slaves of the West Indies were released by Lord Derby. ('True.') He ought to have told them that Lord Derby was a Liberal then. (Hear, hear, and cheers.) Another statement made by General Scarlett was that the Tory party was entitled to credit for the repeal of the Corn Laws; but Sir Robert Peel, before he could pass that measure, had to quit his party and become a Liberal, and that great and honest statesman solemnly declared in Parliament that all the honour and credit of that great and important question was due to Richard Cobden. (Loud cheers.)

Their Tory friends had got the coat, the waistcoat and the brogue of the Liberals. (Hear, hear, and applause.) He thought his honourable opponent was very indiscreet in what he said on that occasion, because when they found that in the last thirty-five years Parliament had been occupied in repealing bad laws, simple folks like themselves asked the pertinent question: if there were so many bad laws, who made them? ('Tories', and cheers.) He told those Tory men who had got those blue ribbons and blue cards that the Tories of the past were entitled to some credit (hear, hear, from the 'blues'); and he wondered his honourable friend did not lay claim to it. He could only attribute it to his great bashfuness. (Hear, hear, laughter, and cheers.) But as General Scarlett had not laid claim to the virtue, he would lay it before them.

They were entitled to the virtue of yielding. (Laughter.) They were wonderful hands at yielding, but it was upon the principle of the pickpocket who gave up the watch he had stolen. (Cheers.) If, then, Toryism had been so black – and black they knew it had been – what were the prospects for the future? What was the policy of Mr Disraeli? (Groans and cheers.) What was the political programme of the present day? It was what it had been in the past and might be explained by one word, and that word was 'resistance'. (Hear, hear.) Mr Gladstone proposed a simple act of justice to reconcile and pacify Ireland, but the Tories said, 'We will resist you'. (Hear, hear.) Mr Gladstone proposed to remove the defects of the Reform Bill from which they were smarting at present, but the Tories said, 'We will resist you'. (Hear, hear.) Mr Gladstone proposed economy and retrenchment, and they (the people) were very green now but they would be more green by and bye. They would not wear their blue ribbons so long when they got to know that, out of every sovereign they earned, four shillings was taken by the government in indirect taxation. ('Shame.')

But, as if that programme was not damaging enough, General Scarlett had added something to it, for he said he would not be responsible for the consequences of the repeal of the Corn Laws. He also told them that the law of primogeniture, one of the most unnatural and wicked laws they had, was the salvation of England. (Cries of 'Shame, shame'.) General Scarlett also told them that the ballot, which poor and dependent men required to protect them, which the interests of society required as a check upon the unprincipled action of partisans, was nothing but a sneaking mode of action. Just and equal laws and religious equality the Tory gentlemen of England had never been accustomed to; they did not understand economy and retrenchment, nor did they care about it. (Loud cheers.)

The issue was in the hands of the people. They had to make choice of one person out of two persons. Would they march under that blue banner ('No', and cheers), which had led those who follow it to an ignominious defeat, which was unfurled in the air today, but was crawling in the mud tomorrow? (Cheers.) Or would they march under that old yellow banner, which would lead them, as it did their forefathers, to a great and glorious victory? (Hear, hear, and applause.) Then, tomorrow they would cast their lot amongst the Liberals. If they would follow Mr Gladstone and Mr Bright (cheers and groans), then he would faithfully and honestly serve them, and zealously support those great men in carrying into effect the great and important measures they had in store for the people of this country. (Loud and continued cheers.)

General Scarlett was received with great cheering, waving hats, &c. He remarked that they were assembled that day under the auspices of the Mayor of Burnley to carry out an Act of Parliament which had been passed by a Conservative Government. ('No, no', and cheers from the Conservatives.) A government with Mr Disraeli at the head of it. (Hear, hear, and groans.) A £7 rental was proposed by Mr Gladstone, but his own party quarrelled and opposed it, and it fell to the lot of the Conservatives to give a much more extended franchise; to give it to every man (laughter and cheers) who had a house and paid rates for it. (A voice: 'Where's the dual vote, then?') It showed them that the Conservatives were not afraid of democracy (cheers); they were not afraid of trusting the people. (Cheers.) On the contrary, it was the desire of the Conservatives to consult the wishes of the people; and, when their wishes had been ascertained, thoroughly mooted and carried through the Houses of Parliament, the Conservatives would carry them into execution.

They had been entrusted by the present government with the franchise, and he was sure they would exercise it in peace and quiet – not by force of hands, but by the exercise of their intellects. (Cheers.) He had had something to do with elections, but he never yet found that any riot, confusion or interruption arose from the Conservative side. ('Shame, shame', and cries of 'Blackburn'.) If they did him the honour to return him to Parliament ('Never', 'No', 'Yes', 'Yes'), it would be by their wishes that he went, for he had had no interest himself in being sent. He neither consulted his own ambition nor his pecuniary interests (hear, hear); on the contrary, he sacrificed the whole of them for the honour of representing the borough with which he had been so long connected. (Cheers.)

Many things had been said of him during the canvass. Some had painted him a great deal too handsome, and some too ugly. (A voice from the Liberal side of the hustings, 'It cannot be.') He had been called an old bigoted Tory and it had been said he was no general and no politician. He would tell them that he was a firm supporter of the throne, a firm supporter of our institutions, of Peers and Commons (hear, hear), because he considered that public opinion was best made known through them, and they had secured for them both freedom of action and personal liberty. (Hear, hear.) He was for the union of Church and State (cheers and groans) because he considered that by Church and State the Nonconformists had the greatest liberty of conscience. ('No', 'no'.) He considered it was a protection to all sects and creeds. ('Hear, hear.') Upon those questions he was a Conservative, or a Tory if they chose to call him so ('hear, hear.'); but upon all other subjects he was as liberal as his honourable opponent, or as any other who might be sent to Parliament. (A voice: 'Ay, what a lie.')

He was as much for the reduction of taxes, and especially would he reduce the taxes that bore heavily upon the working men. (Hear, hear, and voice: 'What about the £3,000,000?' followed by cheers.) It was not upon the poor, but upon the rich, that he would place the taxes. (Hear, hear.) He stated that there was an endeavour being made by the military and naval authorities to carry out reduction. ('But when?') It was true that Lord Derby was on the Liberal side when the Test and Corporation Act was passed (hear, hear, and cheers); but it was Lord Derby who made the Liberals carry it. (Hear, hear.) It was Lord Derby also who made them carry the Act for the release of the slaves in the West Indies.

It was said that the Duke of Wellington carried the Catholic Emancipation Act from fear; but whoever accused the Duke of Wellington of fear? (Applause.) It was also said that when Sir Robert Peel carried the repeal of the Corn Laws he was a Liberal. He was a Liberal from the beginning. When he was a Tory he was Liberal. (Laughter and cheers.) Sir Robert Peel was the most far-seeing statesman they ever had, and he (General Scarlett) only wished he (Sir Robert Peel) was at the head of the Conservative Government, and they might depend upon it the Liberals would have to go with him. He exhorted them to vote according to principle, to be firm and peaceable, and if his supporters were early at the poll he would have the honour of being (a voice: 'At the bottom', and loud cheers) at the head of the poll. (Loud cheers.)

General Scarlett stepped back for a moment, but assuming his position again said they might wonder how his opponent knew so much about the Tories. For some six years he was the Conservative agent for Colonel Wilson Patten.[50] (Loud cheers.)

The Mayor then rose and proceeded to take the show of hands. He called for the show of hands, first on the Liberal side and then took the show on the Conservative side. He then observed that he could not say which side had it for the life of him. He would not swear to either. On whichever side he gave it, he knew he should be in for it. If he knew that either side had a majority of one, he would give the preference to it. He wished one impartial gentleman from each side would assist him.

The Mayor then turned to the Conservative side and spoke with several gentlemen, and afterwards spoke to gentlemen on the opposite side. Several persons called out to him to decide on his own responsibility. He then called for another show of hands, first from the Liberals and then from the Conservatives. Many at the extremity of the Conservative side had retired after the first show of hands, but were soon seen hurrying back when the second show was about being taken. This second show was protested against by the gentlemen on the Conservative side of the hustings.

After this the Mayor said, on his own responsibility, he declared the show of hands in favour of Richard Shaw. The decision was received with loud cheers from the Liberals and groans from the Conservatives, several of the latter protesting against the decision. J. Roberts Esq. demanded a poll on behalf of General Scarlett. The Mayor, having asked who seconded it, G. Slater, senior, Esq., replied that he seconded Mr Shaw.[51] He then proposed a vote of thanks to the Mayor, the returning officer, remarking on the good conduct of the people. As the Conservatives refused to second the motion, Mr Massey seconded the motion and it was carried. The proceedings then terminated with three cheers for Mr Shaw, and in a few minutes the crowd was dispersed, there being not the least disturbance.

The Polling

The polling commenced at eight o'clock on Tuesday morning, in twelve districts, at the following places: St Andrew's district, St Andrew's School; St Peter's; No. 3, Keighley Green, near the Court House; Bankhouse, the Grammar School; St James's, St James's School; Mount Pleasant, Mount Pleasant School; St Paul's, Habergham Eaves; Poor Law Offices, Burnley; St Peter's Infant School, Fulledge; Wesleyan School, Burnley Wood; Towneley Infant School; Trinity, Trinity New School, Lowerhouse, Habergham School, Gannow; National School, Woodtop.

Almost throughout the whole of the day, the greatest excitement prevailed in the neighbourhoods of the various polling places, and in Hargreaves Street and Grimshaw Street, where the Central Committees of the respective parties sat: the Conservatives at No. 12, in the first named street and the Liberals at Cronkshaw's Temperance Hotel in the last named. Messengers on horseback and in cabs ware continually on the road with reports from the various polling places. The mills were closed for the day and thousands of people thronged the streets. The shopkeepers in the principal streets closed their shops, and everywhere in the neighbourhood of polling booths this was case. At several of these, there was considerable disturbance and some fighting.

The windows of the Liberal Committee Room in the Park were smashed in. In St Andrew's district there was some contention between the two parties, who pelted each other with stones. Subsequently the windows in Mr Lomas's mill, Fulledge Road, were smashed. We counted about a

238 General Sir James Scarlett

hundred squares. The windows in Mr Kay's shed were also smashed.[52] In Milton Street the windows in many of the houses were broken; in some a few panes, in others half the number in the window. In Mr John Massey's mill, Trafalgar Street, considerably over two hundred squares were smashed. This was done, as stated, by persons wearing blue favours. Cheering and hooting may be allowed and passed over as a harmless mode of giving expression to feeling, but no reasonable person can have any sympathy with those whose feelings lead them to destroy property. Throughout the day, the police were on the alert, marching to and fro, ready to assist in quelling any tumult likely to result in serious consequences, and in this way, under the judicious direction of Mr Superintendent Alexander, they rendered important services to the town.

As we learn from the police records, four persons were given into custody on the charge personation: John Stanworth by William Nightingale; Thomas Eastwood by William Moorhouse. They were admitted to bail in their own recognisances of £10 each to appear at the Court House on Monday. In Bankhouse district Robert Maudsley by John Riley; and in Mount Pleasant district William Mercer (we did not learn who had given him into custody). These were discharged, it being shown that the charge against them was unfounded.

At the close of the poll at four o'clock, the numbers were given:

For Mr Shaw	2620
For General Scarlett	2238
Majority for Mr Shaw	382

When this result was known, the committee sitting at Cronkshaw's Hotel announced the victory to the multitude outside. Great cheering followed.

Shortly after Mr Shaw appeared at the window and was received with vociferous cheering. He said:

Ladies and gentlemen, I believe that according to the state of the poll I am now your Member. (Cheers.) The state of the poll will be declared by the Mayor tomorrow at nine o'clock in the Cattle Market, and I believe that on that occasion it will be his duty to inform you that plain, humble Mr Shaw is the first Member for Burnley. (Cheers.) If there is one thing that I am prouder of than another it is that I have risen from the people. (Cheers.) I have no handle to my name, and no hieroglyphics at the end of it, excepting what you, the people of Burnley, have put behind it. Gentlemen, I will tell you candidly that I am not one of those who value titles; what I value is the good opinion and confidence of my fellow-townsmen. (Applause.) If I should be returned tomorrow as your Member, you may rely upon this, that I will honestly serve you, and that, as your Member, I will ever support in Parliament those measures which are calculated to promote the happiness and the material prosperity of the people. (Applause.)

Gentlemen, I won't detain you longer this evening. I will content myself by expressing the great honour you have done me. (Cheers.) I beg to tell you that, on the first occasion I met my committee, I told them that if I stood candidate for Burnley it should be on the strictest principles of purity; that I would not have one committee sitting at a beer house. After thanking the canvassers committee, chairmen and vice-chairmen and voters, he said I will only add one word, and that is go home quietly and go home soberly. (Hear, hear, and applause.) There is no Liberal drink; it is all Tory drink, if there is any. I, therefore, beg you will take my advice and go home quietly. (Loud cheering.)

Mr Shaw was escorted through the streets to the residence of his chairman, Alderman Coultate.

The effigy of the Mayor was carried through the streets by the Conservative supporters and then burnt.

Chapter 8

Cliviger

Less than two years after he retired, the General died at his home at Bank after a short illness.[1] His last public appearance was at a soirée of the Burnley Literary Institution on 23 November 1871, two weeks before his death.[2] In early December, having been out shooting at a neighbour's, he caught a chill which turned into pneumonia. This proved fatal because of an existing heart complaint. The course of his final illness was movingly described in detail by Maude Smith, who was staying at Bank Hall at the time.[3] Having fallen ill on Sunday 3 December, he died on Wednesday 6 December. Attended by two doctors, and by the local clergyman and his wife, he remained himself to the end. Reflecting on his life, he said:

> 'Seventy-two years. It is a good life.' 'I have had many years of great happiness and prosperity.' Also, when a blanket was being nailed up outside his door to keep off the draught, he said, 'I don't like that tapping. They will be knocking over me some day.'[4]

His younger brother, Peter Campbell Scarlett, and his nephew William Scarlett, now third Lord Abinger, reached Burnley in time to see him before his death. Their letters from Bank Hall over the next few days add to Maude Smith's account. According to Peter Scarlett, writing to the General's niece:

> The dear General died at half past seven p.m. yesterday or a little earlier. Parker was administering to him the sacrament and he went off as if he had fallen asleep.[5] I will not dilate on our grief, but God's will be done. Charlotte bears up admirably and is quite collected and in want of no assistance. I mentioned your wish to her, at which she smiled, saying that it was not at all necessary to bring you here, more especially as she knew you were not strong; but in point of fact she wants no one except Mrs Parker, who was in the house and passed last night in her room.[6] I go in to see her occasionally and she has Willy on the sofa by her.[7]

Lady Scarlett's calm worried William Scarlett:

Aunt Charlotte bears it too quietly and is too unexcited to be in a satisfactory state. She did not sleep last night but the doctor has given her some soothing medicine, which we hope to get her to take tonight. Mrs Parker has been of the greatest service and, as she was in the house through the whole business, Aunty has got used to her and finds her not only not in the way but is glad to have her. I saw her just now and she desired her love to you and Fanny. She had heard of Fanny's offer to come down and it was in answer to this that she said Mrs Parker was here and kind enough to take care of her.

She went with me at about two o'clock to the General and kissed him several times. She was affected and sobbed a little. When she is more used to the position we will try and find out what she wishes to do and where to live. At present she has not made up her mind, but has intimated that she intends to do as she likes and will have no interference.[8]

In London, Frances Smith expressed the shock caused by his death: 'I cannot realize that he has passed away. What a lesson to us all to watch. No gradual decay, but smitten down in the midst of his strength. The General was the keystone of the family.'[9]

Once his death was announced, his funeral became a matter of great interest to those in Burnley and around. In the *Burnley Advertiser*, admittedly a staunch supporter of the Conservatives, it was reported: 'The sad intelligence gave rise to one general lament, to universal regret and gloom; and fast and full fell tears from thousands of eyes, whilst deepest sorrow filled thousands of grieving hearts to overflow. Each heart felt it to be a *personal* bereavement.'[10] The *Burnley Advertiser*'s Liberal rival, the *Burnley Gazette*, added its tribute, though unable to resist reminding its readers of the General's privileged background and of the result of the Burnley election of 1868:

Sir James Scarlett was in his seventy-third year. Such is the brief account we have to give of the termination of a noteworthy career: the career of a man who had great social advantages to start with, and also personal qualities that enabled him to make the most of those advantages. The respect and affection in which 'The Old General' was held by men of all classes and parties cannot be accounted for by social position merely, nor even military success and personal heroism. There is no doubt that the second son of Attorney General Scarlett was a very amiable, kind-hearted and good man, and these were the qualities for which the people admired and loved him. We say the people, for though, in consequence of the injudicious steps taken during a time of intense political excitement to make the illustrious virtues of the brave old man a stalking-horse for merely party purposes, the great body of the working classes of Burnley rejected him as their representative on purely political grounds, yet they held, and still hold, his personal and private virtues in the highest esteem.[11]

Despite the family's initial preference for a private funeral, they agreed to public attendance along the route.[12] The response to this announcement was extraordinary, despite the short notice given and the fact that the funeral was held on a working day. The funeral, on Monday 16 December, became a huge demonstration of public sorrow, with special trains bringing in parties from throughout Lancashire and beyond. The events of the day were covered in great detail by the *Burnley Advertiser*, which subsequently published a full account of the funeral as a separate booklet.[13]

The local and national obituaries were generous to the General's military record and personal character. At first it was suggested that his memorial should be in Westminster Abbey. This was changed to the Garrison Church in Aldershot, where a statue of the General surrounded by his men stands in the centre of the back of the church. A memorial chapel was also added to St Peter's Church in Burnley.

Sadly, having borne her husband's last illness with stoicism, Charlotte Scarlett's mental health broke down three days after his death. In 1872 she moved to Elfinsward, a house in Haywards Heath in Sussex provided for her by her sister and brother-in-law. She never recovered but lived on another seventeen years, dying on 9 February 1888, aged eighty-two. She was buried, next to her husband, at Holme Chapel

> in the quietude of one of the most beautiful and picturesque of Lancashire churchyard – situate in one the loveliest valleys in England – will rest, side by side, the bodies of two whose lives were fruitful in Christian work and whose memories will be kept green in the locality where they were best known and most highly esteemed for generations to come.[14]

Twenty-eight years after Balaklava, and eleven years after the death of General Scarlett, Tennyson finally wrote about the Charge of the Heavy Brigade. His 'The Charge of the Heavy Brigade' was published in 1882, although begun in March 1881.[15] He had written this at the request of

Alexander Kinglake, the author of *The Invasion of the Crimea*,[16] and was advised on it by General Sir Edward Hamley, who had seen the charge and had written about the Crimean War.[17] In some ways, it was a tribute to Trinity College, Cambridge, which Kinglake, Scarlett and Tennyson had all attended. Unlike 'The Charge of the Light Brigade', which mentions no names, it singles out Scarlett as the hero of the poem.

> The Charge of the gallant three hundred, the Heavy Brigade!
> Down the hill, down the hill, thousands of Russians,
> Thousands of horsemen, drew to the valley – and stay'd;
> For Scarlett and Scarlett's three hundred were riding by
> When the points of the Russian lances arose in the sky;
> And he call'd, 'Left wheel into line!' and they wheel'd and obey'd.
> Then he look'd at the host that had halted he knew not why,
> And he turn'd half round, and he bade his trumpeter sound
> To the charge, and he rode on ahead, as he waved his blade
> To the gallant three hundred whose glory will never die –
> 'Follow', and up the hill, up the hill, up the hill,
> Follow'd the Heavy Brigade.
>
> The trumpet, the gallop, the charge, and the might of the fight!
> Thousands of horsemen had gather'd there on the height,
> With a wing push'd out to the left and a wing to the right,
> And who shall escape if they close? but he dash'd up alone
> Thro' the great gray slope of men,
> Sway'd his sabre, and held his own
> Like an Englishman there and then;
> All in a moment follow'd with force
> Three that were next in their fiery course,
> Wedged themselves in between horse and horse,
> Fought for their lives in the narrow gap they had made –
> Four amid thousands! and up the hill, up the hill,
> Gallopt the gallant three hundred, the Heavy Brigade.
>
> Fell like a cannon-shot,
> Burst like a thunderbolt,
> Crash'd like a hurricane,
> Broke thro' the mass from below,
> Drove thro' the midst of the foe,
> Plunged up and down, to and fro,
> Rode flashing blow upon blow,

Brave Inniskillens and Greys
Whirling their sabres in circles of light!
And some of us, all in amaze,
Who were held for a while from the fight,
And were only standing at gaze,
When the dark-muffled Russian crowd
Folded its wings from the left and the right,
And roll'd them around like a cloud, –
O, mad for the charge and the battle were we,
When our own good redcoats sank from sight,
Like drops of blood in a dark-gray sea,
And we turn'd to each other, whispering, all dismay'd,
'Lost are the gallant three hundred of Scarlett's Brigade!'

'Lost one and all' were the words
Mutter'd in our dismay;
But they rode like victors and lords
Thro' the forest of lances and swords
In the heart of the Russian hordes,
They rode, or they stood at bay –
Struck with the sword-hand and slew,
Down with the bridle-hand drew
The foe from the saddle and threw
Underfoot there in the fray –
Ranged like a storm or stood like a rock
In the wave of a stormy day;
Till suddenly shock upon shock
Stagger'd the mass from without,
Drove it in wild disarray,
For our men gallopt up with a cheer and a shout,
And the foeman surged, and waver'd, and reel'd
Up the hill, up the hill, up the hill, out of the field,
And over the brow and away.

Glory to each and to all, and the charge that they made!
Glory to all the three hundred, and all the Brigade!

76

The Literary Institution Soirée
Burnley Advertiser, 25 November 1871

General Scarlett, who was received with loud and long continued cheering, said the resolution he had to move was one which suited him remarkably well; it was one which required no eloquence on his part to make them all agree with it; and it took him out of the category of speakers because he was by the terms of the resolution forbidden to make a speech.[18] The resolution was that this meeting wishes to return its thanks to the speakers and those who had assisted at this soirée. He was sure they would be most anxious to do this.

Their first speaker was their friend Mr Robinson. He had said one or two good things – as he always did, which were useful and instructive to them. He spoke about the advantage of binding anew the old books rather than buying new ones; and he also spoke of what was natural for him as a banker to speak, that it would be a very good thing if the balance in hand this year were larger.

The next speaker was their excellent Member (Mr Holt); he might say the Conservative Member for Burnley. (Cheers.) He needed not to say one word in praise of his address. He had told them some plain truths. He told them to look out and read the history of the Church, and of its establishment; and hinted as he (the General) thought that some people had taken liberties with the Irish Church, and that they might do this with the English Church. He trusted if this was attempted that they would be prepared to resist it. (Cheers.)

The third speaker was Mr Ecroyd, and I must say that I never listened to a speech with greater pleasure. (Cheers.) He said that with which he was sure the meeting would agree, that one of the first things to be taught in primary education should be the teaching a child its duty towards God and man. (Cheers.)

Their last speaker commenced in a howling wilderness, but he bridged it over and rattled on at a tremendous pace, interesting them by sparkles of wit, like a horse striking sparks as he shyed, and leading to solid and good ground at last.[19] He trusted this speaker would long live to entertain them, giving the benefit of his observation of life, and particularly of his conversations with his wife. (Laughter.)

The General concluded with congratulations on the numerous and respectable assembly gathered in that hall. He had often spoken from that platform and met his friends there; but he never saw a better array of Lancashire witches and Lancashire men than was before him on that occasion. (Loud cheers.)

*   *   *

77

The Last Days of General Sir James Yorke Scarlett

On Sunday 3 December the General did not come down till one o'clock, having passed a restless night, and complained of shivering and pain in his side.[20] He came into the dining room to luncheon and that was the last time he sat at table. He would not eat anything but complained of thirst, and drank champagne and selzer-water, which he liked, and said it was so refreshing. He looked very ill and the bright expression was gone from his face. There was also a catching of the breath which was distressing; one saw he was in pain.

After luncheon he went into the library, drew an easy chair to the fire and, after a few words with Mr Parker, fell asleep.[21] About four o'clock, not feeling any better, he consented to see Dr Briggs, who came and ordered him to bed at once; and, having prescribed for him, desired hot poultices to be applied to the side to relieve the pain and said he should call again at ten o'clock.[22] He then pronounced the attack to be congestion of the lungs and said he could not understand the case alone and wished for further advice.

The General had little or no sleep that night, owing to the constant coughing. Early on Monday morning, Dr Roberts, who is reckoned the Gull of Manchester, was telegraphed for, but was unable to arrive until four p.m.[23] He entirely approved of what had been done. The pain in the side had been relieved and the cough was a little easier, but he said the case was very serious, though not dangerous at that time. The fear was lest bronchitis should set in. He ordered champagne, brandy and soup, saying it was most important to keep up the strength and a little nourishment must be taken every half hour.

That evening Willy and Peter were telegraphed for. At eleven o'clock Dr Briggs came and promised to remain the night at Bank, in case any change should occur. The General passed a tolerably quiet night and had a little sleep. On Tuesday morning, the fifth, when Dr Briggs saw him, he said he certainly was not worse; and, knowing his good constitution, we hoped on.

The General never remained the whole day in bed, though the doctors were anxious he should do so, but he said it was so weakening. He knew he should not get better unless they let him get up; and also the breathing seemed easier when sitting up. His great wish was to take a warm bath; and he actually crawled on his hands and knees (not being strong enough to stand) into his dressing-room in order to get to his bath, when the doctor came in and stopped him. During that day he had a good deal of fever and craved for ice, and complained of the weight of the bedclothes. He said he longed to have a warm bath, then wrap himself in a blanket and roll in the snow.

He did not seem to be aware how seriously ill he was and spoke to Mr Parker about the Conservative Meeting that was to have taken place on the sixteenth. But, later in the evening, he said, as if thinking aloud: 'Seventy-two years. Seventy-two years. It is a good life.' 'I have had many years of great happiness and prosperity.' Also, when a blanket was being nailed up outside his door to keep off the draught, he said, 'I don't like that tapping. They will be knocking over me some day.'

When Dr Roberts arrived from Manchester at six o'clock p.m., he looked very grave and said the case was critical, and the balance was even of recovery or not, an attack of this kind being very serious at the General's age. The great thing was to keep up the strength and give constant nourishment. At the General's request brandy, which he particularly disliked, was discontinued and port wine substituted, which he took readily, and also turtle soup. In the course of that afternoon, when told that Willy was coming, he said, 'He is a capital nurse. He nursed me most carefully through a bad attack of dysentery in the Crimea.' Being also told that Peter was expected, he said, 'Ah, poor Peter. He will make himself ill.' After Dr Roberts left, Willy, who had arrived at five o'clock, went to the General, who said on seeing him, 'Willy, my boy, I am glad you are come.'

Dr Briggs stayed at Bank again Tuesday night. Wednesday morning, his report was that the General passed a quiet night and the symptoms were no worse; but, as the day went on, he grew perceptibly weaker. He expressed a wish that Mr Parker should read to him for a little, at the same time saying, 'I say my own prayers. Just now I knelt down and said them.'

At four o'clock p.m. Dr Briggs, who was with him, observed a change for the worse. The action of the heart was weaker and irregular. When Dr Roberts arrived, soon after, he said there was no hope. About six o'clock Peter took me to see the General. His breathing was short and painful, and the perspiration of weakness was on his forehead. He was sitting up in an easy chair by the fire, his arm resting on a little table by his side. I took his hand and stroked it and kissed it. He looked up at me and said, 'Maudie, I shall see you at breakfast tomorrow.' At that time he seemed aware of his danger but was perfectly calm and sensible to the last.

After Dr Roberts left he went to bed and shortly after he said, 'They will be digging for me at Holme Chapel soon.'[24] He murmured prayers to himself and almost his last words were 'Many mansions, many mansions, great sins and great forgiveness'. He then expressed a wish to take the Communion and turned to Lady Scarlett saying, 'Charlotte, you and Mrs Parker must receive it with me.' Dr Briggs, who was standing by, said he was too weak and advised that he should take a little turtle soup first, but on hearing this the General raised himself in bed and said, in a clear, distinct voice, 'Now. Directly.' While Mr Parker was consecrating the bread and wine, he gave a sigh and died, so calmly and peacefully did his spirit return to God who gave it.

*   *   *

78

The Death of General Scarlett
Burnley Advertiser, Saturday 16 December 1871

The saddest intelligence which for many years past has come to sadden hearts in Burnley has come in this cold and sad winter-time. No sadder tidings could have come than those which filled so many hearts with unfeigned grief, and truest sorrow, upon hearing of the lamented death of General Sir James Yorke Scarlett. The intelligence was startling in its unexpectedness. Tidings of his death scarcely gained credit as it passed from friend to friend, and from house to house. And this because he had so recently appeared in public, to all appearance as well in health as usual. It had become generally known on Sunday that he was suffering from what was reported and believed to be only a severe cold; and loving hope buoyed up the public sympathy that it might prove to be no more than an illness of slight severity and short duration. But to the universal regret and grief it has proved otherwise. Inflammation of the chest increased in severity until the professional skill and unwearying attention of Dr Briggs of Burnley, in conjunction with Dr William Roberts of Manchester, were unavailing. During the afternoon of Wednesday his case was considered hopeless; and at about twenty-five minutes past seven o'clock on Wednesday evening General Sir James Yorke Scarlett, GCB, died at his seat, Bank Hall, at the ripe age of seventy-three years.

No man will be more missed: nor any man longer or more deeply regretted. His death is a national loss; whilst to Burnley and the neighbourhood it is irreparable. Of his distinguished military services we need not speak here particularly; because in Burnley they are so well and universally known and appreciated.

* * *

79

*George, Duke of Cambridge, to William, Lord Abinger
Commander in Chief's Office, 8 December 1871*

My dear Abinger, I have received this morning, by your kind letter, the information of the sad news conveyed by the newspapers yesterday morning, regarding the death of my dear old friend and comrade, Sir James Scarlett.[25] I cannot tell you how this news has overwhelmed me with sorrow and grief. To me personally he was a dear, warm and generous friend. I assure you I feel as if I had lost one of my own family, such are my feelings towards the dear departed one.

Will you assure dear Lady Scarlett how deeply and painfully I sympathise with her in her great grief and overwhelming loss? Pray let me know how she is, for my anxiety on her account is great.

We are under great anxiety at the present moment about our dear Prince of Wales.[26] His state is most precarious. In your sorrow you will share our anxieties. I remain, yours sincerely, George.

*   *   *

80

The Funeral of General Scarlett
Burnley Advertiser, 16 December 1871

Wednesday the sixth of December is a day to be ever deeply and sorrowfully engraven in the annals of Burnley, and on the roll of our national bereavements, for at half-past seven o'clock on the evening of that day one of the bravest of England's soldiers; one of the most high bred and honourable of England's untitled nobility; and one of England's most beloved citizens calmly closed his earthly course and 'fell asleep in Jesus' to enter upon, we doubt not, far higher honour, and more enduring reward than any which this world could confer upon his Valour and his Goodness.

His illness had been short. Few had known that his indisposition was attended with danger. During the afternoon of Wednesday rumour spread, in hushed and halting accent, that it was an illness attended with considerable extent of danger – considering his advanced age – but no reliable information had been received to prepare the public mind for the sad tidings of his death which spread over the town and district with lightning speed, and electric shock, as soon as it was known outside the gates of Bank Hall.

The sad intelligence gave rise to one general lament, to universal regret and gloom; and fast and full fell tears from thousands of eyes, whilst deepest sorrow filled thousands of grieving hearts to overflow. Each heart felt it to be a *personal* bereavement. Each tongue spoke of him as a personal friend; all his grand and noble qualities; what he had been to this town and neighbourhood; his public greatness and his private goodness; his many conspicuous virtues; his unaffected kindness; his frank sincerity; his transparent honour; his characteristic condescension to all, which was no condescension in him, but rather genuine kindness of heart; his universal sympathy and generous benevolence; his large-hearted charity, not merely in ministering to the alleviations of poverty and need, but his charity in kindly judgment upon, and loving construction of, the motives and actions of other men; above and before all, his *blameless* life – these, and many other of his great and noble adornments came at once to recollection, and opened wide the floodgate of general public sorrow and grief.

From the time when his lamented death became known until the day of interment the town and district exhibited the tokens of general and public mourning. The blinds of houses in every position of life were drawn down;

shops were very generally partially closed; flags were hoisted half-mast, and the whole town betokened a depth of wide-spread sorrow such as never has been before, probably never will again be manifested in this town and neighbourhood. When Sunday came the feeling was one of oppression. A felt sense of some heavy bereavement seemed to oppress the very atmosphere. The flag floated heavily and languidly, half-mast on the parish church tower, but no peal of bells was rung, and worshippers went to their respective places in silence; or, holding converse with each other in subdued tones of the one subject of General Scarlett's sudden and unexpected death; and clad, for the most part, in garb of deep mourning.

The funeral had been fixed for Monday, to leave Bank Hall at eleven o'clock precisely. So far as the family wished, the funeral was to have been strictly private – none but the nearest relations to be invited. And, it may, probably, be, that such a quiet, unostentatious funeral would have best harmonised with the deceased General's own wishes, had the expression of his will been known. But public feeling ran deep upon this point. Except in obedience to a clearly expressed desire upon the part of the deceased it is doubtful whether a strictly private funeral *could* have been obtained, so urgent was the general desire, and so universal the instinctive longing, to pay the last mournful offices of heart-felt love to the remains of General Scarlett. This irrepressible feeling of universal regard, and the strong yearning it had to gain public expression upon the day of interment, was conveyed to the family by Captain Commandant Handsley, of the 17th Lancashire Rifle Volunteers, in form of request to be permitted to join in the last sad office of the church.

With that spontaneous kindness, that considerate regard for and compliance with public wish, which has ever been a marked characteristic of the family, all private feeling was at once subdued in reference to the arrangement for a strictly private interment. The expression of the public wish was in the kindest manner deferred to, by no small sacrifice of personal preference; and on Friday Captain Handsley was favoured with a letter of which the following is a reprint: the permission which it conveyed giving much satisfaction to all to whom it became known.

Bank Hall, 8 December 1871

My dear Sir, In answer to your letter informing me that the inhabitants of Burnley are desirous that the funeral of the late Sir James Scarlett should be a public one, I can only express the gratification which the late Sir James Scarlett's family experience at the numerous communications of condolence they have received. The family, as far as they are concerned, are anxious to have Sir James Scarlett's funeral conducted in as quiet a manner as possible, and NO invitations have been sent out, except to the more immediate relations of the family. It is, however, far from their wish to prevent or lessen any spontaneous expressions of sympathy on the part of those who wish to show their respect and esteem for one who was for so many years so intimately connected with the town and neighbourhood of Burnley. The funeral cortège will leave Bank Hall at eleven o'clock precisely, on Monday morning, and it is hoped that all who wish to do so will join the procession. Yours very truly, J.H. Thursby.

This kind concession, from the wish of the family that, to be in harmony with the unostentatious habit of the deceased, the arrangements should be strictly private, came as a great and much desired relief. This restriction removed, 'not to prevent or lessen any spontaneous expression of sympathy on the part of those who wish to show their respect', thousands felt they could not only mourn for, but follow General Scarlett to his grave as a friend.

The Mayor of Burnley (J.H. Scott Esq.) promptly acted upon this permission. The following notice was extensively printed throughout the borough in the course of the afternoon, and nothing could exceed the Mayor's thorough and efficient arrangements in reference to General Scarlett's funeral.

Borough of Burnley. Public Notice

The funeral of General Sir James Yorke Scarlett, GCB, having been fixed for Monday next, at eleven a.m., I have to request the members of the Town Council, the magistrates of the neighbourhood, and the burgesses of this borough to join the funeral procession, as a mark of esteem and respect for the memory of the deceased General. I have also to request that the tradesmen's shops, and other places of business, may be closed during the passing of the procession.

The Town Clerk (A.B. Creeke Esq.), by order of the Mayor, forwarded invitations to the members of the Town Council to take part in the procession. Captain Commandant Handsley issued the requisite orders to the 17th Lancashire Rifle Volunteers to be on duty on Monday, and the staff of the 5th Royal Lancashire Militia were placed under similar instructions. On Saturday evening a meeting of the members of the Burnley Constitutional Association was summoned at the Church Infant School,

Pickup Croft, John Greenwood Esq. occupying the chair, at which it was unanimously resolved that the association, and the members of the Sick and Burial Society connected with it (of which the late General was the founder), should attend.[27]

The directors of the Church of England Literary Institution held a meeting in their library the same evening and resolved to attend, as representatives of an institution of which General Scarlett had been a generous supporter, and in whose welfare and progress he always manifested the deepest interest. General Scarlett's support of the Church of England Literary Institution passed beyond mere pecuniary aim, and since its foundation had been a personal concern. He, as often as he was in residence, was ever ready to take part in its public proceedings; and, it may not now be forgotten that it was upon the platform of this Church Institution, upon occasion of its recently held soirée, that he made his last short, kind and genial speech – rich in that transparent sincerity of thought and utterance which never failed to win the confidence and trust of the hearts of all listeners.

Had Providence given longer tenure of life, his voice would, the very days these lines are being read, have been once again heard within the walls of the institution; little did any think as they looked upon his fine soldierly bearing, his kindly beaming face, his strong, hale appearance, it was the last time he would rejoice them with his commanding, noble presence. Nor did this pervading instinct of respect stir corporate bodies only. Artizans and labourers, factory operatives and industrial occupations of every variety which goes to constitute the daily life of the sons of toil in this hive of industry, gave notice of their resolve, and prepared to give up the wages of the day, to respect the burial of one of whom Burnley 'will never see the like again'.

Saturday afternoon seemed given up to preliminary meetings of various organizations completing their preparations; and Sunday intervened as a day of quiet, of rest, of thought, of recollection. Never were the virtues of lost friend talked of more universally, nor more mournfully, than were those of the late and lamented General Scarlett during the intervening hours of this never to be forgotten 'day of rest'. He whom the people mourned with truest deepest grief 'rested' from *all* his earthly strife; rested yet in his earthly home till the morrow, when he should be carried by sixty thousand mourners to the place of his last long 'rest'; and the people – high and low, rich and poor – *rested*; in resolve to undertake no toil upon the day which saw General Scarlett, Burnley's most distinguished townsman, distinguished not more by public renown than by private worth, carried to his last earthly resting place 'from whose bourn no traveller returns'.

The morning of Monday broke gloomily and sadly – unsunnily and sombrously – as befits a day of funeral. It might deepen into rain; silent and continuous. It was a morning which gave no sign, or possibility, of brightening. All around was gloomy. Shops were closed, flags drooped, saturated with moist and damp, and clung to their flag-staffs; people were on the move, and vehicles passed and repassed in every direction, but it was strikingly observable that there appeared a funereal silence and tone overspreading everything. The Mayor had by authority stopped all traffic upon the road by which the funeral cortège had to pass. Upon this line of road thousands upon thousands of mourners began, at a very early hour, to congregate and obtain vantage ground of position, long hours before the procession was timed to pass. Each succeeding few minutes added density to the accumulating crowd, as one special train after another brought to their destination thousands from other towns, stirred with desire to join in the last offices of respect to a distinguished soldier and townsman, whom, from his long association and tie to Lancashire – and the love he has had for it – we may and *do* regard as a Lancashireman.

Every neighbouring town and village was represented by large and mourning numbers: Nelson, Marsden, Colne, Skipton, Padiham, Whalley, Clitheroe, Portsmouth, Todmorden, Blackburn, Accrington, Haslingden, Worsthorne, Briercliffe and Brierfield were all represented; and so it is estimated that, before the hour appointed for the funeral, not less than sixty thousand had assembled to do respect to the memory of a Good, as well as Great, man. The police arrangements were perfect. But it is even more gratifying to be able to say that, so great was the decorum of this large multitude, and so marked their sense of self-imposed order, the official restraint of the police was in no single instance called for; their services being valuable much more for direction and guidance than for control.

A dense but orderly and most respectful crowd lined the whole of Church Street, the space around the parish church, Fenkin Street, up to the gates and in front of Bank Hall. The body of Volunteers and Militia early took up position in front of the hall. To right and to left, and in front, was one thickly packed crowd. To the right up to the Colne Road carriage after carriage took up position, in order of arrival; after which came the pedestrians stretching out in line beyond the Duke of York toll bar; and all were orderly marshalled into place by the efficient services of the County Constabulary under the able superintendency of Inspector Waling, with silent and effective precision, waiting for the moving of the head of the procession.

An eye-witness thus describes it:

The private carriages, the public carriages, containing representative bodies, the tenantry on horseback and on foot, began to arrive a little before ten o'clock, and fell into their allotted positions on the north side of the hall gates, stretching away for near half a mile on the Colne Road. In the rear of the line marked out for vehicles, the members of the Burnley Constitutional Association, and Sick and Burial Club, had been marshalled, under the general direction of T.C. Holden Esq., by an efficient body of active officers. At the actual moment of starting the members mustered about 1200 persons, of whom about seven hundred were males and five hundred females. The latter had precedence, as a matter of courtesy, and were under the guidance of Messrs J. Singleton, S. Gill and J. Watson. The males were arranged by Messrs J. Eastwood, T. Cross, B. Pate, J. Crossley, J. Wright, C. Wells and J. Jackson; and in superior command along the line was Mr Christopher Porrit. In the rear were the members of the Burnley Fire Brigade under Mr C. Slater, the superintendent.

The procession, it will be seen, fell into the following order: Militia and Volunteers, with their bands, the remains of the deceased General and the mourners; the carriages containing friends and representative men, the tenantry and political society, and the Fire Brigade. Even this interminable line was further extended by the police, under Mr Superintendent Alexander, who fell in along the route and brought up the rear.

* * *

81

The Funeral Procession

As the procession slowly moved along from the gate of Bank Hall, to the time it reached the churchyard gate at Holme Chapel, it wended its melancholy way all the long distance of four miles amidst one dense, and compact, but orderly crowd of onlookers.[28] Whichever way the eye turned in Colne Road, it looked upon a solid, densely congregated sea of human faces. As it passed along Fenkin Street it was the same: the space in front, and the churchyard of the parish church, were densely crowded: every wall had its line of occupants; every tombstone from which a better sight could be obtained was taken possession of; every window along the entire line of the procession was occupied to the last inch.

Church Street and Gunsmith Lane were equally thronged. The banks, and the bridge at the aqueduct, and space around accommodated thousands of spectators; and the garb of mourning was extensively put on. As the body passed St Mary's Roman Catholic Church the bell was heard tolling out its tribute of esteem on behalf of a large number of the deceased General's fellow-townsmen. Fulledge Road to Towneley lodge gate held a like mass of respectful mourners.

Nor was it otherwise when the procession, by kind permission of Colonel Towneley, passed beneath the archway and entered the park. Larger space was available in the park than in the streets through which the procession had previously moved for what may be called the pedestrian followers of the funeral; but through the whole length of the park the throng was inconceivably great. In passing its slow route through Towneley Park the effect was very striking.

Nature herself was as if she mourned; and harmonised by the garb she put on, with the solemnity of the occasion. It was curious to observe how dark and solemnly, in their own leafless nakedness, the very trees stood out, silent, dark and solemn, against the background of white mist which, in further distance, as a curtain, shut out the landscape. The nearer and older trees in the park, by no strained power of imagination, but by easy association and natural suggestion, seemed to grow into the semblance of gigantic sentinels, keeping silent, mournful watch as the Great Soldier was borne to his tomb.

Near the second mourning carriage walked, all the long four miles, an old soldier with an unwandering eye, and soldierly step, his breast showing the medals he had won in the Crimean War; fighting, not improbably, at the side of the deceased; but never mourner went to funeral with firmer purpose. He walked unconscious, apparently, of all and anything except that he, as a soldier, who, in his own rank, had gained glory, was paying the last sad offering of respect to a greater soldier whom he honoured and loved; a soldier also who, in higher rank than his, had won greater glory still!

Emerging from Towneley Park the cortège met another multitude of sympathisers: mourners evidently bent upon witnessing the interment. As Holme Chapel was neared the body of followers increased in numbers, until there was difficulty in finding a way to the churchyard gate. So dense was it, and so deep the lines of the spectators, that the estimate of sixty thousand is, probably, much under, rather than in excess of, the true numbers who paid respect to the departed General.

Shortly after one o'clock the churchyard gate was reached, and the body was taken from the gun carriage and placed upon the bier, and carried just within the gate to await the coming of the officiating priests. Very shortly were seen the Reverend Canon Parker, MA, Rector of Burnley, attended by the Reverend Daniel Sutcliffe, MA, Vicar of Holme; and the Reverend C.J. Besley, MA, and the Reverend B. Jackson Cuppage, MA, Curates of Burnley, vested in surplices, stole and hood.[29]

Having received the body, the Reverend Canon Parker began, in quivering voice, and labouring under strong emotion, that noble office for the burial of the dead, which, as a sacred office for worship, has never been equalled by any other sacred service in any branch of the Catholic Church.

* * *

A week later, on the afternoon of Sunday 17 December, after the service at Holme Chapel.

As the congregation left the church, numbers collected about the grave of General Scarlett, notwithstanding the heavy rain which had fallen continuously during the afternoon. Kindly hands and affectionate hearts had carefully prepared the surface of the hallowed ground for these visitors. A neat bed of the greenest sward had been carefully laid over the opening of the vault, and upon this a neat cross of evergreens and pure white roses had been formed. General Scarlett's remains lie almost directly in front of the doorway into the little church, and distant from it only a few feet.[30]

Notes

Introduction

1. See below, p. 139.
2. Kinglake, *The Invasion of the Crimea: Its Origin, and an Account of its Progress Down to the Death of Lord Raglan*, 8 vols (1863–87), iv, chapter 5, p. 32.
3. Stephanie Barczewski, *Heroic Failure and the British* (2016).
4. 'Horatius', in Thomas Babington Macaulay, *Lays of Ancient Rome* (1842).
5. In a cast which included Trevor Howard as Lord Cardigan, John Gielgud as Lord Raglan and David Hemmings at Captain Nolan, Sir John Scarlett was played by Leo Britt (1908–1979). Lady Scarlett was played by Helen Cherry (1915–2001), the wife of Tony Richardson. Scarlett, Lucan and Cardigan also do not appear in *Balaclava*, a silent film of 1928 made by Maurice Elvey and Michael Rosner, starring Cyril McLaglen as John Kennedy. The film's charge sequences were shot at Aldershot.
6. Orders to 5th Dragoon Guards, 25 January 1855.
7. Below, pp. 138–40.
8. See below, p. 193.
9. See below, p. 55.
10. George Ryan, *Our Heroes of the Crimea: Being Biographical Sketches of our Military Officers from the General Commanding to the Subaltern* (London, 1855), p. 148. Even the *Burnley Gazette*, which strenuously opposed his candidacy in the parliamentary election of 1868, never attacked his personal character. On his death, it admitted that 'General Scarlett was a very amiable, kind-hearted and good man, and these were the qualities for which the people admired and loved him', *Burnley Gazette*, 9 December 1871.
11. Below, p. 174.
12. William Scarlett's letters from the Crimea are at present unpublished. I have a typed transcript of many of them by Boyce Gaddes. A copy of this is in the National Army Museum. The originals of a number of William Scarlett's letters, including some not in the transcription, are in the possession of Sarah Scarlett.
13. Below, p. 68.
14. For a fuller account of the archive and its descent, see the Martin Sheppard, 'In Search of General Scarlett', *War Correspondent*, 36, no. 2 (2018), pp. 36–41. This issue of the *War Correspondent* also contains the first part of extracts from the archive, ibid., pp. 42–45; the following issue of the *War Correspondent*, 36, no. 3 (2019), pp. 8–13, contains a second set of extracts.
15. William Scarlett to Robert, Lord Abinger, 9 June 1855, unpublished letter in possession of Sarah Scarlett.
16. Frances Smith, née Scarlett, 'Family Histories', manuscript in my possession.
17. The archive may have been kept between Harold Smith's death in 1939 and 1947 by Harold's sister, Louise Luard, in Hereford, and between 1947, when Louise Luard died, and 1954 by their brother, Sidney Scarlett Smith, at Dinbren, near Llangollen. Both Louise Luard and Sidney Scarlett Smith initialled parts of the archive as having been seen at dates between 1921 and 1953.

18. These copies are in the archive of King's College, London. Hester and Cilla decided to give Frances Scarlett's diaries to King's College, London, where years earlier Hester had studied theology, together with an eccentric selection of other early family letters. Oddly, they told nobody else in the family about this deposit. Hester also cherry-picked a number of the most notable letters, including those from six Prime Ministers and Nelson, and gave them to Roger Scarlett-Smith, the son of another cousin. This selection contains two original letters from the General.

19. General Scarlett was my mother's father's mother's father's brother; or, in simpler terms, my great great great uncle.

Chapter 1: Early Life

1. Elizabeth Woodstock Campbell (b. 1739) married John Yorke, of The Green, Richmond, Yorkshire, in 1769.

2. His brothers and sisters were Robert (1794–1861), second Lord Abinger; Mary (1796–1860), who married John Campbell, later Sir John Campbell and Lord Campbell (1779–1861), Lord Chancellor, 1859–61. She became Baroness Stratheden in her own right; Louise (1797–1871), who married the courtier Sir Edmund Currey; and Peter (1804–1881), who had a distinguished career as a diplomat. Another daughter, Caroline Scarlett (b. 1801), died in infancy.

3. Abinger manuscripts, Bessie Florence Scarlett, notebook. In private hands.

4. G.E. Cockayne, *The Complete Peerage of England, Scotland, Ireland, Great Britain and its United Kingdom, Extant, Extinct or Dormant*, revised by Vicary Gibbs, 13 vols (1910–59), under Abinger.

5. *A Memoir of the Right Honourable James, First Lord Abinger, Chief Baron of the Exchequer: Including a Fragment of his Autobiography and Selections from his Correspondence and Speeches*, edited by Peter Campbell Scarlett (1877), p. 29. At Cambridge, James Scarlett 'made friends with young Peter Campbell of Kilmory in Argyllshire, and by him was introduced to his relations, a grandmother and sisters living at Tittenhanger. Peter Campbell also took him to visit his aunt, Mrs Yorke, whose maiden name was Campbell, at Richmond in Yorkshire, where she and Mr Yorke lived in state.' Frances Smith, née Scarlett, 'Family Histories', unpublished manuscript in the possession of the editor. Yorke is the family name of the Earls of Hardwicke.

6. Ibid., p. 30.

7. She is referred to both as Louisa and Louise. It is unclear which was her name.

8. Bordering Whitehall and St James's Park, Spring Gardens was demolished in the early twentieth century to make way for Admiralty Arch.

9. Frances Smith, née Scarlett, 'Family History', manuscript in possession of the editor.

10. Notebook in Abinger Collection, 1819, inscribed 'P.C. Scarlett, carissimo filio dedit J. Scarlett magni testimonio amoris', 19 January 1819'.

11. See below, p. 153.

12. *Burnley Advertiser*, 14 August 1869. The chairman announced, 'I believe there is no person in this county who regrets more than Lord Derby that from illness he is unable to come and participate in your contribution this evening.' Rule in this case means medical regime.

13. *The Journal of Sir Walter Scott*, ed. W.E.K. Anderson (1972), p. 43.

14. See below, p. 10.

15. As was then common, he did not take a degree.

16. See below, pp. 11–12.

17. Peter Scarlett was a barrister before becoming a distinguished diplomat. See 'Peter Campbell Scarlett, 1804–1881, Diplomatist', *Oxford Dictionary of National Biography*.

18. See below, p. 10.
19. See below, p. 11.
20. See below, pp. 11–12.
21. George Ryan, *Our Heroes of the Crimea: Being Biographical Sketches of our Military Officers from the General Commanding to the Subaltern* (London, 1855), p. 145. The 'Corner' veterans were professional experts at Tattersalls, the racehorse auctioneers, whose auction yard was at Hyde Park Corner until 1865.
22. James Yorke Scarlett was at Eton from 1811 to 1816. His mother was Louise Henrietta Scarlett (1772–1829). Tsar Alexander I of Russia and King Frederick William III of Prussia visited London in June 1814, following Napoleon's abdication and before the Congress of Vienna.
23. Queen Charlotte (1744–1818), the wife of George III. Frogmore House and Gardens are in Windsor Great Park.
24. Montem was an Eton festival, celebrated between 1561 and 1847, at the Montem Mound, Chalvey, Slough, two miles from the school.
25. His younger brother, Peter Campbell Scarlett (1804–1881), was at school at East Sheen before going to Eton in 1819.
26. Not his elder brother, Robert Campbell Scarlett (1794–1861), later second Lord Abinger, who was already at Cambridge. This aunt was probably Mary Scarlett, née White (d. 1839), the wife of Dr Robert Scarlett (b. 1773), who had a son, Robert James Scarlett, born in 1802.
27. The treaty of Paris, ending the war between Britain and France, had been signed on 30 May 1814.
28. Tear. Words in square brackets supplied. Gardener and Martha unidentified.
29. See above, note 26.
30. His father was James Scarlett (1769–1844), later Sir James Scarlett and then the first Lord Abinger. His sisters were Mary Elizabeth Scarlett (1796–1860) and Louise Lawrence Scarlett (1797–1871). Sir William Anglin Scarlett (1777–1831) was his uncle. Philip Anglin Scarlett (b. 1800), mentioned here, was his first cousin.
31. His brothers Robert and Peter Scarlett.
32. Election Monday at Eton was the day when scholars to go to King's College, Cambridge, were chosen from the Collegers (scholars) at Eton.
33. Louise Lawrence Scarlett.
34. Mary Elizabeth Scarlett.
35. See above, note 26, on the identity of Bob.
36. Tear. Last word 'right' supplied.
37. Probably Alain-René Lesage, *Le Diable boiteux* (1707); possibly Jacques Cazotte, *Le Diable amoureux* (1772).
38. James Yorke Scarlett was at Trinity College, Cambridge from 1816 to 1818.
39. Charles Malorti de Martemont, Professor of Fortification at Woolwich Arsenal, published a commentary on a translation of Dietrich von Bülow, *The Spirit of the Modern System of War by a Prussian General Officer* (1806). He also wrote *The Theory of Field Fortification* (1810).
40. J. Bigge unidentified. The Bigges were Northumberland gentry.
41. At Eton.
42. An early indication of James Yorke Scarlett's professional dedication to soldiering.
43. Unidentified poem.
44. Robert Scarlett became a barrister, but he was never as successful as his father.

Chapter 2: Cavalry Officer

1. The Marquess of Anglesey, *A History of the British Cavalry, 1816–1919*, i, *1816–1850* (1973), pp. 48–63. At Salamanca the 5th Dragoon Guards had charged with the 3rd and 4th Dragoons.

2. H. Moyse-Bartlett, *Louis Edward Nolan and his Influence on the British Cavalry* (1971), pp. 69–93, provides an excellent account of the evolution of British cavalry.

3. The dates of his commissions were cornet, 26 March 1818; lieutenant, 24 October 1821; captain, 9 June 1823; major, 11 June 1830; lieutenant colonel, 3 July 1840; colonel, 11 November, 1851; major general, 12 December 1854; lieutenant general, 9 November 1862; general, 1 November 1870. For the purchase system, see the Marquess of Anglesey, *A History of the British Cavalry*, i, pp. 155–56, 163–66. For the reduction of cavalry numbers after Waterloo, ibid., pp. 74–76.

4. George Ryan, *Our Heroes of the Crimea: Being Biographical Sketches of our Military Officers from the General Commanding to the Subaltern* (London, 1855), pp. 145–48.

5. See below, pp. 22–24.

6. Ryan. *Our Heroes of the Crimea*, p. 145–146. 'In this regiment, when he became captain, he was remarked for attention to the men and horses of his troop.' The Carabiniers were so-called because, from the time of the Napoleonic Wars, they carried a carbine, a shorter version of a musket or rifle.

7. Ryan, *Our Heroes of the Crimea*, p. 146. He was promoted major on 11 June 1830.

8. W.C. Cecil, *A Memorial for Thomas Cecil* (1962), p. 11; quoted in the Marquess of Anglesey, *A History of the British Cavalry*, i, p. 71.

9. Evidence before the Finance Committee, 1828, 4, quoted Charles Clode, *The Military Forces of the Crown: Their Administration and Government*, 2 vols (1869); Marquess of Anglesey, *A History of the British Cavalry*, i, pp. 73–74.

10. Records of the 5th Dragoon Guards, Royal Dragoon Guards Museum, York.

11. Records of the 5th Dragoon Guards, 1830. These agricultural disturbances, known as the Swing Riots, although widespread and marked by the burning of barns, caused directly only one known death. Afterwards, however, nineteen of those involved were hanged and many more transported to Australia.

12. Records of the 5th Dragoon Guards, 1837.

13. Records of the 5th Dragoon Guards, 1839.

14. Records of the 5th Dragoon Guards, 1841.

15. Records of the 5th Dragoon Guards, 1849.

16. Henry Franks, *Leaves from a Soldier's Note Book* (1904; reprinted Doncaster, 2016), p. 11.

17. Ibid., pp 11–12. 'Colonel Scarlett, by the many reforms and improvements that he had introduced into the barrack rooms, and the system of cooking, messing and other matters which I have previously mentioned, had produced a remarkably beneficial effect. It was soon evident the men were determined to let the colonel see that his kindness was duly appreciated, and he soon had the satisfaction of seeing his regiment one of the most contented and best conducted regiments in the Dublin Garrison.' Ibid., p. 23.

18. Ibid., pp. 23–24. 'Colonel Scarlett was a very good judge of horses, and he had taken great pride and pains in having his regiment well mounted. I hope I may say without any boasting that at the time I am speaking of there was not a better mounted corps in the service than the 5th Dragoon Guards.' Ibid. p. 24.

19. 'On the 10th inst. at Burnley Church, by the Rev. W. Thursby, the Hon. J. Yorke Scarlett, second son of the Right Hon. Lord Abinger, and a major in the 5th Dragoon Guards, to Charlotte Anne, second daughter and co-heiress with her only sister,

Mrs Thursby, of the late Colonel Hargreaves of Bank Hall and Ormerod House, in Lancashire. After the marriage the bride and bridegroom started from Ormerod House for the seat of Lord Abinger, Abinger Hall, Surrey.' *Norfolk Chronicle*, 26 December 1835.

20. *Blackburn Standard*, 23 January 1839. A similar notice appeared in a number of other newspapers.
21. Catherine Parker, the wife of the rector of Burnley.
22. *Burnley Advertiser*, 6 February 1869.
23. See below, p. 25.
24. *Hansard*, 3 April 1838. Although slavery had been abolished in 1834, the ex-slaves were still supposed to serve as indentured servants for six years.
25. See below, pp. 41–42.
26. *Lancaster Gazette*, 17 July 1852.
27. See below, pp. 27 and 30.
28. See below, pp. 38 and 39.
29. See below, pp. 31. He retained a strong interest in education, becoming a governor of Burnley Grammar School and donating liberally to the cost of establishing additional schools in Burnley
30. The Duke of Wellington's campaigns in India and in the Napoleonic War.
31. See below, p. 36.
32. A letter, written in Ireland to his brother Robert. No date or place but probably from the first half of 1821, the year when the 18th Hussars were disbanded in Ireland. James Yorke Scarlett, commissioned on 26 March 1818, had joined the regiment as a cornet in 1818. In the letter he refers to having been three years in the army. By 1830 he had become a major in the 5th Dragoon Guards. The regimental collection of the 18th Hussars is held in the Discovery Museum, Newcastle-upon-Tyne.
33. Not the indication of an imminent engagement. Robert Scarlett did not marry until 1824.
34. Italicised passage underlined in the original.
35. Lieutenant Colonel William Davy of the 18th Hussars.
36. Given as Sir D.O. in the original. Major-General Sir David Ochterlony, first Baronet of Pitforthy (1758–1825), was a leading figure in the forces of the East India Company.
37. Possibly the Highland Light Infantry.
38. Returning from Ireland to England before the possible posting to India.
39. For a succinct history of the British cavalry, including the distinction between light and heavy cavalry, see Moyse-Bartlett, *Louis Edward Nolan and his Influence on the British Cavalry*, pp. 67–93.
40. Commissions were mostly bought and sold and became important property rights. An investment in the army by members of the ruling class was seen as a constitutional safeguard against revolution.
41. A reference to a posting to India.
42. Since 1687 the officers in the Guards had held army ranks higher than their regimental ranks. A captain in the Guards would also have the army rank of lieutenant colonel.
43. Nothing is made of nothing.
44. This helps date this letter to the first half of 1821.
45. His father, James Scarlett, later first Lord Abinger (1769–1844), was at the time a leading barrister on the Northern Circuit.
46. Lieutenant Colonel William Davy.
47. According to the *Morning Post*, 23 April 1821, 'Lieutenant John Thomas Machell, who was removed from the Service on the 1st of March, 1821, has been reinstated in his rank'. Machell had been born in Beverley in 1793.

48. Major James Hughes.
49. Frederick, Duke of York and Albany (1763–1827), second son of George III, a major figure in the army even after his resignation as Commander in Chief in 1809, following a scandal over the sale of commissions by his mistress Mary Anne Clarke.
50. James Yorke Scarlett married Charlotte Anne Hargreaves (1806–1888), of Bank, Burnley, and Ormerod Hall, Cliviger, on 19 December 1835. Bank Hall, a large house in Burnley, was his home from then until his death.
51. Sarah (Sally) Smith (1803–1878) had married Robert Scarlett in 1824. Abinger Hall, Abinger, Surrey, was the country house belonging to Robert Scarlett's father, James Scarlett. The letter expresses condolences on the deaths of Anne Smith (1774–1838) and Elizabeth Smith (1776–1838), the sisters of Sarah Scarlett's father, George Smith. They were two of three of Sarah Scarlett's unmarried aunts and lived at Ashtead, Surrey.
52. Charlotte Scarlett was subject to episodes of severe depression. She gave birth to a still-born daughter in Birmingham on 15 January 1839, *Blackburn Standard*, 23 January 1839.
53. Mitchelstown Castle, the largest Neo-Gothic house in Ireland, was rebuilt on an existing site by George King, third Earl of Kingston (1771–1839), in the 1820s. It had eighty bedrooms and three libraries. It was burned down in 1922. His successor was Robert King, fourth Earl of Kingston (1796–1867). The fourth Earl of Kingston was arrested in 1848 for intent to commit an 'unnatural offence', with a young man named Cull, behind Marylebone Police Station. Sent for trial, he failed to surrender to bail, dying abroad in 1867. Two of James Yorke Scarlett's nephews, James Scarlett and Hallyburton Campbell, were both taught for a time by the Reverend John Joyce (d. 1850), vicar of Dorking.
54. Stephen Moore, third Earl Mount Cashell (1792–1883), married Anna Marie Wyse or Wyss (1793–1876) of Bern, Switzerland. They had four daughters and three sons, all of whom became in turn Earl Mount Cashell.
55. Lady Jane Moore (b.1820), the eldest daughter of the third Earl Mount Cashell. John Massey Dawson, rector of Abinger. Others unidentified.
56. Cahir, Tipperary, the site of a barracks.
57. The Chartists were extremely active in Manchester and other Lancashire towns in 1840 and 1841.
58. His niece Henrietta Scarlett (1825–1895). Probably Theresa Villiers Stuart, wife of Henry Villiers Stuart of Dromana, Waterford.
59. John Roebuck MP (1802–1879), a Radical MP. Later the chairman of the parliamentary committee set up, at his instigation, to enquire into the conduct of the Crimean War.
60. Robert Scarlett, acting on behalf of his father, bought a large estate in Lochaber, near Fort William, at an auction in Edinburgh on 21 October 1840.
61. John Joyce (d. 1850). The two sons mentioned here were probably Charles Moore (1826–1898), later fifth Earl Mount Cashell; and Edward Moore (1829–1915), later sixth Earl Mount Cashell.
62. Sir Edward Blakeney (1778–1868), a veteran of the Peninsular War, became Commander in Chief in Ireland in 1836, a position he held until 1855. Doonas or Doonass, Clonlara, Clare, belonged to Sir Hugh Dillon Massey, whose daughter was married to Sarah Scarlett's brother Felix Smith.
63. Captain Abraham Bolton of the 5th Dragoon Guards. John Massey Dawson was the rector of Abinger from 1835–50. His niece Mary had married George Evelyn, of Wotton Hall, Wotton, Surrey, the patron of the living, in 1821. The Massey Dawsons (also Massy Dawson) were an Irish Ascendancy family in Tipperary.

64. Felix Smith (1800–1879), Sarah Scarlett's brother.
65. Dublin Castle, the centre of government in Ireland.
66. Peter Campbell Scarlett became a distinguished diplomat.
67. James Yorke Scarlett was elected Tory MP for Guildford in July 1837, defeating the Liberal candidate by 29 votes. He was defeated in 1841 by a Liberal, despite an overall Conservative victory in the country.
68. Robert Scarlett was MP for Horsham from 1841–44.
69. Although the Scarletts' estate around Inverlochy was large, it was centred on an unsatisfactory house at Torlundie. Over the following years, Robert Scarlett (second Lord Abinger from 1844), rebuilt the house. It was then greatly enlarged, as Inverlochy Castle, by his son, William Scarlett, third Lord Abinger.
70. Colonel Sir Edmund Currey (1778–1842), a courtier married to James Yorke Scarlett's sister Louise, was attached to the household of Mary, Duchess of Gloucester (1776–1857). According to his obituary in the *Gentleman's Magazine* (1842), p. 546, 'He was the fifth son of the Rev. John Currey, Rector of Dartford, Kent, by the only daughter of George Elliot Esq., of Stobbs, N.B., and Wombwell Hall, Kent. He was made a Lieutenant in the Royal Artillery in 1794; served in the campaigns in Holland and Egypt; was appointed aide de camp to his Royal Highness the Duke of Gloucester in 1803, and Secretary and Comptroller of his household in 1805. He retired from the Artillery in 1808, but received the rank of lieutenant colonel from William IV on his accession, and the honour of the Guelphic order on the death of the Duke of Gloucester in 1834.'
71. *Surrey Standard*, a local newspaper.
72. Daniel O'Connell (1775–1847), known as 'The Liberator' the main Irish nationalist leader of the first half of the nineteenth century.
73. O'Connell was the first Catholic Lord Mayor of Dublin, 1841–42.
74. Prince Albert Edward, later King Edward VII, was christened at Windsor on 25 January 1842.
75. Sir Robert Peel (1788–1850), Conservative Prime Minister, 1834–35 and 1841–46.
76. Charles Vereker, second Viscount Gort (1768–1842), of Loughcoole, Fermanagh. Mitchelstown Castle in County Cork. Lismore Castle belonged to the Dukes of Devonshire; Currey at Lismore, unidentified, but perhaps a connection of Sir Edmund Currey, his brother-in-law.
77. 'Henry le Poer Bereford, third Marquess of Waterford (1811–1859)', *Oxford Dictionary of National Biography*.
78. Henry Chetwynd-Talbot, Viscount Ingestre, later eighteenth Earl of Shrewsbury (1803–1868), had married Lady Sarah Beresford, the daughter of the second Marquess of Waterford, in 1828. Rockwell is in Tipperary. Parliament was opened by Queen Victoria on 3 February 1842.
79. The besetting temptation of butlers.
80. James Yorke Scarlett's address in the *Royal Court Guide and Fashionable Directory for 1842* is given as Dartmouth House, St James's Park; and Bank Hall, Burnley, Lancashire.
81. James, first Lord Abinger, lived at 4 New Street, Spring Gardens, Westminster. He recovered in 1842 but died of a stroke in April 1844.
82. Henrietta Scarlett (1825–1895) was seventeen in 1842.
83. This is likely to be a reference to the houses in New Street, Spring Gardens, near Whitehall. The Scarletts lived at No. 4, while their cousins, the Campbells, lived at No. 9. The Bullers, a Devon family, lived at No. 10.
84. Felix Smith and his wife Charlotte, née Massey. She was the daughter of Sir Hugh Dillon Massey, second Baronet (1768–1842) and his wife, Elizabeth, of Doonas,

Clonlara, Clare. The proposed sale followed the death of Sir Hugh on 28 March 1842. Doonas House was close to the Doonas Falls of the River Shannon. Doonas is also often spelt Doonass and Massey often spelt Massy.

85. Peter Campbell Scarlett.

86. Akbar Khan, the Afghan leader in the First Anglo-Afghan War, which led to the massacre on the retreat from Kabul in 1842.

87. Lord Cardigan was unpopular on many grounds. He was blackballed no less than twenty-eight times on 6 July 1841 and another eighteen times seven years later. Saul David, *The Homicidal Earl: The Life of Lord Cardigan* (1997), pp. 178–79. On his return to England after the Charge of the Light Brigade, Cardigan was elected an honorary member of the club. Ibid., p. 328.

88. Major General William Elphinstone, who commanded the British forces in Afghanistan, died there as a captive in April 1842.

89. Sir Edmund Currey, James Yorke Scarlett's brother-in-law, died on 27 August 1842.

90. Sir Edward Blakeney, the Commander in Chief in Ireland.

91. Fitzwilliam Place, part of which makes one side of Fitzwilliam Square, is a handsome Georgian street.

92. Kerrera, an island near Oban. Although there is a ruined castle on the island, there is no large house. Kerrera may therefore be the name of a house on the mainland.

93. John Hely-Hutchinson, third Earl of Donoughmore (1787–1851), of Knocklofty House, Tipperary; Richard Talbot, second Lord Talbot of Malahide (1766–1849).

94. The Duke of Wellington's campaigns in India and in the Napoleonic War.

95. James Scarlett (1830–1845), Sarah Scarlett's younger son.

96. A grace and favour apartment at Hampton Court for his widowed sister, Louise, Lady Currey.

97. Thomas de Grey, second Earl de Grey (1781–1859), Lord Lieutenant of Ireland, 1841–44.

98. The Chartists were active in Lancashire during the economic depression of the early 1840s. A strike in Preston in August 1842 had led to the reading of the Riot Act and four deaths from shots fired by the military.

99. Appleton Hall, Warrington, Cheshire, was built by Thomas Lyon (1786–1859) in the 1820s. James Yorke Scarlett and his wife were living in Stapleford, Nottinghamshire.

100. William Scarlett, the elder son of Robert Scarlett, was James Yorke Scarlett's nephew.

101. His commission was dated 26 March 1818.

102. Robert Scarlett, second Lord Abinger.

103. William Scarlett obtained a cornetcy in the 5th Dragoon Guards but soon exchanged into the Scots Fusilier Guards.

104. Lord Fitzroy Somerset, later first Lord Raglan (1788–1855).

105. The 10th Royal Hussars were sent to India in 1846.

106. His own regiment, the 5th Dragoon Guards.

107. William Scarlett had obtained a commission in the Scots Fusilier Guards. George Duckworth (1826–1854), who was joining the 5th Dragoon Guards, was the son of William Duckworth of Beechwood, Lymington, Hampshire. This letter is preserved in the Somerset Archives, DD/DU/181. See also, below, pp. 156–57.

108. Henrietta Scarlett was the elder daughter of Robert and Sarah Scarlett.

109. Henrietta Scarlett married Otway Graham-Toler (1824–1884), second son of the second Earl of Norbury, on 26 July 1846. Lord Norbury had been murdered by an unknown assassin at Durrow, Queen's County, Ireland, in January 1839.

110. William Scarlett did not marry until 1863, when he married Helen Magruder, the niece of a Confederate general. He was a keen fisherman.

111. Lord George Bentinck (1802–1848), racing enthusiast and leading Protectionist politician. The split in the Conservative Party over the repeal of the Corn Laws in June 1846 led to the resignation of Sir Robert Peel as Prime Minister.
112. Benjamin Disraeli, Earl of Beaconsfield (1814–1881), Prime Minister, 1868, 1874–80.
113. Democritus, pre-Socratic Greek philosopher of the fifth century BC, known as the Laughing Philosopher for his reaction to human folly.
114. John Campbell, first Lord Campbell (1779–1861), James Yorke Scarlett's brother-in-law and the author of *The Lives of the Lord Chancellors*, did not himself become Lord Chancellor until 1859.
115. The Duke of Wellington persuaded the House of Lords to pass the Repeal of the Corn Laws on 25 June 1846.
116. Lord Francis Gordon (1808–1857), son of the ninth Marquess of Huntly (1761–1853), a regular officer in the 1st Life Guards. The Northern Regiment of the Yorkshire West Riding Yeomanry, founded in 1794, became the Yorkshire Hussar Regiment of Yeomanry Cavalry in 1819.
117. Francis Egerton, first Earl of Ellesmere (1800–1857).
118. James Yorke Scarlett's cousins, the Yorkes, lived at Yorke House, Richmond, Yorkshire. His father had proposed to his mother there.
119. Charlotte Scarlett here refers to her husband by his second name Yorke. Unfortunately, Henrietta Scarlett's marriage to Otway Graham-Toler proved an unhappy one.
120. Swinburne Castle, Hexham, Northumberland, demolished in 1960.
121. Captain J. Ireland Blackburne (1817–1893), 5th Dragoon Guards. Mr Johnson unidentified.
122. By his marriage to Charlotte Hargreaves in 1835, James Yorke Scarlett had become the largest employer and highest ratepayer in Burnley, although not the largest landowner. He was naturally interested in local property changes.
123. Eleanor Thursby, her sister. The railway from York to Scarborough had opened in 1845.
124. Ashtead, Surrey, where Sarah, Lady Abinger, had been brought up and where her cousin Lizzie Denshire lived.
125. The Hunt Ball, at the Assembly Rooms, York, was on 7 October, *York Herald*, 10 October 1846. The Yeomanry Ball was at the Mansion House, Doncaster, on 15 October 1846, *York Herald*, 17 October 1846.
126. General Sir Maxwell Wallace (1783–1863), of Ainderby Hall, Northallerton, Yorkshire. He had commanded the 5th Dragoon Guards before James Yorke Scarlett.
127. Thomas de Grey, second Earl de Grey (1781–1859), Lord Lieutenant of Ireland, 1841–44, colonel of the Yorkshire Hussars for forty years. The De Grey Rooms in York, built in 1841–42 by public subscription, were used for the social events of the Yorkshire Hussars.
128. Otterington Hall, South Otterington, North Riding, Yorkshire; Brantinghamthorpe Hall, Brantingham, East Riding Yorkshire, bought by Captain Richard Fleetwood Sharpe (1804–1872) in 1832; Burlington is in Shropshire.
129. Stopping at Bank Hall, Burnley, on his way south from Inverlochy.
130. Peter Campbell Scarlett was Secretary of the British Legation in Florence. This may be a reference to a possible posting to Portugal following the return there of Joao Carlos de Saldanha, duke of Saldanha, in 1846 or even a possible war.
131. Henry Temple, third Viscount Palmerston (1784–1865), Foreign Secretary, 1830–34, 1835–41 and 1846–51; Prime Minister, 1855–58 and 1859–65.
132. A prescient comment on the Crimean War.
133. Lord George Bentinck (1802–1848), a leading Protectionist and sportsman.

134. The Repeal of the Corn Laws, on 25 June 1846, led to the resignation of Sir Robert Peel as Prime Minister.
135. Frances Diana Smith (1781–1866).
136. Elizabeth, Dowager Lady Scarlett (1802–1886); Floors Castle, Roxburghshire, the seat of the Dukes of Roxburgh.

Chapter 3: War with Russia

1. For the events and decisions that led to the war, see Orlando Figes, *Crimea* (2011), pp. 1–129; Trevor Royle, *Crimea: The Great Crimean War, 1854–1856* (2000), pp. 1–127. The first volume of Alexander Kinglake, *The Invasion of the Crimea: Its Origins and Account of its Progress down to the Death of Lord Raglan* (8 vols, 1863–87), is entirely devoted to the origins of the war. Many other books on the campaign in the Crimea begin with shorter summaries of the causes of the war. For perceptive comments on the nature of the war, see Ian Beckett, *The Victorians at War* (2003), chapter 17, 'The First Modern War?', pp. 161–78.
2. For a Russian perspective on the origins of the war, see Albert Seaton, *The Crimean War: A Russian Chronicle* (1977), pp. 17–49. See also, Figes, *Crimea*, pp. 61–99.
3. See William Dalrymple, *The Anarchy: The Relentless Rise of the East India Company* (2019).
4. Or in Burma, conquered in 1824.
5. Royle, *Crimea*, p. 105.
6. For a recent history of this disastrous war, see William Dalrymple, *Return of a King: The Battle for Afghanistan* (2013).
7. George Gleig, *Sale's Brigade in Afghanistan* (1879), p. 181.
8. For the origins of this expression, Royle, *Crimea*, pp. 25–26.
9. Stratford Canning (1786–1880), ennobled as Viscount Stratford de Redcliffe in 1852, was British Ambassador to the Ottoman Empire, 1825–28 and 1841–58. He exercised great authority in Constantinople, where he was known as the 'Great Elchi' or the Great Ambassador.
10. Figes, *Crimea*, pp. 1–9; Royle, *Crimea*, pp. 15–20.
11. Figes, *Crimea*, pp. 107–10, 112–14.
12. Royle, Crimea, pp. 91–97. The destruction of the Turkish fleet at Sinope, where the Turks lost three thousand men and the Russians thirty-eight, demonstrated the devastating effect of explosive shells on wooden ships. Beckett, *The Victorians at War*, p. 170.
13. Andrew Lambert, *The Crimean War: British Grand Strategy against Russia, 1853–1856* (1991).
14. For the formation of the Anglo-French alliance, see Figes, *Crimea*, pp. 157–58.
15. Lieutenant General George Bingham, third Earl of Lucan (1800–1888). For Lucan, see Tom Blaney, *The Notorious Third Lord Lucan: An Embattled Life* (2020).
16. Major General James Brudenell, seventh Earl of Cardigan (1797–1866).
17. For the appointment of Lucan and Cardigan, see Royle, *Crimea*, pp. 130–32, and Kinglake, *The Invasion of the Crimea*, iv, chapter 7, pp. 53–65.
18. As Lord George Bingham, Lucan had married Lady Anne Brudenell in June 1829. They had two sons and four daughters, but Anne hated living on Lucan's estates in Mayo and claimed that Lucan was a tyrant. The couple had permanently separated by 1854. Saul David, *The Homicidal Earl: The Life of Lord Cardigan* (1997), p. 233.
19. See John Sweetman, *Raglan: From Peninsula to the Crimea* (new edn, 2010), pp. 172–73.
20. The Marquess of Anglesey, ed., *Little Hodge: Being Extracts from the Diaries and Letters of Colonel Edward Cooper Hodge Written during the Crimean War, 1854–1856* (1971), p. 6.

21. For Scarlett's appointment, see Kinglake, *The Invasion of the Crimea*, iv, chapter 7, p. 74.
22. Lawrence W. Crider, *In Search of the Heavy Brigade: A Biographical Dictionary* (2012), pp. 587–92.
23. James Yorke Scarlett had been appointed as the Brigadier of the Heavy Brigade on 21 February 1854. While in London in April he had a prolonged interview with the Commander in Chief, Lord Hardinge, and was given a farewell dinner by his sister, Lady Stratheden, and her husband, Lord Campbell. His main worry was how his wife would cope with their separation.
24. See below, pp. 66 and 67.
25. Henry Franks, *Leaves from a Soldier's Note Book* (1904; reprinted 2016), p. 34. James Yorke Scarlett to Sarah, Lady Abinger, 20 June 1854, below, p. 70: 'Almost the whole world are gone to Varna or going today. I am left till some more of my brigade arrive. The 5th went on in the *Himalaya* without disembarking. I went on board and was received with many a cheer.'
26. William Forrest to his brother, Varna, 27 August 1854, National Army Museum, 5804/32.
27. William Forrest to his brother, Varna, 17 July 1854.
28. William Forrest to his brother, Varna, 27 August 1854.
29. See below, p. 83.
30. Cardigan and Lucan quarrelled over the former's claim that he had been told that his command was independent of his divisional commander.
31. The siege of Silistria by the Russians lasted from 4 April to 24 June 1854. Figes, *Crimea*, pp. 172–75, 183–84.
32. See below, p. 70.
33. The Royals arrived from England between 28 June and 14 July 1854. Roy Dutton, *Forgotten Heroes: The Charge of the Heavy Brigade* (2008), p. 28. The 4th Dragoon Guards, sailing from Scutari, landed on 10 July. Ibid., p. 162. The Inniskillings were at Varna by 12 July, 6th Dragoons, Regimental Orders, 1831–1870. The Scots Greys only sailed from England in July and arrived in the Crimea without landing at Varna.
34. Temple Godman's letters from this time repeatedly look forward to his arrival, *A Cavalryman in the Crimea: The Letters of Temple Godman, 5th Dragoon Guards*, edited by Philip Warner (2009), pp. 20, 23, 25. Godman reported from Devna on 12 July 1854 that 'We expect our Brigadier today', ibid., p. 33. On 17 July Godman reported, 'Our Brigadier is come, which we are glad of', ibid., p. 36. Scarlett probably arrived on 14 July.
35. On the south coast of the Black Sea.
36. A military camp about eighteen miles north west of Varna.
37. A makeshift bed, possibly some loose straw and a blanket.
38. William Scarlett to Sarah, Lady Abinger, 18 July 1854.
39. *A Cavalryman in the Crimea*, ed. Warner, p. 53.
40. G.M. Trevelyan, *English Social History* (1944), p. 554.
41. See below, p. 81. According to Temple Godman, 'Devna is a wretched place – any village you saw in Connemara is much better – hardly anyone to be seen, not even chicken', *A Cavalryman in the Crimea*, ed. Warner, p. 26.
42. *Times*, 15 June 1854.
43. William Cattell, 'Bygone Days and Reminiscences by the Way', unpublished memoirs, Royal Army Medical Corps, Museum of Military Medicine, RAMC/PE/1/11-2/ CATT, 'The Crimean War', p. 18.
44. Ibid., p. 17.
45. Ibid., p. 18.

46. At Malta Le Marchant had brought a court martial against a serjeant major for a trivial offence and had then become enraged when this ended in an acquittal. He subsequently, at Devna, told the Duke of Cambridge that his regiment had mutinied. Scarlett did his best to defuse the latter incident. Franks, *Leaves from a Soldier's Note Book*, pp. 30–34, 40–42, 50.

47. Ibid., p. 48.

48. Cattell, 'Crimean War', p. 16.

49. Franks, *Leaves from a Soldier's Note Book*, pp. 56–57.

50. See below p. 138. William Scarlett wrote to his father, 'Our Brigadier is flourishing. His regiment is much more healthy now, but I fear they are going to incorporate it with the 4th Dragoon Guards. Lucan is utterly inefficient and his appointment is admitted on all sides to be the worst in the army.' William Scarlett to Robert, Lord Abinger, 27 August 1854.

51. Kinglake, *The Invasion of the Crimea*, ii, chapter 4, pp. 93–95. Newcastle was Secretary for State for War.

52. See below, p. 80.

53. Godman, *A Cavalryman in the Crimea*, ed. Warner, p. 47. 'Lord Raglan told Uncle Jim that his brigade would embark with the Second Division', William Scarlett to Robert, Lord Abinger, 27 August 1854.

54. Godman, *A Cavalry Man in the Crimea*, ed. Warner, p. 55.

55. For the battle of the Alma, see Figes, *Crimea*, pp. 208–22; Royle, *Crimea*, pp. 217–42.

56. William Scarlett, General Scarlett's nephew, was heavily engaged at the Alma. He described his experiences in two letters to his family.

57. *Crimean Cavalry Letters*, edited by Glenn Fisher (2011), p. 123.

58. Godman, *A Cavalryman in the Crimea*, ed. Warner, p. 60.

59. James Yorke Scarlett. Her brother, William Scarlett, an officer in the Scots Fusilier Guards, sailed from Portsmouth on 28 March 1854.

60. James Yorke Scarlett was appointed to command the Heavy Brigade in February 1854.

61. Peter Campbell Scarlett.

62. The officer charged with buying mules and horses was Captain Louis Nolan (1820–1854), the author of two books on cavalry, later to become notorious as the aide de camp who delivered the order to Lord Lucan which resulted in the Charge of the Light Brigade.

63. Major C.W.M. Balders had been promoted to be second-in-command of the cavalry depôt at Maidstone.

64. For Scarlett's lasting attachment to his regiment, see below, p. 164.

65. Thomas Le Marchant (1811–1873), despite his distinguished cavalry heritage, proved to be a failure when commanding the 5th Dragoon Guards. See above, p. 59.

66. Lieutenant General John Le Marchant (1766–1812) was killed leading three regiments of dragoons in a successful and indeed decisive charge at Salamanca. The Marquess of Anglesey, *A History of British Cavalry, 1816–1919*, i, *1816–1850*, pp. 54–55.

67. 'Among her Majesty's guests have been the Duke of Cambridge, the Duke and Duchess of Hamilton, the Archbishop of York and Mrs Musgrave, the Duke of Newcastle, the Earl of Cardigan, Lord and Lady John Russell, Mr T.B. Macaulay, Brigadier General Pennefather, Brigadier General Buller, the Earl and Countess of Clarendon, Mr and Mrs Sidney Herbert, Brigadier General Scarlett and Captain Sir Baldwin Walker.' *Derby Mercury*, 5 April 1854.

68. Major James Conolly (1818–1885), brigade major of the Heavy Brigade.

69. William Beatson (1804–1872) had a distinguished career as the leader of irregular cavalry in India before the Crimean War.

70. Although he had been Secretary of Legation at Florence since 1844, Peter Campbell
Scarlett only became Minister in Florence in 1858, after three years in Rio de Janeiro.
Henry Lytton Bulwer, first Lord Dalling (1801–1872), was Minister in Florence for
two years from 1852. Constantine Phipps, first Marquess of Normanby (1797–1863),
was Ambassador to France, 1854–58.
71. Trig means exact, neat or tidy.
72. St George's Hospital, Hyde Park Corner, by William Wilkins, 1827–44.
73. James Brudenell, seventh Earl of Cardigan (1797–1868), the commander of the Light
Brigade.
74. In the early days of the railways, there was often provision for coaches to be carried on
trains with their owners in their carriages.
75. Hotel unidentified.
76. Colonel James Yorke Scarlett.
77. James Conolly (1818–1885), who had previously been on half-pay.
78. Versailles, built by Louis XIV (1638–1715), king of France, 1648–1715, known as 'Le
Roi Soleil' and 'Le Grand Monarque'.
79. Louis-Philippe (1773–1850), king of France, 1830–48. After abdicating in February
1848, he left Paris in disguise, travelling in an ordinary cab under the name of
Mr Smith, before crossing the Channel to England.
80. Chalon-sur-Saône, Saône-et-Loire.
81. James Brudenell, seventh Earl of Cardigan; George Hay-Drummond, Viscount
Dupplin, later twelfth Earl of Kinnoull (1827–1897), captain in the 1st Life Guards.
82. Their courier.
83. Hôtel du Louvre et de la Poste, Valence.
84. Uglies were shades projecting from a lady's hat or bonnet.
85. Murray's *Handbook for Travellers to France* (third edition, 1848).
86. The popes were in Avignon between 1309 and 1376.
87. Hôtel de l'Orient, unidentified.
88. A member of the British Legation at Florence, where the General's brother, Peter
Campbell Scarlett, was Secretary.
89. Lieutenant Colonel Charles Townley (1815–1889). His rank was derived from the
Foreign Service rather than army. Some years before, he may have misbehaved
towards Frances Scarlett's cousin, Adelaide Currey. According to Frances's diary for
May 1851, Adelaide 'was young, and innocent, and knew not the ways of this wicked
world. He after the fashion of men cared little for her feelings so long as he amused
himself – the result is he amuses himself now with someone else, whilst life has lost
its brightness for her, her cheek is pale, her spirits gone, and she finds bitterly that
"men were deceivers ever". Poor Adelaide, she did not tell me all this, but I saw it, I
felt it. She is too guileless to keep such a secret, which I fear makes her poor young
head very heavy.' The previous pages of the diary have been cut out, so the matter
is unclear. Arriving on Malta on 19 May, he left for Constantinople on board the
French steamer *Alexandre* on 25 May.
90. A French paddle-steamer of 3910 tons, in service 1846–66.
91. The *Valetta* was a paddle-steamer belonging to the Peninsular and Oriental Steam
Navigation Company (P & O).
92. Varna, a port on the coast of what is now Bulgaria.
93. The *Himalaya*, of 3438 tons, was the largest passenger steamer in the world when
launched by the P & O in 1853. Bought by the Royal Navy in 1854, she served as a
troopship for forty years. Later used as a coal bunker, she was finally sunk by a German
air attack in Portland Harbour in 1940.

94. The Scarletts stayed at Cannes for a month after the General's departure.
95. His wife Charlotte.
96. Robert Campbell Scarlett, second Lord Abinger, his brother.
97. The SPCK's *Saturday Magazine*, 1832–44, provided cheap and useful knowledge.
98. Major James Conolly.
99. The British ruled Malta from 1801 to 1964. The Governor in 1854 was Sir William Reid (1791–1858), Governor, 1851–58. The British Governors of Malta lived in what had been the palace of the Grandmasters of the Knights of St John in Valetta.
100. The large number of Catholic clergy on Malta was often remarked upon by British visitors in the nineteenth century.
101. The French occupied the Piraeus, the port of Athens, between 1854 and 1857 to enforce Greek neutrality during the Crimean War.
102. Most of the French force landed first at Gallipoli, at the mouth of the Dardanelles, as the allies' initial plan had been to form a defensive ring to the west of Constantinople.
103. John and Georgina Drummond were the parents of Hugh Drummond of the Scots Fusilier Guards, William Scarlett's best friend.
104. Probably Major James Conolly but possibly the major of the 5th Dragoon Guards.
105. Koulali or Kulali, a few miles north of Scutari on the Bosphorus and the site of a cavalry barracks, subsequently became one of a number smaller hospitals, besides the main one at Scutari, in early 1855. For an excellent account of medical conditions in the Crimea and Turkey during the war, see Mike Hinton, *Victory over Disease: Resolving the Medical Crisis in the Crimean War, 1854–1856* (2019). For the establishment of the hospitals, ibid., pp. 97–131.
106. Varna, a port on the western coast of the Black Sea in what is now Bulgaria.
107. The 5th Dragoon Guards had embarked in the *Himalaya* at Queenstown, near Cork, on 28 May 1854, arriving without incident at Varna, where they disembarked on 13 June.
108. William Scarlett embarked on the *Simoom* at Portsmouth on 28 March 1854. On 24 May 1854, he had written to his sister, Frances, from Scutari: 'I feel quite well with the appetite of a lion. I will tell you a capital dish which I extemporised out here: boiled fowl smothered in rice nicely boiled; plenty of hard boiled eggs cut in half; boiled raisins and stewed onions in quantities, and garnish the dish with slices of boiled bacon. I should think stewed chestnuts would be an improvement, but I have not tried. Yesterday I went into a Turkish bath. I like the operation and shall insist on the Colonel's trying it.'
109. The 11th Hussars, known as Prince Albert's Own, were part of the Light Brigade.
110. Places near Abinger, Surrey.
111. The Allied landing in Varna aimed to prevent any Russian advance.
112. Frances Scarlett was a talented amateur water-colour artist.
113. The *Europa*, carrying the headquarters of the Inniskilling Dragoons, caught fire two hundred miles from Plymouth on 31 May 1854, leading to the deaths of the commanding officer, Lieutenant-Colonel Willoughby Moore, and eighteen other men and women, and the loss of all the horses, equipment and baggage. The veterinary surgeon was Herbert Hallen.
114. The Turkish garrison of Silistria (modern Silistra), a fortress on the south bank of the Danube, preventing a Russian advance south, was besieged unsuccessfully by the Russians from April to June 1854.
115. Jassy, the capital of Moldavia (now Iași in Rumania). Galaty, Moldavian city on the Danube (now Galați in Rumania). The six-hundred-mile-long River Pruth, well to the north of Silistria, marked the border between Russian and Turkish territory.

116. Devna (modern Devnya), the site of the cavalry camp, was fifteen miles west of Varna on Lake Devna, also known as Lake Beloslov.
117. Mules, essential for transporting equipment and supplies, were in very short supply. The allies had occupied Gallipoli in April 1854.
118. The Sea of Marmara (or Marmora), known in classical times as the Propontis, between the Dardanelles and the Bosphorus. The Bithynian Mount Olympus (not to be confused with Mount Olympus in Greece) overlooks the Sea of Marmara. It is 8343 feet high.
119. Many of the British officers who saw Constantinople were struck by the contrast between its beauty seen from afar and the squalor of its streets. Galata and Pera are areas of Constantinople on the European bank of the Bosphorus.
120. The ancient city walls of Constantinople. Therapia (now Tarabya) and Byukdere (now Buyukdere), on the European shore of the Bosphorus just north of Constantinople, were relatively salubrious resorts, favoured by diplomats during the summer. Therapia became the main base for the wives and families of officers visiting Constantinople during the Crimean War. The Belgrad or Belgrade Forest was an attractive forest park nearby.
121. Mr Helens, James Yorke Scarlett's agent in Burnley.
122. Sarah, Lady Abinger's aunt, Frances Diana Smith, lived at 3 Chester Square. Schumla (modern Shumen) was a fortress town south of Silistria. William Hare, Viscount Ennismore (1833–1924), later third Earl of Listowel, Scots Fusilier Guards. Lord Francis Gordon (1808–1857), 1st Life Guards. He was the son of the ninth Marquess of Huntly.
123. Lake Devna was fed by the rivers Devna and Provadiyska.
124. His old regiment, the 5th Dragoon Guards. Kotlubie is a village on the plain to the north west of Varna.
125. The Royal Dragoons were the 1st Dragoons; the Royal Irish were the 4th Dragoon Guards; and the Inniskillings were the 6th Dragoons.
126. Following the Russian retreat, Austria occupied Moldavia and Wallachia. Words 'in the west' supplied.
127. Viscount Dupplin of the 1st Life Guards.
128. Murray's *A Handbook for Travellers in Turkey* (third edition, 1854).
129. William Shakespeare, *Macbeth*, Act 1, Scene 7, 'If it were done when 'tis done, then 'twere well it were done quickly.'
130. Appleton Hall, Warrington, Cheshire. Light Oaks, Salford, Lancashire.
131. Inverlochy, near Fort William, belonging to Robert, Lord Abinger.
132. A letter to her first cousin and best friend, Mary Campbell.
133. Mary Campbell's younger brother, Dudley, and her sister, Edina.
134. Mary Campbell's mother, Mary, Lady Stratheden. Cecilia Campbell was another of Mary Campbell's sisters.
135. Robert Scarlett, second Lord Abinger.
136. Elizabeth, Dowager Lady Abinger, née Steere (1802–1886).
137. Her sister, Eleanor Thursby.
138. Hallyburton Campbell.
139. Peter Campbell Scarlett was due to visit Torlundie, the centre of the Scarletts' Scottish estate.
140. John Hardy Thursby (1826–1901), the son of William and Eleanor Thursby.
141. He was a widower with two young children.
142. Burnley was an industrial centre. Colonel John Hargreaves (1770–1834), the father of James Yorke Scarlett's wife Charlotte, owned extensive mining interests there. They were inherited by Charlotte Scarlett and her sister, Eleanor Thursby.

143. Named after a family house in Abinger, Surrey.
144. William Duckworth was the father of Captain George Duckworth of the 5th Dragoon Guards. Letter preserved in correspondence about George Duckworth, Somerset Archives, DD/DU/181. The letter is mistakenly addressed to George Duckworth Senior. See also, above, p. 40, and, below, p. 80.
145. George Pitcairn, MD (1805–1854), died at Kotlubie on 16 August 1854.
146. It has been estimated that the British and French forces, including the Royal Navy, lost ten thousand men to cholera in the summer of 1854.
147. William Scarlett had caught malaria on a hunting expedition to Sardinia in December 1853.
148. Captain George Duckworth died on 24 August 1854. According to William Cattell, the medical officer of the 5th Dragoon Guards, 'Duckworth was seriously ill but bore up with wonderful resignation; his features became so changed that Fisher, the vet, who went to sit with him became nervous. I met Fisher in a state of intense excitement rushing out of Duckworth's tent: "Oh! I've got it", pressing his hand against his stomach, then "What is it like?" He was sent to bed, diarrhoea set in and a week after he was buried in a ditch at Varna.' Mark Adkin, *The Charge: The Real Reason Why the Light Brigade was Lost* (London, 1996), p. 50. The regimental surgeon was George Fisher. Lieutenant-Colonel Thomas Le Marchant, 5th Dragoon Guards (1817–1873), the commanding officer of the 5th Dragoon Guards, though not ill, managed to have himself sent home. The *Bombay* was a hospital ship.
149. The siege of Sebastopol, the main Russian naval base in the Crimea, took very much longer than was at first predicted. Scarlett spells the city mainly with a 'b', but often with a 'v'.
150. The Euxine, meaning 'Hospitable' Sea, is the classical name for the Black Sea. It was a euphemism, as the Black Sea is cold, deep and stormy compared to the Mediterranean.
151. See above, pp. 57–58.
152. A fire at Varna on 10 August, following a hot dry spell, destroyed a large part of the British and French stores. Whether the fire was started deliberately remains uncertain. At the time, the local Greeks were suspected of starting the fire. It was believed that the Greeks, in general, were supporters of the Russians.
153. Any advance on Shumla and Silistria was prevented not only by the cholera but by a lack of transport and supplies. It was then made unnecessary by the Russian withdrawal across the Pruth after raising the siege of Silistria in late June.
154. Devna and Kotlubie were both some miles west of Varna.
155. Tsar Nicholas I (1796–1855) ruled from 1825–55.
156. Sultan Abdulmejid I (1823–1861) reigned from 1839–61. In Aesop's fable, the horse allows the hunter to saddle and bridle him so as to conquer the stag. After the stag has been conquered, the hunter refuses to take out the bit or remove the saddle. Scarlett may have meant that now that the Turks had entered in to an alliance with the British and French, they would be likely to be dominated by them in the future.
157. The widow of Colonel Willoughby Moore, who had died on the *Europa*. She became a nurse at Scutari but died there in November 1855. Scarlett's only positive reference to Lucan in his letters.
158. Dr Alexander McGrigor.
159. North Britain was a commonly used alternative for Scotland in the eighteenth and nineteenth centuries.
160. Peter Campbell Scarlett.
161. Mary, Lady Stratheden.
162. The Northern Meeting in Inverness had been set up in 1788. It included dinners, balls, concerts, horse races and Highland games.

163. In a letter of 27 August 1854 to his father, Robert, Lord Abinger, William Scarlett had written, 'God bless you, my dearest Father; I feel more for your anxieties and my Mother's tears than my own danger. If we are properly led and get fair play, we have no fear for the result. I will endeavour to write to you before we start, if not when you hear again it will be from the field of victory.'

164. Psalm 91:6, 'Thou shalt not be afraid of the terror by night, nor the arrow that flieth by day, nor the pestilence that walketh in darkness.'

165. The 4th and 5th Dragoon Guards were amalgamated temporarily due to the losses inflicted by cholera. See below, p. 138. 'They had the misfortune to be highly disapproved by Lord Lucan, reported by him to Lord Raglan, who came at dusk in the evening to see them in their lines, and found them thin and the men dirty. And having no field officers, and their senior captain dead, their surgeon dead and vet surgeon dead, and paymaster absent, his Lordship attached them to the 4th pro. temp, for Hodge to give advice to Captain Burton in command, who was third captain and young in the service. I neither agree with Lord Lucan or Lord Raglan in their opinion, but of that no matter, at least here.'

166. Captain George Duckworth. Major Frederick Weatherley, 4th Light Dragoons.

167. Lieutenant General George Bingham, third Earl of Lucan (1800–1888), the commander of the cavalry division in the Crimea.

168. Edina Campbell.

169. Flora Perry, aged nineteen, was buried at Putney on 11 September 1854. Her father, James Perry (1756–1821), a Scottish contemporary of Cecilia Campbell's father Lord Campbell, was the one-time owner and editor of the *Morning Chronicle*.

170. The whole of this letter is in the handwriting of Charlotte Scarlett. The beginning and end are by her personally, while the central part of the letter is a copy of a letter she had received from her husband.

171. Lieutenant Colonel Charles Doyle.

172. Colonel Edward Hodge (1810–1894), 4th Dragoon Guards, was the author of a diary, edited by the Marquess of Anglesey, *Little Hodge: Being Extracts from the Diaries and Letters of Colonel Edward Cooper Hodge Written during the Crimean War, 1854–1856* (1971).

173. For Le Marchant, see above, p. 59.

174. Balchik Bay, thirty miles north of Varna on the Black Sea, where the invasion fleet gathered.

175. The Heavy Brigade did not reach the Crimea until the beginning of October 1854. Unlike the Light Brigade, they missed the Alma, the first major battle of the war on 20 September.

176. Lord de Ros, Quartermaster General, returned to England in September 1854, when he was replaced by Major General Richard Airey. De Ros's nerves had collapsed. 'My nerves are alas like a child's, and they send me into tears', he told Lord Raglan. Royle, *The Crimea*, p. 190.

177. George Burnand and John Ferguson of the 5th Dragoon Guards; Duncan MacNeill of the 2nd Dragoons.

178. Frederick Swinfen of the 5th Dragoon Guards.

179. George Fisher and George Duckworth.

180. The cholera outbreak of September 1854, starting in Broad Street, Soho, led to deaths of over five hundred people. It also led to the pioneering diagnosis by John Snow (1813–1858) that cholera was spread by water, not air, and the demonstration that the pump in Broad Street was the source of the epidemic.

181. Hartrigge, Jedburgh, Roxburghshire, the Campbells' country house.

182. William Scarlett wrote to his father, Robert, Lord Abinger, on 21 and 28 September and to his sister on 22 September. The letters of the 21 and 22 September survive in transcript, the letter of 28 September in the original.

183. Lieutenant Colonel Francis Haygarth, Scots Fusilier Guards (1820–1911), who lived to be ninety-one.

184. Sir Charles Hamilton, third Baronet (1810–1892), fought at the battle of the Alma.

185. George Moncrieffe, Scots Fusilier Guards.

186. William Shakespeare, *Macbeth*, Act 3, Scene 3, 'Canst thou not minister to a mind diseased, Pluck from the mind a rooted sorrow.'

187. Most of the Heavy Brigade landed at Balaklava at the beginning of October 1854, but the Scots Greys landed at the mouth of the River Katcha on 24 September.

188. Florence Nightingale (1820–1910) went out to the Crimea, with thirty-eight women volunteer nurses, in October 1854.

189. A feeling shared by many capable and educated women restricted in their lives by their gender.

190. Henrietta Graham-Toler, Frances Smith's elder sister.

191. Mary, Duchess of Gloucester (1776–1857), the fourth daughter and eleventh child of George III and Queen Charlotte. The first Lord Abinger had been a close adviser to the Duke of Gloucester and his daughter, Louise, had married Colonel Sir Edmund Currey, a courtier connected to the duke and duchess.

192. The Dowager was Elizabeth, Lady Abinger, widow of the first Lord Abinger.

193. From the Book of Common Prayer, to be said or sung at Matins and Evensong.

194. Florence Nightingale found the military hospital at Scutari, on the eastern bank of the Bosphorus, previously a Turkish cavalry barracks, in an atrocious state on her arrival in Constantinople.

195. William Henry Russell (1820–1907), whose reports for the *Times* led to Florence Nightingale's decision to go to the Crimea.

196. Jane and Georgie West, long-term friends of Frances Scarlett and of Mary ('Polly') Campbell.

197. Robert, Lord Abinger.

198. For nursing during the Crimean War, see Orlando Figes, *Crimea: The Last Crusade* (2011), pp. 293–94, 299–304.

199. Thomas Jones, seventh Viscount Ranelagh (1812–1885).

200. 3885 people died from cholera in Glasgow in 1854.

Chapter 4: Balaklava

1. For the Flank March and Raglan's choice of Balaklava as the British supply base, see Alexander Kinglake, *The Invasion of the Crimea: Its Origins and an Account of its Progress down to the Death of Lord Raglan*, 8 vols (1863–87), iii, pp. 102–5; Somerset Calthorpe, *Letters from Head-Quarters: or The Realities of the War in the Crimea by an Officer on the Staff* (1856), i, p. 220; Trevor Royle, *Crimea: The Great Crimean War, 1854–1856* (1990), pp. 242–44; John Sweetman, *Raglan: From the Peninsula to the Crimea* (2010), pp. 229–33.

2. According to Orlando Figes, *Crimea: The Last Crusade* (2011), p. 229n., Balaklava derives its name from 'Bella Clava', meaning beautiful port, a name given it by the Genoese, who had built much of the port before being expelled by the Turks in the fifteenth century. There was a ruined Genoese castle overlooking the entrance to the harbour. More prosaically, Vladimir Shavshin, *The Valley of Death* (2005), pp. 165–66, considers the name derives from the Turkish 'balyk-uve', meaning a basket for fish, and that the Genoese called it Tsembalo, Tsembaldo or Chembalo.

3. The chaos of the early days of the campaign in the Crimea was slowly rectified. See Parliamentary Reports, House of Commons Papers, xxxiv, 107, 'Copies of Correspondence Relating to the State of the Harbour of Balaklava' (August 1855).

4. Fanny Duberly, *Mrs Duberly's War: Journal and Letters from the Crimea*, edited by Christine Kelly (2007), p. 118. A visiting French officer, Captain Jean-Jules Herbé, wrote, 'I am astonished that the English chose it as their supply base in preference to Kamiesh.' Figes, *Crimea*, p. 288.

5. The anchorage was unsafe due to the considerable depth of the sea outside its entrance.

6. This problem was only solved in 1855 by the construction of a railway from Balaklava to the British lines.

7. William Cattell, 'Crimean War', p. 24 in 'Bygone Days and Reminiscences by the Way', Museum of Military Medicine, RAMC, PE/1/1102/Catt.

8. The 4th Dragoon Guards lost fifteen horses. John Mollo and Boris Mollo, *Into the Valley of Death: The British Cavalry Division at Balaclava, 1854* (1991), p. 20.

9. William Scarlett to Sarah, Lady Abinger, 2 October 1854.

10. Edward Philips, an officer of the 8th Hussars who had been left behind at Varna due to illness, wrote a harrowing account of his voyage on the sailing ship *Rip Van Winkle*. See *Crimean Cavalry Letters*, ed. Glenn Fisher (2011), pp. 246–49. Philips thought, 'The chances are it has buried the Heavy Brigade, and all the steamers were full of horses on deck etc, and when we parted from the *Trent*, several horse boxes and stalls were carried past our vessel, showing she must have been as badly off as ourselves.' Ibid., p. 248.

11. 5th Dragoon Guards, Record of Service.

12. The Marquess of Anglesey, *A History of British Cavalry, 1816–1919*, ii, *1851–1871*, ii, *1816–1919* (1975), p. 54.

13. Ibid., p. 55. Another harrowing account of the storm and the loss of horses on board the *Rip Van Winkle* is in a letter from John Yorke to Etheldred Yorke, 30 September 1854, North East Wales Archives (NEWA), D/E/1545.

14. Mark Adkin, *The Charge: The Real Reason Why the Light Brigade was Lost* (1996), p. 63; Mollo and Mollo, *Into the Valley of Death*, p. 20.

15. See the calculations in Roy Dutton, *Forgotten Heroes: The Charge of the Light Brigade* (2008), p. 5.

16. It was also a far more agreeable base, with hotels, restaurants, brothels and even fashion shops. Figes, *Crimea*, pp. 287–88.

17. Numbers five and six, unfinished and the furthest from Balaklava, were unmanned on 25 October.

18. The Turks were in fact Tunisian recruits. Their numbers are uncertain between one thousand and two thousand.

19. For the defences of Balaklava, see John Barham, 'The Battle of Balaklava', Crimean War Research Society Website, pp. 1–25; Kinglake, *The Invasion of the Crimea*, iv, chapter 5, pp. 78–91. A sloop, the *Wasp*, was also positioned at the harbour mouth, but it would have had difficulty firing over or through the masts of the ships in the port.

20. Tom Blaney, *The Notorious Third Lord Lucan: An Embattled Life* (2020), pp. 140–55.

21. John Yorke to Etheldred Yorke, 20 July 1854, North East Wales Archives, D/E/1545.

22. John Yorke to Etheldred Yorke, 22 October 1854, North East Wales Archives, D/E/1545.

23. Albert Seaton, *The Crimean War: A Russian Chronicle* (1977), p. 138. Prince Menshikov, the Russian Commander in Chief, pressed by the Tsar to act, decided not to wait for their arrival before his attack on Balaklava. Ibid., pp. 137–38.

24. Lord George Paget, *The Light Cavalry Brigade in the Crimea: Extracts from the Letters and Journal of the Late General Lord George Paget, KCB, during the Crimean War* (1881),

p. 57. He added on 21 October, 'If the Russians are clever they will take care that we have no more repose, for they can easily see that we all turn out on the appearance of a few of them.' Ibid., p. 67.

25. Adkin, *The Charge*, p. 80.

26. Among the many accounts of the Battle of Balaklava, see the Marquess of Anglesey, *A History of the British Cavalry*, ii, pp. 62–107; Figes, *Crimea*, pp. 241–54; Royle, *Crimea*, pp. 261–78; W. Baring Pemberton, *Battles of the Crimean War* (1962), pp. 70–116; Adkin, *The Charge*, pp. 67–230.

27. Royle, *Crimea*, p. 265. This may be an overestimate. See Seaton, *The Crimean War*, pp. 138–39; Barham, 'The Battle of Balaklava', pp. 5–7.

28. See below, pp. 117–18.

29. Seaton, *The Crimean War*, p. 142.

30. Ian Fletcher and Natalia Ishchenko, *The Crimean War: A Clash of Empires* (2004), p. 159. See also, Adkin, *The Charge*, p. 70. 'If the enemy took Balaklava the campaign was finished; even if they only cut the roads below the Sapouné Heights they would have to be reopened or the British would face defeat.' Colin Robins agrees: 'It is universally thought by modern British commentators, and by all British involved in 1854, that this was no mere attack on the redoubts, nor a "reconnaissance in force" (another Russian claim sometimes heard), but a determined attempt to take the harbour at Balaklava, which would then have cut off the British Army from its supply route, with catastrophic results.' Colin Robins, '25th October 1854: A Tentative Timetable of Events', *War Correspondent*, 22, no. 2, July 2004, p. 17.

31. Paget, *The Light Cavalry Brigade in the Crimea*, p. 166.

32. See below, p. 115.

33. For more details of the Russian forces, see Adkin, *The Charge*, pp. 80–81; Seaton, *The Crimean War*, p. 138; Barham, 'The Russian Attacking Formations', in 'Balaklava'. The Russians destroyed Redoubt No. 4.

34. Scarlett himself describes the Heavy Brigade as having been near No. 1 Redoubt; see below, p. 138.

35. J.A. Ewart, *A Soldier's Life*, 2 vols (1881), i. p. 264. According to Adkin, *The Charge*, p. 67, Cathcart added, 'The best thing you can do, sir, is to sit down and have some breakfast.'

36. The French forces consisted of two brigades of General Bosquet's First Division, the 1st Brigade under General Espinasse and the 2nd Brigade under General Vinoy; and the Chasseurs d'Afrique under General d'Allonville.

37. Adkin, *The Charge*, p. 91.

38. Ibid., pp. 91–94.

39. Seaton, *The Crimean War*, p. 143; Fletcher and Ischhenko, *The Crimean War*, p. 160.

40. Seaton, *The Crimean War*, pp. 138–56, describes the battle from a Russian perspective. See also, Fletcher and Ishchenko, *The Crimean War*, pp. 155–86.

41. Adkin, *The Charge*, p. 97.

42. The 93rd Highlanders themselves were under Lieutenant Colonel William Ainslie but Sir Colin Campbell was in overall command of the force defending Kadikoi and Balaklava.

43. *Times*, 25 October 1854. Russell described the Russian cavalry as 'gathering speed at every stride, they dash on towards the thin red streak tipped with a line of steel'. His report appeared in the *Times* on 15 November. According to Fletcher and Ishchenko, *The Crimean War*, p. 170, the encounter was 'probably one of the most insignificant skirmishes in British military history'.

44. There was no time for the Russian detachment to join Ryzhov's main force before its encounter with the Heavy Brigade.

45. Adkin, *The Charge*, p. 97. The Royals were left behind with the Light Brigade.
46. Ibid., pp. 97–99.
47. See below, p. 139.
48. Ibid.
49. 'Whilst in no position to execute this movement, the enemy's cavalry appeared on the left flank over the hill in considerable numbers and very near our lines', James Yorke Scarlett to Lord Raglan, 27 October 1854, below, p. 127.
50. The numbers of the Russian cavalry facing the Heavy Brigade have been calculated differently by different witnesses and historians, ranging from 1500 to 3500 and occasionally ever higher.
51. Paget, *The Light Cavalry Brigade in the Crimea*, p. 175. The forward movement of the horns may, however, have been unintentional.
52. F.A. Whinyates, *From Coruña to Sevastopol: The History of C Battery, A Brigade (Late C Troop) Royal Horse Artillery: with Succession of Officers from its Formation to the Present Time* (1884), p. 128, 'this force confronting the Heavies was not more than 2000 at the very outside, probably less'. At the other end of the scale, J.M. Brereton, *A History of the 4th/7th Royal Dragoon Guards and their Predecessors, 1685–1980* (1982), p. 229, states 'Within less than ten minutes his puny force of some 800 men had utterly routed nearly 3500 of the Tsar's finest cavalry.'
53. Seaton, *The Crimean War*, pp. 144–47; Barham, 'The Battle of Balaklava', pp. 6–7.
54. Adkin, *The Charge*, p. 100.
55. Whinyates, *From Coruña to Sevastopol*, pp. 130–31. A shako (chako) was a tall cylindrical military cap.
56. Ibid., p. 147. A shabraque was a saddle-cloth used by light cavalry.
57. For full details of the Heavy Brigade's uniforms, equipment and rank badges, see John Mollo and Boris Mollo, *Into the Valley of Death*, pp. 33–45.
58. Whinyates, *From Coruña to Sevastopol*, pp. 128–29.
59. Tony Margrave, in his newsletters for May, June and July 2020, has compiled and transcribed an admirable and comprehensive collection of letters from officers and men of the Heavy Brigade and Light Brigade published in British newspapers in the aftermath of the Battle of Balaklava. While I have not quoted any of these in this book, none of the letters alter my interpretation of the two charges. Robert Kershaw, *24 Hours at Balaklava: 25 October 1854. Voices from the Battlefield* (2019), also quotes many first-hand reminiscences from those involved.
60. Scarlett was short-sighted, as confirmed by Temple Godman, who refers to him as 'blind as a bat'. *A Cavalryman in the Crimea: The Letters of Temple Godman, 5th Dragoon Guards*, ed. Philip Warner (2009), p. 76.
61. William Montagu, seventh Duke of Manchester (1823–1890) to an unknown recipient, 3 November 1860, reporting a meeting with Alexander Elliot (1825–1909) a few days earlier. Borthwick Institute, Halifax/Derby Papers, box 2.
62. Godman, *A Cavalryman in the Crimea*, ed. Warner, p. 75.
63. Ibid., p. 78.
64. William Forrest, to his wife, 7 December 1854, National Army Museum, 5804/32.
65. Whinyates, *From Coruña to Sevastopol*, p. 147. The eyewitness account may be that of John Branding, the commander of C Troop. See also G. Tylden, 'The Heavy Cavalry Charge at Balaclava', *Journal of the Society of Army Historical Research* (1940), pp. 98–103.
66. Henry Franks, *Leaves from a Soldier's Note Book*, by a non-commissioned officer of the 5th Dragoon Guards who took part in the Charge of the Heavy Brigade, is an important source for Scarlett's command of the regiment, but it was only first published in 1904 and gives more space to the Charge of the Light Brigade than that

of the Heavy Brigade. Ibid., pp. 70–71. He does admit 'It was rather hot work for a few minutes; there was no time to look about you', ibid., p. 70.

67. James Yorke Scarlett to James Chatterton, 7 December 1854, below, pp. 138–40.
68. Ibid., p. 139.
69. Mollo and Mollo, *Into the Valley of Death*, p. 12. See below, p. 139.
70. Below, p. 139. His niece reported him as saying in May 1855 that 'previous to the charge, Lord Lucan had ridden up to him and all the orders he gave were, "Do what you like"'. Frances Scarlett to Sarah, Lady Abinger, 11 May 1855. See below, p. 176.
71. Three letters from Grey Neville, the son of Lord Braybooke, written during the eastern campaign, are in the Royal Dragoon Guards Museum in York. In a letter to his brother Richard, on 7 October 1854, Neville wrote, 'We have most constant alarms with Cossacks, and had a bit of a brush with them this morning; but on a troop of horse artillery coming up they retired. But we are rather in a dangerous position here, having to protect the rear of the army.' His brother, Henry Neville of the Grenadier Guards, was badly wounded at Inkerman. Both brothers died of their wounds on 11 November 1854.
72. The Marquess of Anglesey, *Little Hodge: His Letters and Diaries of the Crimean War, 1854–1856* (1971), p. 49.
73. Temple Godman to his father, 7 December 1854. *A Cavalryman in the Crimea*, ed. Warner, p. 102.
74. Edward Fisher-Rowe, 24 March 1855, *Crimean Cavalry Letters*, p. 153. See also, ibid., pp. 110–11.
75. *Little Hodge*, ed. the Marquess of Anglesey, p. 133, entry for 23 October 1855.
76. Ibid., p. 138, entry for 29 November 1855.
77. Adkin, *The Charge*, pp. 108–9, exaggerates the impossibility of horses galloping up a slope and understates the speed that was reached by several regiments of the Heavy Brigade.
78. Whinyates, *From Coruña to Sevastopol*, p. 132. This was the second squadron of the Inniskillings.
79. Paget, *The Light Cavalry Brigade in the Crimea*, p. 174. 'It must be borne in mind that I was with the second line, some distance in the rear, and that my impressions at the moment were taken from that position, and it is on this ground that I am not tenacious of my opinion.' Ibid., p. 177n.
80. *Little Hodge*, ed. the Marquess of Anglesey, pp. 46–48. Hodge, as he was about to reach the Russian lines, shouted out 'Hard all across', an order given to an Eton longboat about to cross the river.
81. The casualties on the Russian side, however, may have been more than has usually been stated. Relying on a Russian source, Fletcher and Ishchenko, *The Crimean War*, pp. 175–75, put Russian casualties at forty to fifty killed and over 200 wounded, a casualty rate, if the strength of the Russian cavalry is taken as 2000, of over 12 per cent. This compares to the Light Brigade casualties in their charge of around 35 per cent.
82. Tylden, 'The Heavy Cavalry Charge at Balaclava', p. 103. The identity of Major Thornhill is unclear.
83. Astonishingly, Elliot was classified as 'lightly wounded'.
84. Whinyates, *From Coruña to Sevastopol*, p. 136.
85. Ibid., p. 134.
86. Ibid., p. 135.
87. See Kinglake, *The Invasion of the Crimea*, iv, pp. 164–65.
88. Whinyates, *From Coruña to Sebastopol*, p. 137.

89. The Light Brigade incurred losses during the Charge of the Heavy Brigade, but not of men. According to Lord George Paget of the 11th Hussars, 'The attack of the Heavy Brigade was actually in our lines, so we have lost a good deal of property, the answer about everything being, "Oh, it was knocked over in the attack – I cannot find it"; or "The Turks must have stolen it". There is no doubt that the latter did take a good many things from our tents in their retreat in the morning.' Paget, *The Light Cavalry Brigade in the Crimea*, p. 72.

90. Kinglake, *The Invasion of the Crimea*, iv, chapter 5, pp. 210–11.

91. Ibid. According to William Forrest, of the 4th Dragoon Guards, 'We hear my Lords Cardigan and Lucan almost came to blows about the inaction of the Light Brigade after our charge', Brereton, *A History of the 4th/7th Royal Dragoon Guards*, p. 229.

92. Kinglake, *The Invasion of the Crimea*, iv, chapter 5, p. 207.

93. John Yorke to Etheldred Yorke, 5 December 1854, North East Wales Archives, D/E/1545.

94. Adkin, *The Charge*, pp. 121–24.

95. Ibid., p. 124, 'The message was fatally flawed. It had been issued by a man unable to convey his intentions accurately, written by a man without staff training or field experience, delivered by a man without knowledge of its implications and received by a man who had never before been permitted the slightest degree of initiative with his division.'

96. Ibid., pp. 127–37. The Quartermaster General, Richard Airey, wrote the order at Raglan's dictation.

97. Nolan was an expert of cavalry, having published two books on the subject. He had been deeply frustrated by Raglan's previous refusal to unleash the cavalry during the campaign. He believed that unsupported cavalry could successfully charge artillery. He was adamant, when questioned by Lucan, that the battery, not the guns in the redoubts which were out of sight from the north valley, was the intended target. He himself was killed in the very beginning of the Charge of the Light Brigade and was therefore never able to account for what he had said. See David Buttery, *Messenger of Death: Captain Nolan and the Charge of the Light Brigade* (2008); and H. Moyse-Bartlett, *Louis Edward Nolan and his Influence on the British Cavalry* (1971).

98. Commanded by Prince Obolensky, this battery had either eight, nine or twelve guns.

99. William Forrest, letter, 27 October 1854, National Army Museum, 5804/32. John Yorke to his sister, 5 December 1854, North East Wales Archive, D/E/1545. The Marquess of Anglesey, *A History of British Cavalry*, ii, p. 94.

100. 'The French Chasseurs d'Afrique were on our left in rear; we had Royals and Greys in front; 4th, 5th, 6th in support', James Yorke Scarlett to James Chatterton, 7 December 1854, below, p. 140.

101. Adkin, *The Charge*, p. 171. Kinglake, *The Invasion of the Crimea*, iv, chapter 5, pp. 210–11.

102. See below, p. 144. In the absence of Alexander Elliot, who had been wounded during the Charge of the Heavy Brigade, William Beatson acted as Scarlett's aide de camp during the Charge of the Light Brigade.

103. Paget, *The Light Cavalry Brigade in the Crimea*, p. 213.

104. See below, p. 140.

105. Whinyates, *From Coruña to Sevastopol*, p. 144.

106. There were two other charges on 25 October 1854: the abortive charge of the detachment of Russian cavalry against the 53rd Highlanders; and the successful charge of the Chasseurs d'Afrique on the Russian battery on the Fedoukine Heights.

107. An earlier battle involving only cavalry was at Sahágun in Spain in 1808, when the 15th Hussars had defeated two French regiments. Their charge was made uphill, across a

ditch and on rough ground. The Marquess of Anglesey, *A History of the British Cavalry*, i, p. 49. The only British infantry regiment to win battle honours for Balaklava was the 53rd Highlanders. The Turkish infantry defending Redoubt No. 1 had put up stiff resistance, despite being unsupported and greatly outnumbered.

108. The cavalry was intended to act in conjunction with Campbell's force but the charges of both the Heavy Brigade and the Light Brigade were carried out by cavalry acting by itself.
109. Seaton, *The Crimean War*, p. 156.
110. W.H. Russell, *Times*, 15 November 1854.
111. Whinyates, *From Coruña to Sevastopol*, p. 143.
112. Adkin, *The Charge*, p. 127.
113. Ibid., p. 172. 'It remains one of those fascinating "ifs" of military history.'
114. Lord George Paget, *The Light Cavalry Brigade in the Crimea*, p. 69. Paget rode in the charge while smoking 'a remarkably good cigar'.
115. Ibid., pp. 169–70.
116. Ibid., p. 170.
117. 'Colonel Douglas's Remarks on my Account of the Battle of Balaclava', Paget, *The Light Cavalry Brigade in the Crimea*, pp. 247–48.
118. Though the praise or blame would still have been shared by four men with one thing indisputably in common, a name ending in 'an'. Fletcher and Ishchenko, *The Crimean War*, p. 183.
119. For an original and highly stimulating survey of the British addiction to heroic failure, see Stephanie Barczewski, *Heroic Failure and the British* (2016). Barczewski explains the attraction to the Victorians of seeing themselves as plucky, even foolhardy, amateurs at a time when Britain was the dominant world power. For the Charge of the Light Brigade, ibid., pp. 85–113.
120. I.I. Ryzhov, trans. Mark Conrad, 'On the Battle of Balaklava: Notes of Lieutenant General Iv. Iv. Ryzhov', *War Correspondent*, 18, no. 2 (2000), pp. 28–31; and 18, no. 3, pp. 10–12.
121. *War Correspondent*, 18, no. 1 (2000) pp. 14–19.
122. For the timings during the battle of Balaklava, see Colin Robins, '25th October 1854: A Tentative Timetable of Events', *War Correspondent*, no. 22 (2004), p. 17; Douglas J. Austin, 'The Battle of Balaklava: "A Brief History of 25th October 1854"', ibid., pp. 36–40; and Keith Gooding, 'A Review of the Timetable of the Battle of Balaklava', ibid., 23, no. 2 (2005) pp. 16–17.
123. Kozhukov, 'Kozhukov's Account of the Battle of Balaklava', *War Correspondent*, 18, no. 1 (2000), p. 3.
124. For the weakness of the Russian army, see 'A Look at the State of Russian Forces in the Last War', *Voennya Sbornik*, 1 (1858), section 2, pp. 1–15; trans. Mark Conrad in *War Correspondent*, 23, no. 2, July 2005, pp. 24–31.
125. Paget, *The Light Cavalry Brigade in the Crimea*, p. 176.
126. Earl of Lucan to Lord Raglan, 27 October 1954. Raglan, in his own dispatch to the Duke of Newcastle, wrote, 'The charge of this brigade was one of the most successful I ever witnessed, was never for a moment doubtful, and is in the highest degree creditable to Brigadier General Scarlett and the officers and men engaged in it.'
127. Whinyates, *From Coruña to Sevastopol*, pp. 153–54, brings out the contradictions in Lucan's account of his own movements, reproduced by Kinglake.
128. Duke of Manchester to unknown recipient, 3 November 1860, Borthwick Institute.
129. See below, pp. 127–28.
130. The correspondence is in the Northamptonshire Record Office, Brudenell Papers.

131. See below, p. 129.
132. See below, p. 138.
133. Ibid., below, p. 139.
134. William Forrest, letter, 27 October 1854, National Army Museum, 5804/32. Forrest knew what he was talking about, having fallen out with Cardigan while serving in the 11th Hussars. See Saul David, *The Homicidal Earl: The Life of Lord Cardigan* (1997), pp. 135–37, 189–92; Donald Thomas, *Charge! Hurrah! Hurrah! A Life of Cardigan of Balaclava* (1974), pp. 107–9.
135. See below, pp. 142–43.
136. Kinglake, *The Invasion of the Crimea*, iv, chapter 5, p. 149.
137. Doubts about the authenticity of the helmet were first raised by Major G. Tylden in the *Journal of the Society of Army Historical Research*, 22 (1944), pp. 260–61, and then revisited by Major A.M. Annand, 'Helmets of General Sir James Yorke Scarlett, GCB', in the same journal, 56 (1978) pp. 48–51, and by Colin Robins, 'General Scarlett's Helmet: A Note', *War Correspondent*, 14 (1996), no. 3, p. 46. This was based on two images of him wearing in one a forage cap and in another a non-regulation helmet with a horizontal peak. The matter was complicated by there being two undented helmets, in the General's adopted home of Burnley, given to Towneley Hall by Clara Aspinall, the General's great niece in 1934.
138. Godman, *A Cavalryman in the Crimea*, ed. Warner, pp. 76, 79.
139. William Scarlett to Frances Scarlett, 2 November 1854, National Army Museum.
140. See also Cattell, 'Crimean War', p. 34. 'Scarlett, on a sixteen-hands charger at high speed, had been driven between two troopers through the Russian mass, and so was protected from the shock of impending charges. His helmet was stoved in, but the skull uninjured and he escaped with five slight wounds.'
141. Sidney Scarlett Smith, unpublished memoirs, written in 1947, in family archive.
142. Frances Smith, née Scarlett, 'Family History', p. 2.
143. The correspondence to do with this gift is in the possession of the current Lord Abinger.
144. Kinglake, *The Invasion of the Crimea*, iv, chapter 5, pp. 152–53.
145. James Yorke Scarlett to Frances Smith, 4 January 1856, below p. 196. 'I have also got here my Crimean baggage and my horse Silvertail, the best of my stud of six horses and four mules, the remainder having been sold for very fair prices at Scutari. The public not knowing his merits allowed him (Silvertail) to be bought for £59, whereas I value him more than those that sold for £95 and £91, between which prices all the others were sold.'
146. The Royal Dragoons, the successor regiment of the 5th Dragoon Guards, have a hoof mounted in silver in their mess. This, however, was the hoof of Bob, ridden by Captain Desart Burton, who commanded the regiment at Balaklava. The horse painted in Francis Grant's portrait of General Scarlett, commissioned by the officers of the 5th Dragoon Guards, does not have a silver tail, but in this portrait the General is also not wearing the helmet he wore at Balaklava.
147. For the early history of the VC, see M.J. Crook, *The Evolution of the Victoria Cross: A Study in Administrative History* (1975).
148. If the conventions of the day ruled out the award of a Victoria Cross to Scarlett himself, it was the Earl of Lucan who thwarted Scarlett's own recommendations for its award. Scarlett explicitly mentioned Alexander Elliot and William Beatson in his report to Airey, but this was not endorsed by Lucan, who recommended members of his own staff, even though they had not taken part in either the Charge of the Heavy Brigade or that of the Light Brigade.

149. Major General Sir Charles Yorke to the War Office, 21 July 1860, concerning Lieutenant Colonel J. Forbes of the Bombay Cavalry. Crook, *The Evolution of the Victoria Cross*, p. 38.

150. George, Duke of Cambridge, to Sidney Herbert, 24 July 1860, ibid., p. 39.

151. Military Secretary to Commander in Chief, South Africa, 7 July 1900, ibid., p. 39. Hamilton later commanded the landing at Gallipoli in 1915.

152. The first VC given to a senior officer was awarded to Clifford Coffin on 31 July 1917, when he held the rank of temporary brigadier general. Ibid., p. 41.

153. William Scarlett to Frances Scarlett, 2 November 1854.

154. William Scarlett to Frances Scarlett, 28 December 1854.

155. Godman, *A Cavalryman in the Crimea*, ed. Warner, p. 108.

156. A letter to her elder sister, Henrietta Graham-Toler. In October 1854 Balaklava, a small port south of Sebastopol, had become the centre of the British supply chain British in the Crimea.

157. William Scarlett had fought at the battle of the Alma.

158. William Scarlett to Robert, Lord Abinger, 21 September 1854, 'The Russians held a very strong position, they say about 40,000 strong. The French turned it by the sea. We stormed it in front. It was very severe work and our regiment was not well handled. Our loss is 143 killed and wounded, besides ten officers most of them much hurt.'

159. Frances Diana Smith.

160. This report has survived in a Foreign Office file, National Archives, FO 78/1137. It makes no mention of Lord Lucan having ordered the Charge of the Heavy Brigade or of his later cancellation of the Heavy Brigade's advance in support of the Light Brigade. I am most grateful to Tony Margrave for sending me this reference.

161. The Turkish contingent in the Allied army had been entrusted with the defence of redoubts guarding Balaclava.

162. Kamara or Camara, a village to the east of Balaclava. The regiments constituting the Heavy Brigade were the 1st Dragoons (the Royals), the 2nd Dragoons (the Scots Greys), the 4th Dragoon Guards (the Royal Irish), the 5th Dragoon Guards (Princess Charlotte of Wales's) and the 6th Dragoons (the Inniskillings).

163. The Blackwater or Tchernaya, the river which flowed out into the harbour at Sebastopol.

164. These officers were Edward Hodge (1810–1894), Desart Burton (1827–1882), Henry Darby Griffith (d. 1887), John Yorke (1813–1890), Henry White (1820–1886) and Charles Shute (1816–1904).

165. Alexander Elliot (d. 1909) and William Ferguson Beatson (1804–1872).

166. Colonel Thomas Steele, Military Secretary to Lord Raglan.

167. Either Dr James Bright, MD, of 12 Cambridge Square, London W; or Dr John Bright, MD, FRCP, of 19 Manchester Square, London W. Later note by Frances Scarlett: 'As we were travelling up to London on 13 November, a gentleman in our carriage read from a newspaper of the Charge of the Light Brigade. The shock caused my mother a sudden heart seizure. From this dated the trouble she suffered from at intervals and which eventually caused her death in 1878. When she did her mental powers were quite unimpaired and her bodily organs perfect. Only her heart was the weak point.' Sarah, Lady Abinger, died on 3 June 1878. Given wrongly as 1877 in the original.

168. Hallyburton Campbell.

169. Staying with Hester Fraser, née Lomax, their cousin, not at Stratheden House.

170. A nickname for Mary Campbell.

171. Captain Alexander Elliot had received multiple wounds in the Charge of the Heavy Brigade on 25 October 1854, allowing William Scarlett to become his uncle's aide de camp.

172. The siege of Sebastopol lasted from October 1854 to 9 September 1855. The 'compliments' were shells.
173. The Battle of Inkerman, 5 November 1854.
174. Unlike, the Battle of Balaclava, neither the Alma nor Inkerman involved the cavalry other than peripherally.
175. Hugh Drummond of the Scots Fusilier Guards was wounded at Inkerman. Drummond himself described his wound, 'as I was charging with our right flank company, beating them beautifully down the hill, and our men shooting to perfection, I was very much astonished at being sent flying head over heels; the rascals were close in front, and one sent a bullet into my chest to the left of the nipple of my right breast, which, providentially for me, came out under my armpit instead of going through my body; it had followed the bone all round and, I believe, has broken nothing'. Hugh Drummond, *Letters from the Crimea* (1855), transcript by Glenn Fisher, p. 38.
176. General Scarlett was on leave in England in April and May 1855.
177. Sarah, Lady Abinger.
178. If the decision had been made to attack Sebastopol immediately after the Alma, it would almost certainly have fallen. Instead, the Allied delay gave the Russians the opportunity to fortify the city and reinforce its garrison.
179. Dr Andrew Smith (1797–1872), Director General of the Army Medical Department.
180. Lord George Paget (1821–1880), third Marquess of Anglesey, 1869–80, was the grandson of Henry William Paget, first Marquess of Anglesey (1768–1854), a famous soldier who had lost a leg at Waterloo. He was the lieutenant colonel of the 4th Queen's Own Light Dragoons in the Crimea. He took part in the Charge of the Light Brigade while smoking a cheroot. He returned to the Crimea to command the Light Brigade in February 1855, after Cardigan's return to England. He temporarily commanded the cavalry division while James Yorke Scarlett was on leave in 1855 and after the latter returned to England for good.
181. The spelling of Anglesey's title as Anglesea seems to have been standard at this time, as the spelling is also used by Alexander Kinglake, in his *The Invasion of the Crimea*, and by the Earl of Cardigan.
182. The French under Louis XIV never campaigned in the winter.
183. A low opinion of the Turks as allies shared by most of the British Army.
184. The Turks has defended Silistria bravely and successfully. The Ottoman Empire had often relied on the martial qualities of the Egyptian Mamelukes. In the nineteenth century these elite troops became so powerful that they took over control of Egypt from the sultans. Osmanli is another word for Ottoman, derived from their early leader Osman.
185. Abinger Hall, Abinger, Surrey.
186. Louisa Spranger White, née Campbell, was Mary Campbell's elder sister. First paragraph of letter omitted.
187. The *Gazette* was the official government newssheet.
188. St Paul's, Knightsbridge. Henry West, the brother of Frances Scarlett's friends Jane and Georgie West. Lieutenant Colonel George Cadogan (1814–1880), fifth son of the third Earl of Cadogan, was British Liaison Officer to the Sardinian Expeditionary Corps in the Crimea. General Scarlett received two dents on his helmet during the Charge of the Heavy Brigade, on the front from a sabre cut and on the back from the pommel of a sword. The helmet he wore in the charge, with its dents, can be seen in the Royal Dragoon Guards Museum, York. See plates 35–36.
189. Lord Raglan to the Duke of Newcastle, 28 October 1854.
190. W.H. Russell, *Times*, 25 October 1854, in Andrew Lambert and Stephen Badsey, *The War Correspondents: The Crimean War* (1994), pp. 103–17.

191. Peter Campbell Scarlett and Cecilia Campbell.
192. Omitting four other wounds. 'General Scarlett gave his glove all marked with blood to Sarah, Lady Abinger', note in Frances Smith, née Scarlett, 'Family History', p. 2.
193. Inkerman, fought on 5 December 1854.
194. Abinger.
195. See above, note 167.
196. Louise, Lady Currey, and her daughter Mary Augusta, were not going to dine with Mary, Duchess of Gloucester, but with Sarah, Lady Abinger, Frances Scarlett and Peter Campbell Scarlett.
197. Peter Campbell Scarlett was a widower with two young children, Leo and Florence.
198. William Scarlett's part in the battle of the Alma is graphically recorded in his letters to his father, Robert, Lord Abinger, of 21 and 28 September 1854; and to his sister, Frances Scarlett, of 22 September.
199. Probably William Elliot-Murray-Kynynmound, third Earl Minto, and Edward Alderson, Lord Alderson.
200. Major Gilbert Elliot-Murray-Kynynmound, a captain in the Rifle Brigade, and his sisters Charlotte and Harriet.
201. Inkerman.
202. Mary Campbell's father was the Chief Justice of the Queen's Bench.
203. Hensie, second name uncertain, was a German girl who had been a governess with the Campbells in London.
204. Stratheden House, Knightsbridge, the London home of the Campbells. The clothes were for the troops in the Crimea.
205. Charles Pepys, the eldest son of Charles Pepys, first Earl of Cottenham (1781–1851). Charles is given as 'C.' in the original.
206. Dante may have been a portrait of the poet or a cat.
207. Caroline Campbell (1799–1863), a first cousin of Robert, Lord Abinger, on his mother's side. Parkhurst, Abinger, belonged to Peter Campbell Scarlett.
208. Mrs Brigstock, unidentified.
209. John Welstead Powell, rector of Abinger, and his wife Georgiana.
210. Jeremy Taylor (1613–1667), author of *The Rule and Exercises of Holy Living* (1650) and *The Rule and Exercises of Holy Dying* (1651).
211. The Reverend Henry Belmont Sims, vicar of Great Parndon, Essex.
212. Georgina Holme Sumner of Hatchlands Park, Surrey.
213. An account of the Charge of the Heavy Brigade written to Colonel Sir James Chatterton, third Baronet (1794–1874). A veteran of the Peninsular and Waterloo campaigns, Chatterton had commanded the 4th Dragoon Guards at the coronation of Queen Victoria in 1838. He was MP for Cork, 1831–45 and 1849–52. He inherited his baronetcy from his brother in 1855.
214. At the Battle of Balaklava, 25 October 1854.
215. Kotlubie was a village on the plains near Varna in what is now Bulgaria.
216. Lieutenant General George Bingham, third Earl of Lucan, and General Fitzroy Somerset, first Lord Raglan.
217. Lieutenant Colonel Edward Hodge of the 4th Dragoon Guards and Captain Desart Burton of the 5th Dragoon Guards.
218. The Black River was the Tchernaya of which it is a literal translation.
219. Turkish troops had been placed in four redoubts. The troops in the first redoubt to be attacked fought with great courage. The troops in the other redoubts, almost untrained and very poorly equipped, abandoned their positions.
220. The Minié rifle used a bullet invented by Claude-Etienne Minié in 1847. It was adapted first by the French in Algeria and then by the British between 1851 and 1855.

It was the Russians not the Turks who began firing from the redoubt, but only a small number of men in the Russian army had these rifles.

221. The Heavy Brigade consisted of five regiments: the 1st Dragoons, 'The Royals'; the 2nd Dragoons, 'The Scots Greys'; the 4th Dragoon Guards, 'The Royal Irish'; the 5th Dragoon Guards, 'Princess Charlotte of Wales's'; and the 6th Dragoons, 'The Inniskillings'.
222. Lucan's ability to deploy and manoeuvre cavalry was widely criticised.
223. Where the Light Brigade was at this point.
224. The word 'send' supplied.
225. The 93rd Foot, commanded by Colin Campbell, had stopped a dangerous Russian cavalry attack earlier in the day.
226. Sailors from the Royal Navy were manning the guns protecting the heights above Balaklava.
227. A large body of Russian cavalry, commanded by General I.I. Ryzhov. Scarlett, who according to Temple Godman, was 'as blind as a bat', did not see them immediately until they were drawn to his attention by Alexander Elliot. Godman, *A Cavalryman in the Crimea*, ed. Warner, p. 76.
228. The ground where the Heavy Brigade drew up into line was difficult.
229. Only some of the Heavy Brigade, the Scots Greys and part of the Inniskillings and the 5th Dragoon Guards, took part in the initial charge.
230. James Yorke Scarlett placed himself well in front of the leading regiment, with his ADC Alexander Elliot, orderly, James Shegog, and the brigade trumpeter, Thomas Monks
231. The Russians, surprised at encountering the Heavy Brigade, spent crucial minutes preparing to envelop the brigade on both flanks.
232. By failing to advance, the Russians threw away their great advantage of being at the top of the slope.
233. The subsequent waves of the Heavy Brigade completed the rout.
234. C Troop of the Royal Horse Artillery.
235. See Roy Dutton, *Forgotten Heroes: The Charge of the Heavy Brigade* (2008), p. 349, for casualty figures during the Charge of the Heavy Brigade and later on the same day. Dutton estimates that seventy-eight men were killed or wounded.
236. Cornet Grey Neville of the 5th Dragoon Guards.
237. The exact number of Russian casualties is hard to calculate.
238. The famous and much disputed order from Lord Raglan, delivered by Captain Louis Nolan, who was himself killed by a shell at the beginning of the charge.
239. The Heavy Brigade was ready for their second charge of the day.
240. Word 'stay' supplied.
241. Although James Yorke Scarlett drew up his men to follow the Light Brigade's charge, he was ordered by Lord Lucan not to carry this through.
242. Lieutenant Colonel John Yorke of the 1st Dragoons.
243. Chatterton had at one time commanded the 4th Dragoon Guards.
244. Northamptonshire Record Office, Brudenell Papers, xv.9.2.
245. Northamptonshire Record Office, Brudenell Papers, xv.5.3.
246. Northamptonshire Record Office, Brudenell Papers, xiv.9.5. Cardigan commented on Lucan's affidavit, 'This affidavit of the Earl of Lucan is one of the most slanderous and disgraceful calumnies ever written. There is scarcely one word of truth in it. In No. 3 he states that: "As soon as the Light Cavalry moved off, I followed with my staff." The fact is that he ordered General Scarlett to advance, and he having proceeded down the hill with his brigade, suddenly found himself alone in advance, and upon enquiring

why the brigade did not follow him was told that Lord Lucan from the rear had halted and put back the brigade without the order being communicated to General Scarlett.' Ibid.

Chapter 5: The Crimea

1. This result of the Battle of Balaklava may have been blamed too much for the problems facing the British troops during the winter of 1854–55. The route via the Col was in fact more important as a supply line. If control of the Woronzow Road had been a vital factor, it is unlikely that the Russians would have withdrawn from it in December 1854.
2. See below, p. 153. The Guards, including the Scots Fusilier Guards, suffered heavy casualties at Inkerman. Out of twenty officers, two were killed and eight wounded. Frederick Maurice, *History of the Scots Guards from the Creation of the Regiment to the Eve of the First War* (1934), p. 102.
3. *A Cavalryman in the Crimea: The Letters of Temple Godman, 5th Dragoon Guards*, ed. Philip Warner (2009), p. 123.
4. Lord George Paget, *The Light Cavalry Brigade in the Crimea: Extracts from the Letters and Journal of the Late General Lord George Paget, KCB, during the Crimean War* (1881), p. 115.
5. See below, p. 153.
6. See below, pp. 159–61. Perekop is on the Perekop isthmus. This isthmus, which is three miles wide at its narrowest point, connects the Crimea to the Ukraine.
7. See below, p. 167.
8. See below, p. 158.
9. See below, p. 167.
10. See below, p. 161.
11. Tom Blaney, *The Notorious Third Lord Lucan: An Embattled Life* (2020), pp. 160–63.
12. He left the Crimea on 2 April 1855 on board the *City of London*, reaching London on 21 April. For the handover of the Light Brigade, see Paget, *The Light Cavalry Brigade in the Crimea*, p. 89. On 31 March, 'Scarlett came into my room this morning, and announced his departure on account of his wife's death. He stayed a long time with me, lamenting over the whole thing, and I must say was very complimentary to me, saying there was no one to whom he would rather give up the command than myself, and he hoped that I should retain it.' Paget became the temporary commander of the cavalry division on Scarlett's departure until the arrival of William Parlby in the Crimea on 17 April.
13. *Burnley Advertiser*, 5 May 1855.
14. See below, p. 186. Jane West was a long-term friend of Frances Scarlett.
15. See below, p. 176.
16. See below, p. 177.
17. See below, p. 177.
18. See below, p. 174.
19. He was back in the Crimea on 30 June and left, with his nephew William Scarlett, at the end of November 1855. While he was absent, the allies had sent two expeditions to Kertch, which commanded the strait between the Black Sea and the Sea of Azov. The second expedition's success, in May 1855, gave the allies command of the Sea of Azov and made it much harder for the Russians to supply Sebastopol and their army in the Crimea. Royle, *Crimea*, pp. 369, 372, 373–77, 382.
20. Captain C.M.J.D. Shakespear, letter, 15 November 1854, quoted in the Marquess of Anglesey, *A History of the British Cavalry, 1816–1919*, ii, *1851–1871* (1975), p. 121.

21. For these reinforcements, ibid., i, pp. 123–25. In the end there were four brigades.
22. At the Tchernaya, 'the position of General Scarlett on this day was not very clearly defined, with regard to the Sardinian and French armies, further than that he was to cooperate with the allies in the best manner he could', Paget, *The Light Cavalry Brigade in the Crimea*, p. 244. For the risks involved in the proposed cavalry advance, ibid., pp. 232–45.
23. Ibid., p. 234.
24. Ibid., p. 235.
25. See below, p. 190. See also, G. Tylden, 'The Heavy Cavalry Charge at Balaclava', *Journal of the Society of Army Historical Research* (1940), pp. 98–103.
26. Paget, *The Light Cavalry Brigade in the Crimea*, pp. 147–48.
27. Ibid. Viscount Armand-Octave-Marie d'Allonville (1809–1867), the French commander at Eupatoria. For other mentions of Scarlett, ibid., pp. 117–18, 141–42.
28. Godman, *A Cavalryman in the Crimea*, ed. Warner, p. 194.
29. *Little Hodge: His Letters and Diaries of the Crimean War, 1854–1856*, edited by the Marquess of Anglesey (1971), p. 88.
30. Ibid., p. 91. For other references to Scarlett by Hodge, see ibid., pp. 97, 117, 133, 138 and 139. Desart Burton, in his diary for 5 July 1855, Royal Dragoon Guards Museum, York, recorded, 'General Scarlett dined with us here. At all events does not disguise his opinion of Lord Lucan.'
31. *Little Hodge*, ed. the Marquess of Anglesey, p. 97. The 1st Brigade was the Light Brigade.
32. *A Cavalryman in the Crimea*, ed. Warner, p. 151. For other references to Scarlett in 1855, see ibid., pp. 127, 130, 132, 148, 165, 167, 171, 176, 188, 190 and 193.
33. William Scarlett to Sarah, Lady Abinger, November 1854 (day uncertain).
34. Elliot also painted a picture of the Charge of the Heavy Brigade. 'Elliot, the General's aide de camp, has made a capital panorama of Balaklava and it goes home by Mr Glynn of the Crimean Army Fund. Elliot has given me permission to have it copied and I have written to Polly Campbell on the subject.' William Scarlett to Robert, Lord Abinger, 5 March 1855.
35. William Scarlett to Sarah, Lady Abinger, 27 November 1854.
36. *Little Hodge*, ed. the Marquess of Anglesey, p. 78. Even if the room was cold, the dinner was good. After he dined with Colonel Darby Griffith of the Scots Greys, on 30 March, Hodge wrote, 'Griffith gave us a good dinner – a *soufflé* made to perfection, and some good mutton. His cook, however, will not do after Scarlett's.' Ibid., p. 97.
37. William Scarlett to James Yorke Scarlett, 15 May 1855. See below, p. 185.
38. William Scarlett to Frances Scarlett, 12 July 1855.
39. William Scarlett to Frances Scarlett, 27 August 1855.
40. William Scarlett to George Moffatt, 22 January 1855.
41. William Scarlett to Sarah, Lady Abinger, 13 October 1855. On 11 September, Lord George Paget reported that Scarlett was ill, Paget, *The Light Cavalry Brigade in the Crimea*, p. 115. On his deathbed in December, General Scarlett remembered William Scarlett's nursing. 'In the course of that afternoon, when told that Willy was coming, he said, "He is a capital nurse. He nursed me most carefully through a bad attack of dysentery in the Crimea".' See below, p. 248.
42. William Scarlett to Sarah Lady Abinger, 19 October 1855.
43. *Little Hodge*, ed. the Marquess of Anglesey, pp. 133–34.
44. Ibid., p. 134.
45. Sarah, Lady Abinger, and Robert, Lord Abinger.
46. James, first Lord Abinger.

47. Inkerman on 5 November 1854.
48. The Guards, including the Scots Fusilier Guards, suffered heavy casualties at Inkerman. Out of twenty officers, two were killed and eight wounded. Frederick Maurice, *History of the Scots Guards from the Creation of the Regiment to the Eve of the First War*, p. 102.
49. Sebastopol was besieged from the south, while the Russians had open access to the north of the city.
50. After the Earl of Cardigan left for home on 5 December 1854, William Scarlett bought a pair of Cardigan's breeches.
51. William Scarlett, James Conolly and Alexander Elliot shared a hut with James Yorke Scarlett.
52. According to one calculation, the Light Brigade lost 278 men killed or wounded and 335 horses, while 195 men and their horses got back safely from the charge.
53. The brigade referred to in this sentence must be the Heavy Brigade, not the Light Brigade.
54. Many officers were the fortunate recipients of food and clothing sent out by their families.
55. The Russian Orthodox church at Kadikoi was turned into a hospital.
56. Official and unofficial letters in the Crimea often arrived at different times. The official letters, sent via Constantinople, sometimes arrived after the personal letters. From mid-1855, after a cable was laid from Varna to the Crimea, a telegraph allowed the home governments far faster communication with the commanders of their armies in the field.
57. Lord Raglan was made a field marshal on 5 November 1854. James Yorke Scarlett received the accolade of the knighthood of the Bath at a ceremony in the Crimea on 27 August 1855.
58. Earl of Lucan, *English Cavalry in the Army of the East, 1854 and 1855: Divisional Orders and Correspondence whilst under the Command of Lieutenant General the Earl of Lucan, KCB* (1856), pp. cxviii-cxix.
59. See above, p. 40, for a letter to William Duckworth on his son, George, joining the 5th Dragoon Guards.
60. Hallyburton Campbell, later third Lord Campbell (1829–1918), had bought the horse from Major Abraham Bolton of the 5th Dragoon Guards.
61. The Campbells lived at Stratheden House in Knightsbridge.
62. Fortnum and Mason, Piccadilly, founded in 1707.
63. Unloading supplies in the cramped harbour of Balaklava was a major problem, particularly in the first six months of the Crimean campaign.
64. The failure to provide mules to transport supplies the five miles from Balaklava to the front line caused major problems and obliged men and cavalry horses to supply the deficit. A railway from Balaclava to the front, completed by the end of March 1855, greatly improved the supply chain. The Great Crimean Central Railway ran on fourteen miles of track.
65. The Russian cavalry did not appear on the battlefield in force after Balaklava during the severe winter of 1854–55.
66. Lord John Russell (1792–1878), Whig Prime Minister, 1846–52; Foreign Secretary, 1852–53 and 1859–65. The Austrians managed to protect their interests without having to fight. See *Nottinghamshire Guardian*, 14 December 1854.
67. The *Prince*, a storeship carrying much-needed winter uniforms, was wrecked outside the harbour of Balaklava in the storm on 14 November 1854. It was carrying forty thousand greatcoats and boots sufficient for almost the whole army.

68. The Chasseurs d'Afrique were French light cavalry first raised in Algeria in the 1830s. They were recruited from French volunteers and French settlers in Africa.
69. Bourgas, now Burgas, is a port eighty miles south of Varna on the Black Sea coast.
70. Begun in February 1855, with construction coordinated by Sir Henry Morton Peto, the Great Crimean Central Railway was built and allowed ammunition and other supplies from Balaclava to reach the guns bombarding Sebastopol.
71. The Reverend William Thursby and his wife Eleanor, the sister of Charlotte Scarlett. Probably Dr Robert Todd, MD, FRCP, of 26 Lower Brook Street, Grosvenor Square.
72. Abinger Hall, Abinger, Surrey.
73. Sarah, Lady Abinger, and Frances Scarlett.
74. Ormerod Hall, Cliviger, near Burnley, Lancashire, belonging to the Reverend William Thursby and his wife Eleanor. Later note by Frances Scarlett: 'On 15 January 1855, John Thursby came to Abinger, sent by his mother, to ask if some of us would come to Ormerod to assist him in the care of Aunt Charlotte and consult if anything could be done for her benefit. It was decided that Peter and I should go. John Thursby left Abinger the next day and we went to London on 17 January. He joined us at the station the following morning and we journeyed down to Lancashire.' John Hardy Thursby was General Scarlett's nephew.
75. Stratheden House, Knightsbridge, belonging to the Campbells.
76. The 'daily' was presumably a daily train.
77. John Hardy Thursby (1826–1901), the son of Charlotte Scarlett's sister Eleanor and her husband, William Thursby, did not serve in the Crimea but became his uncle's aide de camp from January to June 1856. He inherited Bank Hall and Ormerod House. See Leslie Chapples, *From Ormerod to Thursby: A Chronological Notebook of a Distinguished Family* (1979), pp. 53–84.
78. Henrietta Graham-Toler.
79. Uncertain word.
80. Peter Campbell Scarlett.
81. Michael was not one of children of William and Eleanor Thursby. These were Arthur, John, James, Piers, Richard and William. Perhaps Michael was a dog.
82. As a clergyman, William Thursby was naturally interested in parishes.
83. Regimental order copied into the beginning of the diary of Captain Desart Burton, Royal Dragoons Archive, York.
84. Frederick Campbell (1824–1893), eldest son of John, Lord Campbell, and Mary, Lady Stratheden.
85. The Amateur Exhibition was at 121 Pall Mall and opened on 24 March 1855. It was of 'water-colour drawings and pictures by amateur artists, and art contributions, in aid of the fund for the relief of the widows and orphans of British officers engaged in the war with Russia', *Spectator*, 31 March 1855, p. 19. Felix Smith and Frances Scarlett were amongst the prime movers behind the exhibition.
86. William Evelyn of Wotton Hall, Wotton, Surrey. He was, half seriously, expected to propose to Frances Scarlett but never did.
87. Eliza, Lady Stratford de Redcliffe (1805–1882), the wife of Stratford Cannning, first Viscount Stratford de Redcliffe (1786–1880), British Ambassador to the Ottoman Empire, 1842–58. Mary Stanley (1813–1879) led a party of nurses out to Constantinople, where they worked at the hospital at Koulali near Scutari.
88. Frances Diana Smith. Leith Hill, Surrey, is not far from Abinger and Ashtead.
89. Matthew 2:18, 'In Rama was there a voice heard, lamentation, and weeping, and great mourning, Rachel weeping for her children and would not be comforted, because they are not.' This letter was copied twice by FMS, with slightly different endings. Both endings are incorporated.

90. General Scarlett returned home in April 1855, travelling with his aide de camp, Alexander Elliot. They reached London, via Dover, on the evening of 21 April 1855.
91. Felix Smith, Lady Abinger's brother.
92. Sarah, Lady Abinger, and Peter Campbell Scarlett.
93. Alice Jenkins unidentified.
94. Caroline Campbell of Kilmory, who was living at Parkhurst, Abinger, Surrey, was objecting to the unannounced visit of Peter Scarlett Campbell, the house's owner.
95. The Victoria Soldiers' Lodging House, unidentified. Perhaps a predecessor of the Royal Victoria Patriotic Building in Wandsworth, built in 1857 as an asylum for girls orphaned in the Crimean War.
96. This had arrived by the *Arabia*. Alexander Elliot made a water-colour of its arrival in the hut shared by the General, William Scarlett, James Conolly, James Booth and Elliot himself. William Scarlett sent the sketch to his father on 16 March 1855, 'I enclose a sketch done by Elliot of the excitement consequent on the arrival of eight parcels per *Arabia*.'
97. The 5th Dragoon Guards had arrived in Turkey in the troopship *Himalaya*.
98. The death of Tsar Nicholas I on 2 March 1855.
99. This was for a memorial to James, first Lord Abinger in St James's church, Abinger Common. According to the *Morning Post* of 16 July 1857, 'The church has been decorated by a magnificent east window, painted by Messrs O'Connor, and set up in remembrance of the first Lord Abinger'. Unfortunately, the church was hit by a V1 in 1944, when its interior, including the east window, was largely destroyed.
100. *Peninsula*, unidentified but perhaps belonging to the Peninsular and Orient Line (P & O).
101. Colonel Alexander Tulloch (1803–1864), an experienced administrator and statistician, and John McNeill (1795–1883), a diplomat, were sent out to the Crimea in February 1855 to report on the performance of the Commissariat. They submitted two reports in June 1855 and January 1856.
102. Written from 3 Chester Square, belonging to Frances Diana Smith. William and Eleanor Thursby, Charlotte Scarlett's brother-in-law and sister, lived at Ormerod Hall, Cliviger, near Burnley.
103. Frances Diana Smith.
104. Wylde's Globe, also known as Wylde's Great Globe and Wylde's Monster Globe, was a popular attraction in Leicester Square from 1851 to 1862. It was the brainchild of the mapmaker and sometime MP James Wylde (1812–1887). *Punch* described it as 'a geographical globule which the mind can take in at one swallow', from the inside of which people could see the surface of the Earth.
105. Peter Campbell Scarlett and his future second wife, Louisa Jeannin, née Murray; Alice Jenkins; the Reverend Henry Belmont Sims; John Campbell. Coutts Trotter Arbuthnot (1818–1899), was a member of the Madras Civil Service. His family's home was Elderslie, Ockley, Surrey, near Abinger Hall.
106. Mary and Cecilia Campbell. Ella unidentified, but possibly the musical elder sister of Helen Magruder, the future wife of William Scarlett. William and Helen Scarlett's eldest daughter, Ella Scarlett Synge (1864–1937), was a talented pianist who also pursued a distinguished career in medicine.
107. Algernon West (1832–1921), the brother of Frances Scarlett's friend Jane West. Algernon West was private secretary to W.E. Gladstone, 1861–94. He had visited the Crimea but was not in the army.
108. Hugh Drummond, a captain in the Scots Fusilier Guards, was the best friend of the General's nephew, William Scarlett.

109. William Frederick Campbell, later second Lord Stratheden and Campbell (1824–1893).
110. Rear-Admiral Maurice Berkeley, first Lord Fitzhardinge (1788–1867), survived another twelve years.
111. Frances Scarlett's friend Georgina Holme-Sumner (1831–1897) married Francis Berkeley (1826–1896), later second Lord Fitzhardinge, in November 1867. Francis Berkeley was a captain in the Royal Regiment of Horseguards in 1855.
112. Jane West, Frances Scarlett's long-term friend.
113. Field Marshal Henry Hardinge, first Viscount Hardinge (1755–1856), Commander in Chief, 1852–56.
114. He was at Ormerod Hall, Burnley, having come home from the Crimea earlier in April 1855.
115. James Brudenell, seventh Earl of Cardigan, and George Bingham, third Earl of Lucan.
116. John, Lord Campbell, the General's brother-in-law.
117. Mary, Lady Stratheden, the General's sister and the wife of Lord Campbell.
118. Kadikoi, the camp near Balaclava.
119. Mary Campbell Scarlett.
120. Fox Maule-Ramsay, Lord Panmure, later eleventh Earl of Dalhousie (1801–1874), Secretary of State for War, 1855–58. He did not resign in 1855.
121. At 26 Montpelier Square, Knightsbridge.
122. She and her cousin Cecilia Campbell were going to walk to the Amateur Exhibition.
123. Sir James Yorke Scarlett reached Dover on Wednesday 19 April 1855, *Kentish Gazette*, 24 April 1855. The St George's Hotel was in Knightsbridge.
124. Hallyburton and Dudley Campbell.
125. The Charge of the Heavy Brigade, 25 October 1854.
126. Stratheden House, Knightsbridge, belonging to John, Lord Campbell.
127. Field Marshal Viscount Hardinge.
128. Sarah, Lady Abinger.
129. Robert Ferguson, MD, FRCP (1799–1865), 125 Park Street. He specialised in women's medical problems and assisted Sir Charles Locock at the births of all of Queen Victoria's children.
130. Many army wives went out to Turkey but very few to the Crimea.
131. Therapia on the Bosphorus near Constantinople.
132. Coutts Trotter Arbuthnot, of Elderslie, Ockley, Surrey, near Abinger Hall.
133. Mary, Hallyburton and Dudley Campbell, her first cousins. The New Society for Painters in Water-Colours had split from the original Society for Painters in Water Colours in 1831. It held annual exhibitions of works by its members. Frances Scarlett was a talented artist in water colours.
134. Charlotte Scarlett was clearly in London with her husband.
135. Peter Campbell Scarlett.
136. *Burnley Advertiser*, 5 May 1855. The punctuation has been modernised.
137. At this point the band played, 'See the Conquering Hero Come.'
138. Under an agreement of 26 January 1855, the kingdom of Piedmont-Sardinia sent 15,000 men under General Alfonso La Marmora to aid the allies. The Sardinian troops arrived in the Crimea in early May 1855. Orlando Figes, *Crimea: The Last Crusade* (2011), p. 332.
139. London society hostesses who pressed celebrities to come to their houses were known as 'lion hunters'.
140. Jane West, a long-term friend of Frances Scarlett.
141. Mrs Carew and Lady Dowrich unidentified.

142. Lady Mary Williams, unidentified. Georgina, Lady Alderson (d. 1871), was the wife of Sir Edward Hall Alderson, Baron Alderson (1787–1857).
143. Charlotte Moore, the widow of Colonel Willoughby Moore, who went out to Constantinople to nurse the British troops in the summer of 1854, died of dysentery at Scutari in November 1855. In the original she is spelt 'More'.
144. John Richardson (1780–1864) of Kirklands House, Ancrum, Jedburgh. Richardson was a highly successful lawyer, related on his mother's side to the lawyer and politician Henry Brougham.
145. Frances Diana Smith.
146. Later note by Frances Scarlett: 'The wife of Colonel Willoughby Moore, who perished when the *Europa* was burnt in 1854, carrying cavalry to the Crimea. Every soul was saved, except the Colonel, who was last seen in the midst of the flames, having seen that all his men were in the boats. His widow went out to Scutari and took charge of a Home for Convalescent Officers. The troopship *Europa* caught fire in the Bay of Biscay on 31 May.

    The plan of our going to Constantinople was not carried out. The General left Aunt Charlotte at Erlwood, near Bagshot, in the care of his sister Lady Currey, my dear "Aunt Lou", and he went back to the Crimea in June, taking command of the cavalry. General Scarlett returned to the Crimea on 30 June 1855.'
147. James Yorke Scarlett was promoted to major general on 12 December 1854. He became a knight commander of the Bath on 27 August 1855 at a ceremony presided over by Lord Stratford de Redcliffe. According to his nephew, 'Today our dear General was invested with the collar of KCB and knighted. He looked the most soldierlike and handsomest man of the whole bunch.' William Scarlett to Frances Scarlett, 27 August 1855. Sir James Yorke Scarlett was awarded the Grand Cross of the Bath in 1869.
148. William Scarlett returned to the Scots Fusilier Guards.
149. The Guards were jealous of their leading status in the British Army.
150. John Thursby was perhaps the ADC who was 'sick by the way'.
151. Major-General Henry Robinson-Montague, sixth Lord Rokeby (1798–1883), commander of the First Division in 1855.
152. Lieutenant General Frederick Markham (1800–1855) had arrived in the Crimea on 18 July 1855 and became the commander of the 2nd Division on 30 July.
153. Another example of the jealousies amongst senior officers in the Crimea.
154. The British army, dependent on volunteers, had great difficulty in recruiting the men it needed. Many of the recruits sent out to the Crimea rapidly succumbed to diseases to which hardened soldiers were largely immune.
155. Lord Raglan died in the Crimea on 28 June 1855.
156. General Sir James Simpson (1798–1883) commanded in the Crimea from the end of June to November 1855.
157. In fact, it was the Russians who attacked on 16 August, on the Tchernaya, when they were repulsed with heavy losses. After this last effort, Sebastopol fell on 9 September.
158. The General's sister, Louise, Lady Currey, lived at Erlwood, Windlesham, Surrey. Charlotte Scarlett stayed with her after the General's return to the Crimea.
159. Adelaide Currey married her cousin William Grignon, but died soon after giving birth to a daughter, Adelaide.
160. John Arthur Roebuck (1792–1868), Radical MP for Bath and then Sheffield, chairman of the Sebastopol Committee, which examined the conduct of the war. The vote to set up the committee, on 29 January 1855, led to the fall of Lord Aberdeen's government and Aberdeen's replacement by Viscount Palmerston.
161. Sebastopol fell on 9 September 1855 but the war continued until the signing of the treaty of Paris on 30 March 1856. General Scarlett had left Constantinople on 27 December 1855.

296 Notes to Pages 189–195

162. Peter Campbell Scarlett.

163. Robert, the second Lord Abinger's Scottish estate, centred around Inverlochy near Fort William, had a magnificent view of Ben Nevis, half of which was part of the estate. Frances Scarlett had climbed it the previous September.

164. A letter written after the fall of Sebastopol on 9 September 1855, when the Russians withdrew on a bridge across the harbour. They, nevertheless, kept up sporadic fire from the north side of the harbour.

165. Artillery fire was a major killer during the war, particularly during the siege of Sebastopol.

166. Although Sebastopol had been captured, the war was not at an end. The British were planning operations on several fronts in 1856, but neither side was likely to attempt any major operations until the spring.

167. The public in Britain, reading the *Times*, were in favour of the vigorous prosecution of the war, following up the success of capturing Sebastopol.

168. Charles FitzClarence (1826–1878) of the 10th Royal Hussars (Prince of Wales's Own). FitzClarence, first Earl of Munster (1794–1842), was the eldest illegitimate son of William, Duke of Clarence, later William IV, and the actress Dorothea Jordan.

169. His sister, Louise, Lady Currey.

170. Later photos of William Scarlett show him as stout. The River Lochy flows along the Great Glen from Loch Lochy to Loch Linnhe at Fort William.

Chapter 6: Aldershot

1. See Michael Roper, *The Records of the War Office and Related Departments, 1660–1964* (1998).

2. *Morning Post*, 19 July 1857. Artist's Proofs, £6 6s.; Proofs £4 4s.; Prints £2 2s. Why he was not painted in the helmet in which he charged at Balaklava remains a mystery.

3. *Morning Post*, 27 October 1857.

4. Ibid., 23 June 1860.

5. Mather Brown (1761–1831), American portrait and landscape painter. The picture may have been of another person rather than of Mather Brown.

6. He was writing on Friday, 8 February 1856.

7. To meet the combined family at Brighton.

8. According to the *Saint James's Chronicle* of 9 February 1856, 'The dinner party included her Royal Highness the Duchess of Kent, her Royal Highness the Princess Royal, his Serene Highness Prince Ernest of Leiningen, the Archbishop of Canterbury, Lady Fanny Howard, Baroness de Speth, Lieutenant General the Hon. Sir J. Scarlett, and Colonel the Hon. A. and Mrs. Gordon. The band of the 2nd Life Guards played during dinner. Her Majesty's private band afterwards performed in the Castle.' Colonel Alexander Hamilton-Gordon (1817–1890), an honorary equerry to Queen Victoria, was the son of the fourth Earl of Aberdeen (1784–1860), Prime Minister 1852–55. His wife, Caroline, was the daughter of the polymath Sir John Herschel. Lieutenant General Everard Bouverie (1798–1871). General Sir Edward Bowater (1787–1861), a long-term courtier, had fought in the Peninsular War and at Waterloo.

9. Robert, Sarah, Peter and William Scarlett..

10. The large numbers of horses for sale after the end of the Crimean campaign depressed the price they fetched.

11. Evariste Régis Huc, *Travels in Tartary and Thibet* (1850).

12. Wellington College, in Crowthorne, Berkshire, was founded in 1853 but only opened in 1859. It was endowed by public subscription in memory of the Duke of Wellington.

13. Either James Yorke Scarlett's sister, Mary, Lady Stratheden, or her daughter Mary Campbell. Louise (Louisette) Scarlett (b. 1799) was the daughter of his uncle, Dr

Robert Scarlett (1773–1839). Elly (Elliot) Currey was the son of his sister Louise Currey.

14. The Tchernaya flowed south west into the harbour of Sebastopol. It was the scene of the final battle of the war in the Crimea, on 16 August 1855, which resulted in a heavy Russian defeat.

15. Frances Scarlett had announced her engagement to the Reverend Sidney Lidderdale Smith. The letter was probably sent from Portsmouth, where the General was governor.

16. Louise, Lady Currey.

17. Frances Scarlett and Sidney Lidderdale Smith, rector of Brampton Ash, Northamptonshire, were married at Abinger on 17 December 1857.

18. Both her paternal uncles, Sir James Yorke Scarlett and Peter Campbell Scarlett, were strongly attached to their niece. Robert, second Lord Abinger, died on 24 June 1861.

19. A battalion of William Scarlett's regiment, the Scots Fusilier Guards, was posted in Canada in the early 1860s.

20. The General's niece, Frances Scarlett, had married the Reverend Sidney Lidderdale Smith on 17 December 1857.

21. Peter Campbell Scarlett (1804–1881), the General's brother, had been appointed Minister to Florence on 13 December 1858. He had previously been Envoy Extraordinary and Minister Plenipotentiary at Rio de Janeiro, 1855–58. Their elder brother was Robert, second Lord Abinger (1794–1861).

22. He was a widower, his first wife, Frances Lomax, having died in 1849, leaving him with two children, Frances ('Bina') and Leopold.

23. The General's nephew, William Scarlett, was an officer in the Scots Fusilier Guards.

24. Gomshall Station was opened on 20 August 1849. A mile from Abinger Hall, it was originally called Gomshall and Shere Heath. Sally was Sarah, Lady Abinger (1803–1878).

25. Robert, second Lord Abinger, died on 24 June 1861.

26. Sir Henry Holland, first Baronet (1788–1873), a leading doctor.

27. John, Lord Campbell, died on 23 June 1861, the day before his brother-in-law Lord Abinger.

28. Sidney Scarlett Smith (1861–1954) was born on 15 August 1861. The misspelling of the recipient's name may be a deliberate echo of the name of Whig wit Sydney Smith. Harold Yorke Lidderdale Scarlett was the baby's elder brother.

29. Under the will of Robert, second Lord Abinger, his estate was entailed on the holders of the barony. After the death of his grandson, James, fourth Lord Abinger (1871–1903), without male heirs, the title and estate, including Inverlochy Castle, passed to a cousin, Shelley, fifth Lord Abinger (1872–1917).

30. The General's London house was at 25 Prince's Terrace, later 37 Ennismore Gardens, just south of Hyde Park, near the Albert Memorial.

31. 'I married 17 December 1857.' Note by Frances Mary Smith, née Scarlett.

32. Robert Astley Smith, Frances Smith's fourth son (1865–1945).

33. 'I have a photograph of her on horseback at Portsmouth.' Note by Frances Mary Smith, née Scarlett.

Chapter 7: Burnley

1. See Steve Chapples, *General Scarlett; The Burnley Hero of Balaclava* (2006); and Sam D. Smith, 'A Burnley Balaclava Hero', lecture to the Burnley Historical Society (1955).

2. For the background and effect of the Act, see John K. Walton, *The Second Reform Act* (1987).

3. For the history of Burnley, see Walter Bennett, *The History of Burnley*, 4 vols (1946–1951), especially volume iii, *The History of Burnley, 1650–1850* (1949); and volume iv, *The History of Burnley from 1850* (1951).

4. John Russell, first Earl Russell (1792–1878); previously Lord John Russell during the Crimean War.
5. Edward Smith-Stanley, fourteenth Earl of Derby (1799–1869), and Benjamin Disraeli, first Earl of Beaconsfield (1804–1881).
6. The Reform League demanded universal male suffrage but was more moderate in its approach than the earlier Chartists. Demonstrations in the country's main cities culminated in a crowd so large in Hyde Park in May 1867 that the government, which had prohibited the meeting, dared not enforce the ban.
7. Who exactly was entitled to vote remained disputed, with both sides attempting to add their supporters to the electoral roll and to disqualify their opponents. William Gladstone (1809–1898), Chancellor of the Exchequer, 1852–55, 1859–66, 1873–74 and 1880–82; Prime Minister, 1868–74, 1880–85, 1886 and 1890–94.
8. Burnley, Darlington, Dewsbury, Gravesend, Hartlepool, Middlesbrough, Stalybridge, Stockton and Wednesbury. Chelsea and Hackney were enfranchised with two MPs.
9. Bennett, *The History of Burnley*, iv, p. 137.
10. *Burnley Gazette*, 21 November 1868.
11. There is a great deal more in both newspapers about the campaign than there is room for here.
12. The Abolition of Slavery (1833), which came into effect in 1834, and the Repeal of the Corn Laws (1846).
13. *Burnley Advertiser*, 14 November 1868.
14. *Burnley Advertiser*, 22 August 1868.
15. Bennett, *The History of Burnley*, iv, p. 138.
16. *Burnley Gazette*, 14 November 1868. The Blanketeers were Manchester protesters who planned to march from Manchester to London in March 1817. The Peterloo Massacre of 16 August 1819 was the result of cavalry charging a crowd of 60,000 people attending a rally to demand Parliamentary Reform in St Peter's Field, Manchester. James, first Lord Abinger, had been active in prosecuting Chartists in Lancashire.
17. The radical professor was Thorold Rogers (1823–1890).
18. *Burnley Advertiser*, 21 November 1868.
19. *Burnley Advertiser*, 6 February 1869.
20. In 937 Athelstan, king of England, defeated a combined Scottish and Irish invasion force at the Battle of Brunanburh in Lancashire. The site of the battle is unidentified but was believed to be near Burnley.
21. John Thursby (1826–1901) was the son of General Scarlett's sister-in-law, Eleanor Thursby. He had been the General's aide de camp in 1856.
22. *Burnley Advertiser*, 21 August 1869.
23. John Greenwood of Turf Moor, Burnley.
24. *Burnley Advertiser*, 25 August 1866.
25. See above, p. 210.
26. For Balak and Balaam, see Numbers, chapters 22–24. Balak took the prophet Balaam to the high places of Baal, but Balaam refused to curse Balak's enemies.
27. Probably John Lumley-Savile, eighth Earl of Scarbrough (1788–1856).
28. Catholic Emancipation was passed by a Tory government in 1829.
29. The Corporation and Test Acts were repealed by a Tory government in 1828.
30. Sir Robert Peel (1788–1850), as Conservative Prime Minister, passed the Repeal of the Corn Laws and, in doing so, split the Conservative Party.
31. John Bright (1811–1889), politician and leading promoter of free trade.
32. Richard Cobden (1804–1865), politician and leader of the Anti-Corn Law League.
33. The majority of Victorian Englishmen identified themselves with Protestantism and were suspicious of the Romanising tendencies of the Tractarians and wary of the influx of Irish Catholic immigrants.

34. According to Wellington, 'Educate men without religion and you make them but clever devils.'
35. Governor Clifford unidentified.
36. Adam Townley (1808–1887), born in Blackburn, Lancashire, went to Ontario as Wesleyan Methodist minister in 1835 but was ordained into the Anglican Church in 1840.
37. Professor Greenlove unidentified.
38. Probably what became the Wine and Beerhouse Act (1869).
39. Rear Admiral Sherard Osborn (1822–1875) had served in the Crimean War as captain of HMS *Vesuvius*. Then, in HMS *Medusa*, he commanded the Sea of Azov squadron from August 1855 until the end of the war.
40. Captain Lord William Paget (1803–1873), son of the first Marquess of Anglesey, was a Whig politician.
41. James Folds, as a Conservative, was not made mayor of Burnley in 1867–68 to prevent him from acting as returning officer in the 1868 election. Bennett, *The History of Burnley*, iv, p. 67. Benjamin Chaffer, a builder and quarry owner, was a vocal Conservative.
42. The Literary Institute, strongly supported by General Scarlett, was identified with the Church of England.
43. The *Burnley Advertiser*.
44. Major A.B. Creeke, of the 5th Royal Lancashire Militia, was a prominent Conservative.
45. For the Burnley police at this time, see Bennett, *The History of Burnley*, iv, pp. 88–90.
46. The mayor in 1867–69 was William Lomas.
47. Dr William Coultate (1813–1882) was the leading organiser of the Liberal election campaign in Burnley in 1867–68.
48. John Massey was the owner of a textile mill in Trafalgar Street, Burnley.
49. James Roberts of Tarleton House, Burnley.
50. John Wilson-Patten, first Lord Winmarleigh (1802–1892), MP for North Lancashire for forty-three years.
51. George Slater, a member of the Conservative committee.
52. S. Kay had been active in the Burnley Reform Association.

Chapter 8: Cliviger
1. He had retired on 1 November 1870 with the rank of full general.
2. See below, pp. 245–46.
3. See below, pp. 247–49.
4. See below, p. 248.
5. The Reverend Arthur Townley Parker, rector of Burnley.
6. Catherine Parker (1837–1895), the wife of the Reverend Arthur Townley Parker.
7. Peter Campbell Scarlett to Frances Smith, 7 December 1871.
8. William Scarlett, Lord Abinger, to Sarah, Lady Abinger, 9 December 1871.
9. Frances Smith to the Reverend Sidney Lidderdale Smith, 9 December 1871.
10. *Burnley Advertiser*, 16 December 1871
11. *Burnley Gazette*, 9 December 1871.
12. Ibid. This announcement was made by the General's nephew and one-time aide de camp John Hardy Thursby.
13. *In Memoriam: Records of the Death and Funeral, with Brief Notices of the Life and Military Career, of the Late Lamented General the Honorable Sir James Yorke Scarlett, GCB* (1872).
14. *Burnley Express*, 11 February 1888; *Lancashire Evening Post*, 15 February 1888.
15. There are minor variations between the versions published in *Macmillan's Magazine* in 1881 and in *Tiresias and Other Poems* (1885). In 1885 it appeared with a prologue and epilogue, but neither of these are concerned with the Charge.

16. Kinglake was an admirer of General Scarlett. See above, p. 104n.

17. Sir Edward Hamley (1821–1893) was the author of *The Story of the Campaign of Sebastopol* (1855) and later wrote *The War in the Crimea* (1891), for a long time the standard one-volume account of the war. He also became the first Professor of Military History at the Staff College at Camberley.

18. A speech returning thanks to the speakers at the annual soirée of the Burnley Literary Institution on 23 November 1871. He had been a leading supporter of the institution over the years and had often spoken at its soirées. The four speakers he thanked were the Reverend J.W.W. Robinson; James Maden Holt MP (1829–1911), MP for North East Lancashire, 1868–80; W.F. Ecroyd; and the Reverend W. Stephenson.

19. According to the report of the meeting, 'The Rev. W. Stephenson seconded the resolution in characteristic speech, keeping the audience in a roar of laughter almost from beginning to end.'

20. An account written by Matilda or Maude Smith, the daughter of Sarah, Lady Abinger's brother, Felix: 'Written by Matilda Smith, who was staying with him and Lady Scarlett at Bank when he died.' Note at the end of the account, 'Copied by Harriet Stovold, 12 April 1872. Aged fourteen.' Additional note, 'Letter which Cecily says she expects her brother had copied.' The date of the onset of his illness is given as 'Saturday 3 December' in the original, but 3 December was a Sunday. According to Frances Smith, 'They returned to Bank on Saturday, on which day Maude arrived also, having been on a visit near. There was a dinner party, but the General felt unwell and chilly and left the gentlemen after dinner and went straight to bed. This Maude wrote on Sunday to her people. She seemed to think him seriously ill, but said Lady Scarlett went about as usual and seemed under no apprehension.' Frances Smith to Sidney Lidderdale Smith, 7 December 1871.

21. The Reverend Arthur Townley Parker, rector of Burnley.

22. Dr Henry Briggs, MD, of Burnley.

23. Probably Dr John Roberts, MD, of 14 Grosvenor Square, Manchester. Sir William Withey Gull (1816–1890) had successfully treated the Prince of Wales for typhoid earlier in 1871.

24. Holme Chapel, Cliviger, where he was buried.

25. *In Memoriam*, pp. 29–30. George, Duke of Cambridge (1819–1904), had commanded the First Division in the Crimea. He was Commander in Chief of the British Army, 1856–87.

26. The Prince of Wales suffered an attack of typhoid fever, the illness which may have killed his father the Prince Consort ten years before, in early December 1871 but recovered. Queen Victoria sent, through Colonel Ponsonby, a telegram to Lord Abinger on 8 December: 'The Queen was deeply grieved to hear of the death of Sir James Scarlett, and commands me to convey to you her concern at the news, and her heartfelt condolence with Lady Scarlett.' *In Memoriam*, pp. 30 and 32, also contains tributes from Scarlett's old colleagues, Temple Godman and Charles Shute.

27. General Scarlett had recently given £1000 'towards the foundation of a sick and burial society in connection with the Burnley Constitutional Society'. *In Memoriam*, p. 21.

28. *In Memoriam*, pp. 26–28.

29. Canon Parker preached a funeral sermon at Burnley Parish Church on the morning of Sunday 17 December, *In Memoriam*, pp. 34–41. 'A vast congregation, for the most part clad in deep mourning and numbering not far from two thousand people, filled the parish church, and took devout and reverent part in the morning service.' The Reverend Jackson Cuppage preached a funeral on the same afternoon at Holme Chapel, ibid., pp. 42–50.

30. Ibid., pp. 49–50.

Bibliography

Sources

The originals of the letters and other items in this book are all in the possession of the editor with the following exceptions: *Burnley Advertiser*, Nos 59, 72, 74, 75, 77, 80; *Burnley Gazette*, Nos 71 and 73; James Scarlett, ninth Lord Abinger, No. 19; King's College, London, Archives, GB 0100 KCLCA K/PP168, Nos 18, 20, 41, 53, 62 and 70; Northampton Record Office, Brudenell Papers, XIV.9.2, XV.5.3 and XV.9.5, Nos 42–44; Roger Scarlett-Smith, Nos 30, 55 and 68; Royal Dragoon Guards Museum, York, Adolphus William Desart Burton Diary, 1855, No. 50; Somerset Archives, DD/DU/181, Nos 14 and 27. No. 46 was first published in the Earl of Lucan, *English Cavalry in the Army of the East, 1854 and 1855: Divisional Orders and Correspondence whilst under the Command of Lieutenant General the Earl of Lucan, KCB* (1856), pp. cxviii–cxix. No. 60 comes from my copy of a typed transcript, by Boyce Gaddes, of William Scarlett's letters from the Crimea. Another copy is in the National Army Museum. I am most grateful to Ann Constable for sending me the original of No. 47 and to Michael McGarvie for letting me see the original of No. 27.

Archives

Burnley
Towneley Hall, Burnley, has a sizeable collection of items to do with General Scarlett, including portraits and memorabilia. The two local papers of the period, the Conservative *Burnley Advertiser* and the Liberal *Burnley Gazette*, reported both the Burnley election of 1867–68 and other events involving General Scarlett in great detail. From the online British Newspapers Archive I have made an extensive transcription of articles, covering the election, the presentations to General and Lady Scarlett in 1869, and the General's death and funeral in 1871. The *Burnley Advertiser* published a full report of the last, *In Memoriam: Records of the Death and Funeral, with Brief Notices of the Life and Military Career, of the Late Lamented General the Honorable Sir James Yorke Scarlett, GCB* (1872).

Hawarden
The North East Wales Archives (NEWA), Hawarden, contain a series of letters from John Yorke, the colonel of the Royal Dragoons (the First Dragoons), to his sister Etheldred Yorke, NEWA, D/E/1545. They describe his journey East on the *Gertrude* and his experiences at Varna and in the Crimea, including the wound that led to the loss of his leg while advancing in support of the Light Brigade.

Northampton
The Northampton Record Office contains, in the Brudenell Papers, XIV and XV, an extensive archive of correspondence and other material to do with the Earl of Cardigan's

criminal libel case against Colonel Somerset Calthorpe, which came to court in 1863. General Scarlett was a principal witness for Cardigan.

Taunton
The Somerset Archives, DD, DU/181, contain two letters from General Scarlett to William Duckworth, the father of George Duckworth, who became a cornet in the 5th Dragoon Guards in 1846. The second letter informs William Duckworth of his son's death from cholera at Varna on 24 August 1854.

York
The Royal Dragoon Guards Museum at York has the helmet General Scarlett wore at Balaklava and his medals on display. Its archive, amongst other material to do with the 4th Dragoon Guards, the 5th Dragoon Guards and the 6th Dragoons, includes the Service Records of these three regiments. The archive also holds the diaries and letters of Desart Burton of the 5th Dragoon Guards and three letters from Grey Neville. It also holds transcripts of the letters of William Forrest of the 4th Dragoon Guards and the memoirs of Dr William Cattell of the 5th Dragoon Guards.

In the Borthwick Institute, Halifax/Derby Papers, box 2, there is a letter from William Montagu, seventh Duke of Manchester (1823–1890) to an unknown recipient, 3 November 1860, reporting a meeting with Alexander Elliot (1825–1909) a few days earlier.

Books

Adkin, Mark, *The Charge: The Real Reason Why the Light Brigade was Lost* (London, 1996).
Anglesey, the Marquess of, *A History of the British Cavalry, 1816–1919*, i, *1816–1850* (1973).
Anglesey, the Marquess of, *A History of the British Cavalry, 1816–1919*, ii, *1851–1871* (1975).
Anglesey, the Marquess of, ed., *Little Hodge: Being Extracts from the Diaries and Letters of Colonel Edward Cooper Hodge Written during the Crimean War, 1854–1856* (1971).
Barczewski, Stephanie, *Heroic Failure and the British* (2016).
Baring Pemberton, W., *Battles of the Crimean War* (1962).
Beckett, Ian, *The Victorians at War* (2003).
Bennett, Walter *The History of Burnley*, 4 vols (1946–1951), especially volume iii, *The History of Burnley, 1650–1850*; and volume iv, *The History of Burnley from 1850*.
Blaney, Tom *The Notorious Third Lord Lucan: An Embattled Life* (2020).
Brereton, J.M., *A History of the 4th/7th Royal Dragoon Guards and their Predecessors, 1685–1980* (1982).
Buchanan, George, *Letters from an Officer of the Scots Greys during the Crimean War* (1866; reprinted 2005).
Buttery, David, *Messenger of Death: Captain Nolan and the Charge of the Light Brigade* (2008).
Calthorpe, Somerset, *Letters from Head-Quarters: or The Realities of the War in the Crimea by an Officer on the Staff* (1856 and 1858).
Chapples, Leslie, *From Ormerod to Thursby: A Chronological History of a Distinguished Family* (1979).
Chapples, Steve, *General Scarlett; The Burnley Hero of Balaclava* (2006).
Crider, Lawrence W., *In Search of the Heavy Brigade: A Biographical Dictionary* (2012).

Crook, M.J., *The Evolution of the Victoria Cross: A Study in Administrative History* (1975).

Dalrymple, *Return of a King: The Battle for Afghanistan* (2013).

Dalrymple, William, *The Anarchy: The Relentless Rise of the East India Company* (2019).

David, Saul, *The Homicidal Earl: The Life of Lord Cardigan* (1997).

Duberly, Fanny, *Mrs Duberly's War: Journal and Letters from the Crimea*, edited by Christine Kelly (2007).

Dutton, Roy, *Forgotten Heroes: The Charge of the Heavy Brigade* (2008).

Edgerton, Robert B., *Death or Glory: The Legacy of the Crimean War* (1999).

Figes, Orlando, *Crimea: The Last Crusade* (2011).

Fisher, Glenn, ed., *Crimean Cavalry Letters* (2011).

Fletcher, Ian, and Ishchenko, Natalia, *The Crimean War: A Clash of Empires* (2004).

Franks, Henry, *Leaves from a Soldier's Note Book* (1904; reprinted Doncaster, 2016).

Hamley, Sir Edward, *The War in the Crimea* (1891).

Hinton, Mike, *Victory over Disease: Resolving the Medical Crisis in the Crimean War, 1854–1856* (2019).

In Memoriam: Records of the Death and Funeral, with Brief Notices of the Life and Military Career, of the Late Lamented General the Honorable Sir James Yorke Scarlett, GCB (1872). Published by the *Burnley Advertiser*.

Kershaw, Robert, *24 Hours at Balaklava: 25 October 1854. Voices from the Battlefield* (2019).

Kinglake, Alexander, *The Invasion of the Crimea: its Origins and Account of its Progress down to the Death of Lord Raglan*, 8 vols (1863–87).

Lambert, Andrew, *The Crimean War: British Grand Strategy against Russia, 1853–1856* (1991).

Lucan, Earl of, *English Cavalry in the Army of the East, 1854 and 1855: Divisional Orders and Correspondence whilst under the Command of Lieutenant General the Earl of Lucan, KCB* (1856).

Margrave, Tony, *British Officers in the East, 1854, 1855, 1856* (2009).

Maurice, Frederick, *History of the Scots Guards from the Creation of the Regiment to the Eve of the First War* (1934).

Mollo, John and Boris, *Into the Valley of Death: The British Cavalry Division at Balaclava, 1854* (1991).

Moyse-Bartlett, H., *Louis Edward Nolan and his Influence on the British Cavalry* (1971).

Paget, Lord George, *The Light Cavalry Brigade in the Crimea: Extracts from the Letters and Journal of the Late General Lord George Paget, KCB, during the Crimean War* (1881).

Roper, Michael, *The Records of the War Office and Related Departments, 1660–1964* (1998).

Royle, Trevor, *Crimea: The Great Crimean War, 1854–1856* (2000).

Ryan, George, *Our Heroes of the Crimea: Being Biographical Sketches of our Military Officers from the General Commanding to the Subaltern* (London, 1855).

Scarlett, Peter Campbell, ed., *A Memoir of the Right Honourable James, First Lord Abinger, Chief Baron of the Exchequer: Including a Fragment of his Autobiography and Selections from his Correspondence and Speeches* (1877).

Scarlett, William, 'On Active Service in the Crimea', ed. Boyce Gaddes (1990). A typescript copy is in the National Army Museum.

Seaton, Albert, *The Crimean War: A Russian Chronicle* (1977).

Shavshin, Vladimir, *The Valley of Death* (2005).

Sheppard, Martin, *Crimean Tragedy: George Duckworth, 1826–1854* (2021).

Spiers, Edward M., *The Army and Society, 1815-1914* (1980).

Strachan, Hew, *From Waterloo to Balaclava: Tactics, Technology and the British Army, 1815–1854* (1985).

Sweetman, John, *Raglan: From Peninsula to the Crimea* (new edn, 2010).

Tennyson, Alfred, Lord, 'The Charge of the Heavy Brigade' (1882).

Thomas, Donald, *Charge! Hurrah! Hurrah! A Life of Cardigan of Balaclava* (1974).

Walton, John K., *The Second Reform Act* (1987).

Warner, Philip, ed., *A Cavalryman in the Crimea: The Letters of Temple Godman, 5th Dragoon Guards* (2009).

Warner, Philip, *The Crimean War: A Reappraisal* (1972; reprinted 2001).

Whinyates, F.A., *From Coruña to Sevastopol: The History of C Battery, A Brigade (Late C Troop) Royal Horse Artillery: with Succession of Officers from its Formation to the Present Time* (1884).

Articles

Austin, Douglas J., 'The Battle of Balaklava: "A Brief History of 25th October 1854"', *War Correspondent*, 22, no. 3, October 2004, pp. 36–40.

Conrad, Mark, trans., 'A Look at the State of Russian Forces in the Last War', *Voennya Sbornik*, 1 (1858), section 2, pp. 1–15, *War Correspondent*, 23, no. 2, (2005), pp. 24–31.

Gooding, Keith, 'A Review of the Timetable of the Battle of Balaklava', *War Correspondent*, 23, no. 2, July 2005, pp. 16–17.

Knollys, Henry, revised by James Falkner, 'Sir James Yorke Scarlett, 1799–1871', *Oxford Dictionary of National Biography*.

Kozhukov, 'Kozhukov's Account of the Battle of Balaklava', *War Correspondent*, 18, no. 1, (2000,) pp. 14–19.

Robins, Colin, '25th October 1854: A Tentative Timetable of Events', *War Correspondent*, 22, no. 2, (2004), p. 17.

Ryzhov, I.I., trans. Mark Conrad, 'On the Battle of Balaklava: Notes of Lieutenant General Iv. Iv. Ryzhov', *War Correspondent*, 18, no. 2 (2000), pp. 28–31; and 18, no. 3, (2000), pp. 10–12.

Sheppard, Martin, 'Extracts from the Scarlett Family Archives, 1', *War Correspondent*, 36, no. 2 (2018), pp. 42–45.

Sheppard, Martin, 'Extracts from the Scarlett Family Archives, 2', *War Correspondent*, 36, no. 3 (2019), pp. 8–13.

Sheppard, Martin, 'In Search of General Scarlett', *War Correspondent*, 36, no. 2 (2018), pp. 36–41

Tylden, G., 'The Heavy Cavalry Charge at Balaclava', *Journal of the Society of Army Historical Research* (1940), pp. 98–103.

Website

Crimean War Research Society Website: *cwrs.crimeanwar.org*

John Barham, *Journey through the Crimean War.*

Index

Abdulmejid I, sultan, 275 n. 56
Aberdeen, George Hamilton-Gordon,
 fourth Earl of, 53, 54, 195
Abinger, Surrey, 28; church, 170, 293
 n. 99
Abinger, Lords, *see* James Scarlett;
 Robert Scarlett; William Scarlett
Abinger Hall, Abinger, Surrey, xix, 2, 3,
 18, 25, 30, 32, 37-39, 43, 63, 86, 122,
 133, 137, 161, 165, 167, 169, 171, 173,
 175, 187, 195, 197, 200, 201, 263 n. 19,
 plate 25
Abolition of Slavery, act, 209
Ackbar Mahommed, 34
Adkin, Mark, 118
Admiralty, 223
Adrianople, treaty of (1829), 52
Adriatic Sea, 64
Africa, 48
Afghanistan, 49; Kabul, 49
Agriculture, 29; prices, 46
Airey, Major General Richard, 97, 110,
 136
Albert, Prince, 40, 195
Albert Edward, Prince of Wales, 251
Aldershot, xix, 193, 194, 205, plate 38;
 Forest Lodge, 205, 206; Garrison
 Church, 242
Alderson, family, 136
Alderson, Georgina, Lady, 186
Alexander I, emperor of Russia, 5, 7, 262
 n. 22
Alexander, police superintendent, 228,
 238, 257
Algeria, 48
Alma, battle of the, xxi, 60-61, 88, 89n.,
 90, 91, 94, 95, 113, 124, 125, 132, 154,
 182; Bourliak, 61; Great Redoubt, 61;
 Kourgané Hill, 61
Alma, river, 60
Alexandria, 69

Amateur Exhibition, 165, 166, 175, 178,
 292 n. 85
America, 29, 220, 221; New England,
 221; New Orleans, 199; war with, 29
Anglesey, Anglesea, Henry Paget, first
 Marquess of, 133
Anglo-French naval force, 52; *see also*
 British navy; French navy
Apollo, statue, 41
Appleton, Cheshire, 38, 754
Arabs, 68; Arab horses, 160
Arbuthnot, Coutts, 172, 178
Army, as profession, 5, 11-12, 23-23, 38,
 39, 40, 47; purchase of commissions,
 6, 22-23, 38, 39; ranks, 22-23; letter
 from James Yorke Scarlett to Dudley
 Campbell, 156-57
Army, *see* British Army; Russian Army
Arnold, Nottinghamshire
Artillery, 93, 185; Royal Artillery, 93;
 C Troop, 101; W Field Battery, 93;
 Russian Army, artillery, 108
Ascot Races, 7
Asia Minor, 70
Athens, 69
Australia, 222, 263 n. 11
Austria, 47, 48, 52, 57, 72, 74, 80, 159
Azov, Sea of, 51

Baidar, village, 96
Baidar bridge, 96
Balaklava, battle, 90-125 passim, 180,
 182, 183, 190, 193, 194, 227, 242,
 plates 16, 30-32, 37, 38; medal, 182;
 vulnerability of port of Balaklava, 90,
 91, 92; Russian army after the Alma,
 95; rumours of Russian attack, 95;
 attack, 96, 97; slow response of allies,
 97; fall of redoubts, 98; Russian attack
 on 93rd Foot, 98; Ryzhov's advance,
 99-101; Russian cavalry's appearance

above Heavy Brigade, 100; Charge of the Heavy Brigade, 101-9; Scarlett's account of it, 104, 105, 138-40; pace of charge, 107, 108; Russian retreat, 108; Royal Horse Artillery's part in Russian defeat, 109; failure of Cardigan to support Heavy Brigade, 109; Raglan's orders to the cavalry, 98, 99, 110; Charge of the Light Brigade, 109-13; Heavy Brigade's part in the Charge of the Light Brigade, 109-13; Scarlett's recollection of the Charge of the Light Brigade, 112, 141-44; nature of the battle, 113; losses, 114; orders to cavalry division, 115; failures of support, 115, 116; Lucan's role, 105, 109-13, 115; possible victory of Light Brigade, 116, 117, 121; strategic importance of Charge of Heavy Brigade, 118-20; result of the battle, 120

Balaklava, port, xv, xvii, xx, xxi, 17, 21, 90, 279 n. 30; described, 90-91; name, 277 n. 2; cattle pier, plate 10; graves, plate 33; harbour, plates 10, 11, 26, 33; landing wharf, plate 11; *see also* Balaklava, battle

Balchik, 51, 85

Balkans, 48; mountains, 51

Ballot, 210, 230

Balls, 30, 83, 89; Clonmel, 30; De Grey, 45; Hunt, 45; Northern Meeting, 83; Tower of London, 201; Yeomanry, 45

Baltic Sea, 53

Bank Hall, Burnley, home of James Yorke Scarlett, xix, xxiii, 18, 36, 64, 70, 73, 74, 76, 77, 78, 84, 85, 86-88, 89, 126, 130, 131, 132, 162, 170, 205, 210, 240, 241, 247, 248, 250, 252, 253, 254, 256, 258, 259, 263 n. 19; description 78; Bank Hall meadow, 211; plates 20, 39

Bath, order of the, 124, 125, 151, 192, 193, 227, 250; presentation, 295 n. 147

Bath, Somerset, xxii

Bathing, 57; Turkish bath, 273 n. 108

Bathurst, Mrs, 186

Beards, 57, 58, 78, 194, plates 8, 9; James Yorke Scarlett's beard, 58, plates 28, 29; William Scarlett's beard, 28; *see also* Moustaches; Sidewhiskers

Beatson, Colonel William, aide de camp to James Yorke Scarlett, 64, 111, 112, 123, 125, 128, 129, 144; recommended for VC, 125

Beechwood, Hampshire, 79

Beer Houses, 222

Belgium, 221

Belgrade, 72

Ben Nevis, 190, 191

Bentinck, Lord George, 46

Berkeley, Colonel Charles, 173

Berkshire, Ascot, 7; Eton, *see* Eton; Slough, 8; Windsor, *see* Windsor

Berlin, 64

Besika Bay, 52

Bessarabia, 51, 72, 95

Besley, the Reverend C.J., 259

Bethlehem, 50; Church of the Nativity, 50

Bewley, George, quartermaster, plate 19

Bible, Balak, 215, 216, 298 n. 26; Psalms, 276 n. 164; Rachel, 167; St Matthew, 292 n. 89

Bigge, J., 11

Bingham, Lord George, 95

Birmingham, Warwickshire, 15, 18, 222; riot in, 15

Biscay, Bay of, 54, 72

Black Sea, Euxine, 47, 51, 54, 56, 80, 81, 92, 275 n. 150; map of 51

Blackburne, Captain, 43

Blackburne, Richard, 75

Blackwater, river, *see* Tchernaya

Blakeney, General Sir Edward, 28, 35, 265 n. 62

Blanketeers, 210

Bolton, Captain Abraham, 28, 157

Books, 21, 36, 69, 137, 245; *China*, 196; *Fanny Scarlett*, xxii; *In Memoriam*, 258, 259, 299 n. 13; *Le Diable*, 262 n. 37; *Letters from Headquarters*, 122; Murray's guides, 67, 74; *Paradise Lost*; *The Invasion of the Crimea*, 243

Booth, James, servant, 150n., plate 28

Bosphorus, 47, 51, 54, 55, 73, 191

Bouverie, Lieutenant General Everard 195

Bowater, General Sir Edward, 195

Brampton Ash, Northamptonshire, xxii, 199, 201

Surrey, 2, 15, 209, 219; Abinger, *see*
    Abinger; Abinger Hall, *see* Abinger
    Hall; Ashtead, 45; Dorking, xix, 2,
    27, 161, 175, 187, 195; East Sheen,
    3, 262 n. 25; Erlwood, 189, 196-98,
    204; Ewhurst, 70; Farnborough, 197;
    Gomshall, 201; Guildford, xix, 19,
    28; Hampton Court, 36; Holmbury,
    70; Leith Hill, 70; Richmond Park,
    60; Wellington College, 196-97;
    Windlesham, 1189, 196-98, 204
Sussex, 15; Battle, 15; Brighton, 36,
    194; Cuckfield, 15; East Grinstead,
    15; Hailsham, 15; Haywards Heath,
    242; Horsham, 28; Mayfield, 15;
    Rothersfield, 15; Uckfield, 15
Sutcliffe, Reverend Daniel, 259
Swale, river, 2
Swinburne Castle, 43
Swinfen, Lieutenant Frederick, 85
Swing Riots, 14, 263 n. 11
Syria, 50

Talbot, James Talbot, third Lord, 36
Taxation, 29, 33, 222, 236; borough rate,
    29; tithes, 15; *see also* National Debt
Taylor, Jeremy, 137
Tchernaya, battle of 196, 197
Tchernaya, Blackwater, river, 95, 96, 112,
    117, 138, 145, 148
Temple Grove, East Sheen, Surrey,
    school, 3, 262 n. 25
Tenedos, 58
Tennyson, Alfred, Lord, 117, 242-44;
    'The Charge of the Heavy Brigade',
    242-44; 'The Charge of the Light
    Brigade', xvii, 243
Test and Corporation Acts, 233, 236
Therapia, 72, 74, 84, 85, 178
Thin Red Line, 98
Thornhill, Major, 107
Thursby, Eleanor, 18, 44, 73, 77, 161,
    162, 163, 170
Thursby, family, 165
Thursby, John, nephew of Charlotte
    Scarlett, aide de camp to James Yorke
    Scarlett, 77, 78, 163, 211, 222, 254
Thursby, the Reverend William, 18, 77,
    161, 162, 163, 181, 184, 215, 263 n. 19
Tilsit, treaty of (1807), 49

Tittenhanger Park, Hertfordshire, 2, 261
    n. 5
Todd, Dr Robert, 161, 292 n. 71
Todleben, Eduard, 90
Toler, *see* Graham-Toler
Tories, 2, 20, 26, 210, 213, 225-27, 233;
    see also Conservatives
Torlundie, Torlundy, house near Fort
    William, later Inverlochy Castle, 77,
    80, 86, 88
Torquay, Devon, 172
Towneley, John, of Towneley Park,
    principal landowner in Burnley, 180-
    82, 184
Townley, the Reverend Adam, 220, 221
Townley, Lieutenant Colonel Charles,
    68, 272 n. 89
Trade, 29, 221; Free Trade, 29; *see also*,
    Corn Laws
Trade Unions, 221, 222
Traktir bridge, xvii, 96
Trafalgar, battle 47
Transport, 158
Treasury, 218
Trebizond, 57
Trevelyan, G.M., 57, 58
Trieste, 64
Trinity College, Cambridge, xix, 1, 3, 5,
    11-12, 243, 262 n. 38
Tulloch, Colonel Alexander, 170, 171
Turkey (Ottoman Empire), 29, 47, 51,
    63, 85, 89; Besika Bay, 52; Bosphorus,
    47, 51, 54, 55, 73, 191; Byukdere,
    72; Constantinople, xx, 47, 50, 51,
    52, 54, 55, 56, 57, 58, 64, 68, 69, 73,
    89, 91, 160, 187, 274 nn. 119 and
    120; Dardanelles, 51, 52, 54; Galata,
    72; Gallipoli, 51, 54, 56, 63, 69,
    72; Golden Horn, 72; Koulali, 70,
    91; Marmara, sea of, 51, 72; Pera,
    72; Scutari, 51, 54, 72, 89, 10, 140,
    149, 152, 176. 186; Seraglio Point,
    72; Sinope, 52, 269 n. 12; Tenedos,
    58; Therapia; 72, 74, 84, 85, 178;
    Trebizond, 57; *see also* Bulgaria
Turks, Turkish army, 47, 49-53, 56, 57,
    70, 81, 91, 93, 96, 98, 99, 119, 127,
    138, 150, 159, 160, 177, 183; Turkish
    navy, 52; *see also* Balaklava, battle;
    Redoubts